Asylum Ways of Seeing

ASYLUM WAYS OF SEEING

Psychiatric Patients,
American Thought and Culture

Heather Murray

PENN

UNIVERSITY OF PENNSYLVANIA PRESS

PHILADELPHIA

Published by
University of Pennsylvania Press
Philadelphia, Pennsylvania 19104-4112
www.upenn.edu/pennpress

Printed in the United States of America on acid-free paper
10 9 8 7 6 5 4 3 2 1

A Cataloging-in-Publication record is available
from the Library of Congress
ISBN 978-0-8122-5357-3

CONTENTS

Asylum Ways of Seeing

Introduction

In 1928 the matron of the Racine County Asylum in Wisconsin received a letter from a mother asking how her daughter was doing in the hospital. Since the matron had told this mother previously that her daughter was "extremely nervous and hard to handle," this mother wanted to know if her daughter had "quieted down any."[1] The matron offered reassurance that her daughter had been "down to our Christmas party and seemed to enjoy it very much. She received a package from her husband the day before Christmas and we gave her all the fruit and candy and nuts we thought good for her."[2] Still, the matron was obliged to say that "we do not see any change in your daughter. . . . She does not take an interest in anything. She seems to be perfectly contented to sit and look out of the window all day."[3]

This image of an indifferent psychiatric patient, lost in her own private world and staring out an institutional window, would come to have a completely different valence between the interwar era when these letters were written and the post–World War II period. The characterization of a psychiatric patient as oblivious, or even an automaton, a figure that would become so chilling and troubling to patients' rights advocates of the late twentieth century in their critiques of mental hospitals, was not so terrifying from the standpoint of the earlier twentieth century but instead was more neutral, simply a way of being in the hospital. As difficult as it may be for twenty-first-century readers to imagine, this figure was considered a soul at peace, in an accepted, if not a coveted, emotional state. It is the changing nature and observation of the patient that is the subject of this book.

Images of the automaton patient—passive, resigned, and absented from the world in the cloistered setting of the hospital—animated psychiatry over the course of the twentieth century, often serving as a metonym for the nature of mental illness of any kind as experienced in an institution. For Swiss psychiatrist Eugen Bleuler, writing in 1911, the affect of emotionlessness and acquiescence was especially characteristic of patients hospitalized with dementia praecox or "the schizophrenias," as it was known at the time. In a well-known passage from his book on dementia praecox, he observed that those who were institutionalized for long periods of time "sit about the institutions in which they are confined with expressionless faces, hunched up, the image of indifference. They permit themselves to be dressed and undressed like automatons, to be led from their customary place of inactivity to the mess hall and back again without expressing any sign of satisfaction or dissatisfaction."[4] These kinds of observations have been made not just about patients with schizophrenia but also in reference to the institutionalized population writ large, as though the mental hospital environment itself was inherently atrophying and life draining to its denizens. By the 1950s some social scientists had even given this phenomenon a name: "institutionalitis."[5] Neurologist and author Oliver Sacks evoked this kind of patient figure too when he reflected upon abandoned asylums from his vantage point in the early twenty-first century, noting that it was once "perfectly permissible" for patients to "just stare into space."[6] Perceptions of these institutionalized automatons have not always been stagnant, however, and neither have the sensibilities associated with them, most particularly resignation.

This is a book about people with mental illnesses and distress and those in their orbits who cared for and observed them—what I call patient cultures. I focus on the institutionalized, as well as those facing the prospect of institutionalization, their ideas, and their cultural and emotional expression in the face of this. What kinds of cultures, sensibilities, and concepts did an array of psychiatric hospitals as institutions create and facilitate? And how did these both resonate with and generate more widespread thought and culture beyond the hospital? I uncover here the voices of patients, their family members, psychiatrists, and hospital observers, and I consider both state and private institutions, as well as biological and psychoanalytical psychiatry. I explore the lives, writings, and politics of those who faced hospitalization owing to a range of emotional and cognitive afflictions and suffering, among them depression, bipolar disease, and schizophrenia, in their various incarnations over time, as well as "conditions" once treated in psychiatric hospitals, such as alcoholism and dementia in old age, not to mention distress that patients themselves had difficulty discerning, identifying, and categorizing. I recognize the amorphous quality of a term such as "mental illness," and patients' ambivalence about the very idea, whether this took the form of uncertainty about the boundary between sickness and moral character during the early twentieth century, the initial enthusiasm about a more pronounced medicalization of mental illness at midcentury, more rigorous political questionings of labels in the late twentieth century, or a proliferation of psychiatric identities at the turn of the millennium. I also recognize the abstraction of the category of "the patient." While I do not wish to elide important differences regarding class, race, and gender among patients, I suggest that once a patient identity becomes created, these distinctions also matter in relation to the transformative experience of being hospitalized, or being ill, or simply feeling alienated or internally tumultuous, all of which can change an individual's capacity for observation, sharpen political ideas, and initiate more conscious considerations of the emotional lives of others.

In addition to patients and their caregivers, the setting in which care was administered is a central character here, hovering in the background even when a patient had not yet been hospitalized or if a place for treatment was uncertain. The difficulty of writing about these institutions is that they are so freighted with a past of well-documented cases of neglect and abuse, whether this took place in the asylums of the interwar period, the overcrowded "snake pits" of the early postwar period, or the underfunded state hospital, the "cuckoo's nest," of the final third of the twentieth century. Poignant narratives of exploitation animate both this book and the narratives of other historians. And yet, acknowledging and analyzing the nature of this particular kind of institutional violence does not preclude an analysis of the styles of personhood and institutional citizenship that ran parallel to broader styles of selfhood and citizenship in society. It is in these hospitals that patients gave more conscious thought to the unfolding of time, to the physical and the built environment, to the nature and needs of communities versus those of individuals, and to scientific modernity. Psychiatric hospitals are contradictory in the sense that they require withdrawal from society but emphasize sociability among patients, and they have an intriguing ambiguity about them as places, since they can be simultaneously zones of intensified intimacy and sites of oppression. They can be fleeting, transient "non-places," while at other times sites where chronic illnesses played out and where patients lived out their days.[7] The individuals encountered in them offer personal, emotional assessments not just about the nature of violence but about community, individualism, conformity, science, and human rights, all themes that have animated twentieth-century America but that have been especially urgent in the reflections of patients and their observers. As such, these institutions suggest a unique way of seeing and imagining.

Within the patient culture of mental illness, resignation has been a central demeanor of the psychiatric institution—captured most poignantly in the automaton patient—as well as a response to institutionalization, and even a strategy within it. I trace a shift over the course of the twentieth century from a resigned, tragic sensibility that this patient embodied to a more possibility-seeking, utopian sensibility that shaped not only demeanors of and attitudes toward mental illness but other political or daily life realities. Resignation contrasted starkly with the institutional and emotional citizenship and community required of one in hospitals, something that became ever more pressing over the course of the postwar period. In insisting upon this style of active citizenship, and in introducing a patient to scientific concepts, the hospital itself had a hand in undermining the automaton that it was purported to create. The hospital interacted with and fashioned forces outside the institutional walls that also upheld and deepened a need for active citizenship and self-transformation: most particularly, scientific modernity in the interwar years, the heightened fears of totalitarianism in the early postwar years, and the political agency of the counterculture and rights culture during the late twentieth century.

I suggest that a sense of inevitability was more likely to define ideas about mental illness within the confines of institutional psychiatry particularly during the interwar era, and this posture toward one's lot in life had its parallel in a larger sensibility and mode of engagement with life: a sense that one was powerless to change the way things are, that what can't be cured must be endured. I do not seek to disparage resignation as a sensibility; as philosopher Susan Neiman reminds us, a synonym for "resigned" is "philosophical."[8] Instead I wish to understand how it is that resignation went from being interpreted as wisdom in the early twentieth century, to being understood as a capitulation to dubious scientific and political forces by midcentury, to being viewed as a profound violation of selfhood and the integrity of emotional expression by the century's end. How did the automaton, accepting of one's lot in life, both in the psychiatric hospital and beyond, come to assume such an unsettling and menacing valence over the course of the twentieth century, an aspect of freakery—a human, but not quite—rather than a particular perspective on reality?[9]

Throughout this book, I cover distinctive eras in American psychiatry and in societal sensibilities and ideas. The period between World War I and World War II is an especially intriguing starting point for thinking about the theme of resignation. During these years critics and observers of American hospital psychiatry suggested that the mental hospital or asylum was more custodial than caretaking, a departure from the reformist attempts to create humane, bucolic institutions during the nineteenth century. This custodialism in itself suggested an irretrievability of the mentally ill. Interwar asylum psychiatrists were often isolated from the intellectual currents in both broader professional medicine and psychoanalysis.[10] Confronting these institutions, patients were forced to take a pause from the clamor, speed, sensory shocks, and newness of modernity, and some saw no choice but to simply "be" in the hospital. If medical observers and sometimes even patients themselves accepted mental illness and institutionalization as an unrecoverable fate and as part of the inherent pain of the universe, they could conflate this inescapability with a sense of tranquility and suspended time that characterized resignation. Feeling benumbed, oblivious, and sequestered could even be compelling as a response to the tumults of modernity.

At the same time, during the interwar years, the hospital as an institution ironically destabilized the demeanor of the automaton that it helped facilitate for management purposes, or that patients adopted simply to exist in the asylum. As an emotional demeanor, resignation contrasted with the emotional citizenship of the hospital. The psychiatric hospital as an institution could intensify a patient's powers of observation and introspection. But it also powerfully suggested and enforced an institutional citizenship that emphasized association, voluntarism, participation, civic obligation, belonging, community, and solidarities among the suffering. It was a contradictory atmosphere of withdrawal that emphasized sociability.

Resignation expresses itself passively—or, more charitably, as peacefulness—while curing and the pursuit of possibilities express themselves more actively, perhaps even as unrest. Incurability has its most striking parallel in resignation and the institutionalized automaton, and curability has a parallel in more utopian thinking and the active, seeking agentive individual, who had no need for hospitalization. The ideational realms of psychiatric hospitals also could introduce patients, and by extension their families, to scientific modernity, whether this took the form of psychoanalysis, diagnosis, or, particularly by midcentury, psychosurgeries and psychotropic drugs. The sense of unrecoverability that characterized the interwar period changed when more institutions offered biological psychiatry and psychosurgeries at midcentury, lobotomies and electric shock therapy most prominent among them, that located mental illness in brain anatomy and were thought to cure everything from chronic schizophrenia to chronic depression.[11] As scientific modernity came to be seen as something that the individual could engage with and possibly manipulate, autonomy and self-possession deepened as ideals in the institutional setting. And when psychiatrists, patients, and family members alike began to have more faith in biological cures for all forms of mental illness at midcentury, they embraced an ideal of activity and transformation over passivity and resignation.

But psychosurgeries also demonstrated the fraught relationships between individuals and a scientism that potentially reduces people to automatons, the very archetypal figures of the mental hospital that patients and their families thought they could avoid by turning to biological psychiatry. The zombie figure in particular inhabited an early post–World War II American imaginary, and psychiatric hospital populations felt they had a firsthand acquaintance with this specter. While the rejection of the conformist and the embrace of authenticity over the course of the postwar period have figured in historical discussions about the impact of totalitarianism on American thought and culture, the history of psychiatry can uniquely illuminate the disconcerting figure of the automaton, often read as a passive bystander, who haunted so many areas of American culture, from political writings to popular culture.

Critics of hospital psychiatry became more vociferous during the early postwar era, and not just because the promises of psychosurgeries seemed more uncertain then. Some observers focused on mental hospitals themselves and called for reforms, writing exposés of these overcrowded, underfunded, and sometimes virtually uninhabitable institutions.[12] In turn, the "lonely crowds" that animated the social science landscape at midcentury had their most intriguing laboratory in the mental hospital. These institutionalized patients themselves came to embody styles of postwar era personhood and citizenship that rendered the hospital a site much more freighted with perceived American national character and ideology than it had been a generation before. As passivity and resignation became more politicized, a patient was no longer being wise by simply accepting her fate as an institutionalized mentally ill person; instead, she was being an automaton, a figure now viewed more disparagingly as one who had dubious political commitments and was perhaps even prone to totalitarianism.

In the name of reform, psychiatric observers and critics helped prepare a social and intellectual foundation for deinstitutionalization during the 1960s, a movement that posed a more powerful repudiation of resignation and a commitment to individual rights, possibility seeking, and emotional fulfillment beyond the hospital. Some historians have charted a parallel evolution of "grand expectations" in American society in personal as well as social and political life, and they have explored, sometimes from a conservative political perspective, the evolution from a duty-bound consciousness to a more rights-based one. According to this perspective, this shift was shaped by postwar consumer culture and the promises of personal happiness that it offered, by the postwar civil rights movement and its compelling suggestion that the downtrodden of all guises identify with African Americans seeking rights and restitution, and by an emerging countercultural emphasis on self-realization.[13] Patient writings during this era suggest that the counterculture may have flourished and been heightened in direct tension with the hospital setting, which served as a glaring example of an oppressive societal structure that coerced the individual into acquiescence. By the 1960s and 1970s, the tranquil, resigned psychiatric patient came to be viewed as a tragic violation of individual authenticity.

In no era were psychiatry's critics bolder than during the last third of the twentieth century, when they called into question many forms of psychiatric and medical authority, with the mental hospital often at the center of their critiques. In this vein of thinking, a patient's lot in life was more than just a tragedy, and something could—indeed should—be done to rectify or eliminate oppressive societal structures. Psychiatric patients of this deinstitutionalization era also offer a particularly striking insight into neoliberalism, in this instance meaning the displacement of state institutions by political and economic privatization strategies. In stark contrast to the midcentury liberalism that mental hospitals embodied, exhibiting a faith in social welfare, social institutions, government, and the behavioral sciences to solve problems, late twentieth-century neoliberalism was distinctly unwedded to social welfare and to institutions, participation, and citizenship.[14] What happens when the hospital as a reflective context is gone? What happens to ideas without a place to express them? The newly placeless patient could repudiate the institutionalized subject, and seemingly a life of resignation as well.

Especially by the century's end, some patients and caregivers were embracing a new era of biological psychiatry based on curing biochemical mental illnesses, which was perceived as potentially liberating the mentally unwell from the institution.[15] But amid this remedicalization, some also longed for a better hospital, or simply a refuge from suffering; this desire became more prominent when the promises of biochemistry seemed uncertain. This yearning was not as direct or literal as seeking reinstitutionalization; instead it expressed itself more as an amorphous need for community, diffuse forms of care, reciprocal intimate relationships, sympathetic witnessing from public authorities, and creativity in day-to-day life. The psychiatric institution was still, by definition for many observers, antithetical to this kind of fulfillment.

Once perceived as a necessary "pause" during the early twentieth century, this sense of being absented from the larger world in a mental hospital came to be viewed as a punitive halt that simply enforced the creation of a self-evacuated subject, the precise opposite of the liberal, autonomous, self-possessed individual. By the century's end, the more passive, resigned institutionalized subject was displaced by a more active, politically engaged, rights-bearing patient who questioned the given-ness of life and who was by nature institution-less. Over the course of the twentieth century, emotional vibrancy and animation displaced serenity and imperturbability as ideals for care and treatment and a way of being, as personal demeanors and political ones alike. The seemingly acquiescent and dormant psychiatric hospital patient, once seen by cultural observers as inevitable during the early twentieth century, came to be viewed, during the mid- to late twentieth century, not only as a mechanical figure disturbingly stripped of an interior life but as politically, personally, and aesthetically dubious.

Still, aspects of resignation lingered, often expressed as a kind of ambivalence about the institution of the psychiatric hospital itself or simply as a means to make the unbearable bearable. And resignation was not incompatible with patient intellectual curiosity, which was often shared by their caregivers when assessing psychiatric hospitals, and the science, biological concepts, therapy, and citizenship routines that these institutions embodied. Though other areas of intellectual inquiry, especially cultural history, have been quite keen to think about the critical capacities of groups once considered simply acquiescent, whether consumers or TV watchers or radio listeners, this reflection has not been as prevalent in the history of medicine, which has been more interested in the tensions between exploitation, social control, and agency.[16] To suggest that patients can be intellectually interested in their illnesses or in the experience of being in an institution is not to belittle their suffering or to presume a certain class and education elitism. The patients and their family members who wrote to, for example, their governor or their local state hospital psychiatrist often were by their own admission not formally educated and did not mince words about the depth of their suffering, but at the same time their intellectual curiosity as well as their emotional and political intelligence are apparent. Though the cultural cachet of self-knowledge has been traditionally thought of as the province of the bourgeoisie, especially during the modern era when intellectuals and the upper-middle class embraced psychoanalysis, broader swaths of the American population have shared in the desire for self-knowledge and engagement with science and medicine.[17]

"We need to talk about mental illness,"[18] exhort public health campaigns in contemporary America, as if to suggest that the taboos surrounding mental illness are still so entrenched that few would dare discuss this aspect of the human condition, beyond the dimly imagined afflictions and gothic curiosities that feature so prominently in contemporary horror films and novels. And yet, patients have been talking about mental illness with their family members, hospital psychiatrists, and fellow patient communities, as well as representing their thoughts and experiences in an array of intimate and cultural genres, over the past century. Moreover, the mentally "well" have been visiting and beholding the unwell and have been captivated, especially by hospital environments, and recording these perceptions in ways that manifest both fascination and revulsion, exoticization and fear, sympathy and callousness, care and repudiation. And mental hospitals as institutions have long been faced with huge expectations, dissected, complained about, lavishly praised when helpful, and condemned when insensitive or abusive, like families themselves. These caregivers and the potential need for them all still inhabit and animate the American imaginary.

Historians of medicine have long been encouraging more chronicling of the patient's perspective to the point that this call has become a truism.[19] In turn, some scholars have called for more attention to responses to madness in the community;[20] others have decried the "absent entity" of the caregiver in medical history;[21] and still others argue that the family's role in caregiving has not been given enough emphasis.[22] Historian Gerald Grob famously invoked the figure of the "invisible patient,"[23] lost to historians because of the mostly aggregate data of psychiatric statistics of illnesses from the twentieth century. These patients are also "invisible" because psychiatric archival sources can be frustratingly fragmentary and elusive to researchers working on the twentieth century owing to restricted access to case notes and patient records.

Despite this displaced patient subjectivity, patient voices survive in revelatory letters to psychiatrists at both state hospitals and private institutions, as well as to public officials, and in intimate correspondence—a corpus that historian Michael Pettit has called a "therapeutic archive."[24] Their voices also animate anthropological and sociological ethnographies of patient life in psychiatric hospitals, advice literature and films addressed to larger mental health publics, hospital publications, patient newsletters, medical textbooks, medical periodicals, and memoirs or "autopathographies,"[25] not to mention creative venues: novels, documentary films, plays, poetry, and patient drawings. Their caregivers' voices, be they family members or hospital doctors, also survive in these kinds of sources, allowing a glimpse into the moral and emotional economies surrounding the patient over time.[26]

These sources demonstrate that patients and their intimate observers have been creators of culture and producers of ideas in their own right, particularly in their narrations and analysis of emotions, illnesses, selfhood, and hospital experiences. Ideas were not just imbibed from the outside world and adapted within the institution; they flowed outward as well. Intellectual histories of psychiatry need not solely derive from the perspective of psychiatrists, just as patients are not solely the embodiments of "lived experience."[27] The kinds of sources that I take up here allow me to connect the history of psychiatry in the United States to intellectual and cultural history broadly construed. Social histories of psychiatry and its institutions have been and continue to be foundational in the field, particularly in the United States, and have explored themes of institutionalized captivity, the carceral state, coercion, exploitation, social control, and surveillance, as well as forms of power and resistance, both subtle and overt, and engagement with the state, in fascinating ways.[28] I depart from these somewhat in that I am not trying to verify a social reality or engaging in a case study of an individual hospital but rather focusing more on the representations of these hospital experiences and feelings in both intimate and creative venues.[29]

Historians as well as popular culture have tended to present, with good reason, fairly limited possibilities for the existence of a person with mental illness in the context of a psychiatric hospital, often in an atmosphere of social control. A 2009 YouTube upload called "Shocking Paranormal Imagery!" at the Milledgeville State Hospital in Georgia, which was notorious for its overcrowding and patient exploitations at midcentury, also showed some photos that were distinctly un-shocking, such as lingering shots of the grounds or the trees, or just prosaic things like laundry facilities.[30] These kinds of everyday details also come to life readily in the cultural and imaginative outputs about the hospital, as well as instances of comfort or whimsy or sweetness, perhaps heightened in an overall atmosphere that offered these moments only sparingly, such as patient puppet making and puppet shows at Central Griffin State Memorial Hospital in Oklahoma, pet shows at Osawatomie State Hospital in Kansas, and song fests at Eastern State Hospital in Tennessee during the 1950s.[31] These moments demand our attention, just as instances of inhumanity and systems of cruelty do, perhaps especially because of the existence of those systems.

The relationship between history and acts of violence, or historical narrative and the unfolding of a particular tragedy, is deeply ingrained, though in less sensationalized forms than in homemade paranormal videos.[32] These thematic frameworks make sense in the history of psychiatry, too, given the breadth of the carceral state and the well-chronicled instances of patient suffering in institutions. In exploring the idea of the hospital as an imaginative space, in which not solely patient captivity or agency can unfold, I uncover surprising and complicated instances of human connection, as well as often unresolved yearnings for community life, themes that have animated histories of other captive communities but have not been as prevalent in the history of psychiatry.[33] Wartime and prison contexts are not the only ones in which unusual solidarities between people can develop, and expanding the lens to the hospital allows for more thinking about the emotional intensities within an array of subsocieties.

This reflection also allows for the insertion of "sick" individuals into the more common race, class, and gender paradigms of human and social difference, categories that have a contentious basis in biology or that have been biologized against the will of those they purport to represent. The "mentally ill"—and even the "disabled" writ large—do not tend to inhabit diversity conversations in the same way that race, class, gender, and even sexuality have.[34] As such, people with mental illnesses constitute an unusual "minority" who can sometimes "pass" and at other times cannot and who are sometimes willing to see themselves among the ranks of other oppressed groups. Perhaps because mental illness in particular can be considered more purely a personal misfortune rather than a subject position, it is often relegated to fantastical realms or quiet conversations among those who face similar suffering, despite the pleas of patient activists to see it as more of a political or social identity. This sense of minoritization is often more heightened and urgent in the physical context of the hospital or when someone is facing the prospect of institutionalization, which reinforces a sense of existing in a parallel society.

"Minority" consciousness is central to the question of resignation, as this has been a disposition for both working-class and racialized people, at times a strategic one. Sociologist Lillian Rubin has written about resignation in white American working classes, an attitude of "things just happened."[35] Abstract comments about the problems of human nature—often a brutal, white human nature—made within a sensibility of resignation, of "the way people are," also have a voice in early twentieth-century African American novels. In Jessie Redmon Fauset's 1924 novel, *There Is Confusion*, one of her characters, Brian, both acknowledges and contests this as a truism when he notes that often a "time comes when [a Black man] thinks, 'I might just as well fall back . . . a colored man just can't make any headway in this awful country." Of course, it's a fallacy. And if a fellow sticks it out he finally gets past it, but not before it has worked considerable confusion in his life."[36] Expressions of resignation as responses to suffering, often the only conceivable responses to suffering, were quite important among vulnerable populations in the early twentieth century but became complicated and sometimes disavowed as the century wore on. The psychiatric realm has yet to be inserted into this conversation. Moreover, exploring a history of sensibilities in this way can illuminate those that have been seemingly discarded, and why, as well as how they might linger through traces, be resurrected, or simply exist by other names in the contemporary moment.[37]

The archival sources that I draw from here, particularly intimate correspondence between patients and family members and their psychiatrists, are fragmentary and often subject to censorship.[38] Moreover, the records from various state hospitals are inconsistent and vary by hospital and by state. Some records are held by state hospitals that are still in operation, some have been destroyed due to destruction schedules to ensure patient privacy, and some simply have been lost. What does exist in hospital records, from scattered private correspondence, to annual reports, to patient newspapers, to architectural plans, allows for some reflection about the chasm between what has been documented and what has not, or what has been preserved and what has not. These sources are not meant as a repudiation of medical archives, such as doctors' notes or patient records; they are meant to suggest that those sources do not always reveal the moods, perceptions, and introspection that I am interested in here, such as representations of what it feels like to be in a mental hospital, or patient longings and fantasy lives, or their political consciousness within institutional environments.[39] Patients and their intimate observers' correspondence and testimonials are distinct genres in the same way that doctors' notes are. At the same time, I recognize that the patient voices I have had access to are themselves curated samples, by their families, by government officials, by psychiatrists, or by other institutional authorities. Whether a patient was expressing gratitude for care, or outrage over abuse, or something much more ambivalent, these sources illuminate patients who had at least some level of engagement with the medical establishment.

Privacy regulations have had something of a decontextualizing effect on my sources, sometimes stripping patients of not only identifying factors but clues as to their class background, generational cohort, and ethnoreligious or racial background. Moreover, all states have varying policies about what can and cannot be seen, as well as different twists on privacy laws, and this has had a shaping factor on the evidence that I present.[40] Not all hospitals kept such correspondence either in their own or in state archives, and I have tried to be cognizant of all the evidence that has been forgotten, erased, or never recorded.

I also recognize that privacy laws and archival attempts to preserve patient privacy and preclude patient identification are relevant to understanding a desire for anonymity, so powerful for those who are vulnerable for a host of reasons, among them mental illness, disability, sexuality, and race, and is perhaps even more compelling now in an era of more pronounced surveillance states and cultures and hypervisibility.[41] On the one hand, anonymity is a necessary protection against physical and psychological violence, perhaps even against emotional and political superficiality. Historian Susan Lawrence reminds researchers that privacy laws are only concerned with the rights of the living and their relatives rather than the "non-existent legal status of the privacy of the dead" who only have a "symbolic existence."[42] Perhaps it is not always possible to project the privacy desires of the dead from one historical moment to another. In 1941, a young African American woman who was a patient at Searcy Hospital, a segregated Alabama institution then exclusively for Black patients, wrote a stirring letter to the governor of the State of Alabama, Frank M. Dixon, to testify to the appalling patient living conditions there, as well as physical and emotional abuses. "I have been informed not to sign my name to any letter I write you, but since I write the truth the whole truth and nothing but the truth I deem it unnecessary to write an anonymous letter!" she said. "I am willing to shout the truth to a nation! We need help! Now!"[43] There is an irony in anonymizing this powerful voice.

The impulse to protect patient privacy has been noble insofar as it protects a patient, even as a non-living historical subject, from stigma and malicious gossip, but it is also contradictory and certainly imposes a constraint on discussion, the very factor that many patient advocates say is also necessary to destroy the stigma of mental illness. Some vulnerable groups have considered privacy anathema and fought against it, in the name of pride (racial pride or gay pride, most prominently), or as is more often the case for those with mental illnesses, in the name of dignity.

Perhaps because so many patients have died nameless and seemingly anonymous, an eagerness to do justice to their existence also suffuses historical reflections about them. An intriguing example is a collection about the Willard State suitcases: four hundred suitcases filled with patients' belongings were discovered in 1998 in the attic after the Willard Psychiatric Center closed in 1995. The authors explored the contents of ten suitcases and noted that "spirits of the suitcase owners had been awakened without their consent, and we felt that we owed them our utmost effort to do them justice."[44] They take up this kind of spiritual language throughout the book, writing that when the abandoned suitcases were first discovered, curators and state workers who were roaming the grounds of the abandoned buildings trying to collect things that might be worth preserving before the demolition crews came were struck by the "awesome sight" of "crates, trunks, hundreds of standard suitcases . . . all neatly arrayed under the watchful eyes of the pigeons who had come to join the lost souls and their worldly possessions."[45]

Of course there is something spiritual about history, and this is particularly the case when exploring such deeply personal effects of the dead. Perhaps, too, preservationists are animated by a protest against the namelessness and dehumanization of bureaucracy that so frightened many prospective psychiatric hospital patients and their families, especially during World War II and the postwar era. Thousands of state hospital patients were buried in anonymous, often numbered graves in the United States. Sometimes patients did not have coffins, and their bodies were simply buried in shrouds. At other times they had no grave markers, or if they were cremated, their ashes might be left in random locations throughout the hospital grounds. Many hospitals harbor these "friendless" patients whose families did not collect their bodies to buried.[46] Organizations have formed to put names on the gravestones of patients who have died in asylums, in a sense reclaiming them from abstract bureaucracy and powerfully announcing that they are not just "numbers," akin to the work being done now at genocide sites.[47] Preservationists want to at least mark the asylums as important sites for death and, by putting names on asylum gravestones, restore the possibility of grieving and mourning for these individual patients.

I do not want to diminish the importance of this historical preservation work so much as to call to mind larger questions about who can be seen as a respectful observer, chronicler, and interpreter of these patients, or a bestower of "dignity." A historian reading archival sources is not an inherently more reverential observer than a preservationist, but I do suggest, following historian Elizabeth Lunbeck, that observation through study has the potential to be a mode of empathy, while recognizing how freighted observation of the vulnerable has been historically.[48]

Beyond these archival sources, there is also an extant body of creative works and memoirs written by people with mental illness, as well as their caregivers, well-known ones to be sure, but also those that few people have read.[49] These sources, in combination with therapeutic archives—and I do not wish to establish a hierarchy between the two—allow for an illumination of the public, communal self of the asylum era who told very different stories about mental illness than the more amorphous "cerebral subject"[50] that characterizes turn-of-the-millennium era psychopharmacology and de-institutionalization.

Such sources also allow for a meditation on more abstract questions: How have people given narrative form to and why have they metaphorized mental illness and the experience of hospital life throughout the twentieth century? In what ways did they convey suffering, their fantasy lives, and their sense of rights in their institutional environments—if they thought of themselves as having them—over time? The institutional contexts in which patients composed these reflections—and the moment when these contexts were gone—are central here.

One of the appeals of an immersion into writings of all forms by patients and those who cared for them is that they offer their readers a form of emotional and even moral intensity. Perhaps this is why university medical humanities programs try to make doctors more morally aware and emotionally responsive by reading literature.[51] But part of that project of humanizing medicine also could be to historicize it, to illuminate how basic medical decisions, such as leaving patients alone to live out their days in a hospital, or attempting to cure them and to liberate them from the institution, have both shaped and been shaped by broader ideas and emotional dispositions about what the individual could and should accept in life or try to change.

CHAPTER I

What Can't Be Cured
Must Be Endured

During the 1920s, when writer Jane Hillyer was just twenty-four years old, she was diagnosed with dementia praecox and placed in a sanatorium.[1] Many praecox patients simply lived out their days in institutions; historian Richard Noll has referred to it as a diagnosis of hopelessness during the early twentieth century, the "terminal cancer of mental diseases."[2] Hillyer was a white woman of means and in a private sanatorium, and yet she spent four seemingly interminable years there. As distinctive institutions from state hospitals, sanatoriums tended to harbor affluent patients whose mental illnesses were not necessarily debilitating and went there to have a restorative rest cure through an array of treatments in diet, exercise, hydrotherapy, massages, and the like.[3] Yet in her 1926 memoir, she said that "my condition had been pronounced incurable. There was no use . . . to make further effort. I would be comfortable in this institution. . . . The situation was accepted as one must accept inevitability."[4] Even when offered rehabilitative treatment that emphasized environmental and emotional factors in healing,[5] patients like Hillyer appeared to accept a kind of inevitability of tragedy, a sense that utopian possibilities simply did not apply to the personal realm and that this was especially true for mental illness. These larger modes of engagement with life accepted devastating illness as the way things were, as the inherent pain of human existence that had to be borne stoically.

Hospital psychiatry both shaped and was shaped by this larger sense of resignation. American mental hospitals were often at a crossroads during the interwar years, between concepts of Victorian benevolent patriarchies and refuges and institutional homes of modern biological psychiatry, such as psychosurgeries. The optimistic "moral treatment" and the "cult of curability" of the early nineteenth century were waning, particularly at state institutions, in favor of custodialism and chronicity during this period, which continued into the interwar era.[6] By the 1920s, mental hospitals were becoming the most common kind of custodial institution in the United States, and their construction was more robust than that for both almshouses and prisons. In this period, and until the late twentieth century, they were mostly populated by white people and had higher proportions of women.[7] Psychoanalysis was still unusual in many of these institutions, even as psychoanalytical ideas, the popularization of Freudian concepts, and the commodification of psychological concepts were becoming a part of the larger cultural conversation of American modernity.[8] Instead, psychiatrists worked in asylums and state hospitals and were often severed from the ideas animating broader professional medicine and psychiatry.[9]

This sense of being on the cusp of modernity had its facsimile in broader American society, still situating itself between Victorian traditionalism and modernity. A widespread medical characterization of mental illness as unrecoverable and incurable during the interwar years paralleled broader dispositions of resignation that accepted a prognosis of inevitability in medical spheres and sometimes beyond. These sensibilities are evident in the ways that patients and their families wrote about and represented mental illness as experienced in an institution. They did not just discuss illness but the sorrows of life as well; they also made observations about the natural world and the passage of time. A strategy for understanding institutionalization and the suffering of mental illnesses, as well as broader forces of modernity, was to consider all of the natural forces beyond one's control.

Serenity, resignation, and even apathy and quietude could be particularly cherished emotional states from the vantage point of this self-consciously modern moment. An idealization of peace, idleness, and even the figure of the automaton constituted a desire to locate spaces of suspended time, observation, and meditation amid the clamor, speed, and sensory and political shocks of modernity, and the asylum provided an institutional setting for this slowed-down inwardness.

But that same mental hospital environment also unsettled the very emotional strategies it was purported to create, or at least to need for management purposes, and that patients and their families sometimes adapted so that they could carry on. The hospital by its nature intensified patients' capacities to observe and notice things and feelings, and this ironically could make them more critical of the environments and the illnesses to which they were also resigned. The institution also at least sometimes introduced patients to psychiatric concepts, facilitated by a larger post–World War I context wherein the wider American public was becoming more aware of and educated about the existence of "mental illness" broadly construed, such as "shell shock" and neuroses, and where postwar organizations in the vein of the National Committee for Mental Hygiene were enabling conversations about psychology and psychiatry.[10] And the hospital encouraged patients to consider certain civic ideas, almost always promoting, as part of institutional citizenship, communal values and participation in a community of fellow sufferers, something that had a distinct resonance in the interwar years when "community" was a vaunted social ideal. Active participation existed in tension with resignation in the hospital, suggesting an ideal of hospital citizens rather than hospital subjects.

During the late nineteenth and early twentieth centuries in particular, the presence of the health-care system deepened in Americans' lives, both in the rise of the modern hospital and in scientific and technological values, and perhaps nowhere was this made so manifest as when a family member faced spending a period of time in a residential hospital.[11] Sometimes families were involved in the institutionalization process, in addition to doctors, police, and other state workers, and commitment laws varied between the states.[12] Vengeful relatives and dubious commitment practices have become such a prominent part of a cultural story and collective memory about the asylum that it is possible they have drowned out the voices of families who found the commitment of loved ones a genuine quandary or who were more ambivalent about the process. Some parents might have simply doubted their capacity to care for a loved one experiencing a mental illness. One mother whose daughter appeared to be suffering from depression and was living in Bellevue Place, a private sanatorium in Batavia, Illinois, catering to upper-class white women, owned to the superintendent (asylum administrator) there that her daughter had been a "great problem" for years. The mother worried that she had not "always handled the case just right. I have done the best I could, except for the few times when my nerves have undone me and I have [given] way to irritation. It has not been often, but there have been times when I have told her what I thought of her in no uncertain terms. For this I am sorry and have told her so many times."[13]

The idea of doing the "best I could" emblematizes a larger mode of parenting, caring, and way of getting through day-to-day life, but it was especially helpful when families were dealing with the suffering, potential stigma, and blatant medical intervention when their loved ones were patients. In this vein, one common feature in the intimate correspondence of families who had hospitalized loved ones was an acceptance of one's lot that ran alongside a yearning for the return of a family member to life outside the institution. This is exemplified in a series of letters that an adult daughter living in Florida wrote to her mother at Racine County Insane Asylum in Wisconsin, a facility whose inhabitants were often working-class whites.[14] Multigenerational families were no longer common during this period, among the poor or working class, but families still were saddened by and felt guilty about the prospect of leaving older relatives in particular in institutional settings; the majority of patients in American asylums of this period were over the age of sixty-five.[15] This daughter confided to her mother that "I feel so bad and unhappy. I have written so often that we wanted you to visit us this winter, and I hope yet that you will come. It is so nice here in winter." She signed off with these words: "Don't grieve and worry Mother, it could all have been different, but nothing can be changed anymore. Lots of love."[16]

This poignant, seemingly futile acknowledgment that "nothing can be changed" seems reminiscent of an idea of religious resignation in the nineteenth century and even earlier, but it endured into the twentieth century.[17] Novelist John Williams captured this sensibility when he wrote of a family of Missouri farmers in the early twentieth century that they "regarded [their lives] patiently, as if it were a long moment that [they] had to endure."[18] But resignation was not unique to agricultural workers or working-class people. Henry Collins Brown, a man of means who would become the founder of the Museum of the City of New York, had a mental breakdown in 1928. He wrote a memoir called *A Mind Mislaid* in 1937, recalling his time at Bloomingdale Asylum, a private hospital that was among the first to experiment with moral treatment in the nineteenth century and still harbored this heritage of rehabilitation when he was a patient there.[19] Brown wrote that "my progress was slow. . . . I could see no improvement. I resigned myself to my fate and gave way to settled melancholia."[20]

The ultimate hope of nineteenth-century moral treatment was a cure. However, by the interwar era, some patients and their loved ones, in both private and public institutions, sought something considerably humbler than a cure: the subtler and less dramatic solace of the bearable over the unbearable or of comforts over discomfort. In 1924, a woman wrote directly to a "dear friend" in Racine County Insane Asylum and asked her: "How have you been and how is the world to you? Is it any better than it was. This is a cold cruel world. You can give all you have, but when you need help alas where is it?"[21] In a sense, she attributes mental illness to simple, undeserved ill luck. The absence of family members from the home was particularly difficult during holidays and festivities that disrupted the routine and monotony in regular life. Another woman wrote to the matron of Racine in 1924 about her adult son, noting that "today is [my son's] birthday it has been a sad one for me. There is no use to remind him of it he probably has never thought of it it is the best way."[22] Even while on the verge of expressing a slight grievance about her son's lot, she ultimately does not protest it. The matron tried to emphasize the rhythms of daily life inside the asylum, the activities and simple pleasures that provided comfort. She wrote that the son "seems very much brighter and is outside a great deal." She also noted that "we have had some very nice pictures lately, some of which were 'The White Sin', 'The Dawn of a Tomorrow', and good comedies. Our people all seem to enjoy them all."[23] Addressing the mother's sorrow over missing her son's birthday, the matron said that her son "does seem to enjoy being outside. . . . He received a bday letter from his Aunt . . . and seemed to enjoy it very much. Was sorry to have your letter sound so lonesome, but please don't worry about [him]. . . . Hope you are well." She signed this letter "Lovingly."[24]

If there was hope expressed in these personal letters, it took the form of a hope that the comforts of the outside world could permeate the asylum. Family members sometimes struggled in their own conception of the hospital. One father asked of the Racine asylum in 1931: "How does she like the place she is in. What does she think it is. A 1st class hotel. Let us know. How she is? And greatly oblige."[25] He went on to offer some nutrition suggestions from his home to the public sphere of the "hotel." The hotel image is intriguing, because these institutions were ambiguous in their self-conception and promotion: were they resorts, spas, elite colleges? Psychoanalytic hospitals referred to themselves as "campuses"; private hospitals tended to gravitate toward the hotel model.[26] The mother of the young woman living in Bellevue Place mentioned earlier wrote that "I feel that she [the daughter] needs to be there, or in a similar place, and yet it is sad to have her there. I believe yours is just the place she needs, as I like the attendants and doctors and the beautiful grounds. I trust you can do something for her." Still, to try to make Bellevue more comfortable and perhaps a happier place for her daughter, she wrote: "I want to ask if she may have her Corona typewriter there. She is fond of writing and it would help pass time if there is no objection. I could bring it over some day."[27] Sometimes families simply wanted something more abstract than material objects from home, in the vein of assurances given to their family members that they still cared for them and loved them from afar. In 1926, two sisters wrote to the superintendent of Bellevue, where their third sister was being treated: "She used to be very much attached to her family. Does she wish to come home again?"[28] The woman writing to her "dear friend" at Racine asked: "Did you have any Christmas doings? I hope you had some Christmas joy. . . . Do not think I have forgotten you, for you are in my thoughts very often. . . . I send you loving greetings and wishes for a brighter new year."[29]

In the 1920s, the possibilities for staying in touch with dispersed loved ones beyond letter writing were more palpable and more celebrated than ever before. During this time, AT&T billed itself as the "annihilator of space," but perhaps the ease of communication highlighted the isolation of the institution as a world apart and added to the anguish of being separated from loved ones.[30]

Families with members in an asylum also embodied the tensions between loss and absence: a dead but not dead loved one. A means of understanding and perhaps coming to accept this was simply contemplating the natural world. A year later, in 1923, the Florida daughter wrote her mother in Racine another letter, this time talking about her gardening. Here too she expressed love in quotidian details. "It rains here every day now," she wrote. "Some days it is real hot, and then the ants are so bad. But the nights are always cool. We have lots of turnips planted." Then she wrote: "Wish I could hear from you Mother how you are. . . . I will close with lots of love. I think of you every day."[31] Literary critic Gail Caldwell has written of the "bland executioners of the human connection" being time and distance, the means through which many friendships simply peter out and come to an end.[32] Yet having a loved one in the asylum was neither this "bland executioner" nor the definitive reality of death. Instead it was a confusing borderland.

Families must have felt this ambiguity especially when receiving letters not from their own relatives but from the superintendent and matron of the asylum. They sometimes were forced to confront and accept the idea of their loved ones' potential state of oblivion. Such letters do not reveal what these patients were suffering from: it is not clear if they were seemingly benumbed owing to a state of depression or melancholia, or the "flat affect" of dementia praecox; if they appeared as such owing to a particular kind of treatment such as the sedative paraldehyde, which induced sleep; or if it was simply institutional life that was atrophying.[33] To a woman who was inquiring about her husband's welfare at the Racine asylum, the superintendent wrote in 1924: "[I] would say that he seems about the same as when he came here. Can see no change to speak of. His mind seems to be a blank and he shows no interest in anything. Gave him your letter but cannot tell how much he will get out of it."[34] Was this a blunt letter that would emotionally devastate the families who received it, or was it simply a descriptive state of affairs that family members would accept as the given reality of mental illness or the institution?

It is entirely possible, of course, that the superintendent was being insensitive in addition to being resigned. During the early twentieth century and interwar years, some observers of American psychiatry characterized asylum superintendents and employees—and even American psychiatry on the whole—as both anti-humanist and anti-intellectual. The nineteenth-century view that insanity was a brain disorder was still prevalent, and during that period medical students studied psychiatrist Emil Kraepelin's diagnostic scheme; most of his diagnoses did not include the concept of a cure. His emphasis instead was on categorization and description.[35] Perhaps a psychiatric legacy of diagnosis in part accounts for the superintendent's tone and apparent lack of sympathy—this transformation of a patient into a description of an ailment—though he hardly offered a technical, scientific description either.

Perhaps it is also the case that, of necessity, most superintendents and state hospital employees in particular were preoccupied with management and custodial functions, and this involved more attention to symptoms rather than psychotherapy.[36] In a 1921 article, the superintendent of Kings Park State Hospital in New York wrote that the daily exigencies of the "thousands of poor unfortunates committed to our care" meant that the superintendent could become "somewhat calloused both as to our own feelings toward patients and also with respect to our attitudes toward their friends and relatives." He noted that it was much easier to state "the patient's condition is unchanged since your last visit" in a letter home rather than to "convey the idea to the recipient that we actually have a personal interest in the patient." He was sympathetic to how the family must feel: "we can well imagine the effect upon the relatives of a brief reply to . . . inquiries."[37] However, he did caution that many family members of patients were "ignorant of our aims and purposes, often speak our language poorly, have little education, or are peculiar personalities. Further, their conceptions of State institutions are often colored by the lurid accounts of ill treatment of patients gleaned from sensational newspapers or from badly informed friends." Still, to "secure trust" and "eliminat[e] suspicion and prejudice," he believed that superintendents needed to employ "tactful, sympathetic and humane wording."[38] "Bald truth," in his view, such as a patient's prognosis being hopeless, might "better be left unsaid."[39] This ideal of discretion might have been a kind of "benevolent deception," which was still quite common for physicians vis-à-vis their patients with serious illnesses during the early twentieth century.[40]

Still, it is not clear whether saying a patient was not taking an interest in anything was indeed a "bald truth" or whether a description of disinterest could simply be perceived as "the way things were" inside a state hospital. And it was not just superintendents at public hospitals who used this language. At the Sheppard and Enoch Pratt Hospital in Towson, Maryland, a private psychiatric hospital outside of Baltimore where psychoanalysis was prominent, the superintendent, Ross Chapman, wrote in a letter to a man inquiring about a female relative in 1932 that though she was "quiet, pleasant, [and] friendly," she "takes no particular interest in anything."[41] In another letter a week later he noted that she "shows no particular interest in things going on about her, though she takes part in various hospital activities."[42]

Physicians' judgments about patient "rationality" were important because those who were deemed irrational were often diagnosed with mania or dementia; the three primary psychiatric diagnoses of the early twentieth century were mania, dementia, and melancholy.[43] Still, the tone of these letters is quite unceremonious, comments that might have been written in a doctor's note rather than in a note to a family member since they do not bear the markings of intimacy or emotional reciprocity often associated with letters. It seems that this style of writing in the third person from ward notes addressed to a medical readership also could blob out into what psychiatrists wrote to family members. In fact, it is difficult to discern what sort of genre or narrative form these letters to families actually are, particularly given that during the early twentieth century letters to and from the hospital superintendent were published as entertainment, in the form of captivity narratives.[44]

Whatever the motivation for the tone of the letters, it is striking that disinterested, oblivious patients could be presented as comfortable, even satisfied. The nineteenth-century insane asylum, too, once harbored the ideal of a state of peacefulness, in the form of enforced idleness, in a bucolic setting, so that the image of rest held some benevolent connotations. Even if the early twentieth century was an age of disillusionment with asylum medicine, some observers still held onto the nineteenth-century ideal of the asylum as a placid retreat and refuge, a place where one could escape an overstimulating environment and get "re-set," and they grafted this ideal onto the patients. This view also entailed a charitable reading of confinement as seclusion and a pause from the intensity of the pace of life outside the asylum.[45]

The extreme form of this peacefulness and resignation was the patient who became an automaton. This figure has a striking resonance with a legacy of often ambivalent images of the individual as a windup toy that animated modernist American thought and culture, appearing in reflections on the second wave of American industrialization at the turn of the century, and mechanized production, made famous in paintings such as Thomas Anschutz's *The Ironworkers' Noontime* (1880), in Thorstein Veblen's turn-of-the-century theorizing about the merging of bodies and machines, and in Frederick Taylor's conflation of man and machine in *Principles of Scientific Management* (1911), something that gained new life in the Fordist standardization of the 1920s.[46] Here, the mechanical individual is both a revered and a discomfiting figure, embodying the all-encompassing nature of capitalism, but also an exciting futurism. To be alive in this period was to have a unique consciousness about time and newness, including new technologies, new ideas, new experiences, and the overturning of tradition and received wisdom, all of which suggested powerfully that the modern era was fundamentally different than any other.[47] Perhaps an underacknowledged emotional ideal in this period of social upheavals is serenity.

Patients at times yearned for a sense of peace and a refuge from the intensity of modern life, as well as from their own feelings. Perhaps this was particularly the case for Depression era writers who were disillusioned with the commercialism of the "jazz age" and its excesses, or simply its discomfiting pace. The novelist Millen Brand evoked a reverence for tranquility and an understanding of inertia as peacefulness in his novel of Depression era New York City, *The Outward Room* (1937). This is the story of Harriet, a young woman who had been living in an unnamed mental hospital outside of New York City for seven years with a diagnosis of what was then called manic depression. The novel begins with this arresting passage: "She always woke up early. . . . This morning . . . she followed the receding sound [of a nurse's step]. The air was gray, sunless just before dawn. . . . In its half-light, clean of thought, she lay looking at the indistinct furniture . . . but hardly seeing it. More than not seeing. It was peace."[48] The passage is a kind of embrace of an in-between world, of sleep and consciousness, night and day, and emotion and emotionlessness. Still, if there are hierarchies of emotional states in this novel, lows predominated over highs: "Sitting on the edge of the bed, she looked downward passively at the floor . . . she was able to think more quietly . . . what she feared [most was] any return, even by implication, to the 'manic.'"[49]

Journalist William Seabrook's memoir, *Asylum* (1953), also repudiates the manic quality of modern life for a therapeutic sense of sequestered peace. In

1933, he committed himself to the Bloomingdale Asylum in Westchester, New York, to treat his alcoholism. He stayed there until 1935, writing an autobiographical account of his experience that became a best seller.[50] When first admitted, he confessed that "I came here for seclusion. I came here to be locked up. I thought I had rented a nice, quiet cell." He appreciated the therapeutic technique of being in a wet pack, which felt to him like a "cocoon" and made him think of the "womb . . . how nice and safe and warm it was." In the distance he could hear some "ordinary, living, human sounds way down the corridor somewhere, but they didn't disturb or concern me. I sweated, time passed, and the tension was gone and the jangling nervousness disappeared too, faded slowly as it does under a strong soporific. I was soon as peaceful as a four-month fetus."[51] The image of confinement, in what some called the "modern day straitjacket" of the wet pack, or what was known in "asylum colloquialism as an 'ice cream sandwich,'"[52] is here conjured not with a sense of coercion but with appreciation for the interlude of introspection it offered. How the modern world does or does not permit a reckoning with inner life was an urgent theme for interwar Americans, particularly as the turn inward was something of a modernist preoccupation in both the sciences and the arts.[53]

The sense of peace that Seabrook discovered here was felt within the body; it was not an abstract state of being. It was not just a rest from a feeling of "cognitive overload"[54] that some patients sought but a sense of peace that was sensual as much as it was mental. Historian Otniel Dror has argued that a powerful shift occurred between the Victorian era and the modern era in America in terms of how scientists understood the relationship between the body and emotions. While the Victorian era prized an emotionally excited organism for laboratory-centered physiological research, the ideal scientific subject of modernity was both a de-emotionalized and anesthetized body.[55] This too sounds something like an automaton, stripped of an interior life.

Perhaps the divide between life inside the asylum and in the outside world can be expressed, in the modern period, as a contrast between the sloweddown spaces of introspection and the sped-up spaces of non-introspection. This perception perhaps was more urgent during the Depression when a desire for spaces untouched by or transcending industrial capitalism and the producerist ethos was quite pressing, perhaps a reimagining of the mental hygiene impetus at the turn of the century that urged industrial capitalists to slow down and take time to rest before suffering nerve damage or "business depressions."[56] The idea that if one were "released" from the struggle to make money one could find psychic freedom was a long-standing one in

American psychiatric thought, and some interwar era asylums were relatively self-sustaining communities, a holdover from the nineteenth century.[57] Historian Howard Brick has described a widespread embrace of a "postcapitalist" vision during the interwar years that, in its American incarnation, tended to be quite optimistic in the attempt to free "economic man" from the more suffocating parts of competitive, economic individualism while still being individualistic.[58] Is there a way in which the interwar asylum can also be described as "postcapitalist," or at the very least nonproductive? Lying in bed one night Seabrook reflected, implicitly, on this idea. He noted that life in the asylum "require[s] no effort, payment, money or responsibility. My pockets are empty. I have no money here. I need none. Here all things are free as salvation."[59]

These kinds of asylum therapeutic techniques, especially divorcing patients from activity and the work world, held a more complicated legacy for women than they did for men. The very concept of monotony and relationships to a range of domesticities were more freighted for women than for men, particularly for turn-of-the-century "new women." Writer Charlotte Perkins Gilman famously felt forced to submit to the "rest cure" for a month in 1887 under the care of neurologist S. Weir Mitchell. In her rest cure she was asked to be as domestic as possible and not to write or be creative. She used this experience as the basis for her famous short story "The Yellow Wall-Paper," which depicts a decline into psychosis under such conditions.[60] Zelda Fitzgerald had a similar experience in the mid-twentieth century. In 1934, when she was in her thirties, she underwent treatment after having "breakdowns" and what was speculated to be schizophrenia. One institution she was treated at was Craig House, a sanatorium in Beacon, New York, where she too was denied a rigorous creative life.[61] Her psychiatrist there noted that it had been a struggle to get Zelda to stop writing her short stories. However, he noted that "she gets a certain amount of definite recreation out of her painting, and do not think that should be curtailed."[62] Here it was the psychiatrist who decided what constituted leisure and peacefulness and what constituted more mentally taxing work. A lesser-known writer and memoirist, Margaret Wilson, spent more than five years in a sanatorium after her nervous breakdown in 1931. Wilson was a professional woman with a PhD from Columbia who had taught, quite happily, in a "well-known vocational college for women." She described the "business atmosphere" and the producerism of the outside world as one that "buoyed" her up, with its "clacking typewriters, constant telephoning, dictating through Dictaphones, rushing salesmen, and various interruptions." But the "air of the sanitarium was different." She calls it alternately "unpleasant" but also "exciting" and "disturbing."[63]

While Wilson's portrait of the asylum is much more ambivalent than that of writers in the vein of Jane Hillyer, neither is it as purely repressive as it was for Gilman and even for Zelda Fitzgerald. The captivity narrative was well known in the mythology of the asylum thanks to such highly publicized nineteenth-century accounts as *The Trial of Ebenezer Haskell* (1869) and Elizabeth Packard's *The Prisoners' Hidden Life, or, Insane Asylums Unveiled* (1868), and it endured into the interwar years.[64] What Margaret Wilson offers is a subtler kind of asylum captivity narrative than the ones so deeply entrenched in the American cultural imagination. She damns the place with faint praise when she writes: "like a modern jail . . . there were some good points. The ward was thoroughly aired, cleaned, shined, and the walls and ceilings were nicely painted."[65]

Still, mental hospital patients and their families must have been acquainted with these kinds of popular portraits, and these historical cultural scripts might have weighed heavily on them. Accordingly, sometimes patients and families were simply grateful when the physical torture and oppression they perceived to be characteristic of an earlier, more benighted age were not present. A similar sense of gratitude toward science and modernity can be located in broader American narratives regarding the "march of man toward progress" popularized in the post–World War I period.[66] Henry Collins Brown, for instance, writing in the 1930s, found that Bloomingdale Hospital was more modern than it had been in his imagination. "In olden times it was considered perfectly good form to dig holes in the ground as prisons for such unfortunates as myself, and throw them into it like rats in a pit," he wrote. "It is only within recent years that this problem of mental treatment has become a department of medical activity under the State."[67] Another mother felt indebted to Racine for the fact that it was not one of these "rat pits" that Brown describes. When her daughter returned home from Racine, this mother rejoiced in her daughter's everyday accomplishments. She wrote to the matron in 1922 to let the hospital know that her daughter was "doing just fine so far and I hope she will keep it up. She is having her teeth fixed just at present and goes down town and back alone just as well as any sane person. I am very much pleased." This mother said of Racine: "It pleases us to hear her speak so well of all you people up there. She sure thinks you people are just it. She tells us what she did up there and how she was her own boss. Nobody was cross or mean to her."[68] The letter is perhaps indicative of not only the generally meager expectations of even the "modern" asylum but also a more general hopelessness or at least a dearth of possibilities about one's prospects in life.

The mental hospital all but compelled its patient inhabitants to become observers of the quotidian details of the day to day, a habit of mind mirrored by their witnesses and loved ones outside of the hospital. Often the only solace and gestures of empathy that loved ones could give to patients were news of day-to-day life and the acknowledgment of the passage of time in the outside world, suggesting a sense of inevitability about the separation between those inside and outside the asylum. "Life continues" is a cliché that, although perhaps the ultimate of resigned observations, could be reassuring in this context. The Florida daughter who wrote to her mother in the Racine asylum during the 1920s often talked about the weather, including one hot, dry summer they had been having. She had just sent her mother a care package and asked: "How did you like the mangoes, isn't that a queer fruit." She said that she had "planted a date tree" and she "heard, but I don't believe it, that it must be 1,000 years old before it bears dates. Now that long I can never live."[69]

The feeling of disjuncture between the world of the sick inside institutional environments and the world of the well outside them has been remarked upon and metaphorized across time. But there is also something historically specific about noticing the passage of time during a historical moment that was so self-consciously modern. Interwar Americans could scarcely help but register swift changes surrounding them, part of a vast swath of disorienting developments in a society that was detraditionalizing, perhaps best expressed by technological transitions.[70] "Screaming airplanes, bearing the night mail for the Far West, used to zoom past my window just at sleepy time,"[71] Henry Collins Brown wrote of his stay in the asylum. Few Americans had experience on airplanes, and they could be evoked with a particular kind of violence.[72] The Florida daughter was also noticing these developments punctuating her landscape: "Last week an airplane turned over half a block from our house [and] the man wasn't hurt, but the airplane is a wreck. I am always afraid one will fall on our house ... sometimes there are a half dozen flying around, and they make such noise." Only at the end of her letter does she move from acknowledging the passage of time and changes in the physical environment to concern for her mother: "How are you feeling Mother, I do hope much better. I can think of nothing more to write this time, I close with lots of love and hope."[73] A patient at Racine also simply observed the rhythms of daily life in the asylum in one of her letters, giving her writing almost a stream-of-consciousness tone, perhaps enforced by the environment of the hospital itself. "I just looked at the clock, it is quarter to one. Hot Dog! I hear the radio say. Hot Dog! again."[74] Her life, too, featured these reminders of outside life, even as the radio here might have acted as an enforcer of disinterest rather than a link to that world: "The patients <u>do not</u> talk much here. I guess they are a bunch of radio listeners."[75]

Just as there was a particularly modernist way of observing and experiencing time, so too was there a time-bound, asylum way of seeing, often experienced with the same ambivalence. Jane Hillyer noted that "my powers of observation became very acute, more acute than they had been before—or have been since. This was partly because I had unlimited leisure to look." During the summer, she "looked and looked and LOOKED ... I was alone and the passage of time seemed particularly slow. I began to watch the grass. ... I had just discovered the minute shadow that one grass blade ... throws against another. ... No one had ever called my attention to this."[76] As psychiatric theorist J. H. van den Berg wrote in his phenomenology of sickness, *The Psychology of the Sickbed*, "What healthy person ever saw a flower open, a caterpillar pupate or a butterfly spread its damp wings?"[77] In both of their evocations, the experience of hospitalized sickness, in its structurelessness, offered an intensified sense of both time and place.

The sharpening of observation, though, also could breed a more critical posture toward the hospital and a less passive style of noticing that clashed somewhat with resignation. The sense that the hospital was inherently institutional and transient rather than domestic and enduring, for example, was palpable in patient reflections. Wilma Wilson, a former actress who had been known as Wilma Carnes during her acting days, was an alcoholic sent to Camarillo Hospital in California in 1939 for, as she calls it, "drinking when I should have been thinking." Here she was given to noticing, and not simply passively, small details of daily institutional life. She said of their bath towels that "we never had any other towels than those small, grayish, exceedingly hairy squares."[78] While most wards had a "magazine rack, and the inevitable locked radio ... there were no rugs or pictures or other knickknacks dear to feminine hearts."[79] Such "knickknacks" were traditionally absent in mental hospitals; this was a source of distress for some patients and even for hospital architects and designers.[80] In addition to what she took as being divested of femininity, smells were also quite powerful for Wilson, forcing her to confront, simultaneously, odors of embodiment and deodorization. She noted that the hospital was "scoured" each day with "antiseptic" but still "there always emanated from [the patients'] rooms a sour, revolting stench. ... The buildings were clean and modern … [But there] is an indefinable odor to insanity, an identifying scent as unmistakable as the odor of death, and far more unpleasant. Once smelled, it is always recognizable."[81] Richard Noll also discusses the unique smells of turn-of-the-century asylums, a distinctive combination of bodily odors, ammonia, and the sedative paraldehyde.[82] Such reflections about bedrooms, towels, and caged radios demonstrate a strong ambivalence about the domestic reassurances of institutions.

Emotional pragmatism and resignation were also not dispositions that meshed well with psychoanalysis, and the tensions between these different sensibilities—one seemingly emotionally and analytically terse and the other more emotionally extravagant and analytically playful—also characterized patient reflections of the hospital when psychoanalysis was on offer. Dr. William Alanson White was the superintendent of Saint Elizabeths Hospital in Washington, D.C., from 1903 to 1937. This hospital was a federally run, public hospital, at this time for soldiers and sailors, founded on the nineteenth-century "moral treatment" model. He made some revelatory remarks about psychoanalysis in this vein, as he was somewhat dubious about the individual's capacity for self-understanding. This seems counterintuitive coming from someone who had been part of the "new psychiatry" of the turn of the century, a group of psychiatrists who had faith in psychotherapy, did not ascribe wholeheartedly to the disease model of scientific medicine, and were prevalent in a shift in thinking from diagnosing insanity to preserving mental health.[83] Still, in 1920 he pronounced that the "average person goes blundering on through life without any realization or at least any adequate realization of what various forces are behind his conduct which urges him forward."[84] Patients at times at least privately resented this posture of psychiatric knowingness about hidden motivations.

While Freud and his colleagues, from their vantage point in the early twentieth century, debated the role of empathy, objectivity, and emotional presence in the consultation room, as well as the analyst's opacity, in personal accounts patients complained not just of psychiatric coldness but of intrusiveness and, implicitly, of overinterpretation, of being denied the "right to reticence,"[85] as Erving Goffman called it. James Duffy, for instance, wrote a rather damning booklet in 1939 about his stay at the Gallinger Insane Hospital in Washington, D.C., called *The Capital's Siberia.* Though he is careful to say that the conditions he describes inside Gallinger were due "largely to carelessness and neglect than to anybody's desire to be cruel," he also indicts the hospital as a "concentration camp."[86] He notes that the "the sights I saw were heart breaking, cruel, and cold blooded," including aged, bedridden patients calling out in pain who were "told to shut up you old s.o.b. you ought to be dead long ago."[87] But what also discomfited him, beyond the crowding, the frightful sounds, the nauseating smells, the fear of assault, and loneliness, was something far more abstract than the material conditions at the hospital: the way psychiatrists treated patients. "I cannot understand how Dr. . . . Silverman [the staff psychiatrist at the hospital] can ask such intimate questions that have nothing to do with the mind," he wrote. "When a good doctor of psychiatry sees that a patient resents certain questions, he knows it is not right just to keep asking those questions that . . . [cause] the patient to be ill at ease. Particularly, he has no right to ask them in a brow-beating or domineering manner."[88]

Ironically, perceived psychiatric voyeurism might have stimulated a greater desire for discretion, subtlety, and reticence—postures that resisted, rather than accepted, the psychoanalytical mores offered in some institutions. Wilma Wilson was taken aback when she met her first psychiatrist in prison in Lincoln Heights Jail in California. She described the psychiatrist as an "ancient little man" who asked her bluntly: "How's your sex life?" (see Figure 1),[89] and her general impression of him was that he was a dirty old man. Another memoirist, Marian King, also found that psychiatrists were rather invasive, at least at first. King had been hospitalized after an overdose of veronal, a commercial barbiturate to induce sleep, and she wrote a memoir, *The Recovery of Myself* (1931), about her experiences at the Phipps Psychiatric Clinic at Johns Hopkins University. Here she describes a psychiatric "quizzing":[90] "Now, young lady," her psychiatrist said to her, "I want you to tell me the story of your life as far back as you can remember . . . begin with your infant days and come up to the first day that you entered this hospital, and DON'T stop until I interrupt." He wanted "all the facts, true ones. Everything relating to your family which concerns you; your associations; your schooling, and general interests in life."[91] In another session, the psychiatrist asked King if she knew what "petting parties" were and whether or not she "believed in them." She said of course she knew, but she "resented such questions. They seemed unnecessarily vulgar to me." When she expressed her disgust, he responded with, "You are a bit prissy, I see."[92] In fact, sexuality was something King found particularly reductive about psychiatry. She recalled the curious pairings of questions in a survey that her doctor had asked her to fill out: "Do you ever think of suicide? When you are on the top of a high place do you feel like jumping off? Did you ever love a woman? Do you like men? Which do you like better, men or women? Why?" She called these questions "useless."[93]

"How's your sex life?"

Figure 1. Wilma
Wilson, *They Call Them
Camisoles* (Los Angeles:
Lymanhouse, 1940), 25.

"Useless" suggests both a pragmatic and discerning posture toward psychoanalysis and confessional culture as encountered in the hospital. Lawrence M. Jayson wrote an autobiography of his year in Kings County Hospital in Brooklyn; he was taken there after he "tried to get to Europe by walking across the ocean"[94] and heard a voice that said "you are worthless. You've never been useful and you've never been any good."[95] He had been diagnosed with dementia praecox.[96] Jayson was not opposed to psychoanalytical interpretation or even his doctor's overtures: he was in fact quite "touched" by his psychiatrist's "kindness and soft-spoken manners" but "to him I could say nothing, shaking my head at all his questions, continuing to sob as he patted me gently. I was past the state of wishing to be dead. . . . Telling him could not help."[97] When Carl Jung delivered a series of lectures at the Fordham University medical school in 1912, he argued that "everyone likes to unburden himself of painful secrets" and that confession brought about a "tremendous feeling of relief."[98] Confession has been an especially fraught concept for historians and theorists of psychiatry, but neither relief nor, exactly, coercion to confess best describes the dilemmas seen in these writings.[99]

All of this attention to private or psychic life seemingly reinforced individualism. And yet something of a communal spirit also could be found inside the asylum of this period, with all the suffocating and liberating qualities of a commune, and this tempered that individualism while being somewhat incompatible with resignation or passivity. During the interwar era, the idea of community and participation still had a generally positive connotation in

American thought and culture—before the emergence of a more foreboding one in the post–World War II period—a sense that communities provided fellowship, companionship, cooperation, and spaces of learning and a way of tempering crass consumption and materialism. Interwar era political associations emblematized communitarianism more than individualism; and a "participatory ethic" and even collectivism commanded sociocultural prestige particularly during the 1930s.[100] Perhaps this helps explain why patient unreachability—a perennial medical concern in psychiatry—was particularly troubling from the vantage point of the interwar years. A psychiatric textbook published in the United States in 1934, *Modern Clinical Psychiatry*, discussed, in a section on psychotic disorders, "a state known as *depersonalization*. The patient has feelings of vagueness, of unreality, of detachment, or of being a spectator of life instead of taking part in it."[101] This statement pathologizes an observer mode of being over a participator mode of being, or a failure to "take part" in the community. This kind of diagnosis culturally resonated at a moment when civic engagement, commitment, and belonging were privileged modes of being or citizenship.[102]

A paradoxical ethos of the mental hospital was that the institutional culture it created did not easily encompass the introspection its space was also purported to offer. Patients were not "allowed" to stay unreachable. Lawrence Jayson found a patient culture of constant activity to be somewhat overwhelming. During his hospital stay, "our social events began to take all my time and I had no opportunity to think of the past. Dances, games, moving pictures, arts and crafts were crowded into our days' activities. We were not allowed to stand still. Life became fun."[103] As a 1930 silent film about Utica State Hospital in New York noted, "busy hands drive cares away" and "Dr. Exercise and Dr. Fresh Air" had curative benefits.[104]

Even William Alanson White concurred. He wrote to a prospective patient in 1930, who, in White's estimation, suffered only from mild neurosis, "You are no doubt inclined to think too much about yourself; your thoughts are too introspective, which naturally tend to aggravate your condition, and if it were possible to pull yourself together and find an interest outside of yourself I feel sure that you would begin to note an improvement." He recommended "some kind of work that will get you away from yourself."[105] Ironically, here a superintendent who was open to psychoanalysis took up the freighted language of "pull[ing] yourself together," precisely what cynical observers of psychoanalysis might say. Colonel Bell Burr commented upon this in a 1921 textbook designed for psychiatric nurses and attendants. He wrote that inside the hospital, "routine itself is favorable" because there was "less to stim-ulate, less to annoy." Moreover, in a hospital the patient was not "threatened or punished for disorderly conduct," and "if depressed he is not adjured by everyone he meets to 'brace up'. . . . In a hospital he becomes less introspec-tive. He is thrown into the society of those similarly afflicted, and finds that his trouble is not more deep and abiding than that of his neighbor."[106] But was the culture of enforced fun in the hospital not doing its own version of "bracing up," perhaps reconstructing broader social values of self-reliance and activity? As historian Matthew Gambino has noted, a marker of mental health in early twentieth-century America was a "combination of personal responsibility and civic engagement," an ideology that was in fact steeped in early twentieth-century racial ideology and whiteness, one that placed Afri-can Americans in particular outside of larger civic life in its attempt to delin-eate models of socially acceptable behavior.[107]

Striking in Burr's passage also is the language of being "thrown" into a community of people with parallel illnesses. Asylum communities were not chosen ones, and patients could feel powerless in the face of them, resigned to their existence. At other times, these communities could be intriguing to patients, as well as baffling and discomfiting, so much so that they were moti-vated to write about them and often question them. Sometimes this reflec-tion was simply to resist the human diversity on offer in the hospital: not all of these institutional encounters encouraged kindness or empathy. Jane Hillyer noted that at mealtimes the patients "all sat down together, all kinds and conditions and colours. A law exists in that State to the effect that in no public institutions can negroes be segregated. A sulky looking 'yellow gal' sat opposite me. I was stunned. Though race prejudice has never been a thing with which I have had to contend, this was of course unheard of."[108] In her telling, race is on the same plane as a "condition." Generally, asylums were racially segregated until midcentury, and even then, as with many other insti-tutions, they were slow to desegregate. The customs of the larger community in which the hospital was located tended to reflect policies on racial integra-tion. The mixing of races at the dinner table, an intimate space, was often more troubling to whites when desegregation did occur: hospitals, swimming pools, restaurants, and schools were more controversial to whites than tran-sient spaces such as buses.[109] Hillyer not only felt she had to take her place among other races, but in her telling she also was relegated to the "vulgar" lower classes. When she started a rumor that one of the nurses, Miss Wil-lis, was secretly a man, Miss Willis confronted her: "'You darn fool . . . what do you mean by saying I am a man? You idiot, you haven't the sense you were born with.'"[110] Miss Willis then banged Hillyer's head into a wall and this too was something new, as Hillyer was not used to physical violence. "'Spanking may be necessary for poor mothers who have no time to give to their children, but it will not do for women of leisure,' was my mother's dictum. I had looked upon any kind of corporal discipline as simple barbarism, not for our world. 'It has come to this,' I thought."[111] Hillyer is quite judgmental of her fellow patients, and goes well beyond simply noticing her hospital surroundings, to being voyeuristic about them. Henry Collins Brown also admitted that he used to visit mental hospitals as a young person on a "slumming expedition."[112] "Slumming" was a term taken up by turn-of-the-century wealthy white urbanites who engaged in "slumming parties," where they explored immigrant and working-class districts or areas where sexual minorities might congregate.[113] Clearly the boundaries of this activity were quite broad, and the mentally ill have been an underacknowledged factor in the phenomenon. Indeed, even by the 1930s, visitors still went to the asylum to observe, part of a long-standing tradition of medicine as spectacle, a nineteenth-century practice that had not withered away by midcentury even though, in the words of literary critic Susan M. Schweik, modernity deemed disability an "improper object to be looked at."[114]

One thread that animated some patient reflections in this period was irony, which also could be nurtured in the asylum, perhaps again a more critical, sometimes affectionately so, reaction to the hospital environment than simply reconciling oneself to be there. Henry Collins Brown was able to make light of the delusions of his fellow patients during his stay at Bloomingdale: "We had some really distinguished guests—General Pershing, Napoleon . . . Herbert Hoover, Mussolini . . . and Henry Ford. On the women's side there were the Queen of Sheba, Mary Pickford, Greta Garbo, Ethel Barrymore . . . Lady Astor . . . and Edna Ferber." Brown felt, simply, that there were some "queer fish in a state hospital,"[115] and this was something that Wilma Wilson noticed, too. At first, she hoped that she would be segregated from the other "nuts" at Camarillo, because she had been committed as an alcoholic. She was bemused to meet a fellow patient, Elsie, who found everything about the hospital better than she expected. "'Isn't this nice?' [Elsie] purred. 'For a long time I won't have to worry about going to work and my husband WILL HAVE TO find a job." Elsie kept going around saying, "'Gosh, isn't this a beautiful hospital?'" When Wilson asked her, "'What about all these maniacs knocking about?'" Elsie responded, "'Oh, them! . . . I got used to nuts up in Psycho.'"[116] Wilson stayed in this fairly bemused register when discussing her fellow patients, even those with more profound delusions. When she attended a patient dance, she said she had a "marvelous" dance partner and she would have "enjoyed myself completely had he not talked to himself the entire time, interspersing meaningless words with the low, ominous laughter usually reserved for the Black Coffin program on the radio."[117] Perhaps this mood of irony, seemingly without reverence or pity, was fostered by the genre of the captivity narrative as well as the sentimental novel, which historically have contained moments and a tone of romantic melodrama.[118] In Margaret Wilson's memoir, *Borderland Minds* (1940), for example, one chapter is titled "Escapes and Suicides!"[119]; the punctuation indicates the hospital experience is narrated as something of an adventure.

These ironic patients, and even reflectively critical ones who eventually wrote memoirs about their experiences, were relatively privileged ones, though, those with the capacity and insight to reflect upon their time in the hospital. Other patients were more chronic, and some of course died during their stay in the asylum. The institutionalized mentally ill during this period had much higher mortality rates than the people who lived outside of them, often because they were sites of epidemics of infectious diseases such as tuberculosis, diphtheria, typhoid, and dysentery.[120] Death in the asylum illuminates a lingering nineteenth-century idea of a "good death," in addition to an ethos of resignation, because the asylum was a place that ideally should have provided time to take stock of life and to prepare spiritually for death.[121]

But it could not always serve as this kind of site, and especially created doubt and deepened anxiety about the moment of death for the loved ones who could not be there. The family and friends of a middle-aged female patient at the Racine asylum knew that she was not doing well. Her elderly father was still living, and a female friend of his wrote to the matron to ask why his daughter had died in the asylum. The friend asked: "Did [she] ask for anyone as she passed out of life? . . . [Her] father ask me if I saw [her]. I told him yes. So as not to hurt his feeling. I am very gentle with old people in my manner toward them. But I was not with [her] or near that place at the time she died." Ultimately, though, her attitude about death paralleled—and perhaps informed—a resignation about mental illness so prevalent in this period. "There are lots of sorrow in this World," this woman concluded, "we can not understand."[122] Here the superintendent wrote back to provide details about this woman's death. Spare and stripped of sentiment, this letter nonetheless was offered in the spirit of bestowing a sense of peace. Though her death was caused by myocarditis, the superintendent reminded this inquirer that the patient also had long been "extremely nervous and melancholy and always depressed." This emotional state was asserted as a condition, in the same vein and in the same sentence as her heart problems. As to the moment of the death itself he wrote that: "No, she did not ask for any one before she passed away, seemed very content and reconciled saying she was prepared to die, and waiting for the end. Yes she knew her father when he visited her last time, seemed glad to see him, altho very weak and not able to talk much."[123]

Family members also experienced this sense of quiet surrender in the face of a loved one's death in an institution. A man whose mother was at Racine wrote to the matron about his mother's eventual death there, saying: "It was my wish to have been with her at the end but perhaps it is just as well."[124] In response, the matron wrote to tell him that she "regret[ted] that we did not wire you in time that it would have been possible for you to be here at the time of her death." She continued, "Without a doubt you are anxious to know how your mother passed away . . . very quietly, just got weaker and weaker, she made no comments or any requests of any kind. She was completely helpless during her confinement in the Hospital."[125] What is perhaps most revealing here, though, is that, again, hospital superintendents and managers conflated an image of weakness and helplessness at the verge of death with peace, another version of oblivion, akin to being perfectly content to sit and stare out the window all day.

CHAPTER 2

Biological Psychiatry
and the "Happy Drone"

Sociologist Paul Starr has argued that most modern people's central encounter with science comes in the form of personal medicine.[1] Much as interwar era mental hospitals were often custodial and their conditions varied, often drastically, they also had at least a veneer of science: they had a chief psychiatrist, nurses, and physicians, even if not always enough of them. They offered medication and diagnosis, even if sparingly, and embodied, though the institution often chose to mute them, medical identities. During the interwar years they also increasingly offered biological psychiatry in the form of psychosurgeries, which reached their apex in the United States between the late 1930s and the 1950s.

It was often patients themselves and especially their family members, not just their psychiatrists, who were purveyors of what medical philosopher Anne Hunsaker Hawkins has called the "militant ideology of the cure."[2] Biological psychiatry seemed to contain a promise of possessive individualism, in that the patient and families could potentially "have" their old selves, and family members, prior to mental illness and institutionalization, back.[3] The cures offered by biological psychiatry did not always promise a huge amount, sometimes just a state of peacefulness, or even acquiescence. But as patients and families gradually attached hope to psychosurgeries, and the restoration of the patient beyond the institutionalized automaton figure, they helped accelerate a shift away from a broader sensibility of inevitability and tragedy about life, mental illness in its hospital incarnation in particular. Those who contemplated drastic biological interventions were often sorrowful, to be sure, but they also sensed dramatic curing possibilities in a way that their forebears, who lacked a biological psychiatric option, did not. Patients, families, and cultural observers who experienced biological psychiatry were more precisely focused on science and cures in their writings rather than on aspects of the world that were not under their control: the weather, the physical and built environment, the unfolding of time. Just as resignation has a passive affect, embracing scientific modernity has a more active one. Peacefulness as a vaunted and coveted emotional state inside the hospital was transforming into activity and animation beyond the institution.

Still, as promises to "fix" the mentally ill brain emerged, contradictions also surfaced about the expectations of scientific modernity. Especially by the early post–World War II period, doctors, patients, and families alike were both fascinated by the potential of biological psychiatry and fearful of scientific modernity, as a new view of it as excessively rationalizing, bureaucratizing, and politically nefarious took hold. An emerging anxiety questioned what would become of the "true self" amid biological intervention, something that dovetailed with a new intellectual uneasiness about the figure of the automaton. While some patients and those who cared for them desired psychosurgeries to allow for a sense of relief and peace, and a life beyond institutionalization, ironically these very interventions would also be condemned for rendering the individual lifeless and enshrining the archetypal automaton patient of the institution.

In the interwar era, however, engagement with science in itself complicated the inevitability of tragedy, whether this was mental illness or losing one's loved one to an institution, by also offering the possibility, even if a faint one, of improvement or cure. In the post–World War era, psychiatric, and increasingly, public knowledge that soldiers could be temporarily afflicted with mental illness suggested that it was not solely hereditary but contextual, and as such could be treated and possibly alleviated. This kind of thinking challenged the idea of the heritability and inescapability of mental illness, as well as mental illness as an unfolding family tragedy over the generations, as early twentieth-century eugenics, still prevalent in the cultural imagination, had suggested. Moreover, by the 1920s, the mental hygiene movement was attempting to unite the human sciences and social activism, suggesting a salutary social power in behavior modification, while a broad conceptual change from insanity to poor adjustment in this period encouraged an interest in personal health and enrichment.[4] And scientific utopianism as a broader cultural trend animated American modernity.

Some families actually preferred to think of their loved ones as having specific biological illnesses because they thought that the possibility of change and recoverability was greater. As Edward Shorter notes, nerves are physical structures that can be said to heal naturally and in that respect it might be comforting to think about illnesses of the nerves. Moreover, the connotations of problems of the nerves were relatively mild.[5] Patients and families in the interwar years thought about domestic cures for maladies of the nerves and engaged in dialogues with scientific authorities about their domestic intuitions, common sense, and folk wisdom, even in the face of institutional taxonomy and scientific language. In 1931 the father of a female patient at the Racine asylum wrote to the superintendent and the matron to say that he believed that life in the hospital was too sedentary and that his daughter "sits down too much. How can any blood or organ work, if she is so lazy. She get dried up and hard if she don't work at something." He also suggested that "if she had raison she get some iron in her blood. And if she ate yeast . . . it put her in fine order. And she come home."[6] In another letter, the same father asked, "Has she much improved. Did she get doctored up? Did she get any yeast to eat every day that is good. For any one its mean good blood good health. Did she get blood from iron tablets. They are good too. Write us soon and let us know how she is?"[7] This man's letters are unvarnished and direct. While they could be read as an instance of a long-standing, populist strain in American health, circumspect about the wisdom of experts, they also could be seen as a kind of domesticization of science. Moreover, self-improvement through exercise or diet or mind cure, or simply the individual will, suggests a kind of lay health practice that endured from the nineteenth century and earlier in American spiritual traditions. In addition, during the previous century nutrition was also posited as a cause for mental illness and that idea carried over into the twentieth century. Moreover, an interest in lay healing was perhaps uniquely accommodated in psychiatry since as a discipline it shared at least some roots with this popular practice.[8]

While domestic and "natural" remedies were some of the only hopes of curability during the interwar era, they often were not enough when institutional life was more unbearable than tolerable. One thirty-two-year-old woman wrote to Dr. White at Saint Elizabeths in 1921 about her thirty-three-year-old husband, who had been a "very smart capable fellow and foreman of the cutting room in the Overall Factory here and was liked by everyone."[9] Here she described her husband's mental illness in terms of a physical condition. Three years prior she noticed that he started getting sore throats constantly. He became worn out and then "lost his mind" and "has been so ever since." After her "town doctors" pronounced his case hopeless, her recourse was to nature: "I took him camping to see if fresh air and being quiet would help and it seemed to a little." Since they were "poor people," she put her baby in "care" and went out to work. She kept her husband home but he "acted so strange" that she put him in Worcester State Hospital in Massachusetts since "there was nothing left for me to do." She went on to describe his state of misery there: "he was so home sick and said he didn't get food to eat," and he could not "have his own clothes."[10] Institutional clothing was still quite common in this period, and the prospect of wearing them was distressingly dehumanizing to some beholders. And even a psychiatrist at Worcester State during the interwar years admitted that the food was so deplorable that the back ward patients there verged on having scurvy owing to such low levels of vitamin C in their blood.[11] This woman decided that even if it "cost my life and baby's he's coming home he's suffering enough."[12] However, this sojourn at home did not work out and in fact was the start of a repeated pattern of hospitalizations, withdrawals, and then more hospitalizations. She underscored the toll this took on her: "my nerves are well worn out as I have a hard position in the shoe shop and then my house work and care of baby after work. I could bear it no longer."[13] If only the hospital could provide "plenty of fresh air," she said, but they "get so little of it there." Instead they are "fed, bathed and then walk the floor or rock until time to go to bed." The hallways of the asylum here assumed a particularly ominous and depressing significance as the dreary substitute for going outside: he was only walking in "those long corridors."[14]

Even if her husband's recurring institutionalization easily could have suggested hopelessness, this woman harbored some faith in scientific remedy. She noted that she wanted her husband's tonsils removed and examined, "but they say no that he will never be any better that his insanity is dementia precox which can never be cured."[15] During the early twentieth century, state hospitals tended to host a mixture of incurables and those whose prognosis was more hopeful, though the hopefuls also could be in psychopathic hospitals, wherein the emphasis was on mental health rather than chronic care.[16] This woman believed that things would be different if only her husband could be treated elsewhere, as she had heard that dementia praecox could be cured at the Trenton State Hospital in New Jersey. But she did not have the money to take him there.[17] Instead she described her sense that her husband was withering away; he believed that the hospital and doctors "don't do nothing to help you." But she ended her letter on a resolute note: "doctor I shall never be satisfied to know that my husband is incurable until these tonsils and teeth are removed"; she wrote that "I feel so bad for those poor patience I'd do most anything to make them happy . . . as you say doctor I think every one of them ought to have a chance the same as any other sickness."[18]

While Dr. White did explicitly ask his patients and their families to view mental illness in the same way as any other sickness,[19] this woman insisted upon an etiology of mental illness from bodily somatic locations, as though seeking an unintentional self rather than something that her husband could will away. Ironically, during the interwar years, American psychiatrists were gradually shifting from somatic models of illness to more social and environmental ones, a trend that would intensify greatly after World War II as the importance of psychoanalysis in institutional psychiatry deepened.[20] Still, her ideas were not just fantastical thinking: scientific psychiatrists who sought to fuse psychiatry with scientific medicine, such as Superintendent Henry Cotton at Trenton State Hospital, practiced body part removals during the interwar era, premised on the idea that toxins produced by bacteria in certain organs caused mental illness, or the "doctrine of focal infection."[21] In this woman's letter the idea of diseased body parts is not a reduction of the individual to clinical material but seems a profound consolation. While William James feared at the turn of the twentieth century that "medical materialism" was belittling, a way of conveying complex emotions as simple biological phenomena, this was not always the case for patients or their families.[22]

The idea of simply evacuating mental illness from the patient undergirded biological psychiatry, as well as the fantasies of many other social observers, families, and patients. Some family pleas were simply for cures, though, and they were more steeped in a language of re-possessed selves that would prevent repeated cycles of institutionalization, as well as the perceived oblivion of mental illness. In 1939, one woman wrote to Dr. Winfred Overholser, the superintendent at Saint Elizabeths beginning in 1937, who lived on the grounds of the hospital, was an advocate of close relationships with the patients, and continued the eclectic tradition of Dr. White. The woman was worried about her nineteen-year-old son, who had "become afflicted five years ago with schizophrenia."[23] Schizophrenia was the most common psychiatric diagnosis of the midcentury, so perhaps this family had some knowledge about the disease.[24] She told Overholser that she would be "deeply grateful" to be kept informed of "newer treatments" and "possible cures"[25] as they developed. "Of course I am heartbroken,"[26] she went on, describing a son who was a high school success, an excellent student, and an athlete but who had become "confused" during high school, losing his "initiative and speech." He was now "terribly tired all the time and occasionally gets stubborn spells," which his mother described as "Foreign to him!" as though he had been invaded by something. He only spoke in "monosyllables,"[27] even after some treatments at a Maryland hospital, including twenty-eight shots of insulin, another somatic therapy popular from the late 1930s to the 1940s in the United States, administered under the premise of salutary mental health benefits after an insulin coma.[28] Her son also had been observed at Sheppard Pratt Hospital and at the Phipps Clinic in Baltimore, both private institutions, but she described her means as "limited" so she "took him to my sister's farm in Virginia."[29] When all else failed in the way of biological cures, she tried for a bucolic retreat, which was resonant of the nineteenth-century asylum ideal. But this option was not satisfying to her because "at present nothing special in way of a cure is being tried."[30]

This mother ended her letter beseechingly in language that was decidedly not resigned to her son's fate: "I can't sit day after day and not try to find something to cure him! We just have not hit on the right medium in his case. I can't let him deteriorate."[31] The final plea was to restore both her son's character as she had known it before he became "foreign" and his sense of animation and enterprise. "[He has] no initiative!" she wrote. "I guess he needs dynamite under him to arouse him!! He was a brilliant boy—always leaned towards sciences and deep subjects, astronomy and such! . . . Please keep [him] in mind . . . and if a possible cure is discovered . . . a cure that is not too dangerous I beg your help and co-operation. I love him so!"[32]

Having family members cured so that they could live outside of institutions was a particularly urgent need during the interwar era and continuing into the war era when the prospect of chronic institutional life was forbidding and in some cases terrifying. Some social experiments with patients seemed viable alternatives to institutional life during the Depression, a time when more and more elderly people were being committed.[33] In this spirit, Harlem Valley State Hospital in Dover, New York, had some of its patients try living in family situations as "foster children" of sorts, an experiment that had also been tried at the turn of the twentieth century, in an effort to separate chronic patients from those showing signs of improvement. The premise of this experiment suggests an idea of people with mental illnesses as orphans during an era when the figure of the orphan had a pervasive cultural presence. In a laudatory 1936 article on family care of psychiatric cases discussing Harlem Valley, Harry A. Laubert noted that a county attorney who employed Anna H., a "young manic," claimed that "'she is the best maid they ever had.' She is practically an adopted daughter of the family, plays and goes skating with the young children and assumes the role of 'big sister' to them." Meanwhile, the caretakers of Rose D. said "they always wanted a daughter and now they have one." And the caretakers of Henry S., "an old senile, are very grateful for his presence in their home as he keeps 'grandpa' occupied at chess at every day. They are now 'buddies.'"[34] Such undertakings allowed, in this case, white families to experience alternate kinship strategies already well established, sometimes to mitigate the severity of racism, in African American and immigrant families.[35]

Still, not all families had access to a social experiment in the vein of Harlem Valley State, and the majority of patients with mental illnesses were hospitalized in the 1930s rather than in the care of families.[36] The overcrowding, disease, seclusion rooms, and use of cuffs as well as the image of patient inertia, dependency, and atrophy in the state hospitals all created incentives to find fast, effective biological treatments. As Martin Summers notes in his study of Saint Elizabeths Hospital, many of these problems, particularly overcrowding, were heightened in the segregated wards in the interwar years. Jack D. Pressman also notes that in many hospitals, patients with various medical conditions were all housed together in the same ward. A patient who was an alcoholic could live next door to a patient suffering from schizophrenia.[37] Moreover, in the 1930s, there was a dearth of medications available to American patients in state hospitals, apart from sedatives such as paraldehyde and barbiturates.[38] This medicine, while perhaps of dubious value to any patient, was especially not helpful for those suffering from extreme depression, psychoses, or schizophrenia. Outside of these drugs, somatic psychiatry also consisted of radical experimental methods, such as the infamous body part removals at Trenton State Hospital.[39]

Popular exposé literature about state hospital conditions in the 1930s and 1940s such as reformist journalist Albert Q. Maisel's well-known piece in *Life* magazine titled "Bedlam, 1946" and journalist Albert Deutsch's *The Shame of the States* (1948), as well as novels in the vein of Ellen Philtine's *They Walk in Darkness* (1945), all painted damning portraits of these institutions, though in the liberal, reformist name of generating more funding for them and a more robust welfare state. Philtine powerfully evoked the "stark bareness" and the suffocating "mingling of human odors with disinfectant," the infestations of insects and rodents, the overcrowding, and the denigration of the human spirit at the fictional Farland State Hospital.[40] Maisel's article emphasizes overcrowding, public neglect, despair, abandonment, depredations, anonymity, dehumanization, violence, abusive attendants, and incompetent doctors. The pictures of shivering, miserable, naked bodies resonate, startlingly, with Holocaust photographs, and he calls the Philadelphia State Hospital at Byberry, one of the largest mental hospitals in the United States at the time, "little more than [a] concentration [camp] on the Belsen pattern."[41]

Deutsch's book, in a similar vein, was written at the behest of state hospital superintendents who were seeking more funding for the hospital system.[42] As such, Deutsch emphasized the dilapidated character of the buildings and the depressing atmosphere inside the institution. He described Byberry in the 1940s as hosting "sick minds" who were "salvageable through proper treatment" but instead "were allowed to rot into hopeless decay and death."[43] Rotting away was a central image in this book, along with more horrific, atavistic, and almost ghoulish images, even when he is careful to set himself apart from more sensationalistic exposé literature. He writes about a family who went to claim their member at the morgue of Manhattan State, only to find "a big rat right on the chest of the corpse."[44] He, too, offers chilling Nazi imagery, saying of Byberry's wards that they reminded him of "pictures of the Nazi concentration camps at Belsen and Buchenwald. I entered buildings warming with naked humans herded like cattle and treated with less concern, pervaded by a fetid odor so heavy, so nauseating, that the stench seemed to have almost a physical existence of its own."[45] He reminds readers that Hitler's personal physician had declared at Nuremberg in 1947 that the "'life of an insane person is not in keeping with human dignity'"[46] and challenges his American readers not to sink to these depths, echoing a stirring injunction made by several American intellectuals in the early postwar era to prevent Nazism from "happening here."[47] "We are not like the Nazis," Deutsch pronounces. "We do not kill off 'insane' people coldly as a matter of official state policy. We do not kill them deliberately. We do it by neglect,"[48] indicting America as a subtler and more insidious Nazi. Here, he condemns a sensibility of passivity by invoking a kind of bystanderism, a theme that was also emerging in transnational conversations about human rights.[49]

Deutsch was mostly sympathetic toward the psychiatrists and staff at these institutions; he simply saw them as hamstrung by a dearth of resources.[50] These portraits were more helpful in engendering anti-institutional sentiment than in generating demand for further funding, however. By the 1950s some social scientists were claiming that institutionalized life did not encourage recovery but instead worsened patient illnesses, even suggesting a condition called "institutionalitis."[51] And throughout his account, Deutsch is unapologetically modernist in his approach, disparaging the past and its treatment of the mentally ill as benighted.[52] He anticipates an enthusiasm for medical cures that would take hold more broadly during the early 1950s, an age of celebrated medical progress, including the Salk vaccine, which contributed to a renewed sense of confidence about the powers of American medicine.[53]

Psychosurgeries were once considered modern themselves. And given the perceptions and realities of interwar, war, and early postwar era institutional life, in this context, a lobotomy might have seemed a necessary intervention, despite its invasiveness and its connotations of tampering not just with the brain but the soul as well.

Lobotomies were introduced in the United States in 1936, though their apex was in the mid-1940s.[54] Before the operation fell out of favor in the mid-1950s, an estimated 20,000 lobotomies had been performed on American psychiatric patients.[55] Most were done in state hospitals, though some were performed in private hospitals or in the psychiatry or neurology department of university medical schools.[56] As an operation, lobotomy was premised on the idea that altering the frontal lobes of the brain could produce a sense of peace and contentment that would calm agitation, or relieve profound depression. This idea was derived from the Portuguese neurosurgeon Egas Moniz, as well as Yale neuroscientists Carlyle Jacobsen and John Fulton in the 1930s, who had witnessed the emotional changes in chimpanzees after altering their frontal lobes. While before the alteration the chimpanzees had been prone to temper tantrums, afterward they appeared as if they had joined a "happiness cult."[57] The operation produced the most significant results on people with schizophrenia and chronic depression, though it would come to be used more indiscriminately between 1945 and 1950 on patients with neuroses, hyperactivity, neurological disorders such as Parkinson's, and perceived sexual disorders, homosexuality among them.[58]

Lobotomy's most famous American practitioners, Walter Freeman, a professor of neurology at George Washington University Medical School (affiliated with Saint Elizabeths Hospital), and James W. Watts, a neurosurgeon, who operated at the George Washington University Hospital, acknowledged that the main relief a lobotomy could offer was from "emotional tension." When a newly lobotomized patient was asked about his worries, he would respond: "'what worries?'"[59] In 1937, Freeman and Watts did admit that in the wake of lobotomy every patient "loses something . . . some spontaneity, some sparkle, some flavor of the personality,"[60] and there is a "bleaching of the emotional tone and the quieting of anxiety."[61] However, in their view, this did not mean that these "patients are apathetic, lacking all emotion."[62] The fact that they sought to defend the operation from the charge of emotionlessness indicates that though peace was still a preferred emotional ideal—especially over a state of agitation—outright apathy was also something to be guarded against. By 1942, Freeman and Watts admitted that in a "considerable portion of cases," especially among those with schizophrenia, hallucinations and delusions persisted, but they hoped that these symptoms would be "lacking [in the] emotional force" they once had.[63] A patient who was less emotionally tortured after a lobotomy was considered a success.[64] This ideal dovetailed nicely with official hospital culture in the interwar years, in which psychiatrists expressly advised their patients to become less introspective.

Accordingly, some observers noted that lobotomized patients were not just affectless but more tractable and manageable in institutional settings.[65] In a 1951 study of sixty-two lobotomized male veterans at the Veterans Hospital in Northport, New York, Lester Drubin noted that these patients, without the "spark" of their psychoses, were now more likely to exhibit "apathy, inertia, and lack of spontaneity." Newly "detached" and "more like automatons," they were now "better institutional citizen[s]."[66] Here being a part of the institution is itself defined as a kind of acquiescence.

Lobotomies were initially quite popular in the American media, and the proclamations made about them were both miraculous and modest, something that both subverts and reinforces acquiescent resignation as a medical and personal mode of being. While the surgery received a powerful imprimatur from the influential *New England Journal of Medicine* in 1936, at a more popular level, patients such as Harry Dannecker, a toolmaker from Indiana who had become tense and nervous and suicidal after losing his job, praised lobotomy by declaring that "psychosurgery cured me" in *Coronet* magazine in 1945.[67] The *Saturday Evening Post* proclaimed famously in 1941 that lobotomies literally "cut worry out of the mind."[68] This article in particular endorsed oblivion as a preferred emotional state by saying that even if the operation transformed a "morbidly anxious man into a careless happy drone . . . it is better so, than to go through life in an agony of hate and fear of persecution."[69] That the words "happy drone" could coexist easily in 1941 and were not contradictory indicates that peace, perhaps even at the risk of emotionlessness, was deemed a possibility worth risking from the vantage point of the war era.

A laudatory article in the *Washington Evening Star* in 1936 even invoked resignation as the ideal that lobotomy could achieve: "It seems unbelievable that uncontrollable sorrow could be changed into normal resignation with an auger and a knife,"[70] as if resignation was the only achievable or livable state anyone could hope to have, perhaps a reimagination of the Freudian logic of "ordinary unhappiness." In fact, though, this is how many psychiatrists represented lobotomy: not necessarily as a cure but as the best attempt to make life more livable for the tortured,[71] almost an extension of the logic of the hospital.

On the one hand, lobotomies seem purely and extremely biological in nature and, at least in their initial years, a modern form of treatment. According to historian Jack Pressman, lobotomy had a symbolic function in linking psychiatry to the rest of medicine and ushering in a more scientific discipline, legitimizing psychiatry in the eyes of other physicians, while again helping relieve the burden on crowded and besieged state hospitals.[72] During the early post–World War II period in particular, American psychiatrists were trying to distinguish themselves from social workers and psychologists, whose professions also had grown in the wake of the war, given these therapeutic professions' increasing importance, especially in relation to the screening of new military recruits.[73] The long-standing debate between those who believed in bodily origins of mental illness and those who believed in environmental, structural origins of mental illnesses, or simply life experiences, was more pressing during World War II and the early postwar era, when some social and medical observers noted a growing rift between biological psychiatry and psychoanalysis. Psychiatrists with a psychoanalytical orientation such as Harry Stack Sullivan, who had treated patients suffering from schizophrenia with psychoanalysis, faulted lobotomy for failing to distinguish between the mind and the brain.[74] David Rioch, a neuroanatomist who later became a psychoanalyst, said in 1947 that a psychosurgeon was "treading on dangerous ground when he decides that a patient without a soul is better than a patient with a sick soul."[75]

Historians of psychiatry, in turn, have themselves emphasized both lobotomy's inherent barbarity and its attempt at scientific modernity, and sometimes in stark contrast to each other. Gail Hornstein, for example, notes that lobotomy's central practitioners were never deterred, despite "serious technical difficulties (the type of blade they were using often broke off and lodged in the brain during the operation)."[76] This sort of narrative instills a chilling image of lobotomy as a symbol of scientific recklessness and sadism. Jack Pressman, by contrast, emphasizes not only that doctors genuinely believed that they were helping patients by performing the operation but that lobotomy could be said to have built a basis for a more "scientific" psychiatry, including psychopharmacology.[77] He notes that doctors "were prodded into ever more aggressive modes of intervention,"[78] but the historical actors here are not clear. Who was doing the prodding? Historian Mical Raz also has tried to determine why lobotomies were ever popular or could have been viewed as sound medical practice during the early and even mid-twentieth century. She notes that the practice of lobotomy was a more eclectic one than how many have come to understand it retrospectively. For instance, psychosurgery adopted elements of psychoanalysis and did not divide the body from the mind in such a stark way as it might seem today.[79] These foci do not capture the daily realities of lobotomy within the institution. For example, in a 1952 article titled "Post Lobotomy" published in the patient newsletter at Mendocino State in Talmage, California, the supervisor of rehabilitation is mentioned as having planned a special program for the patients of Ward 1 who had recently had lobotomies to facilitate their rehabilitation in the form of "orientation, habit training and re-education."[80] This newsletter acknowledges lobotomy's potentially devastating effects, including loss of social judgment, loss of social skills, and inability to understand social cues.[81]

When trying to contextualize lobotomies historically beyond issuing outright condemnations, some historians have referred to family members as desperate to help their loved ones, or doctors as desperate to help their patients, often in the name of shortening or preventing institutionalization. Other medical historians divorce the question of morality from lobotomies through historical contextualization, only to then insist that doctors and family members have nonetheless been moral actors and meant no harm.[82] As historian Joel Braslow notes, it is also not easy to gauge doctor desperation, even if it is a comforting thought that "emphasizes the benevolence of their forebears, who labored in the dark ages of therapeutics with the best of intentions, and at the same time reassures them of the enlightened nature of present practices."[83] Still, it was not always the psychiatrist who wished to proceed with the operation, desperately or recklessly or even neutrally. Family members, too, could be enchanted by the prospect, the clarity, and the chimerical nature of the cure.

An example is a man who wrote to Saint Elizabeths Hospital in 1948, "anxious to pay for anything which might cure my wife." This woman was twenty-seven years old and "schizophrenic paranoiac," a diagnosis she received "5 months after childbirth." While she had received treatment in a "sanitarium" before, including "insulin shock treatment" as well as "electroshock," her "hallucinations still continue."[84] The psychiatrists he consulted had recommended "a Freeman and Watts prefrontal leucotomy operation." He wanted to know what exactly would happen to her after this operation, as well as the "percentage of complete cures"[85] and partial ones, putting his trust in statistics. The assistant superintendent at Saint Elizabeths at the time wrote back to him, saying that though the hospital had used the treatment of prefrontal lobotomy or leucotomy, this operation "should not be performed except as a last resort." Patients who had received the operation sometimes showed improvement, "but even those showing good improvement have continued to manifest symptoms of brain damage from the operation itself, so that the operation is primarily used to lessen the distress of the mental symptoms rather than in hope of full recovery."[86] Many patients were placed in the disheartening and hopeless category of "last resort" during this historical moment, and this made the operation a viable option.[87]

For some, lobotomy was simply a means of avoiding a more profound deterioration and a life in the hospital, perhaps just slightly different from accepting the way things were. And some family members were quite defensive about their choice to have their children undergo a lobotomy; in fact, they appeared to subscribe to the purely intentionalist view that "what is done out of love is beyond good and evil."[88] One mother wrote to Dr. Overholser in 1956 about her son, who had had a lobotomy performed just two years earlier. She noted that during the early 1950s he had been diagnosed as a "paranoid schizophrenic" and "this I understand is the most serious in a mental patient."[89] She had also consented to electroshock treatment for her son and he was "doing very well," but the staff at his hospital "deemed necessary the lobotomy operation . . . after weighing it carefully I decided on it since I had been informed he would only go from bad to worse." Yet her "reason for writing you is I read [you don't] approve of this type of operation."[90] While William Alanson White had not permitted lobotomies at Saint Elizabeths, Overholser did permit them after other therapies had been tried, including psychotherapy.[91] The mother noted later in the letter: "As for the operation I did what I considered the only thing to do under existing circumstances that time. I also would if possible like to know does a patient stand a chance of being close to normal after this operation." Her main fear was that "the question arises within me—could the patient become dangerous that he might consider his life or others?"[92] This last concern signals some deeper worries on her part, as though she had tampered with her son's moral being.

Lobotomies can illustrate what some medical historians have called a "conspiracy to believe,"[93] a subtle pact between doctors and patients that allows them to believe a painful remedy might result in a cure, and these beliefs deepened with the promises of scientific modernity especially during the war and postwar eras. In 1946, one mother asked Overholser plaintively: "I have been told that lobotomy operations should be a last resort but when does one reach the point when they consider they should use the last resort?" This mother was inquiring about her twenty-two-year-old daughter, who had attended college but had been diagnosed as "Dementia Praecox of the Paranoid type."[94] She had been in a sanatorium a year earlier where she had "50 insulin comas and 20 electroshock treatments. These did not help her but seemed to make her worse." This mother added that "some tell me that lobotomy is the only thing left that might help her and others of the school of psychology seem to think she would recover by letting her wait." For a family in this situation, the idea of beholding a twenty-two-year-old deteriorating and "letting her wait" might seem unbearable. The mother said that "now she seems to be considered a case of long standing in spite of the fact that I tried to get the best for her from the first."[95] This letter is not especially hopeful, but neither does it demonstrate blind acceptance of a chronic medical condition. Rejecting the "letting her wait" idea was also a departure from the sensibility of acceptance more characteristic of patients and those who cared for them in an earlier era.

Overholser's letters to families of patients about lobotomy do allude to the kinds of emotional states the operation was said to alleviate and the kinds of emotional demeanors that resulted, and the implications for the patient's selfhood were implicit. These kinds of reflections are perhaps more explicit in doctor's notes of the war era, however. In 1944, Dr. Hugh T. Carmichael, a psychoanalytical psychiatrist, kept a series of lobotomy notes from eight patients who had undergone the procedure. His notes suggest why a state of passivity could be deemed preferable to a state of profound agitation. One case was that of a thirty-three-year-old "twice married" woman who had been admitted in 1943 to the Illinois Neuropsychiatric Institute, which offered an array of therapeutic techniques and was known for its neurosurgeries.[96] While in 1941 she had received electroshock treatments at a state hospital, two years later she found herself plagued with "thoughts of hitting someone, hurting her daughter, killing her husband, committing suicide, and of screaming. She realized that something was wrong with her and that these thoughts were strange to her real self and became very worried and anxious."[97] However, after her prefrontal lobotomy in 1944, she "at first seemed somewhat passive and rather indifferent and said that her obsessive thoughts no longer seemed important to her. . . . This indifference, passivity, and lack of spontaneity continued." While there is no pretense here of restoration to her "real self"—even though it is presupposed that one does exist—"she no longer complained of bodily aches and pains or of her obsessive fears."[98]

Not only did patients have a "real self" to lose but a wariness of biological treatments is suggested here, at least those that might alter the patient's insight or creativity, an emphasis that would deepen over the course of the postwar period. Freeman and Watts's reflections on lobotomy in the 1940s acknowledge the potential loss of creativity in a patient. They noted, for example, that "literary expression drops off in quality and quantity following prefrontal lobotomy."[99] They used the example of a lobotomy patient who had been a "virtuoso" on the violin at the age of fifteen whose musical compositions had been published. Diagnosed with schizophrenic psychosis, she spent two years in a mental institution during 1933–1935 and did not touch the violin. She spent ten years after that at home with her mother, and Freeman and Watts note that during her period of convalescence after her lobotomy in 1946, she "played the violin with a certain technical excellence" but "became more interested in listening to the radio and watching her mother do the housework." They noted that "creative capacity in artistic, literary, musical, theatrical and other fields undergoes a decided reduction after prefrontal lobotomy."[100]

While Freeman and Watts's notes are more matter-of-fact, Carmichael's notes also suggest the stirrings of hesitation about the ideal of peace that verges into oblivion, or at least some reluctance to see biological psychiatry as an emotional regulator. However, the "calculus of suffering" that he offered, the risks that were worth taking to ease mental pain and the risks that were not, seemed to some an acceptable trade-off from the vantage point of psychosurgery during the 1940s, and perhaps a more livable alternative than long-term treatment in a mental hospital.[101] While Carmichael's notes have the feeling of self-evident truths, as diagnoses and medical narratives directed at medical readerships often do, they also contain certain rhetorical flourishes that render them part of a broader sphere of emergent cultural conversations about authenticity so prevalent in popular sociology during American sociology's "golden age" in the 1940s and 1950s.[102] While physicians' notes and psychiatric case studies are often studied for their literary qualities, perhaps these notes also can be considered a species of sociology themselves and as such commentary on the styles of selfhood within a given moment.

Carmichael's evocation of the "real self" would become a more pressing concern during the early postwar era when a broader American public was becoming aware of the unsettling implications of tampering with the brain, or brainwashing. The word "brainwashing" first appeared in the American lexicon in 1950 in an article by journalist Edward Hunter. In his 1951 book titled *Brain-Washing in Red China*, regarding the mental manipulations of

American soldiers during the Korean War, he wrote that "brainwashing" was something that could transform them not just politically but racially into the "emotionless Chinese."[103] Other writers, such as psychoanalyst Joost Meerloo, in his 1956 work *The Rape of the Mind*, suggested that psychological authority could be manipulated by dictators to make people into "zombies" in the service of a "menticide." In Meerloo's words, menticide could create a new, robotized community called Totalitaria.[104] His rhetoric has a parallel in other images of totalitarianism in this period, such as Hannah Arendt's *Origins of Totalitarianism* (1951), which evokes a political system capable of invading and colonizing inner life, destroying individuals and creating lifeless, mechanical objects.[105] As historian Matthew Dunne demonstrates, this brainwashing narrative was not just a figment of a paranoid, Cold War imagination; it became a broader American habit of mind, made manifest in the growing awareness of the "hidden persuaders" who attempted to influence American consumers in advertising and political campaigns alike as more subtle forms of mind colonization.[106]

By the early postwar era, the automaton had taken on a more political and sinister valence than it had before. Medical onlookers had a sense that despite the therapeutic benefits of biological psychiatry, these treatments could be used in the service of submission to authoritarian politics. This fear was growing in the 1950s as greater exploitations were being imagined, perhaps enough to upend the logic of the medical utilitarianism of lobotomies or the idea that these operations benefited, at least ultimately, both the individual and the community.[107]

The anxious preservation of the real self, even if the price of authenticity meant institutionalization, was even more striking in early postwar cultural portraits. A particularly damning depiction of lobotomy is in the best-selling 1958 novel *Daybreak* by Frank G. Slaughter, set in the fictional Leyden State Hospital. Slaughter's novels have an expository and didactic feeling to them, perhaps because he was a physician who tried to introduce medical concepts in the forum of the novel. His central characters are James Corwin, an assistant resident in neurosurgery, and a psychiatrist named Alex Goldschmidt who serves as a humanist voice and the conscience of the novel. He chastises Corwin for participating in lobotomies by saying, "'You've no right to seal off a section of a man's brain, just because his emotions don't operate by normal rules.'"[108] Goldschmidt's protest takes on a political valence when he says that a superintendent's idea of a "'solution for mental illness is to turn a psychotic into a machine that does as it's told.'" Even when challenged that psychoanalysis does not necessarily provide a cure, Goldschmidt says that his patients are "still experiencing emotion. They're alive, in every sense of the word."[109] Finally Goldschmidt declares, "'If the spark is still there . . . isn't it worse than murder to snuff it out?'"[110] Having a spark inside the subsociety of the hospital was presumably better than living without one in the more manifest world of broader society.

This language of being "alive" and having a "spark" presages an emerging emphasis on the experience of emotion in all of its incarnations, a repudiation of the tranquility ideal and a more explicit political icon of the automaton, which would deepen as the postwar period wore on. As historian Michaela Hoenicke Moore points out, the German people, perceived to have been taken advantage of by the Nazis, often themselves were depicted as automatons, with the capacity for both naiveté and aggression, not to mention total submission to an evil authority figure.[111] While the fear of the "masses" was present during the interwar years, it was becoming more glaring in the postwar period, expressed by the Frankfurt School, among others, and their fears of the "semi-automatic" spectator in culture and politics. This idea of the massification of the individual resonated strikingly with critiques of biological psychiatry.[112]

The dissent voiced in Slaughter's novel also has synergies with psychoanalytically oriented psychiatrists of the early postwar period. Psychoanalyst Harry Stack Sullivan, for example, was a critic of physical therapies, as befits a "neo-Freudian" who focused on the inner self and its relationship with social institutions. In 1947 he claimed that lobotomies made one into a "contented imbecile."[113] Some went even further than he did. In 1949 Nolan Lewis, a psychoanalytical psychiatrist specializing in schizophrenia who was open to biological treatments and interested in biochemistry, addressed the New York State Psychiatric Institute, questioning whether the "quieting" of a patient was a cure. He believed that lobotomized patients "act like they have been hit over the head with a club and are as dull as blazes. . . . It disturbs me to see the number of zombies that these patients turn out."[114]

By 1951, the valence of the "drone," described as potentially "happy" just ten years earlier, had now changed more definitively to something human but not quite "there." The lobotomized also could be considered unproductive. As psychologist Stanley D. Porteus, who studied fifty-five lobotomy cases in Kaneohe Hospital in Hawaii in 1951, noted, a lobotomized population would mean that "industry . . . would cease" because "cheerful drones could hardly carry out the complex business of modern living."[115] There could also be a menacing quality to this drone. Irving Wallace indicated that lobotomy could convert patients into "docile, inert, almost useless drones" stripped of their "soul and conscience."[116] The image of the "soul" was a stirring one in the early postwar period, when questions of human nature, spiritual or political or ideological, held a renewed and heightened urgency.[117] At the level of popular culture, the soul was often conflated with the brain, and the preservation of the brain was all the more poignant in fending off the brain's "invaders" or "eaters," symbols and mythologies that became more popularized in 1950s American science fiction.[118]

It is not surprising, then, that lobotomies would take on a more nefarious quality in cultural portraits, especially as the understanding of the side effects of these operations deepened. Perhaps it is the case too that fiction as a form is most vitally interested in the preservation of the human capacity for creativity. For example, in Tennessee Williams's 1958 play, *Suddenly Last Summer*, the power of lobotomy to ensure peacefulness takes on a most menacing twist as a profound violation of autonomy and compromiser of truth, a demeanor perhaps befitting only an institutionalized subject. The play was at least semi-autobiographical, in that Williams was ruminating upon his mother's decision to allow a lobotomy to be performed upon his sister, Rose, without his knowledge.[119] This is the story of a poet, Sebastian, who has been gruesomely murdered after seeking sexual favors from men while on vacation in Europe. His cousin, Catharine, has had a breakdown in the wake of his death and is "babbling" constantly about the circumstances of her cousin's death, ones that Sebastian's mother, Mrs. Venable, wants to keep quiet so as to protect Sebastian's reputation. It is Mrs. Venable who consults with Catharine's psychiatrist to arrange a lobotomy for her. While the doctor emphasizes the risks of the operation, and the unknown waiting in its wake, Mrs. Venable extols the operation because it "pacifies [the patients], it quiets them down, it suddenly makes them peaceful."[120] Despite his protests, Mrs. Venable insists that a lobotomy would be a "blessing" to Catharine "to be just peaceful, to be just suddenly—peaceful."[121]

By 1958, however, being "peaceful" was much more contested as an ideal disposition, and it was the disposition most likely to circumscribe a patient in an institution. In her novel *The Bell Jar* (1963), Sylvia Plath offers an array of images of compliant robot patients at McLean Hospital outside of Boston, among them Valerie, a patient who had had a lobotomy. McLean is a private hospital that was then known for its patient writers, artists, and scientists, and for treating, at least in the early postwar period, schizophrenia and more severe mental illnesses. Plath's protagonist, Esther Greenwood, a twenty-year-old poet, describes Valerie as an eerie statue and having a "perpetual marble calm." When Esther asks Valerie how she's doing, Valerie says that she is "fine" and "not angry any more." And in response to Esther's inquiries about when Valerie is leaving, she responds, "'Oh, I'm not leaving . . . I like it here.'"[122] This passage resonates intriguingly with an exchange included in one of Freeman and Watts's articles from 1937 wherein a sixty-three-year-old patient who had been "high-strung" and "emotional" before her lobotomy said after her operation that she "seem[ed] to have forgotten" why she was upset beforehand because "it doesn't seem important now."[123]

As a form of treatment, electroconvulsive therapy had some of the same ambiguities as the lobotomy. As with the lobotomy, patients and families sometimes perceived electroconvulsive therapy as a biological treatment that could be potentially violent and dehumanizing. But alternately it was perceived as a modern treatment that promised a clear and uncomplicated cure, a restoration of patient vibrancy, and a repossession of the old self, untouched by mental illness and liberated from the hospital. "Shock" therapy refers to three different treatments: insulin shock, Metrazol shock, and electric shock, alternately called electric convulsive shock or electroconvulsive therapy (ECT).[124] Here I discuss electric shock therapy only, which started to be used in the United States in 1940. This involved shocking the brain with a brief electrical current to the point of convulsion. This kind of treatment was thought to help profoundly depressed patients, though there was hope, initially, that this technique would help those with schizophrenia too.[125] In the early days of electroshock therapy, ECT was often administered without anesthesia or muscle relaxants, and this would not change until the late 1950s.[126] In larger state hospitals, patients were often given ECT en masse, a disconcerting image of a patient herd. Still, during the 1940s, shock treatments, as with lobotomies, were quite popular and written about optimistically in popular media such as *Time*, *Reader's Digest*, and *Newsweek*.[127]

A measure of a treatment's success was sometimes how reinstated family members seemed in its wake, and this was no less true for ECT than it was for the lobotomy. In a letter that a psychiatrist at Rochester State Hospital in Minnesota received in 1953, the writer told him: "I am glad that you have started the electric shock treatments on my wife. . . . Her paranoid delusions were getting more realistic to her every day. It seemed to me that she was getting just about as bad as she was before she had her lobotomy operation. She always seems glad to see me when I go over there."[128] The writers of these letters did not simply accept losing someone to mental illness. With newer treatments came a firmer sense of optimistic hope for the patient, not to mention an intensifying sense of individualism in that the patient might be seen to be making progress when she seemed to exhibit some traces of her old self.

At times it was psychiatrists, especially those with a psychoanalytical orientation, rather than family members who called for a more nuanced understanding of electroshock cures as well as the experience of hospitalization. In 1955, Dr. John Whitehorn, a professor of psychiatry at the Johns Hopkins University School of Medicine and an advocate for psychiatry in medical education, was giving a third-year course in psychiatry to students who wanted to become doctors. As a psychiatric educator, Whitehorn also was interested in psychoanalytic psychiatry and the process of psychotherapy.[129] In a lecture hall, he presented this audience of prospective doctors with an elderly woman suffering from a debilitating depression that had left her "totally unable to function in the household." She had been hospitalized and had received shock treatments, but "the trouble was that the minute she began to respond at all, she demanded that she be released from the hospital, and immediately relapsed."[130] He noted that in the past she had been quite dependent on both her husband and her housekeeper.[131] After she left the lecture hall, Dr. Whitehorn told the class that what they had seen was a "pathetic old lady, almost grotesquely dramatizing her need for some human contact."[132] He noted that this "clinging dependency . . . is quite a characteristic phenomenon in these depressed patients."[133] On the one hand, his presentation of this patient reads as objectifying, as if she were an artifact in a museum. And yet his pedagogical purpose in presenting her this way was to make a plea for psychiatry as a humanizing force. As he addressed his students, "You may ask why I put any importance on this matter of trying to establish with her a mutual understanding of her problem in life before we relieve her with the electrical treatments. Wouldn't the main thing be to quick put in the plug and give her a shock treatment and make her feel better?" "Quick put in the plug" is a challenge to his students to see beyond reductive and instantaneous biological psychiatry. He suggested instead "combin[ing] that kind of symptomatic relief of the depressed feeling with some kind of . . . therapeutic assistance which will help a person face up to and deal better with the actual life situation."[134]

Patients and those who cared for them, too, often felt ambivalent about electroconvulsive therapy, as though they were caught between older ideas of resignation and just "getting through" and newer ideas of remedying ills through scientific modernity. Sometimes dispositions about treating and curing mental illness clashed within the same household. A fifty-year-old woman wrote to Dr. Overholser in 1956 to say that her husband had just had a bout with depression and had been recommended for "shock treatment" but he refused. "I am at a loss to know what to do from now on as he is letting himself believe that he is mental," she said. "A few days ago he said, 'there is no sense in me hanging around, do what you like with the farm. . . . The way I feel now I am not up to running it—I guess I'm crazy as a bat!' I should go away."[135] This woman did not know what to do in the face of this sort of fatalistic surrender.

Other prospective patients clung to the hope that they could manage their emotions on their own without a psychosurgical intervention or a hospitalization through endurance and emotional stoicism, values that were present though waning in the face of medical modernity. In 1956, an old friend of psychiatrist Fredric Wertham's wrote to ask him his opinion about biological psychiatry. Wertham was the senior psychiatrist at the New York City Department of Hospitals at the time and was known for his work at the Lafargue Clinic in Harlem, a volunteer-run facility of psychiatrists, psychologists, and social workers that treated mostly African American patients, as well as for popularizing psychiatry in works such as *Seduction of the Innocent* in 1954, which lamented the impact of comic books on children. He also maintained individual therapeutic relationships and kept a set of letters documenting these. In this particular letter, a woman indicated that her psychiatrist had asked her whether or not she wanted to do ECT treatment and she had a "strong instinct against it." Instead, "I keep feeling if I can 'get by' till it is over, there is some gain; but that may be wrong."[136] The vicissitudes of her depression were quite excruciating: "I usually have two or three hours a day when I feel pretty awful, and sometimes a whole day."[137] She wanted to know how she might evaluate cures in the face of pragmatic emotional stoicism: "I know the pills are only a palliative and no cure but neither is the ECT a cure is it? Nor is it certain that it achieves improvement? Does one pay any price, medically or physically, by just sticking it out? If I am willing to stand the bad times and painfulness?"[138] She noted that the ECT treatment "scared" her because she had heard it impeded memory, because she knew that Dr. Wertham was "so against it," and because she was afraid of "'interfering' with bodily processes in a way no one quite seems to know much about."[139] The letter is painfully honest about what depression feels like: "I've gone on now over 3–4 months, only half alive and really sometimes quite miserable."[140] It was an "awful illness, to be in the grip of something you can't handle and that robs you of your energy and ability to manage."[141] And yet she does not contemplate hospitalization as a therapeutic measure but all manner of biological psychiatry instead. There must have been many more people like her who resolved to simply "stick it out." But by the postwar period, when presented with more scientific treatment possibilities, this posture was harder to maintain.

As with lobotomies, though, electroshock treatments also could be perceived as reducing people to automatons and made the "getting by" option seem more livable. This apathetic figure populated the mental hospital in both cultural portraits and patient reflections. Harold Maine's autobiography, *If a Man Be Mad* (1947), discusses his experiences working as an attendant in a V.A. hospital during World War II among psychiatric patients before he himself was committed at Bellevue Hospital in New York for psychiatric treatment. Of his schizophrenic patients he noted that sometimes they became "lucid" after electric shock treatments, but at other times they simply "settled into catatonic torpor."[142]

Electric shock could even be portrayed as a more willfully violent treatment, presaging a more nefarious view of these treatments that would deepen over the course of the postwar period. One activist who thought of it in this way is Kenneth Donaldson, who would become a famous figure in the landscape of post–World War II era psychiatry in 1975 when he was at the center of a Supreme Court case that ruled against the involuntary commitment of psychiatric patients. But Donaldson's problems with state hospitals began long before 1975, and he had always insisted that he did not need to be hospitalized. In 1956 when he was in his late forties he wanted to tell his story to the *Daily News* of Philadelphia, a tabloid newspaper. He told the paper that his problems had begun fourteen years earlier "when I was railroaded to the insane asylum and given electric shock treatments at Marcy State Hospital, Marcy, New York." In a more conspiratorial tone, he said that "my enemies tried to make a mass of jelly out of my mind."[143]

Some patients felt that electroshock treatments were recriminatory measures to keep recalcitrant patients passive and ensure their compliance, ensnared in the hospital, at a moment when passivity was becoming perceived as a potential form of suffering rather than a potential solace. Over the course of the twentieth century and even before, whether in personal protest letters, published captivity narratives, or cultural representations of the hospital, attendant cruelty and sadistic pleasure are legendary.[144] Peter G. Cranford noted in his diary in 1952 that one night the patients at Milledgeville State Hospital, where he was the chief clinical psychologist from 1951 to 1952, were "jumping around laughing, hugging each other as if celebrating a football victory. Walter F, the cruel attendant, had gone berserk! Shock treatment was ordered. He resisted wildly."[145] Cranford noted that the other clinical staff had long believed that this particular attendant was "psychotic" and that the patients now felt that justice had been served through shock treatments.[146] Cranford readily admitted that managing patients and trying to keep them tranquil could still be the primary goals, but many patients lived in "constant terror of being shocked."[147] After a patient play one night in 1952 that became especially boisterous, he reported that one fellow psychiatrist said to him, "'Let's go. I've seen enough. By the time my patients get back to the building, I'll have to shock them down.'"[148] This dynamic was also captured quite arrestingly in unpublished personal letters and testimonies to government officials. A patient at Hastings State Hospital in Minnesota, for example, wrote to Minnesota governor Orville Freeman in 1957 about the purely retaliatory biological psychiatry that she felt was practiced there. The use of ECT was at its height in the 1950s at Hastings State; in 1952, for example, there were 23,317 ECT treatments delivered to 590 patients, for an average of 40 per patient. She complained that one of the psychiatrists in the hospital, "a fearsome man," was "electro-shocking well people for nothing at all just for a chip-on-the-shoulder personal diversion—such is outright dangerous recklessness."[149]

Electric shock was frightening not only as a perceived way to enforce patient passivity but as a symbol of the cold-hearted scientist. Patients depicted this figure during the war and postwar periods as having the power to render the patient emotionless. While the associations between scientists and emotional frigidity are long-standing, especially in the form of the nineteenth-century "scientist at the bedside" figure, this valence would be reinforced during the war and early post–World War II eras when cultural images of the "mad scientist" proliferated.[150] In 1945, the psychiatric journal *The Attendant* published a remarkable document, "A Subjective Account of Electroshock Treatment" by a "Former Patient" that described the process chillingly within a general medical atmosphere of emotional sterility. The author evoked the long waiting period before the "ordeal ahead" wherein the "'doomed ones' wander about restlessly." At the "zero hour" another period of waiting began, wherein the patient could hear "loud and sometimes agonized noises" that reinforced the idea of imminent "electrocution."[151] The patient describes the "six strong pairs of hands holding me down" and the "thick roll of gauze and cotton thrust between the jaws" and the "long-handled electrodes" in addition to "numbers being read off, everything being carefully, scientifically, maddeningly checked." Then: "electrodes to the temples again.

All set. Blank."[152] The depiction of science here is one of coldblooded robotics, a total dearth of empathy, of numbers being obliviously and mechanistically read aloud in the face of a human being enduring terrible suffering.

The suffering in this piece was a prelude to an ultimate void or "blankness." Judith Kruger recalled something similar in her memoir, *My Fight for Sanity* (1959), detailing her time in an unnamed state hospital two months after her son had been born and she became an unbearably nervous new parent. During the shock treatments themselves she asked if it "would have killed" the orderlies, nurses, and doctors "to say a word of comfort? Do they think it's easy, this submission to oblivion?"[153] In her portrait there is a gendered component to her frustration, as though unfeeling science has a particularly male character, something to which female patients had to submit. Biological treatments such as lobotomies and electroshock treatments were more likely to be administered to women than to men.[154] But at the very least white women were considered appropriate subjects for modern medicine and were not deemed to fall outside of the category entirely. In his 1952 novel, *Invisible Man*, Ralph Ellison creates a character who undergoes electric shock treatments in a factory hospital. But the doctors debate whether to give a Black man this treatment at all, saying that in "primitive instances" a cure might not work and that "simple prayer" might be better for him.[155] While whites were at least permitted the identity of being a patient, this was not always extended to Black people. The portraits of the doctors administering the shocks are equally cold and bloodless, and the descriptions of getting "blasted" are also terrifying, only here with the addition of a degrading racial mocking as the doctors describe his convulsions as "dancing" and "hav[ing] rhythm."[156] There is, however, a parallel with other ECT depictions in the description of his mind after the shocks, which was "alternately bright and blank in slow rolling waves."[157]

Edward Shorter has argued that electroshock in particular has negative connotations because of its associations with the death penalty by electrocution in the United States. It could never be accepted as fully therapeutic, given the very nature of what happens to the human body when electrocuted, the state of robotic acquiescence that ensues, and even the sadistic control of populations envisioned through such a practice.[158] He also notes its terrifying depictions in cultural sources such as the film version of *The Snake Pit* (1949), based on the 1946 novel by Mary Jane Ward, about her experiences at Rockland State Hospital in Orangeburg, New York. In the book, which was particularly influential in establishing the literary genre of the asylum novel, Ward's protagonist,

Virginia, believes that "they were going to electrocute her, not operate upon her."[159] Ralph Ellison created this sort of portrait as well when the narrator describes his head as being "encircled by a piece of cold metal like the iron cap worn by the occupant of an electric chair."[160] Medical officials themselves were at times cognizant of the disturbing cultural images that might have populated the patient imagination in the face of biological psychiatry. In 1950, the chief clinical psychologist at Mississippi State Hospital was prompted to tell prospective patients in a booklet that electroshock had been "falsified by popular writers since its invention" but really was just "another method of inducing relaxation and relieving nerve tension." He further advised patients that they would "feel no pain . . . you will go to sleep, and wake up in a few minutes feeling much better. The treatment is not dangerous. . . . It does not burn the skin, the brain, or any part of the body. It will not injure your brain. You may not be able to recall details for a few hours after shock, but your memory will always return."[161] The fact that patients needed this kind of reassurance indicates just how terrifying the idea of passing an electrical current through the brain is. Of course, patient treatments, especially the physical act of surgery—of necessity mutilating—are always freighted with patients' preconceived notions about them. In her memoir about brain surgery, neurosurgeon Katrina Firlik admits that "surgery is trauma, but it's intelligent, controlled trauma, and it's done in the patient's best interest, despite appearances."[162] But it is not always easy for a patient to separate their preexisting ideas from realities, intentions, or even beneficial consequences.

Historian Jonathan Sadowsky argues that therapy and control are not mutually exclusive and that sometimes both disciplinary and therapeutic goals can comingle.[163] But the fear of control could become more pressing, particularly in relation to the ambient political culture. Cultural portraits of electroshock therapy in a hospital context became more prevalent in the postwar period, sometimes expressly likening biological psychiatry to a political authoritarianism seeking to create a population of acquiescent automatons. Sylvia Plath famously traded in these kinds of images in *The Bell Jar*. The experiences of her protagonist, Esther, with shock treatments, at least as described in the early part of the book, are particularly ghastly and are equated with the electrocution of the Rosenbergs.[164]

Patient fears and their imaginings about biological psychiatry and scientific modernity shaped how their family members reacted to their hospital treatments in the early postwar period as well. One mother was quite distraught after seeing the effect of electric shock treatments on her son at Napa

State Hospital from 1943 to 1946 and then at Stockton State Hospital, both in California. When she visited her son she found him in a weakened state, which she attributed to electric shock treatments. She wrote to the governor of California, Earl Warren, in 1949, decrying the treatment her son had received. Warren was known for his commitment to mental health issues and even convened a conference on mental health during that same year.[165] He sought to bring "California out of the asylum age and into the hospital age" by modernizing the California mental health system, especially after his visits to some of these institutions during the late 1940s.[166] However, this mother rejected these "modern" treatments, noting that electric shock "is dangerous and sometime[s] death occur[s]."[167] In fact, she felt that the doctors "gave him a treatment just to put [him] to death."[168] She further accused the hospital of leaving the medicine cabinets unlocked, giving her son access to "poison pills."[169] This letter can be read as purely conspiratorial, but the notion that medicine is poisonous rather than therapeutic was in fact becoming a mainstream idea in the postwar period. As psychiatrist Robert J. Lifton argued in his analysis of Nazi doctors, physicians work along the border between life and death, so the idea that they might shift under a totalitarian regime from being life-savers to euthenists is not necessarily implausible. More people were becoming aware of the manipulations of science during World War II and had to reckon with this idea of the potential perversions of medicine.[170]

What was supposed to obviate the need for biological psychiatry in the vein of lobotomies or electroshock by the 1950s—and hospitalizations and custodial care altogether—was psychopharmacology, but this also would become implicated in the idea of a menacing automaton, even while being hailed for freeing people from a life in the institution. "Major tranquilizers" such as chlorpromazine (brand name Thorazine) and reserpine (brand name Serpasil) began to be used in 1954 and were said to help patients with psychoses regain contact with reality, while "minor tranquilizers," such as Miltown, were introduced in 1955.[171] As medical reporter Albert Q. Maisel wrote somewhat optimistically in 1958, tranquilizing drugs have "speeded up the recovery of tens of thousands" but also had changed conditions inside the hospital dramatically, eliminating the need for patients to be confined to the "back wards," receiving "custodial care" instead of "therapeutic care."[172] Indeed, these psychotropics were said to free patients from physical restraints such as shackles or straitjackets and even to propel a shift from asylum to community-based care.[173] According to Dr. Henry Benjamin, the director of psychiatry at Northampton State Hospital, the introduction of Thorazine also resulted in a decline in the use of electroshock treatment and the "geriat-ric wards [are] quieter and cleaner as a result of more extended use of these drugs."[174] It is telling that the novel *Daybreak* reaches a hopeful denouement when reserpine is discovered, thus delaying a lobotomy on a sensitive, intel-ligent patient.[175] While psychiatrists and family members alike had fretted during the interwar years about the capacities of individual care versus insti-tutional care, this idea was shifting subtly now in the early postwar period toward the merits of deinstitutionalization as psychotropic drugs in particu-lar seemed to promise life beyond the hospital.[176]

These drugs solidified, but also complicated, the notion that a sense of peace—even if it meant being tranquilized into stupefaction—was prefer-able to a state of agitation. Psychiatrists and patients alike expressed some reservations about tranquilizing drugs, in the form of a wariness of all-out apathy, something that undergirded the deepening reservations about lobot-omies and electroshock as well and served to highlight the idea of a need for patient management in a hospital setting. Chlorpromazine was in line with other biological treatments, a "medicinal lobotomy," in the words of some doctors.[177] David Walton Allen, a psychiatrist and psychoanalyst, wrote in his autobiography that during the 1950s, before the introduction of the new tran-quilizing drugs, he did a tour of southern mental hospitals for the Univer-sity of North Carolina. He noted that after the introduction of psychotropics, hospitals "became much quieter," and while there were fewer "difficult-to-control" patients, there was also "a lot more catatonia."[178] The woman from Hastings State Hospital noted to the governor in another letter that she was glad that her husband refused to give consent to electroshock treatments and "thorazine over-dosage treatments" because these things had the effect of "crumpling human bodies." Her husband felt that they were nothing short of "outright murder."[179] Even if tranquilizing drugs were supposed to be "chem-ical lobotomies," and less disturbing than psychosurgeries, they still could embody more subtle connotations of soul murder.

The idea that science was too invasive, too omnipotent, and too arro-gant was becoming more widespread as the postwar period progressed. In fact, grave uncertainties were starting to be voiced about science for science's sake—the idea that everything can and should be known and understood and, as in the logic of the cure, potentially conquered. The Cold War was transforming medical science as a profession, ushering in what some have called a "medical-industrial complex."[180] Some observers of American science dreaded what scientific medicine could become, as expressed in the futuristic medicine of Nazism. As biologist Benno Muller-Hill notes, the values of science, especially objectivity, were seen to have "opened the door to every conceivable form of barbaric practice."[181] Other historians have followed in this vein, suggesting that science was becoming most centrally an "agent of fear" widely perceived to be in need of a larger ethical framework, pointing to public intellectuals' powerful critiques of scientism in the early postwar period.[182] Historian David Serlin suggests that in the wake of the horrors of Nazism and the atomic bomb, science needed to be rehabilitated or redeemed in order to mitigate a profound cultural uneasiness of its hubristic and destructive capacities vis-à-vis destructive technologies.[183] Art historian Peter Bacon Hales, in turn, notes that in the wake of atomic culture in particular, Americans had to acknowledge and make sense of a particular kind of terror, things that sounded like science fiction, such as "invisible death rays" and "rogue unseen particles"[184] that annihilated entire populations.

Intellectual enthusiasm about biological psychiatry, a sense that it could offer comforts, intellectual engagement, renewed selfhood, and the hope of panaceas, ran alongside these anxieties about the unconstrained powers of science during the war and early postwar eras. The engagement with biological psychiatry at least initially seemed to offer midcentury patients and their families a glimpse of a life beyond institutionalized patienthood and chronicity. But more profound doubts were beginning to emerge about the meanings of cures during the early postwar period and about what, exactly, was being cured. Drastic biological interventions, or any enforced psychiatric treatments that flattened emotions, would come to be seen as a means of enforcing passivity and even tampering with a natural or authentic self. Ironically, modern biological interventions that were initially perceived as ensuring possessive individualism, in the sense that embracing biological selfhood could allow patients to retrieve their selves as they had existed prior to mental illness and envision a life beyond hospitalization, were beginning to be perceived as forces that ensured a mass conformity characteristic of the institution and the benighted relics of a more barbarous medical moment.

CHAPTER 3

====

Communities, Selfhood, and "Lonely Crowds"

Being cured through psychosurgery and then leaving the hospital seemed a radical departure from the image of the chronically institutionalized patient who was lost to her own internal world, until some observers began to question whether these scientific panaceas themselves were ways of enforcing the very institutional oblivion that patients were trying to transcend. But biological psychiatry existed alongside the custodialism of the mental hospital during the war and early postwar eras, and patients and families sometimes felt they had no choice but to accept the institution's capacity for care. None of this changed. What did change was the intensification of ideas and conversations about individualism and community, particularly by the early postwar period when conformity, consensus culture, and the nature of democracy were becoming more widespread concerns of American intellectuals, psychiatrists, and patients alike. Where better, as an imaginative space, to seek out the "lonely crowds" that allegedly populated the postwar American landscape than communities of fellow sufferers inside a mental hospital? Here were the ideal subjects through which to explore the tensions between late modern articulations of possessive individualism and community, and between the passivity of conformity and the more active citizen of a democracy.

Hospital communities loomed large in patient and caregiver reflections. During the war and early postwar periods, institutional citizens embodied, and their very existence intensified, some of the larger contradictions about late modern American liberalism, communal participation most particularly, and the emotional demeanors associated with this form of association. Institutionalized people and their onlookers at times embraced these communities for their caring capacities but also feared them for their more authoritarian possibilities in a way that paralleled the often simultaneously hopeful and uneasy attitudes toward science during the same modern moment, and that was more critical of the resigned solace these communities could provide for an earlier generation. In the moral universe of many American social observers, questions about what the role of the individual could be in the midst of a swelling bureaucracy and sprawling postwar institutions, the mental hospital among them, were quite pressing. These dilemmas about being an authentic individual, an observer somewhat scornful of the herd, and yet also being a participant in the community, were especially compelling ones within the subculture of patients in the mental hospital's therapeutic community.[1]

On the one hand, social critics and intellectuals were quite wary of the privatization of emotional life and culture, whether this took the form of suburbanization; feelings of atomization and uprootedness; the loss of the war as an instance of moral community; withering ties to extended families, religious organizations, and other community organizations; and a dearth of forms of association and civic participation. Purposeful and edifying community, as well as transcendence of the banalities of the everyday, perhaps had its most powerful example in the African American civil rights movement, revered not just by Black activists but by some white liberal onlookers as well.[2]

But running alongside this pursuit of communitarianism was an anxiety about the "public" and the masses when seen as social conformity, quiescence, unthinking performance and consensus, passive bystanderism, participation in nefarious associations, or politically freighted notions of coercive collectives. This critique was made manifest in anxieties about the emergence of a popularity culture that quashed individualism, which extended, in a postwar political culture anxious about the fate of democracy, even to the existence of American totalitarianism.[3] Doubts about an ethos of solidarity in the form of a community had implications for the world of the mental hospital, as it could cast suspicion upon the very concept of care within a communal setting.

Psychiatric observers, families, and patients themselves were also ambivalent about the notion of community, especially the kinds of idiosyncratic associations that formed in the mental hospital. Their ideas resonated with all of these fraught assessments of postwar communitarianism and individualism, the public and private, performance and authenticity.[4] An insistence upon genuine individualism of the late modern era had to compete with the ideal of interdependent selfhood within the mental hospital community and older ideals of these kinds of communities that lingered. Patients of the mental hospital inhabited the ideal laboratories in which to observe all of these styles of personhood and citizenship, rendering the hospital a site much more freighted with perceived American national characters and ideology by the war and early postwar eras than it had been in the interwar era, and again complicating resignation as a demeanor of or strategy within the institution.

In a departure from the interwar era, a patient was no longer being wise by simply accepting her fate as a mentally ill person within an institutional setting—instead, she was potentially being an automaton, a figure viewed more disparagingly in this period. Intellectuals and social critics alike increasingly scrutinized the emotional expression of the automaton, as this figure came to embody a more explicit political valence, as one uniquely prone to totalitarianism. While official institutional culture, as represented by hospital writers and representatives, offered contradictory advice regarding the experience of mental illness within the confines of a mental hospital, encouraging patients to be both resigned to their fates and active participants in their hospital community, the meanings of resignation were shifting by the war and early postwar eras. Hospital and patient life once meant philosophical cooperation with the innate sorrows of life; however, early postwar era writings about institutional life exhibited a more explicit and pronounced political consciousness, a waning sense of embeddedness in the natural universe, and, gradually, still less a sense of the possibilities of scientific modernity. Patients and their observers now gave much more consideration to the emotional vibrancy of the patient. Where once emotionlessness in a patient could be considered an expression of peace or even wisdom, now that sense of peace, including submitting to the passage of time, was more likely to be called into question as political and moral inertia.

One common narrative of American psychiatry during the war and early postwar periods is that psychoanalysis dominated the discipline, rather than hospital psychiatry, and it could be argued that the renewed popularity of psychoanalysis during this late modern moment was a factor that contributed to a deepening interest in authentic emotional expression. The bailiwick of psychiatry, especially psychoanalysis, as noted, expanded greatly during World War II and the immediate postwar period, given the success of psychiatrists at screening recruits for the conflict.[5] One basic idea that World War II reaffirmed was simply that mental illness had its origins in environmental factors. Accordingly, after the war, American psychiatry was reoriented toward psychoanalysis rather than Kraepelinian diagnosis. Karl Menninger, an advocate for the integration of psychoanalysis into mainstream American psychiatry, pronounced that "only a person can heal a person."[6] Psychoanalysis dominated the American Psychiatric Association in this period, psychoanalysts chaired medical school psychiatry departments, and prospective doctors learned from psychoanalytically oriented textbooks. Even the first Diagnostic and Statistical Manual in 1952 had a psychoanalytical inflection.[7] Hannah Decker notes, too, that the boundary between the sick and the not sick was becoming less rigidly defined.[8] And after the war, more psychiatrists went into private practice, distancing themselves from the asylum, though even by 1957 there were only about a thousand analysts practicing in the United States.[9]

While being treated by a psychoanalyst was not necessarily common in early postwar America, psychoanalytical ideas were infiltrating postwar culture and politics, as many cultural historians have vividly documented. Hollywood and its producers, for their part, were keen on understanding and representing psychoanalytical ideas in their films, including striking representations of the subconscious mind. Psychoanalysis had a presence in the popular media, and psychoanalytical concepts were also popularized in psychology books such as Robert Lindner's sensationalistic *The Fifty-Minute Hour* (1955) which contained case studies of a "rapist-murderer, a fanatical communist, a compulsive glutton, a native American fascist, and a schizophrenic missile scientist."[10] And it was not just a pop culture phenomenon: many literary critics in the vein of Lionel Trilling and Alfred Kazin took up psychoanalysis as a theoretical framework.[11] Moreover, psychoanalysis was also implicated in the health of nations. The social sciences in general gained intellectual prestige during this era as areas of intellectual inquiry that held the capacity to explain human behavior and broader society: psychiatrists increasingly formed collaborations with psychologists, anthropologists, and sociologists.[12]

And yet, hospital psychiatry that was not particularly psychoanalytical in orientation still characterized the therapeutic landscape for many Americans. Most state hospitals did not offer psychoanalysis, and some five hundred thousand people were in state hospitals in 1946.[13] Other observers questioned whether psychoanalysis was helpful for patients with chronic mental illness. As mental health lobbyist Mike Gorman noted in 1956 when making a case for better funding for mental hospitals, "What does the psychoanalyst do when he is confronted with a hysterical, anxiety-ridden patient who is smashing the furniture in a blind attack of rage? He calls the police."[14]

Despite the popularity of postwar psychoanalysis and therapeutic culture broadly construed, institutionalized psychiatric patients still were confronted with ideas and attitudes of both self-reliance and resignation, sometimes even proffered by their loved ones. In one example, journalist David Maraniss wrote a retrospective reflection titled "Uncle Phil's Brain" in 2002, based on a collection of correspondence he found between his uncle and grandfather. His uncle had been hospitalized at the age of twenty-two for schizophrenia in 1942, at Highland Hospital in Asheville, North Carolina. This facility employed an array of therapeutic techniques overseen by Duke professors of neuropsychiatry.[15] Phil wrote to his father in 1945 to admit to him that "after four years of so-called hospitalization, I just feel that I am doomed to incapacitation of a more or less general nature, being regarded as something of a subhuman species halfway between a gorilla and a man." He continued, "I am pretty much all by myself in the world, have difficulty in making friends and adjusting myself . . . [and have] nothing to say and [am] getting no enjoyment or satisfaction out of anything I do. I am tired most of the time, worried, apprehensive, and very unhappy. It's just downright torture, that's all it is." His father responded to this cri de coeur by reassuring his son that a "reasonable amount of happiness would come" and that "nobody probably is happy all the time."[16]

Adjust your expectations, his father suggested, as though a complaint of unhappiness could only come from somebody with too great a sense of emotional entitlement. In another letter in 1946, Phil's father told him: "I would suggest that you concentrate the mind on something other than yourself. You will feel better and time will go faster. . . . Effort I believe will make it possible to minimize the pain . . . DON'T GIVE UP. Also try to see as many funny things in life as you can . . . I'm making a collection of jokes."[17] Here Phil's father encourages self-reliance, self-improvement, and self-motivation. After years at Highland Hospital, and after a topectomy in 1949 at Columbia-Presbyterian Medical Center, Phil endured many cycles of "hope and despair"[18] until eventually he went to live in Maraniss's house, "living out his days as the uncle in the basement."[19]

Perhaps there was a particular early postwar era class mentality embodied in Phil's father's attitudes. As the authors of *Family and Class Dynamics in Mental Illness* argued in 1959, working-class families attributed to their family members with mental illness "some willful and innate tendency to cause trouble. They considered the patients to be 'lazy', 'mean', 'ornery', or 'trouble makers', rather than sick."[20] These ideas were not just class-bound but even deeper shibboleths about mental illness that illustrate how stagnant ideas about the human character can be and how deep the desire is for an individual to have free will. This is reminiscent even of medieval thought, such as Dante's *Inferno*, wherein despair is something of a moral failing; acedia was "the sin of sloth."[21] American transplant psychoanalyst Karen Horney felt that these attitudes were particularly American in character. In 1942, she claimed that there was a widespread belief in the United States that "self-discipline is the uppermost virtue. To give much thought to himself in any way is self-indulgence and selfishness."[22] This fear of self-absorption and the desire to "pull oneself together"[23] suggest moral doubts about attention to interiority and a certain emotional pragmatism that did not easily jibe with psychoanalysis.

Public mental health campaigns of the early postwar era dealt with the persistence of suspicion of the reality of mental illness by comparing mental illness to other common ailments, which emphasized a neutral biologization to elicit sympathy. This was akin to a strategic and rhetorical move that gay activists made in the early postwar period in likening homosexuality to a neutral sickness model.[24] In the words of advice writer and activist Edith Stern, another author of exposé literature about mental hospitals, blaming someone with mental illness for the "torrent of abuse he pours forth upon you, for his 'stubbornness,' his dirty habits, or the 'lazy' way he sits staring for hours instead of going about his business" would be like "blam[ing] him for vomiting if he had stomach trouble or for lying idle if he had a broken back."[25]

Even if there is a resignation in accepting mental illness as a sickness that could befall anyone, these same public mental health campaigns were also more optimistic about institutional care. The mental institution was, in the words of postwar hospital architects, not merely a "neutral setting for custodial care, but . . . a positive and significant element in a total program of therapy."[26] Part of this program could be emotional management. For instance, early postwar psychiatrists believed it was imperative to try to link a proportional emotional expression to the individual circumstance.[27] In psychiatric textbooks of this period, prospective psychiatrists were told that they needed to "evaluate the appropriateness of emotions to given situations." This seems perennial advice, but it was also a time-bound and even a racialized pursuit. The same text reminded prospective psychiatrists that "to the Scandinavian, the Italian may appear wildly emotional, while the Italian may think the Scandinavian cold and unfeeling."[28] These ideas take on more urgency within a context of a larger distrust of emotional extremes or emotions divorced from rational will during the war and early postwar eras and a moment when psychiatrists played a role in the education of proper emotional expression, again more pressing in a wartime context. After 1945, social observers increasingly conflated excessive emotionality with political irrationality and fascism, but underemotionality and submissiveness were politically charged demeanors as well and were thought to have the potential to lead one politically astray.[29]

Emotional expression proportional to the immediate context became particularly problematized when psychiatrists noted listlessness or a zombie affect. This might have been a result of the deteriorating reputation of the lobotomy in the postwar period and the perceived emotionlessness of the lobotomized. An intriguing example of an interest in the automaton's affect is in the clinical notes from the Serpasil study, or the Serpasil geriatric project, which doctors at Saint Elizabeths Hospital conducted from 1954 to 1955. Serpasil, the market name for reserpine, is a minor tranquilizer and anti-psychotic in the same vein as Thorazine.[30] By the 1950s, Saint Elizabeths no longer treated veterans; it began transferring these patients to the Veterans Administration system, and of the hospital's seven thousand patients, some two to three thousand were above the age of sixty-five, making it a good place for a geriatric study.[31] According to a physician's notes on one patient in the study, he stated "in an extremely bland and almost nonchalant manner that he wishes to obtain some poison in order to kill himself" because "'I'm so unhappy I'd be better off dead—I get no results in existing as I am.'"[32] It is not just what this patient said that appeared troubling in these notes but that his bland affect and demeanor did not align with what he said. As Henry Davidson, the superintendent of Essex County Hospital in Cedar Grove, New Jersey, noted in 1958, psychiatric words and euphemisms to describe withdrawal or indifference were legion and included "aboulia," "apathy," "bovine," "cataleptic," "depersonalized," "flattened," "stuporous," and "untidy," among others.[33]

According to the documents from the Serpasil study, aligning emotional expression with a patient's words and repudiating the affect of the automaton were both considered necessary to be able to exist both in and out of the hospital. In the study notes, another man was described as a "slovenly dressed, moderately obese middle aged colored male" who "sauntered into the examining room, spontaneously shook hands limply, stated that he feels 'just medium' today and slumped down into the indicated chair." He reported in "an off-hand, rather nonchalant manner" that he had come from a hospital where he had "attempted to electrocute himself." At the end of this medical interview, the patient "stood up, stretched . . . yawned . . . hitched up his trousers and slouched slowly out of the room."[34] In a meeting a month later, this same patient described the feeling that he was being "'crucified' but as he describes his torture he shows very little affective force."[35] He is noted as saying, "'All I know is that I'm in my grave,' [in a] rather listless voice with a peculiar mechanical property."[36]

Medical observers have long monitored African American patients in particular for their perceived emotional expression and affects, reading them as overly emotional and violent or as underemotional and passive. As Martin Summers notes, psychiatrists have postulated a distinctive Black psyche that tended to infantilize or primitivize, and the legacy of these turn-of-the-twentieth-century ideas were still present at midcentury.[37] Moreover, during the 1950s and 1960s African Americans were widely believed to experience higher rates of mental illness, and Black patients were much more likely to be institutionalized for life, which might have provided more impetus and opportunity for the monitoring of even basic emotional expressions.[38] The Black patients at Saint Elizabeths experienced not just segregated but inferior facilities and were expected to show deference to predominantly white attendants, nurses, and medical staff, a deference that many might have had to perform simply to allay white hostility and violence outside of the hospital.[39] Desegregation was not widespread in 1954, and this kind of racial legacy was not easily shaken.[40] Moreover, a contextual imagination is not evident in these Serpasil observations in terms of a discussion of the material conditions that might have contributed to feelings of depression. A unique contradiction that early postwar African Americans faced was that at the same time that they were being overdiagnosed they were not always recognized as therapeutic subjects. Sometimes racism was simply not acknowledged, and at other times the psychic lives of African Americans were reduced to being interpreted simply as the outcomes of American racism. In 1948, psychiatrist Fredric Wertham said that "'Negroes are not allowed the luxury of neuroses. The official view is that they are just unhappy, or they need housing, or they feel downtrodden.'"[41] In 1949, *Ebony* magazine captured the paradox in disparaging the bloated numbers of African Americans in institutions while decrying the difficulty Black Americans faced in finding adequate mental health treatment.[42] In 1950, writer and anthropologist Zora Neale Hurston made a plea to acknowledge the emotional lives of people of color. In "What White Publishers Won't Print" she said she was "amazed" by the "Anglo Saxon's lack of curiosity about the internal lives and emotions of the Negroes, and for that matter, any non-Anglo Saxon peoples within our borders."[43] Even if midcentury American racial liberalism was focused squarely on the rights of the individual, this focus tended to elevate political selfhood and did not necessarily include a nuanced understanding of emotional life.[44]

Still, the midcentury American public was more educated about mental illness and its institutions, and arguably the concept of mental health, than their forebears had been. Psychiatric care was now becoming more of a federal than a state responsibility, and mental illness as a political issue was gaining visibility. In 1946, the National Mental Health Act was passed, with the imprimatur of President Truman, to support research into the diagnosis and treatment of mental disorders.[45] Novelist Mary Jane Ward published *The Snake Pit* during the same year, which chronicled her experiences as a patient in a state mental hospital. After her book became a best seller she became a speaker for the National Mental Health Foundation and advocate for patients, giving a number of lectures to health-care workers and patients alike.[46] At the very least, the government was now more involved in the field of mental health awareness, reaffirming an early twentieth-century shift in thinking about mental illness to thinking about mental health instead and addressing a reading and viewing public through an array of educational films and pamphlets. These official sources have their limitations, of course. They are not at all nuanced and can be condescending and seem outdated and corny to twenty-first century sensibilities. But they address a public that had been largely unaware of these issues and that would not be addressed in this systematic way again.[47] Much as these official sources interpellate or meddle sometimes quite moralistically, they also offer a kind of witness to suffering and suggest an ethos of care that exists outside the family. They did so quite reverently, as well, and encouraged viewers to take mental illness seriously, rather than receive it ironically, a sensibility that interwar era patients sometimes could find a solace. And these official sources encouraged an openmindedness about the mental hospital as an institution.

The domestic care versus institutional care debate continued from the earlier interwar era, but early postwar families and patients were more determined to advocate for patient engagement and activity and sought a hospital environment, if one was necessary at all, that could ensure this. Even if family members knew outside intervention was necessary, they also often grasped for a third way. As an example, in 1946, a mother wrote to California governor Earl Warren about her twenty-five-year-old son's predicament at Camarillo State Hospital. He had been hospitalized there owing to a "nervous breakdown." He had run away once, "trying to come home." She did not feel that her son's living conditions were acceptable: "No sunshine, no exercise, no vitamins, no cheerful words from anyone! I say it is enough to kill one." She asked poignantly: "I am trying to find some kind people to love and care for him, but where is such a place?"[48]

Indeed, where is such a place? This woman "could not bring him home if they would allow it, have neighbors who seem to think it funny to taunt him, etc."[49] She wondered: "What is being done to help him? . . . He is quiet, bothers no one, and seems rational to us when we speak to him, just despondent, nothing to interest him, not allowed what little entertainment they have—only those with yard permits attend entertainments."[50] Here, not taking an interest in an institution is a quandary, not a solace. Her entreaties grew quite desperate and more abstract and pertained to anyone who suffered as her son did: "I beg of you to help these unfortunate people, no one loved now."[51] Her thoughts are emblematic of a subtle shift in sensibility in the kinds of demands and expectations that some patients and their onlookers sought from the medical establishment, as well as more entrenched sentiments about the humanity of the sick.

Perhaps what is most poignant about these testimonies is the fact that a patient's care and engagement within the institution often depended on the kindness and competence of one or a few individuals and could be as random, and as profound, as that. In 1949, for example, the patient newsletter of the Mendocino State Hospital in Talmage, California, included a cartoon praising a nurse as a "one-woman rehabilitation program" (Figure 2).[52] These capsules of kindness speak to Jack D. Pressman's point that conditions varied profoundly between hospitals, even within wards of hospitals, since the mental hospital was a "fragmented environment composed of many subworlds."[53] This idea is made manifest in therapeutic archives, wherein letters of complaint, or simply outpourings of longings, are often countered by letters of praise. In addition to inquiries and life stories, Dr. Overholser of Saint Elizabeths received letters of appreciation during the 1940s and 1950s. One woman who was a patient at the hospital during the early 1950s said that she received "wonderful treatment," that Saint Elizabeths was not "the average State Hospital," and that she was appreciative of "the kindness" shown to her by her doctors. She notes that she was grateful for "having a clean bed and room. Never once have I seen any form of insect life in my room, and the nice clean sheets each week are deeply appreciated. I appreciate the good reading material available to us."[54] Cleanliness and a lack of bugs is setting the bar quite low, but such assessments of mid-twentieth-century Saint Elizabeths diverge strikingly from other contemporary early postwar accounts. Sociologist Erving Goffman did his fieldwork at this hospital, posing as an employee there between 1955 and 1956, and famously pronounced it a "total

Figure 2. "Mrs. Buchanan to Work with Group Affairs," *Pomo News* 1, no. 46 (March 22, 1949): 7. State Archives of California.

institution," one that "untrained" its patients for life outside, creating a "tension between the home world and the institutional world."[55]

The active, community-oriented patient citizen was never a certain prospect even at a hospital invested in this ideal and even with families committed to making this happen. Attention to domestic details was supposed to help ensure satisfactory patient community life. Herman C. B. Denber noted in 1960 that at Vermont State Hospital the patients enjoyed an ambience that was as "non-custodial as possible" with wards that were "pleasantly decorated and furnished, [with] television, laundering facilities, etc. The patients have pets, make popcorn and plan parties. In short, we try to provide a more normal, homelike atmosphere."[56] There is no discussion here of the home being a potential problem. Advice writer Kathleen Doyle acknowledged this in her *Public Affairs Pamphlet* in 1951, which was written for patients' families: "whenever anyone tells you he would be better off at home, remember it was in home surroundings that his illness developed."[57] But the spirit of the age was captured better by an observer like New York City mayor Fiorello LaGuardia, who said that "the worst home is better than the best mental hospital."[58]

Even as the domestic atmosphere of the psychiatric hospital was supposed to ensure a degree of emotional vibrancy, psychiatry as a discipline was implicated in emergent, larger cultural conversations about social conformity and the emotional demeanors of passivity that could result and lead to questionable political proclivities. In 1957, psychiatrist J. Sanbourne Bockoven captured an essential contradiction in psychiatric treatment when he noted that "psychiatry itself rises in status as the means by which the individual can be cured of nonconformity. By the same token, individuals who go to mental hospitals are not welcome back to the community unless they have become good conformers."[59] Such comments also suggest a certain cultural "type" of the era and of the mental hospital, one evoked by Albert Deutsch in *The Shame of the States*. He noted that while we might imagine "unfortunates who have seemingly descended to animal levels of existence . . . sluggers, biters, spitters, pushers, screamers, and even killers . . . most patients are perfectly harmless folk." In fact "they are, if anything, too passive, too frightened, too beaten, too withdrawn. Among them are many of our most sensitive types—people so tender, so delicate, that they could not stand the tough, harsh, brutal reality of modern life."[60] This image of the too-sensitive-for-the-modern-world mental patient was becoming a recognizable figure in a host of sources in this period, anticipating the celebration of the nonconforming, artistic mentally ill person in the late twentieth century. Journalist Mike Gorman evoked this in his 1946 *Daily Oklahoman* piece when he wrote that many patients in state hospitals "possessed sensitive, high-strung minds. In their escape from the painful jungle of human conflict, they have retreated into private worlds."[61] Here again was a uniquely sensitive but lonely individual that modernity had cast aside.

Hospital onlookers thought that if a patient could be unburdened of her loneliness, she could be integrated into a broader patient community, becoming active, engaged, and productive. Loneliness was a prominent early postwar era preoccupation for American artists and intellectuals, instantiated in the haunting photographs of Robert Frank's *The Americans* (1958), wherein the dominant sensibility is alienation. Psychoanalyst Frieda Fromm-Reichmann, for her part, believed that loneliness could lead to the "development of psychotic states" and leave a person "emotionally paralyzed and helpless."[62] She made a distinction between loneliness and restorative, creative solitude, such as immersing oneself in the natural world.[63] In a pamphlet about the development of vocational activities on therapeutic wards, Herman C. B. Denber extolled these "purposeful activities"[64] as reprieves from loneliness inside hospitals, a disavowal of what Deutsch saw as the pitiful spectacle of patients rotting away in "enforced idleness,"[65] which interwar era observers might once have perceived as peace. As Mike Gorman wrote of Oklahoma's state hospitals in 1946, what he witnessed there was a "terrifying atmosphere of hopelessness in institutions where thousands of patients are penned in day after day and night after night endlessly staring at blank walls."[66] Where once the image of a patient staring out the window all day was considered reassuring, it now again marked the frightening nature of idleness and aloneness, or what Goffman described as the "patient's sitting all day in one place, with a vacuous expression on his face."[67]

Official institutional culture of the early postwar period placed a renewed emphasis on staying busy and allaying a state of oblivion. Advice writer Edith Stern pronounced that the "dangers of idleness are far greater than the dangers of exploitation or overwork."[68] A 1953 film titled *Mental Hospital*, produced by the University of Oklahoma for the Oklahoma State Department of Health and Mental Health, showed patients at a fictionalized version of Norman State Hospital dancing, getting their hair done, reading books, playing baseball, and attending religious services. The film noted likewise that "boredom" was the "enemy of the mentally ill."[69] The activities offered at hospitals varied widely: vocation camp for psychiatric patients in remote areas, library visits, special events such as picnics, movies, and pet classes (see Figure 3), and "industrial therapy" such as shoe and coat repair.[70] At Saint Elizabeths Hospital, patients could receive radio therapy, dance therapy, film therapy, and psychodrama therapy and were encouraged to draw and share their creative works.[71] Allaying a state of hospital lethargy was again paramount. As psychiatrist Mortimer Gross noted, at the Elgin State Hospital in Illinois, patients had an array of activities to choose from: Chinese checkers, jigsaw puzzles, singing and rhythm band, walking, softball, volleyball, and fishing trips. And though it was not surprising to him that some patients participated "as so many automatons," others did "seem to enjoy what they do and are less mechanical in their participation."[72]

Figure 3. "Collie Classes Held at Anoka State Hospital," *Mental Hospitals* 7, no. 7 (September 1956): 18.

Mental hospital officials were anxious to promote a sense of active hospital community. Cultural programs and other leisure activities can be read as evidence of a deepening emphasis on sociability and interdependent selfhood during the war and early postwar periods, a kind of community building from within institutional culture that was intended to encourage individual engagement. An idealized example of this is the documentary *Mental Hospital*, which centered around a patient who had been diagnosed with paranoid schizophrenia. When he emerges from the hospital, presumably feeling relieved if not cured, he looks as though he has just finished a refreshing run. He notes that even though people in his small town might "sneer" at the thought of his sojourn in a mental hospital, "this place here has given me my life back." And "now that I am well, I can't help feeling just a little sad, the way you always do when you leave a place." On the surface, this is hardly a ringing endorsement of the attachment he formed to the hospital, but the hospital was still a "place" in this view, rather than something more subterranean and oblique.

The pressure to join patient communities was perhaps difficult, though, for sentient, introspective patients who were anxious to preserve their sense of authenticity. One such patient spent some time at the Brattleboro Retreat in the 1940s and early 1950s; this became a chance for him to meditate about work, leisure, and boredom. As a private mental hospital in Vermont, the Retreat was committed to a nineteenth-century ideal of "moral treatment," such as patient-produced newspapers, theater, book clubs, and the like.[73] Still, in a series of letters to a family friend in 1949, he referred to his stay at the Retreat as a "tedious period . . . I am still supposed to be a voluntary patient but between my family and others, I can hardly call my soul my own." He "thought . . . the primary purpose of any type of hospital is to try and cure as many patients as possible and to restore as many to life beyond its walls." Yet he felt that "staying here too long unfits anyone for life outside. It is as if my family were resigned to my staying here for the rest of my days,"[74] a thought that resonates with Erving Goffman's ideas of the "disculturation" or the "untraining" that occurs inside the asylum walls that renders patients "incapable of managing . . . daily life on the outside."[75]

Even if the Retreat patient's family seemed to inhabit an older sensibility, he was not resigned, though neither was he especially active and engaged in hospital community life. For him "many of the social activities seem childish. . . . Not enough time and thought is given to rehabilitation of patients so that they may be restored to a useful existence instead of living a parasitical and futile one."[76] His assessment resonates with Anne Sexton's 1960 poem "Ringing the Bells," which evokes patient culture in a psychiatric hospital, specifically a Tuesday morning music lesson that she went to "because the attendants make you go / and because we mind by instinct, / like bees caught in the wrong hive." This lesson only seemed to underscore that they were a "circle of crazy ladies / who sit in the lounge of the mental house / and smile at the smiling woman / who passes us each a bell."[77]

The sense of time passing undergirded the idea of "futile existence" and was perceived to be more tortuous by patients and their observers in the early postwar period than it was in the interwar era, and both were now less likely to discuss the hospital as a welcome pause or an interlude of introspection. H. Warren Dunham and S. Kirson Weinberg noted in *The Culture of the State Mental Hospital* (1960) that, for patients who were not engaged in work at Columbus State Hospital, "time and monotony hung so heavily on their hands. They had little, if anything, to do except sit continually upon hard chairs."[78] For the patient, "time marches on. One year passes, then five, then ten and nothing has happened but the initial examination, ward transfers, a couple of physical complaints, and a visit from her husband." This was why, in the hospital, "time ceases to have meaning."[79]

The passing of time could even be perceived as an early postwar era enforcer of conformity. Russell K. Hampton, a psychologist, wrote an account of his personal breakdown in 1961 when he was a twenty-nine-year-old graduate student suffering from depression. He entered the psychiatric ward of his university's general hospital. He soon found that the "days plod by. Have I been in this place only a week? Have I ever been anywhere else? Already the days and nights have become depressingly predictable. They are anesthetizingly the same."[80] Paul Hackett, who spent a year in a Veterans Administration Hospital in New Jersey diagnosed with schizophrenia, noted in his 1953 account that he was continually aware of time. Even on the first day, when he was not sure exactly where he was and was in something of a delusional state, observing just a corridor, hearing dishes in the background being stacked and washed, or sitting in a large room with a red leather chair, he focused upon a clock on the wall: "the blank hands were chasing the wild red hand. I wanted to break the glass. Time was in prison on the face of the clock. It couldn't escape."[81] As he became less delusional throughout the course of his treatment, he expressed his thoughts on time less elliptically. "Like a prisoner awaiting parole," he wrote, "I counted the days and the nights of the passing time, and slept away as much of it as I could to make it pass sooner."[82]

There is an intriguing resonance between writings about white, middle-class conformity, domestic time, and solitude and those of mental illness during the postwar period. Accounts of the surfeit of time and boredom in the domestic realm mirror the psychology of the sickbed. Betty Friedan famously referred to the suburban home as "the comfortable concentration camp" and fretted that tranquilizer use during the 1950s had lulled women into passive acceptance of thwarted dreams.[83] Friedan did not believe there was anything liberating about the sense of peace and quiet that prevailed when children went off to school and men went off to work, nor did she experience the house as a place of introspection. Instead she described housewives taking to drink at "11 am to hide the clunking whir of the dishwasher, the washing machine, the dryer, that are . . . the only sounds of life in that empty house."[84] In psychiatrist Richard Gordon and psychologist Katherine Gordon's descriptions of the mental life of suburbanites in 1960, the conditions sound similar to those in a mental hospital. They refer to a crying young mother, who experiences "voices in the walls . . . telling her she is worthless." In another house, a "middle-aged woman is also weeping. . . . Finally she gets up, takes a bottle of sleeping pills from the bathroom cabinet, empties the pills into her hand and swallows them."[85]

The feelings of depression these writers were describing might have been exacerbated in an early postwar era consumer culture of abundance, optimism, and buoyancy, ideals that were inherently middle class, and often white, particularly at the level of cultural representation. Passivity and lacking energy could be pathologized in this climate in particular. Even in the face of suffering, avoiding hospitalization altogether was still an imperative for some. For example, a young woman who approached Saint Elizabeths superintendent Overholser in 1956 was in search of a drug that might help her and might prevent her from being institutionalized. She was nineteen years old, married to a twenty-two-year-old, and expecting a baby. She had a history of mental turmoil, which she had told her husband about, including a "nervous breakdown" when she was fifteen, at which time she had been hospitalized for three months.[86] She mentioned experiencing "weak[ness], dizziness, can't get out of bed to do my housework till one or two o'clock in the afternoon, no matter how early I go to bed. . . . I want to sleep all the time. When I do get out of bed I have no energy." In fact, her husband had "threatened to leave if I can't have more energy than I do now."[87] Psychiatrist Peter Kramer has suggested that there was a historical shift in American culture's preference for certain gendered personality types, noting that socially favored women of the late twentieth century were much more energetic, assertive, and outgoing than midcentury women, particularly those who took "mother's little helpers" during the 1950s.[88] This is an intriguing idea but one that has been complicated by historians of psychopharmacology who show that tranquilizers were originally marketed to men during the 1950s, though they tend to be remembered now as white, middle-class housewife drugs.[89]

Still, letters like this one show that women were very much aware that appearing listless and lacking energy could be undesirable in an era of renewed domesticity, a kind of flip-side of the uncertainties and trepidation that animated the early postwar era "age of anxiety" of a new era of nuclear weaponry and feared nuclear apocalypse.[90] The woman who wrote to Dr. Overholser asked if the "new drug [Meratran] will help me? If so, could I possibly get it and try it? . . . From what I read . . . it sounds very encouraging and my hopes are up very high because I think maybe I can get well [and] have one of the most happy homes and family that has ever existed."[91] This comment also suggests that she ascribed to an early postwar ideal of the nuclear family. Ambivalence about domesticity also abounded in the 1950s and early 1960s, if novels such as Richard Yates's *Revolutionary Road* (1961) reveal anything about the era; the book's central character complains constantly about feeling suffocated by his family life.[92] What was the place of the hospitalized mentally ill, or potential hospital patients, in these postwar families, be they happy or miserable or simply ambivalent ones?

While Friedan located woman's selfhood in the marketplace or in fulfilling work in the public sphere, the idea that time drifted along amorphously in the hospital seemed to offer a setting that could shield a patient from having to be productive and from the social roles of the workplace. Perhaps this was a more poignant reflection during the early postwar period when the commercialization of public spaces was becoming ever more apparent, though this was again a gendered reflection, as a hospital pause for middle-class men could be more appealing than for women like Friedan who did not have the chance they wanted in the work world.[93]

The surfeit of time in a mental hospital could lend itself to spiritual reflection, though it could also hover between meaningful and anesthetizing. On an official level, some mental hospitals, as institutions, wanted to suggest that they too could be sites for spirituality. The Brattleboro patient kept with his letters a fascinating document called "How to Keep Sane in a Hospital for Mental Patients." This document advised his fellow patients: "Cling to the belief that God reigns in the universe, and that communion with spiritual forces is just as possible within hospital walls as it is outside."[94] In the 1950s, the United States experienced a broad religious revival in the form of traditional Protestantism, televangelism, an upswing in Catholic and Jewish participation in traditional practices, and rising popularity of Christian existentialists. Psychoanalysis and religion, in turn, were sometimes crudely pitted against one another in pop culture sources during the early postwar period though this document encourages a combination of the two.[95]

Perhaps what prevented the Brattleboro Retreat from being a site for spiritual reflection was precisely a lack of solitude and being nagged to participate in activities. An inherent condition of living in a hospital is the stress of being in the public sphere at all moments—even if it was made to feel like domestic space. The mental hospital never left patients truly alone and demanded a constant performance, in effect offering a surfeit of privacy yet without solitude. Social observers such as Goffman have commented on the performative dimension of patients in the public sphere of a mental hospital: they perform their illnesses so as not to disappoint their psychiatric doctors and nurses.[96] But some performances in the hospital might have been a bit more banal than this and came simply at the cost of personal authenticity. In a 1943 letter to a friend the Brattleboro patient wrote that "of course hospital life is largely artificial by its very nature. A person has to be courteous and pleasant to others although there is so little in common. That is the difficult part."[97] This patient embodied a larger reverence for and preoccupation with authenticity, which disparaged putting on airs, social phoniness, and small talk, all the pleasantries that one might need to employ in public. Mental illness, as literary critic Abigail Cheever argues, has always been a vital site of pondering authenticity,[98] but this seems to be a preoccupation that was most intense during the war and especially by the early postwar era. It is not that interwar era patients never thought about authenticity—Seabrook and Brown, for example, praised the authenticity of the asylum inmates as exceeding that of those on the outside. But by the early postwar period these reflections were becoming more commonplace and were implicated in a rejection of the automaton as a way of being.

Psychiatrists at times even believed that the mental hospital could be a space of emotional authenticity for patients. At Saint Elizabeths Hospital in 1954, a psychiatrist was asked to address the matter of patients who were being noisy on the hospital porches and disturbing the neighbors. Mental hospitals in the United States were traditionally set apart from the "sane" world, in the "curative space" of the asylum,[99] often in bucolic settings, and yet the two worlds occasionally caught glimpses of each other when patients were taken into town for visits and through transitional spaces such as asylum porches and balconies. At times this created tension regarding the "proper" sphere of the expression of mental illness. In this particular case the psychiatrist wrote, "My own private feelings about the matter is that if people cannot holler in a mental hospital, where can they holler?"[100] Another neighbor complained during the same year that the hospital should curtail the "hollering, screaming, profanity, and obscene language."[101] Dr. Addison M. Duval, Saint Elizabeths' first assistant physician, replied to this neighbor that "I hope you will remember that it is sometimes good for our patients to 'let off steam', and that a good mental hospital does not place too severe restrictions on its patients."[102] These kinds of complaints speak to a long-standing position that insanity is not the province of the public sphere and must stay confined to its realm "offstage." Dr. William C. Woodward, a physician and lawyer, noted in his testimony before a congressional subcommittee regarding the voluntary admission and treatment of patients at Saint Elizabeths in 1947 that if someone suffering from mental illness simply "stays in his hotel room or his room in a boarding house, he is perfectly safe from the police or from commitment,"[103] which he regarded as unfortunate. In the vision of these doctors and some other observers, the mental hospital could be a necessary haven for bizarre and eccentric behavior that the public sphere simply could not accommodate otherwise. These voices also suggest a right to emotional expressiveness, one that the hospital could accommodate, and can be considered political articulations of a sort.

In fact, ideas about authenticity informed many areas of intellectual inquiry beyond psychiatry. These ideas were bound up with the need for "true" emotional expression rather than passively going through the motions. The popularity of existential philosophy in the United States in the 1950s caused Americans to think about authenticity more consciously, including the moral role of the individual in a hostile and threatening world, as characterized in popular works such as Walter Kaufmann's *Existentialism from Dostoevsky to Sartre* (1956) and Christian existential philosophers such as Reinhold Niebuhr and Søren Kierkegaard.[104] Moreover, the need to attain authenticity was particularly urgent in a society that had just witnessed and was contemplating how the extreme circumstances of warfare could be de-individuating. American social observers at midcentury were also quite aware of the changes to the presentation of the self in different contexts and in front of different audiences, as well as the chasm between the private and public selves, often reflecting on the remaining true self. They were attuned especially to false appearances, scrutinizing those who were "passing" for other than what they seemed; these included those with an ambiguous race or sexuality, the upwardly mobile poor, and the politically dubious.[105] The mentally ill could be added to this list, and perhaps they were the most disturbing because they most embodied the threat that anyone could end up like them, especially if institutionalized.

Goffman is most well known for thoughts on this array of selves, especially his ideas on the self that one wants to become,[106] but they had a much broader ambit than this. These ideas were fundamental to reflections about the "internal migrations" that the individual was forced to make in wartime contexts, for instance. Bruno Bettelheim showed how authenticity was tainted in the concentration camps and how selves split into the real and the social, with the real here taking on a sort of sacred quality, as the true self that got preserved.[107] These ideas were also prevalent in ethnographical and psychiatric writings on postwar African Americans, especially regarding the gap between the performance of public deference to white mores and an internal, more authentic sense of private disillusionment. In 1950, anthropologist Hortense Powdermaker evoked a deep and seething anger that she theorized lurked beneath an ostensible African American deference to whites.

Her writings suggest white observers feared African American authenticity and found it unsettling. These kinds of observations of African Americans would only intensify in the face of desegregation when the emotional "rituals of segregation" were displaced by more unknown ways of being.[108] But these writings also emblematize the increasing attention in the 1950s to the true self and its vicissitudes, which might include anger, among other emotions.

Certain styles of selfhood also were becoming freighted with a dire politics by the war and early postwar period in a way that they were not in years prior, and this reflection was easily transposed onto mental hospitals. Social critics fretted over the passivity of the American "masses," perceived as passive citizens whose intimate relationships were not conducted in real communities but in Hollywood films.[109] Frankfurt School thinkers such as Theodor Adorno alluded to the passive American recipient of popular culture and mass media as a "pseudo-self," uniquely susceptible to fascism, something that America also could be vulnerable to in the 1950s.[110] As Carol R. Murphy, a Quaker writer and thinker, wrote in a 1955 pamphlet, a "healthy person" with a "healthy ego" could be likened to a "secure and democratic government," but a "neurotic person" has a "defensive ego, which represses what it cannot handle" and could be likened to a "dictatorship, where freedoms are repressed, often in the name of a tyrannous conscience, and the populace is rigidly controlled by a secret police."[111]

The image of the automaton, a figure devoid of an interior life, had widespread circulation during the war and postwar periods among hospital psychiatrists to be sure, but also in larger intellectual conversations about authenticity and the problems of conformity as a social evil in daily life, popular culture, and politics.[112] Was the mental hospital immune to the social conformity that so bedeviled the workplace and other theaters of social life during the war and early postwar eras? While postwar American cultural representations suggested a sense of intrigue about cybernetics and the relationship between men and machines, these were often laced with a fear that a heartless, mechanical, automaton-like thing was going to turn on human beings.[113] Perhaps this perspective reflects an awareness of the mechanization of warfare during World War II, of soldiers who had to perform mechanized tasks and were reduced to the level of automatons. Or perhaps it reflects the reality that the A-bomb instilled of the dreadful capacities of technology and people's powerlessness in the face of it.[114] In 1958, family psychiatrist Nathan Ackerman warned somewhat direly that "we must be continually vigilant against the cultivation of machine-like efficiency, against the development of trained technicians who operate with precision but are numb to the sufferings of people. . . . We must not allow ourselves to be seduced by the sick values of the machine age."[115]

As early as his 1941 book *Escape from Freedom*, psychoanalyst Erich Fromm, also of the Frankfurt School, had ascribed the state of robotization with a grave political significance, one that rendered the self vulnerable to external manipulations and totalitarianism. "The person who gives up his individual self and becomes an automaton identical with millions of other automatons around him, need not feel alone and anxious anymore," he wrote, discussing why totalitarianism could be appealing to people to begin with.[116] World War II provided an intellectual and political context to be wary of this automaton and passivity. In *Escape from Freedom* Fromm explores the psychological conditions that allowed Nazism to flourish, the idea of "authoritarian characters," and conformity in the United States. He received a number of letters from American readers in response to this work. In 1942 a woman wrote to say how moved she was by this book, especially by Fromm's description of the automaton because "here, I believe, is a greater threat than Fascism to the American dream of freedom for the individual."[117] This acquiescent character, in her view, was a "more imminent danger" to the United States than Nazism.[118] She also transposed this kind of thinking onto individual lives, especially what she considered the circumscribed lives of American women at midcentury. She admitted that "for forty years I submitted and conformed to other people's ideas of what I should be. In so doing I believe I let 'them' kill a potential artist." She continued: "My life is richer and I am less a burden to society than my mother—the most negative person I have ever known. Her beauty-hungering soul was completely crushed by conformity to what 'they' think and say."[119] A critic of the privatization of politics would say that this woman simply wanted historical events to be somehow about her, as if her superficial mother could possibly be compared to the hollowness of the "masses" of Germans who sought solace in fascism. And yet this letter also demonstrates an appreciation that the failures in private life could now have a momentous and dire political import, as well as new, quite damning, political valences beginning to be ascribed to the automaton who just blindly accepts social mores.

In 1956, after Fromm had been living in the United States for more than twenty years, he wrote that "human relations are essentially those of alienated automatons, each basing his security on staying close to the herd, and not being different in thought, feeling or action."[120] Walter Freeman praised this kind of sameness because he felt the lobotomy could be a great social equalizer: after the procedure the IQs of highly intelligent patients went down a bit while those of less intelligent patients went up a bit.[121] Yet during the 1950s especially, observations of the automaton began to be laced with a fear of submission to political authorities, which embodies both emergent civil rights discourses of the postwar period and a more abstract consciousness about the brutality of "man." Exposé literature and advocates for the mentally ill at midcentury tended to speak in abstract language about this universal "man." Historian George Cotkin argues that modernist intellectuals of the late 1940s and early 1950s believed in the "commonality of the human condition," which he attributes to a temporary decline in racialist thinking, a growing interest in cultural anthropology, and Freudian thought.[122]

Patient communities were not immune to discussions about their own potentials for fascism in microcosm. These associations could be fraught, owing to a hierarchy of illness among the patients, a popularity politics no less conformist than in other social settings and ascribed with the same dire political implications. A major study of the internal politics of a mental hospital ward community, *The Mental Hospital*, was published in 1954 by psychiatrist Alfred H. Stanton and sociologist Morris S. Schwartz. The floor under study here was a disturbed women's ward with a fifteen-patient capacity in Chestnut Lodge, a sixty-bed hospital in Rockville, Maryland. This facility was a sanatorium for those suffering from "mild and nervous mental diseases," one that prized psychoanalytical psychiatry and a range of different therapeutic techniques from dance to drama therapy. Chestnut opened in 1910 after being transformed from a luxury hotel and marketed itself still as this sort of inviting hotel.[123] From the standpoint of the early postwar period, the hospital is perhaps most well known for being the home of the psychoanalyst Frieda Fromm-Reichmann, who used psychoanalysis as treatment even for patients with schizophrenia. Gail Hornstein notes that the Lodge was quite an emotionally intense community because so many people were being simultaneously psychoanalyzed: the doctors, the nurses, occupational therapists, and even some attendants.[124]

Despite these innovative intentions, in *The Mental Hospital*, Stanton and Schwartz depicted a rather authoritarian institution, even referring to the hospital an "inexorable propaganda machine,"[125] one that had a hand in creating the pathologies of its patients. A fear of lurking institutional authoritarianism was part of a larger postwar propensity to believe that social reality potentially manifested a struggle between democracy and freedom on the one hand and totalitarianism on the other.[126] "Can it happen here?" derived from Sinclair

Lewis's well-known satirical novel of 1935, *It Can't Happen Here*, became an animating question of American postwar intellectuals when considering the possibility for fascism emerging at home. Why, as Jean-Christophe Agnew asks, in the midst of America's postwar triumph, did American intellectuals develop a "tragic sense of itself?"[127] This interpretation of social reality illuminated many different areas of intellectual inquiry; in education, for example, creating innovative, democratic thinkers who would safeguard American democracy was paramount. As an institution, the mental hospital could find itself in a landscape of a "democratization of culture" undertaken by American social scientists and wanted to be seen as active democracies in microcosm.[128]

Private institutions in the postwar period like Chestnut Lodge also were anxious to designate themselves as places that offered patients leisurely activity and fulfillment; they did not want to be in the same category as grim institutions with lifeless denizens. The Lodge's architects were particularly attuned to the ambient atmosphere of the hospital, even at the level of sounds and smells, so as to avoid a languid "sick atmosphere." Architect Chloethiel Woodard Smith wondered if "daily 'normal' sounds" such as a "cock's crow, wood being sawed, rug shaken, broom sweeping, dog's bark" might help to "'reach' the patient, and should be consciously provided." Odor, she noted, was particular anathema in the context of a mental hospital since the "horrid miasma of the mental hospital back ward is evoked. . . . This, too, is architecture's business—to build in good ventilation, to admit the fresh smell of outside and even the strong, pleasing odors of good food."[129]

Commenting on the social architecture of Chestnut Lodge, Stanton and Schwartz noted with surprise that the patients of the ward did not gravitate toward specific leisure activities such as listening to the radio, even though the radio as a cultural form seems particularly fitting for a version of domestic culture offered in the hospital.[130] Instead, the female patients preferred to congregate and simply talk. Their observers noted that the porch gave the ward a feeling of spaciousness and that patients did sometimes go out on it, but the "social center of the ward" was actually the "corridor between the nurses' office and the living room."[131] Hallways have been a subject of debate in American asylum architectural discourse since the nineteenth century: all long corridors were to be eschewed because the hospital would then feel institutional and not like "home."[132] Perhaps these patients rejected the hospital's domestic spaces that seemed like bad copies of home, grasping this strange incongruity. Instead they lingered in the corridor like coworkers chatting with each other in the workplace, unsure of what they were to each other.

Stanton and Schwartz criticized patients for forming cliques and for clique-ish conformity and praised them for community and emotional solidarity. They noted that the patients they observed "ate their meals together regularly. They exchanged confidences with one another, most significantly, confidences about occurrences in their therapeutic treatment [and they offered] mutual sympathy and support."[133] For example, when "one member disparages herself the others tried to counter this picture of herself." Stanton and Schwartz recorded a conversation along these lines between two members of the ward clique, a Miss Michels and a Mrs. Stillman:

MISS MICHELS: I have a lot of hair [on my body].
MRS. STILLMAN: I have, too!
MISS MICHELS: But I have more than anyone else.
MRS. STILLMAN: Oh no. I've seen women with more hair than you have.
MISS MICHELS: Oh, no, you haven't! They weren't women. They must be apes!
MRS. STILLMAN: One of the happiest and best-adjusted girls I know has electrolysis done time and time again.
MISS MICHELS: There are many hairy women, but no one has as much as I have. I got it all over my chest, my hands, my legs, and my face.
MRS. STILLMAN: You look attractive, you know.
MISS MICHELS: I'm not attractive. . . .
MRS. STILLMAN: I'm a woman and I can tell.[134]

This conversation seems depressingly universal as one among women who scrutinize each other's physical appearances, yet it is significant that Mrs. Stillman offered her fellow patient a reassurance laced with her potential for conformity. Miss Michels was not in fact freakish for having hair all over her body; she was just like any other woman. Much as their observers criticized patients for conformity, the perils of nonconformity were also evident inside the mental hospital. According to sociologists H. Warren Dunham and S. Kirson Weinberg, most mental hospital patients knew that "conformity is essential for their welfare."[135]

Much as an ethos of social conformity was derided by intellectuals and cultural critics during the early postwar era, at the same time an ethos of social integration was also quite morally powerful, whether this was expressed by the Black or gay civil rights movement.[136] Integration was also poignant inside the asylum community among those who were also notably stigmatized and separated. Patients widely commented upon and dissected the profound pain of feeling like an "outcast," which departed from the romanticism ascribed to individualism in popular culture about rebels, or in intellectual culture, such as the Beat Generation.[137] *Ebony* magazine even quoted Mary Jane Ward in 1949 as saying that she did not think there was race prejudice among the white patients in mental hospitals because "I think the average white patient regards the average Negro patient as a fellow sufferer."[138] This view seems quite romantic at best—this very article noted that the conditions that Black patients had to endure were like those in "concentration camps," and patient testimonies themselves show plenty of instances of hierarchizing by race, by illness, or by class, even among the fellow sufferers, not to mention overt examples of racism such as white patient minstrel shows with actors performing in blackface, a nineteenth century practice that persisted even in the mid-twentieth century.[139] Nonetheless, her comment does suggest at least an ideal of fellowship among the hospitalized stigmatized and a developing minority consciousness.

If integration was sought and sometimes strategically needed, the same could be said of resignation, even amid hospital ideals of activity that do not dovetail easily with it. Resignation quietly endured in the same way that it had animated psychosurgeries: to make bearable the unbearable. And hospitals ironically also encouraged it as an ideal, which suggests that this sensibility lingered, at least in a diffuse way, into the war and postwar eras. The first rule of "How to Keep Sane in a Hospital for Mental Patients" was "never try to reform the institution in which you are a 'guest'. Do your best to cooperate with the authorities, however unnecessary and burdensome the regulations may appear to you to be." Perhaps in recognition of all the exposé literature about mental hospitals that animated the early postwar era, the document advised patients "not to take too seriously all the tragic tales" they had heard about the hospital environment. The document further told the patient: "'Cheer up; Twont last; Nuthin does'" and urged her to cultivate a sense of humor.[140] Elgin State Hospital near Chicago furnished its patients with a similar pamphlet during the postwar era, written by Anton T. Boisen, the chaplain there, who was a well-known figure in the hospital chaplaincy movement and had been hospitalized himself during the 1920s for psychosis. He had become quite interested in exploring schizophrenic thinking for its parallels to religious visions. The pamphlet, addressed to "Our New Guests," acknowledges that "entering the mental hospital is often a trying experience. One feels lonely, fearful, discouraged and desperately in need of help."[141] However, the "Prayer for the Hospital" that this pamphlet offers does not sound particularly hopeful, beseeching "Almighty God" to give "those who are ill . . . patience and courage, and, if it may be, the recovery of their health."[142] The pamphlet reinforces this vision of "if it may be" by also offering a version of Reinhold Niebuhr's serenity prayer from the 1940s: "grant us the serenity of mind to accept that which cannot be changed, the courage to change that which can be changed and the wisdom to tell the one from the other."[143]

In turn, the pamphlet that the Brattleboro patient kept both encouraged a sense of therapeutic community, and it did not: "In the 6th chapter of Galatians there are two apparently contradictory passages: 'Bear ye one another's burdens;' 'Every man shall bear his own burdens.' Both are equally true."[144] Perhaps some patients did find solace and the social bonds of a community in the mental hospital, but the Brattleboro patient simply observed a mishmash of humanity, an unchosen or forced community. In the fall of 1944 he wrote that "there is no congeniality or companionship but only a most morbid, peculiar atmosphere among a group of people who have practically lost all enthusiasm (if they ever had any). After dinner . . . there is only time to write a letter or visit the library, or both before retiring."[145] Here were some limits of institutional emotional solidarities or what Harold Maine has called the "loyalty of suffering" that he experienced among patients during his psychiatric hospitalizations for alcoholism during the 1940s.[146] A disquiet about a dearth of community was something that American social critics of this period complained about as well: a lack of a sense of "neighborliness" in America's cities and towns.[147] Perhaps these perspectives were more specific to whites born in America than immigrants or people of color, who may have developed stronger communities in the face of hostility from the larger society.[148] But the idealization of community participation also speaks to a historical moment in which the communitarian spirit of the interwar or even war era was perceived to be waning, a void that a mental hospital community ideally was designed to meet.

At the same time as social conformity could be considered an evil in this period, somewhat paradoxically, grave warnings about the dangers of too much individualism were also a feature of American social and intellectual life during the War and early postwar period. Although the communities that developed in the hospital were at times ambiguous, psychiatrists in the early postwar period were concerned that their patients were fundamentally unreachable, passive to the point of being unintelligible to others, not amenable to social integration, and too intensely lost in their internal, individual worlds. This was a perennial therapeutic frustration that became more acute during the 1930s when the community as an entity was held up as an ideal, but during the early postwar period it continued to be a concern: patients had become too socially withdrawn, were immune to psychoanalysis and other forms of therapy, and failed to engage with larger community life. Of course, many mental illnesses can render patients somewhat remote, at least for a time, but the fear of this unreachability was amplified during the early postwar era; this was somewhat paradoxical since psychiatry textbooks from the 1950s were also preoccupied with the superficial conformity that they felt had beset American society at large, even amid the pragmatic necessity of conformity in the institution.[149]

A fear of emotionlessness and being out of "contact" was also gaining ground in the 1950s among psychiatrists and psychologists. Bruno Bettelheim furthered and popularized this kind of thinking in his well-known 1959 essay, "Joey: A Mechanical Boy," about a boy with autism who functioned "as if by remote control."[150] Postwar psychiatrists did not allow their patients to stay in the realm of fantasy; they sought a return to "contact" and a return to social integration, and this heightened the importance of the institution's role.[151] Ideally, a patient was to be "reachable" and a participating citizen within the hospital community. Silvano Arieti, a psychiatrist who specialized in schizophrenia and who subscribed to a trauma model of schizophrenia rather than a purely medical one, noted in a 1959 American psychiatry textbook that "schizophrenia may occur in every type of society [but] it tends to be more common in that type of society which [David] Riesman calls other-directed."[152] This is quite a damning thing to say about other-directedness, or taking one's cues from the group and peer culture rather than the individual, an idea made famous by David Riesman's The Lonely Crowd (1950), a book that encouraged a broader cultural conversation about "other-directedness" throughout the postwar period.[153] However, there is a more positive side to other-directedness, one that the National Association for Mental Health tried to capture. In a 1951 pamphlet, "Mental Health Is… 1,2,3," mentally healthy individuals were defined as people who can "feel they are part of a group." In fact, "mentally healthy people are good friends, good workers, good mates, good parents, good citizens."[154] Both too much other-directedness and too much inner-directedness were problematic for psychiatrists, and this reflects a wider dilemma in the American polity that was especially pressing at midcentury: the desire to create authentic individuals who would stand strong against totalitarianism, resist becoming meaningless participants in the herd, and yet not teeter over the edge into excessive privatization and the abandonment of families and communities. Public health sources that addressed themselves to audiences interested in mental health in the 1950s tried to straddle this line between community and fascism by minimizing the importance of the collective and placed their accent on companionship instead.[155]

Still, broader societal concerns about government omnipotence and government persecution were more prevalent during the war and early post-war eras as patients, too, began to see totalitarianism as a lens through which to understand—and to protest—their institutional environments. Grievances about the patient condition during this period were more politicized than they had been during the interwar era: their sorrows were starting to be viewed as not inevitable and amenable to change. In addition, there began a subtle shift from a belief in natural rights, or a preservation of their moral beings, to a more explicitly politicized and a broader gamut of rights, not to mention a less deferential patienthood.[156]

The very act of writing letters to government officials suggests a faith in the power of patient testimonials to effect change. In 1941, the governor of Alabama, Frank M. Dixon, an avowed and doctrinaire segregationist, received letters from a young African American patient at Searcy Hospital in Mount Vernon, Alabama, a segregated and exclusively Black institution until the end of the 1960s. She attested to appalling, "almost unbearable" living conditions there and evokes a kind of protective posture toward the patients around her who were "deteriorated, disturbed and distressed" and in need of "immediate attention." Suffering from insomnia while in the hospital, she wrote the governor long letters about what she observed there.[157] She detailed to him brutal patient beatings administered by white nurses and attendants.[158] Patients were compelled to work, demeaned while doing it, and not given even the most basic of comforts; "only a few patients [were] given anything to prepare" for their "monthly periods."[159] If a patient should die on the floor, "the one who happens to find her kicks her to see if she is dead."[160] She felt compelled to note to the governor that "we are human . . . we have feelings and are the fruit of some mother's womb!"[161] The entire situation, particularly witnessing people at their most vulnerable—and here she highlighted mental suffering—moved her to write because she could not "rest contented knowing that such brutality exists in the authorities of any institution, especially in one for insane people."[162] For her, the institution was potentially redeemable, as were the lives of her fellow patients; if only they were "placed under the care of a therapist [then] they would not, possibly, wade into the depths of insanity!"[163] Perhaps a remaining faith in better institutions and government enabled her to say that she was still "anxiously waiting for you to take the necessary steps to set the situation straight."[164]

By the early postwar era, patient pleas about the oppressions of the hospital environment also took up totalitarian imagery: personal, existential tragedies could become blurred with larger political ones. As a rhetorical strategy, the Nazi metaphor and broader metaphors of racism resonated with midcentury American hospital denizens and added a certain heft to a posture of objection beyond the expressions of sorrow of an earlier generation.[165] A mother who felt that her daughter was virtually imprisoned at Patton State Hospital in California pronounced that "this is United States not Hitler's Germany" in her 1953 letter to Earl Warren.[166] She also invoked the Civil War, noting that: "1860 to 1865 Civil War was to end slavery and Persecution. My daughter of white race."[167] This comment also reveals the kinds of racial hierarchies that existed within the mental hospital and the desire to assert one's whiteness as something that could be cherished even in the face of hospitalization. And it suggests an awareness of entitlement to citizenship rights on the part of white patients, something that might have made the idea of hospital citizenship more complicated for Black patients. Edward X. Lane, an African American psychiatric patient who had spent thirteen years in the Criminal Building, the State Hospital in Trenton, New Jersey, during the 1950s, noted that attendants regularly said things to him like "'you crazy black bastard, you'll never get out.'" And he too invoked the Civil War, only here to explain racial prejudice, because he felt that bigoted whites, "these soulless creatures," in vulnerable or unenviable circumstances were "still trying to prove their superiority—an obsession held over from the Civil War," one that called into question Black citizenship.[168] In other letters, there was simply a mishmash of totalitarian and tyrannical imagery from popular culture: the Soviet Union became a kind of epicenter of the loss of individual liberty and an emblem of the automaton in these writings, and patients and those who cared for them took up the concentration camp as a metonym for the Holocaust as liberally as it often is today. For example, a woman wrote to Governor Warren in 1952 about her husband's captivity in Agnews State Hospital in California, saying of a psychiatrist there that "just about everyone claims [he] is a dirty communist and this place a concentration camp! He walks around like Lucky Luciano nervously swinging a cigar from his mouth."[169]

How can these captivity narratives be reconciled with those who found instances of community inside the hospital? Were those instances of solidarity or affiliation only brief moments within a more generalized ambience of captivity? Was life in mental hospitals much like life on the outside—plodding along, for the most part, with moments of happiness and serenity and epiphany and community, but also with great swaths of boredom and lacklusterness, punctuated by periods of tragedy, not to mention exploitation?

An intriguing example of a collision of these kinds of narratives is in a 1960 letter from a woman to Minnesota governor Orville Freeman, who was interested in liberal policies such as civil rights, to protest that her son had been placed in Fergus Falls State Hospital under what she felt were false circumstances. She wrote of her son's value as a person and his kindness and equanimity: "he is a quiet obedient person. People say he is a very nice person and kept to himself and minded his own business."[170] She also spoke of her loneliness: "Why do they keep him locked there like an animal when he should be home to help me." She was enclosing letters from her son so that the governor could see that "nothing is wrong with him."[171] However, the son's letter, while perfunctory, is not a captivity narrative per se. It is simply a slice of fairly neutral daily life at the hospital. On Thanksgiving Day 1960, he wrote, "Dear Mother, Wishing Mom a happy thanksgiving and holiday pleasantness. A man who works for Patient Activities asked me to make a bridge to use for the pool table. . . . Doctor Moran talked to me and spoke as though there will be some help for me. Such as medicine and consultations. I am getting a pill every morning. Probably for my nerves. They have helped me quite a bit. Regards to friends and hoping Mother is well. Your son.[172]

This was not the cry for help that the mother's letter was; in fact the letter does not have an especially emotional tone, other than reassurance that he was being cared for through therapeutic activities and medicine. Patient newsletters show other instances of this sort of matter-of-factness as well. In "Ward News" from a patient newsletter from Mendocino State Hospital in 1951, for example, they note that a patient was a "lucky 'gent'" because in one day "his father, mother, wife, and two daughters paid a visit."[173] Was a new face of resignation in this period, in the wake of the disappointments surrounding biological psychiatry and the cures they proffered, as well as a more palpable postwar fear of totalitarianism, simply a quiet observation of care? This kind of source serves as a reminder of the quotidian of the hospital environment and institutionalization, perhaps a relentless dailiness with small breaks in monotony and routine that take on an extra weight in these contexts, yet still a poignant one that contributed toward the perception that the institution made human beings into automatons.

The story of hospital psychiatry could be bleak in the war, and early postwar periods, no matter what the genre. And yet another shift from the interwar era—and something that also profoundly altered the way resignation was felt and represented—is an inchoate sense in the early postwar period that grievances could be heard, that complaints could be aired, and perhaps even that injustices could be redressed. There was an emergent hope that some sympathetic witness would indeed pay heed to the trials of institutionalization and even the vagaries of mental illness itself. Perhaps this sprang from the creation and diffusion of particular psychiatric publics in this period—a public addressed in advice pamphlets, mental health films, and exposé literature in addition to official government channels. If injustices in the treatment of the mentally ill could be redressed, then, in this reasoning, so too could the experience of mental illness, of feeling lifeless, or even feeling like an outcast. The expectations for sympathetic witnessing, emotional reciprocities, justice, and rights grew just as the expectations for the institution were waning.

CHAPTER 4

From Possessive to Expressive Individualism

A patient at St. Peter State Hospital in Minnesota wrote a letter to the governor, Orville Freeman, in 1956 to say that he was being "imprisoned wrongfully" and wanted to have it on record that "I need no Institutional care. I need no doctor. I need no nurse. I take care of myself."[1] He continued by asserting his moral rectitude, as if to say that this was incompatible with mental distress: "I'm no mental ill, committed no crime, have no violent temper and fight, no shock treatments, need none, want none, taken no medicine, have not been up in the sick room, do not smoke, drink liquors, beer, and swear." But he also suggested that basic medical tests were a violation of his very being: "There is no law in Minnesota that states I had to be forced into city hospitals and institutions . . . to take examinations, tests, conferences, psychiatrist tests, chest x-rays . . . that's my own personal affair." He signed off on this same self-reliant note: "I have never asked for charity. I want no charity."[2] State hospitals have often been bound up with charity, something that was true of the nineteenth-century heritage of some state institutions.[3] But this letter also invites a reflection upon what it was that the individual believed the state owed him and what services were being forced upon him, a question that would become more urgent by the late twentieth century when American political thinkers were pondering this relationship, and the welfare state, anew.

Social observers have attributed deinstitutionalization in the United States to psychotropic drugs such as Thorazine, as well as changes in government policy,[4] but deinstitutionalization is also a cultural and sensibility shift. The drift toward self-reliance and deinstitutionalization in the 1960s can be understood as an extension of mid-twentieth-century social reform liberalism that perceived the phasing out of institutions for the mentally ill as a corrective to the dilapidated and depressing mid-twentieth-century "concentration camps" that exposé writers evoked so vividly in their works. And yet, midcentury American liberal government policies were ideally supposed to correct social abuses by intervening with the market when necessary, sometimes through social institutions.[5] The awareness that many mental hospitals were corroding meant that they would require massive infusions of money to be sustained, which even ideologically liberal policymakers were not prepared to spend.[6]

There were nonetheless some attempts to improve the institutional therapeutic landscape in this period, something thought would be best accomplished by deemphasizing the mental hospital as the principal institution for treating mental illnesses. In 1963, the Kennedy administration's Mental Retardation and Community Mental Health Centers Construction Act (Community Mental Health Act), which transferred funding from large mental institutions to nonresidential community mental health centers, something both activists and community psychiatrists had sought, helped reduce the number of individuals in mental hospitals and decrease the overcrowding that had so bedeviled the social observers of the 1950s.[7] Lyndon Johnson's Great Society programs and the passage of Medicare and Medicaid during the mid-1960s, in turn, included psychiatric benefits for the elderly and poor people.[8] Advocates of community psychiatry from within the psychiatric profession continued to urge fellow psychiatrists throughout the 1960s and 1970s to explore the relationship between psychiatry and the vulnerable, among them the poor and "minority" groups.[9] Still, the ethos of community care offered more of a focus on general mental health and the prevention of illness rather than caring for, let alone curing, people with more severe mental illnesses.

To the libertarian way of thinking, the mental hospital could only ever be a punitive institution, and the only social bonds it could offer were ones of power rather than citizenship. The central reflection about the individual and the community that was so prevalent at midcentury was changing, in the late twentieth century, to a reflection about the often fraught relationship between the individual and society's structures, and with a deepening pessimism about those structures, often loosely defined as "the system" and perceived as dissolving the individual. Countercultural observers of the 1960s and 1970s in particular, steeped in an array of social, political, and cultural oppositional stances, highly politicized these structures and, as an earlier generation had done, tended to interpret them in totalitarian terms.

But the tenor of these critiques and metaphors was changing in that patient writings and their advocates displayed and embraced a more atomistic individualism than the communal selfhood of the hospital. In turn, critical patients and their onlookers also harbored deepening doubts about scientific language, medicalization, and the culture of medical experts, particularly as threats to the sanctity of individual emotional expression. In fact, the fear of tampering with the uniqueness and authenticity of the self reveals a wider anxiety about the perceived coercive and hubristic qualities of medicalization and science more broadly as the ultimate source of knowledge. Patients were more likely to embrace the individual's uniqueness, irreducible to categorization, and were less likely to engage with and play with scientific modernity in the way that their interwar forebears had done. In turn, doubts about the "militant ideology of the cure" multiplied even in a moment when curing ideology animated the broader late twentieth-century medical establishment, such as the "war on cancer" and cryonics, as though aging and death were things to be conquered.[10] Instead of these cures, a generation of countercultural thinkers were more invested in the sanctity of emotional expression itself and emotional extravagance rather than parsimony. Social movements of the 1960s and 1970s promised dramatic shifts in intimate mores, among them the gay liberation movement, the second wave feminist movement, and the patients' rights movement more broadly conceived, which all provided new and more collective repositories of emotional expression.[11]

An intensified fear of scientific modernity did not translate into a reembrace of the extreme realism of resignation or a demeanor of inevitability. Instead, patients developed a heightened interest in the individual as an active agent, living beyond society's structures, and the mental hospital loomed large here. While on the surface a rejection of medical authority can be seen as a kind of anti-modernism, or simply anti-scientism, what is unique about the renouncement of medical authority and the culture of experts in this era is that patients also still sought great things of therapeutic cultures broadly conceived, in the form of empathy and emotional witnessing.

An idealization of a full range of emotional expression symbolized yet another, distinctive, repudiation of the figure of the automaton of the hospital and passivity within the medical sphere and in broader social and political realms. During the late twentieth century, the dread of the automaton was not always directly politicized as it was at midcentury when this figure was so politically dubious as to be a potential fascist—it did not have to be. Instead, the fear of the automaton could be just as much about the inability to feel in itself, and to be emotionally fulfilled, as though emotionlessness in itself was a tragic violation of personhood. A countercultural ideal was an individual who was engaged, active, and productive rather than indifferently staring into space or even seeking the bearable over the unbearable, respites in an otherwise dreary hospital routine. Writings of patient and countercultural observers alike placed a heightened value on the expression of an array of emotions—anything but being inactive, passive, and oblivious in a place of suspended time.

A disquiet about the automaton as a way of being, as well as a reimagining of the concept of the "insane" and medical unreachability, informed the ways that patients and broader cultural observers affirmed the value of the mysterious, at times exoticized, inner life of the "mad" and their insights during the later 1960s and the 1970s. The celebration of the uniquely sensitive, nonconformist individual in the mental hospital deepened in this period, not unlike Albert Deutsch's characterization, only by the late twentieth century this figure did not need more money from state authorities to survive but needed to be set free from the hospital to lead a more natural existence in a society that did not have carceral institutions. This iconic wise, interesting, authentic madwoman/madman directly animated American countercultural sources during this period, given their emphasis on self-expression rather than self-control and the tendency to see all institutions as instruments of social control. Countercultural critiques of medical logics, systems, and institutions were animated not just by liberal, possessive individualism but by a shift toward expressive individualism in writings about psychiatry and perceptions of care in the late twentieth century. As American political philosopher Marshall Berman wrote in 1970, the "politics of authenticity" is a "dream of an ideal community in which individuality will not be subsumed and sacrificed, but fully developed and expressed."[12] And this shift is on display in patient and observer writings that became much more focused on the emotive self rather than the institutional or physical and natural world.

In the 1960s and 1970s, sentient, activist Americans suggested that they were emerging from a time of a tyranny of reason in the earlier postwar period to explore pure, unfiltered emotional expression, and it is no wonder that the "mad" were prestigious here, especially from the standpoint of aesthetic expression.[13] There were glimmers of this idea earlier, a sense that the "queer fish" of the mental hospital were more authentic and original than those superficial and boring patients outside of it. But these ideas lacked a larger cultural and intellectual apparatus, in the form of psychiatric survivors'

movements and the counterculture, to bolster them as they would come to
have in the late 1960s.

A veneration of personal authenticity also entailed a humanist respect for
emotions in all of their incarnations, from withering lows to maniacal highs.
Countercultural writers valorized deep feelings, spontaneity, and intuitive
realms and were suspicious of Western rationalism, prescribed social roles,
and institutions.[14] In *Views of a Nearsighted Cannoneer*, a collection of essays
published in 1968, countercultural writer and literary critic Seymour Krim
suggested that "much that used to be called 'insanity' is almost an emotional
necessity for every true feeling, reacting, totally human person in America
at this time."[15] Even the expansive and common reference book *The Comprehensive Textbook of Psychiatry*, the world's leading textbook on psychiatry,
first published in 1967, showed an understanding of mysticism in relation
to science, as well as how the two could be combined from the standpoint
of official medical culture. Psychiatrist Norman A. Cameron here admitted,
when discussing mental illness, that "there is in everyone always an under-
current of magical and superstitious thinking that is not released except in
dreams ... we all live deeply irrational lives; but we have all been schooled
in childhood to develop an overlay of realistic, logical thinking and a relatively impersonal attitude even about deeply personal matters."[16] Perhaps it
was not a coincidence that Hans Prinzhorn's quirky 1922 book, *Artistry of the
Mentally Ill*, was reprinted in 1972 for American audiences; it validated the
intensity and authenticity of asylum inmates' feelings, as well as the aesthetic
value of their drawings.[17] Author David Maraniss, whose uncle lived in his
family's basement after a series of unsuccessful treatments for his mental illness, instantiated these ideas when he said of his uncle Phil that "during the
60s I even began to romanticize him, putting him in my pantheon of rebels.
If insanity was the only honest response to an insane world, then Phil was the
most honest person I knew."[18] As literary critic Lionel Trilling said in his 1971
work *Sincerity and Authenticity*, the romantic view that "madness is liberation and authenticity" was not just the province of radicals but widespread
among educated people.[19]

This romanticization of the "mad" could verge into exoticization. In her
feminist critique of the psychiatric system, *Women and Madness* (1972), psychologist Phyllis Chesler recalled being in a bookstore in Greenwich Village
beside a "frizzy-haired woman" who was "talking to herself out loud." She
notes that her professors would have labeled this talk the "word salad" characteristic of schizophrenics. And yet to Chesler it was "wonderful to listen to:

deep and golden and endless. At some point, I said something like 'Amen' or 'Right on.'" The woman "stared at me suspiciously," but Chesler believed that this was owing to the woman's implicit sense that "where the hell did I get off taking her seriously when the world had already made it plain to her that her safety lay in being misunderstood and not noticed."[20] Chesler projects a certain pride in nonconformity onto a woman with schizophrenia—which this woman may or may not have felt—and presumes a superficial wider society.

The perceived authenticity of madness also entailed a deepening rejection of the automaton within the hospital and beyond. American medical textbooks and cultural representations were so thickly populated with images of the automaton that by now it had become something of a cliché of the mental hospital. And yet the fear of the automaton was even more deeply entrenched by the late twentieth century than it had been at midcentury, even if the figure was not as explicitly politicized as it had been in earlier postwar incarnations. In 1968, psychologist Erich Fromm claimed that a "new specter" of contemporary society was in fact not politics or the "old ghost of communism or fascism" but instead the "completely mechanized society" wherein the human was simply a part of a total machine, "passive, unalive, and with little feeling."[21] In 1967, psychiatrist Simon H. Nagler wrote that an automaton was created when an "entire personality is dependent on the cultural pattern, and the individual becomes what others are and expect him to be. His fear of aloneness is overcome by thinking, feeling, and acting exactly like everyone else in his culture or group. A pseudo self is created."[22] In this depiction, the automaton was not necessarily vulnerable to fascism or other dubious politics; it was merely a pseudo-self, and a tragedy in that sense.

The automaton was also not "natural" in the way that embodied, emotive beings are, and this was bound up with a countercultural renunciation of a style of rationalizing and objectifying and depersonalizing science, emblematized in the hospital and institutional environments. In psychologist Buryl Payne's popular 1973 book, *Getting There Without Drugs*, he indicts a worldview of "nineteenth century science" for leading "us astray" since it advocated "treating people like things and manipulating them as though they were objects—so many tin soldiers and mechanical clerks—and this subtle and pervasive philosophy of squeezing everything into rational schemes has actually made people more thinglike, more robotized and dehumanized."[23] Mental health patient advocate Anthony Brandt took up this same language of objectification in his 1975 work, *Reality Police: The Experience of Insanity in America*. In the book he tells the story of a young adult at the

Menninger Foundation in Topeka, Kansas, who was openly rebellious against
the routine there and subsequently confined to her room for long periods of
time. She then became the "nonperson the hospital assumed her to be" and,
"accorded the status of a thing, she became one."[24] Though these observations
are drawn from a personal account he received from this woman, Brandt also
makes many general observations about mental hospitals. He even expresses
sympathy toward the nurses and aides within these institutions, seeing them
as fellow victims of the system: "Functionaries in an enormous bureaucratic
organization, they were half robots themselves."[25]

The automaton was also an aesthetic problem of the hospital within patient
portraits and remembrances, and this aesthetic disgust could have been a factor
in the sensibility shift toward deinstitutionalization. Actress Frances Farmer
published her now famous account of her mental illness in 1972, a retrospective look at the 1940s and early 1950s. She spent eight years as an "inmate" in
Western Washington State Hospital for the Insane, an asylum south of Seattle,
starting in 1945, diagnosed as paranoid schizophrenic.[26] What she describes
about her fellow women in the state hospital is so steeped in the language of
the automaton that one wonders how conscious her use of it was or if it was
simply implicit, given the more widespread disquiet that observers felt upon
beholding this now chilling figure in the 1960s and 1970s. In the showers she
remembered that "some of the women stood blank and motionless even when
the lather from their hair poured white stinging foam into their eyes. They
were beyond feeling." She also refers to her fellow inmates as "mechanical
toys ... shuffled through long and unfamiliar corridors,"[27] conveying something eerily robotic or doll-like. In Susanna Kaysen's memoir of her time as a
young woman at McLean Hospital, a private psychiatric facility, from 1967 to
1969, she, too, describes the expressionlessness of some of the women around
her. She remembers that many women congregated around the television set,
which was often perceived as an instrument of American inertia since cultural
critics began to comment upon it in the 1950s.[28] She noted that at McLean
watching TV was mostly for the "catatonics and depressives."[29] After her friend
Lisa came out of seclusion, all she could muster the energy to do was watch
TV, and before that she had scorned this medium.

Critics of institutionalization in the vein of Anthony Brandt invited
readers to ponder the nature of intense emotionality, as if anguish and tor-
ment outside of the mental hospital would be better than oblivion, the very
opposite of the argument posited by psychosurgeons at midcentury. To
observe hospitals from the inside, he simulated his own mental breakdown

and committed himself to Hudson Valley State Hospital in Poughkeepsie, New York, for eleven days. He said that the patients on his ward had nothing: "no hope, only the dulling of consciousness that comes with months and years of tranquilizing drugs and an endless dehumanizing routine." He learned that despair is "voiceless. It quietly watches the television all day long. It reads a real estate handbook over and over again. It sleeps a great deal. All its days are the same."[30] The patients became "impenetrable, emotionless shells" and as such "lose interest in leaving the hospital."[31]

Hospital time, in turn, was now not perceived as a peaceful interlude but instead as more plainly depressing. According to Brandt, "The day wears away. The day is rock eroding. Time becomes geologic in scope. . . . The day accumulates, ice building up on the surface of a lake. There is nothing to do."[32] While interwar era patients and observers also described the physical environment, they did so with a sense of inevitability about it and sometimes an interest in it, rather than a sense of protest, and this underscores a late twentieth-century ethos of dissent where even the "given" can be questioned. Such a depiction is yet another degree removed from the early twentieth-century appreciation of zones of suspended time and observation. By the late twentieth century there was a reimagination of dailiness in the hospital, and the passage of time therein could just be tortuous. As Kenneth Donaldson wrote retrospectively in his 1976 memoir of his fifteen-year hospitalization at Florida State Hospital in Chattahoochee between 1957 and 1971, which perhaps again reveals just as much about his 1970s self as it does his 1950s self, "Day followed monotonous day. From seven to five I sat in the dust of the yard or in a back window or on the porch."[33]

In confessional and retrospective accounts, some former patients spoke of an enduring distress just at the thought of their past institutionalized selves, and this too was bound up with the specter of the automaton. Another memoirist, Barbara Field Benziger, wrote in 1969 of her stays in two unnamed urban hospitals, one of which she called the "bad hospital" and the other the "better hospital." She had been hospitalized for depression and suicidal tendencies. At the "bad hospital," the "other patients were really very sick there, sicker than I. They had vacant and unseeing eyes, and I felt they had been put away for keeps. They were silent and perpetually withdrawn."[34] After being released from the hospital, she was burdened with the fear of "going back."[35] After the publication of *Women and Madness* in 1972, which among other themes discussed dubious psychiatric diagnoses of women and their experiences in mental hospitals, Phyllis Chesler received an array of letters from women who often relayed their own experiences of therapy and the hospital. One woman told Chesler that the "humiliation, trauma, horror, degradation, and suffering" she experienced at mental institutions had left her finding it "hard to laugh" or to "take delight in living." She had "tried to hide my past as well as I can, but it must be obvious that something has happened to me."[36] Her experiences had caused her to question the very existence of institutional psychiatry: "Was being strapped down on a pillow for over ten hours in a maximum security ward [worth] it? Was being confined in a ward next to screaming, singing old women [worth] it?" She asked Chesler: "How does one purge these memories in order to get on with life?" What she faced in the hospital was "months of unproductivity, sitting and doing nothing, knowing that your dreams have died."[37] Perhaps this interpretation was still inflected by the complicated legacy of a surfeit of time for women, whether the stifled women artists of the modern period or the white, middle-class housewives that animated second wave feminism. But it was more than just a historically freighted experience: here the boundary between enforced suspended time and violence was thin or barely existed.

Yet these critiques were not limited to women, even if they held an extra urgency for them. Russell K. Hampton, the psychologist mentioned earlier who suffered from a debilitating depression and was hospitalized in 1961 as a twenty-nine-year-old graduate student, wrote his retrospective account of hospitalization in his university hospital's psychiatric ward in 1975. From his vantage point in the late twentieth century, he noted feeling a "hospitalization syndrome" wherein his "initiative" and "drive" had been "consumed" in the "ward routine" as the "mechanics of bathing, dressing, eating, reporting to the various activities, and ostensibly participating in the group and individual therapy sessions became ends in themselves."[38] His use of "ostensible" is striking, suggesting an increasing doubt about the good of institutional participation. It is also harder to imagine an interwar era patient referring to "hospitalization syndrome"[39] in a way that disparages a lost capacity to be productive when business depressions and productivity were more commonly then considered causes of emotional distress.

Critics in this vein saw it as unfortunate and tragic if institutionalized individuals, reduced to puppets, did not experience the gamut of emotions, even negative or destructive ones. The automaton was the ultimate passive spectator of society during a moment when political action and the agency that accompanied this were revered, especially in communitarian and New Left circles of the late 1960s and the 1970s.[40] In 1970, an associate of Kenneth

Donaldson, who was at this time in the last part of his hospitalization at Florida State Hospital in Chattahoochee, wrote in an essay condemning involuntary confinements that the "main rationale" for having enforced hospitalization or the existence of a carceral state was to "rid society of its strange acting members, its burdensome nuisance and its purported dangerous characters. It is to rid the streets of the violent." However, "it is the joke of our times to equate our mentally ill people with violence. They are the opposite: passive, bereft of spirit." She then juxtaposed the mentally ill with the social tumults of the 1960s: "Have we witnessed any riots or burnings in mental institutions? Of course not. They are the safest places in America today." She admitted that while "we don't know what causes mental illness, we suspect that undue repression of the human spirit is somewhere involved in its genesis. It is the ironic tragedy of our world, then, that 'therapy' is further repression."[41] On the one hand, this characterization reaffirms Deutsch's portrait of gentle souls of the early postwar period. But this letter also equates mental illness with an authenticity of spirit and hospitalization with the crushing of said spirits. Though early postwar era social critics repudiated the automaton as well, they did not do so by claiming that automatic behavior stifled anger and potential criminal elements that perhaps should not be stifled.

But by this period patient advocates considered even those kinds of repressions potentially harmful. Other ambient alternative therapeutic practices of the 1960s and 1970s, such as consciousness raising, leftist radical therapy, therapeutic communities, experimental wards, feminist clinical practices and therapy, and self-help and first-person testimonials echoed this sentiment and dovetailed nicely with philosophies of artistic and personal liberation of the late 1960s and early 1970s.[42] One source in this vein was Arthur Janov's *The Primal Scream*, first published in 1970. Janov was a psychologist and inventor of primal therapy, a technique that involved reclaiming and reexperiencing childhood anguish and repressed feelings, often socially unacceptable ones—primal screams. After primal therapy, one was supposed to experience life in a new way, full of richness and depth. One patient he writes about, Elizabeth, was a speed-addicted lesbian who "looked, even walked, like a man."[43] During the day she dressed conservatively and worked in a bank but at night she would "let [her] hair down and join the gay crowd at the local gay bar."[44] She defended her speed usage by saying, "I take pills to keep from feeling life . . . I feel less with pills . . . I'm so sensitive to life I can't stand it. I need pills to dull life. The pill makes me feel dead." However, she went to primal therapy to reclaim this lost sensitivity. She had become "so

sick of not feeling at all . . . I'm sure that at least the pain will let me know that
I am alive . . . 'cause I really feel dead."[45] After primal therapy, though, "everything was becoming real to me. Colours were vivid. Landscapes looked like
paintings. I no longer saw the world through a telescope."[46] Renewed intensity
and vividness were here therapeutic goals in themselves, and these ideas resonated with the emotional tenor and intensity of gay liberation movements
that emphasized authentic feeling rather than repression.

Gone, then, was the mental health ideal that the early postwar period
had offered of the individual who was well-adjusted and rejected emotional
extremes, the perfect citizen for early postwar American liberalism and consensus culture and for the hospital striving to embody these ideals. Activists
increasingly called this emotional citizenship into question, seeing it as bound
up with the hypocrisies of Cold War American liberalism, perhaps most centrally in Vietnam War. By the late twentieth century, authenticity required
perhaps some extremes of behavior, and emotional extravagance was not the
self-absorption or self-indulgence that Karen Horney believed Americans
were uneasy about from her vantage point in 1942. The vicissitudes of emotional experience rendered one fully human, artistically engaged, and authentic. Where in the early postwar period mental health pamphlets emphasized
good citizenship and being a member of a group, now emotions in all their
guises were seen as indispensable to human fulfillment, perhaps especially
anger, and particularly in the context of the sociopolitical movements of the
1960s and 1970s. Second wave feminists, for example, encouraged the open
expression of anger because its suppression had contributed to oppression
and compromised authenticity.[47] Works by such Black psychiatrists as William Grier and Price Cobbs, including *Black Rage*, a best seller in 1968, asked
white Americans to appreciate that African American cultural demeanors,
especially the "playing-it-cool style," which white people were so fond of emu-
lating, were inauthentic in the sense that "a man may be overwhelmed with
conflict, threatened with an eruption of feelings, and barely maintaining his
composure, but he will present a serene exterior . . . an important aspect of his
containment is the fear that his aggression will be directed against the white
world and will bring swift punishment." Maintaining this front came at a high
"cost and suffering."[48] This book's subject is the tension between passivity and
aggression, with rage emerging as an understandable and honest response.

In fact, American social critics of the late 1960s and 1970s were quite preoccupied with the idea of "rage" and how this manifested itself socially, and
psychiatry was no stranger to this broader discussion. In the summer of 1967,

for example, when African American psychiatrist Alvin Poussaint offered commentary on the motivations behind urban riots, he claimed that what united the rioters was "rage,"[49] suggesting that politics could be understood as reenactments of psychic conflicts. However, the medical implications of these ideas could be quite troubling for African American men. Historian Jonathan Metzl notes that by the 1960s schizophrenia was becoming a disease characterized by rage rather than docility. He notes that psychiatric journals of the 1960s increasingly argued that schizophrenia was a condition most likely to afflict Black men who were involved in Black activist groups such as Black Power in all its incarnations rather than upper-class white women, as was more commonly thought in the interwar era. This viewpoint pathologized activism as "protest psychosis," even when the men in question had no involvement in the civil rights movement.[50] Was unfettered emotional expression a luxury that not all could afford?

The American anti-psychiatry movement ran alongside the broader counterculture; it too advocated not just unfettered emotional expression but the need for patient withdrawal from mainstream society and medical systems, turning away from a midcentury ideal of integration. It was also a movement that framed the more politically sentient patient conversations and imaginative works produced during this period, serving as a radical iteration of individual rights. The basic critique of radical psychiatry or anti-psychiatry was that society needed change—in economic, political, and social systems rather than in the individual.[51] The movement embodied a broader intellectual posture of the 1960s and 1970s that suggested that meanings of phenomena such as mental illness were socially created and constructed rather than "real" or "given," which is itself a rejection of a sensibility of resignation that is more likely to be accepting of actualities. This intellectual demeanor is exemplified by Michel Foucault's *Madness and Civilization* (1964). Foucault problematizes not only the reification of madness but paternalism, domination, and power, as embedded in the figure of the psychiatrist and in institutions such as asylums. He advanced a structuralist point of view that asylums did not represent progress but were emblematic of modern, industrial states.[52]

In the United States, the anti-psychiatry movement comprised a group of former psychiatric patients, intellectuals, and writers who adapted these structuralist ideas. They advocated for more humane treatment of the mentally ill and questioned the social control inherent in the psychiatric system, as well as the very idea of madness. As their ideas gained momentum during the late 1960s and throughout the late twentieth century, these thinkers and writers suggested that psychiatrists had been too keen to medicalize eccentric behavior, inhibiting both individuality and unconventional thinking. As such, the anti-psychiatry movement was quite critical of biological psychiatry, especially psychosurgeries, shock treatments, and psychotropic drugs, as well as Freudian psychoanalysis, even though psychoanalysis was starting to have less institutional power by the mid-1970s.[53]

Anti-psychiatry repudiated objectification and human experimentation while embracing feeling for the sake of feeling, yet another disavowal of the automaton. Moreover, anti-psychiatry dovetailed well with deinstitutionalization and its blurred boundary with anti-institutionalization of the late twentieth century. The anti-psychiatry movement also resonated with a medical public perhaps more amenable to their ideas in the wake of more widespread knowledge about the history of American medical experimentation. Most famously the revelations in 1972 about the Tuskegee syphilis experiments offered a powerful indictment of the "medical-industrial complex," illuminating anew medical experiments performed on African Americans that were long embedded in the history of the American medical establishment.[54] This came on the heels of something even more relevant to psychiatric patient populations: a 1966 article by physician Henry K. Beecher detailing the extent of medical experimentation in American institutions: in prisons, orphanages, and homes for people with cognitive disabilities, as well as mental hospitals.[55] And by 1977, a former state department intelligence officer, John Marks, made public CIA documents that offered evidence about how Americans had been exposed to behavioral modification techniques in the MKUltra program. This involved administering LSD to one thousand American soldiers in Edgewood, Maryland, to see how the drug influenced them, something envisaged as a diplomatic weapon for the American government, or at least to keep pace with Soviet brainwashing techniques. He also exposed Dr. Ewen Cameron's "psychic-driving" experiments: putting patients in electroshock- and insulin-induced comas to erase their negative memories and previous psychological patterns and create new ones through the use of suggestion.[56] Literary critic Michael Staub has shown that this fear of the fragility of the self in the face of totalitarian governments was a concern most associated with the American right during the 1950s, one that would be reimagined by American radical social movements of the 1960s and 1970s, in this case anti-psychiatry.[57]

The revelations of these experiments diminished the trust that socially conscious patients and prospective ones had in psychiatry, who were, after all, members of an increasingly cynical American public. Why should there not be crime at the heart of psychiatry when broader reckonings with the Watergate scandal during the 1970s revealed that crimes were being committed at the heart of government, a government that had lied about the Vietnam War and demonstrated that deceitfulness existed at a wider and deeper level than previously imagined?[58]

While anti-psychiatry critiques could be raw and blunt and can seem conspiratorial, these activists nonetheless had genuine concerns about the real and systematic past abuses of mental health patients. The movement was in keeping with a larger trend toward medical rehumanization, humanist "positive" psychology, and patient-centered therapy.[59] These ideas resonated with both alternative health movements and feminism, especially by the 1970s, when these, in combination with homeopathy movements and back-to-nature movements, gave deeper consideration to the "whole patient" in illness as well as experiential knowledge.[60] An anti-psychiatry vision suggested a fundamental incompatibility between science and empathy, perhaps again reflecting a broader American questioning of scientism and science's perceived allegiance with the military in the late twentieth century, as well as a deepening recognition of the integrity of emotions in and of themselves in the face of science. This is not to reinforce a rigid dichotomy between science and countercultural movements but to suggest that anti-psychiatrists were trading in something of a monolithic view of science themselves and placed the realms of intuition and romanticism above rationalistic, scientific, technocratic, and bureaucratic values.[61]

Feminist anti-psychiatry probed more specifically the gendered dimensions of medicalization and hospitalization. The letters that Phyllis Chesler received in the 1970s have synergies with this tradition, as they illuminate the feminist dimensions of deinstitutionalization. These testimonials evoked a bureaucratic nightmare worthy of Deutsch, or even nineteenth-century captivity narratives, only here with a late twentieth-century feminist twist in the midst of a movement gaining momentum toward voluntary institutionalization. Chesler argued that nonconformist women, particularly women of color, often were misdiagnosed or exploited by male therapists, often sexually, a portrait common within second wave feminist critiques of psychiatry.[62] She asked: "How did American women get into asylums in the past?" In her portrait, it was: "Suddenly, unexpectedly, a perfectly sane woman might find herself being arrested by a sheriff; removed from her bed at dawn, or 'legally kidnapped' on the streets, in broad daylight." Either that or "her father or

husband might ask her to accompany him to see a friend to help him with a
legal matter. Unsuspecting, the woman might find herself before a judge or a
physician, who certified her 'insane' on her husband's say-so."[63]

Some of Chesler's female correspondents felt that they had been pathologized and hospitalized for unorthodoxy or for artistic temperaments that were
more readily tolerated or perhaps even revered in men, though this thinking
was not necessarily or solely feminist and was analogous with the ideas of
libertarian writers, too, who characterized schizophrenia as potentially a form
of "super sanity" in the context of a deranged world.[64] A reclamation of the
affects of rebellion and nonconformity was urgent here, rather than the apparent passivity of submitting to the medical establishment. One woman who
wrote to Chesler was a member of the American Association for the Abolition
of Involuntary Mental Hospitalization. She said that she felt she could talk to
Chesler, now that her previous experience of institutionalization was receding
into the past. "I can speak, come out of the closet, to use the popular phrase,"
she said, a phrase that indeed was increasingly taken up not just in relation to
sexuality but to mental illness.[65] She directly implicated her family in her captivity: her "misguided and not well-off parents" had incarcerated her involuntarily from 1965 to 1968 at Dayton State Hospital and Longview State Hospital
in Cincinnati.[66] She avowed that "I am high-strung, nervous, a low achiever,
but the experiences and memories I carry from some of the horrible places I
was in will, I'm afraid, stay with me all my life."[67] She called herself a "nervous
Nellie,"[68] as if to soften the medical diagnostic terms by using plain language,
an implicit critique that was becoming especially trenchant as the numbers of
possible psychiatric diagnoses expanded within the DSM-II in 1968.[69]

This intuitive language and rejection of diagnostic categorization and the
institutionalization that often accompanied it in these accounts suggest that
attitudes against psychiatry in this period were perhaps part of a larger "culture war," one that pitted masses versus elites, populism versus education,
or perhaps simply common sense, folk wisdom, and intuition against formal education, a reprisal of some of the sentiments expressed in the interwar
era, only without the interest in scientific psychiatry that some interwar era
patients harbored, if only for its newness. This populist flavor was not just
part of a broader intellectual critique of scientism but befitted a more general
populism in American politics in this period and an active renunciation of
the culture of experts, something that animated not just political radicals but
also the New Right's creation of the "silent majority" as a category of hard-
working, law-abiding, commonsensical, underappreciated Americans.[70] The

woman who wrote to Chesler mentioned just above was not alone in making self-characterizations in everyday language. Another woman who wrote
to Chesler in 1973 said that "I'm one of the local crazy ladies and the local
shrinks would love to get me in their clutches, but I'm determined not to
submit."[71] "Local crazy lady" makes her sound like a harmless eccentric, a
weird but lovable and potentially wise feature of a small town's landscape. She
also noted that she was "continually amazed at the childish attitudes of the
so-called 'educated' people."[72]

Perhaps this discussion reflects a larger democratization of the professions
in this era, or even a withering distinction between psychiatrist and patient.[73]
The woman who called herself the "nervous Nellie" admitted that she was
not doing all that well emotionally: "inwardly, I am a million pieces of jagged
glass."[74] While she embraced non-medical or at least non-technical names for
her feelings, she was also, somewhat paradoxically, disappointed by the lack
of medical attention she had received in the mental hospital. She said that
"trying to pry from a doctor in a state hospital your diagnosis (or prognosis)
is an exercise in futility. I was never told either."[75] It could be that not receiving a diagnosis was just as troubling as receiving one, perhaps a microcosmic
reflection about why psychiatry as a system of ideas was an unsettling prospect. Patients could spurn psychiatry, especially its more patriarchal incarnations, and yet still crave some more empathetic version of it.

Still, the women who wrote to Chesler knew that they would find a ready
audience for their doubts about institutionalization and psychiatric diagnosis, bolstered by a broader intellectual atmosphere of the 1970s that tended to
view categorization as an instrument of political oppression and a crass, reductive, dehumanizing quantification. This disquiet became a pressing question
among sociologists in the 1960s who argued that labeling was a reductive
epistemology, wielded against those who were unconventional, potentially
incarcerating them for it.[76] This critique was highly individualistic and traded
in an affect of activity over passivity. In 1972, Chesler received a letter from
a woman who said that "I have been diagnosed as schizophrenic but have
always been suspicious of this diagnosis. I have always been rebellious."[77] Her
sense that diagnosis was a kind of social control to police nonconformists was
not unique to her. Libertarian psychiatrist Thomas Szasz wrote in *Ideology
and Insanity* (1973) that "to classify another person's behavior is usually a
means of constraining him. This is particularly true of psychiatric classification, whose traditional aim has been to legitimize the social controls placed
on so-called mental patients."[78] The woman who wrote to Chesler hoped

that she would be "responsible for the liberation of hundreds of thousands of women from the wrong diagnosis. Disobedient women were once burned at the stake. Now they are made prisoners in mental hospitals. I want to see a bloody revolution."[79] The outrage over misdiagnoses and wrongful hospitalizations resonated with broader intellectual reassessments and the problematization of biological psychiatry and hospitalization on display in the 1972 Rosenhan experiments, wherein eight healthy actors, claiming to hear voices, received diagnoses, mostly for schizophrenia, and were hospitalized, an experiment that was supposed to expose the dubiousness of psychiatric medical diagnosis.[80] But perhaps it simply underscored the uneasy boundary between being mentally ill and mentally "well." The premise of the Rosenhan experiments is quite positivist in its apparent craving for scientific precision: Would these critics have preferred something like a blood test that indicated schizophrenia?

Diagnoses now appeared more blatant infringements upon feeling for the sake of feeling as well as agents of estrangement, perhaps the precursors to the ultimate estrangement of institutionalized life. The willingness to question and reevaluate diagnosis entailed not only a more definitive claim to individual emotional integrity and uniqueness but also a reimagining of biological psychiatry in this period, here thought to instill simply emotionlessness and inertia. In an interview in 1988, neurosurgeon James Watts reflected that during the 1960s, given the social tumult and violence in many American cities, fears had emerged that lobotomies would be used for political purposes to quell "violence in the streets."[81] The New Left student activist organization Students for a Democratic Society (SDS) expressed their disquiet over this very idea in a 1973 protest pamphlet about the establishment of a UCLA Center for Psychosurgery whose aim was the reduction of social violence. The organization feared that this center would "study the causes of unrest among the poor and try to develop techniques to stop the mass expression of that unrest." The authors of the pamphlet pronounced that "docility [is] defined as health, and protest as sickness."[82] They likened lobotomies to harsh punishments in the same vein as the medical discipline of slaves in antebellum America: "cutting off the toes of a runaway slave and cutting out part of the brain tissue of a militant rebel are both clear attempts at suppression rather than treatment."[83] The reference to race is striking here since, as Martin Summers points out, the medical profession tended to think of Black "madness" as uniquely violent, particularly early in the twentieth century.[84] It is no coincidence that an organization that demanded direct, participatory democracy would be appalled by medically instilled peacefulness, read here as inactivity and acquiescence.

Cultural sources offered a reading of biological psychiatry as it was practiced in the hospital as a force that quells individual uniqueness as well, and this included ever more vivid and chilling depictions of electroshock treatments in particular. The most terrifying and iconic scene of electric shock treatment in the late twentieth century is in the film version of *One Flew over the Cuckoo's Nest* (1975), which advances the novel's central themes. Here the central, rebellious character in a mental hospital in Oregon, Randle McMurphy, faces a particularly brutal, unanesthetized electroshock treatment.[85] In surveys of audience members post-screening, viewers attested to how barbaric they found the practice of electric shock and insisted that they would not let a family member undergo the treatment.[86] It is a frightening scene in the novel, as well, though there perhaps is some respite in the written description of the treatment as it is interspersed with McMurphy's attempts at resistance and his singing, which the doctors "try to hush."[87]

When not depicted as sheer torture, electroshock treatments were portrayed simply as nullifiers of emotions and disturbing on this account alone. In the 1964 film *Shock Treatment*, in which the protagonist, an interloper in the world of the mental hospital, receives a punitive treatment from a sadistic psychiatrist as a form of torture, his flailing body is filmed from above, while the camera focuses on his blank, vacuous expression afterward.[88] That electroshock was a barbarous treatment that churned out zombies was an idea gaining currency in the wake of the Tom Eagleton scandal of the presidential race of 1972, which made both depression and ECT a part of a broader social conversation. Eagleton was a senator from Missouri who withdrew from the vice presidential nomination with Democratic candidate Senator George McGovern when the public became aware that he had been voluntarily hospitalized for "nervous exhaustion" and had undergone two courses of electric shock treatments during the 1960s. To many, this made Eagleton unfit to hold national political office.[89]

In Ellen Wolfe's memoir, *Aftershock* (1969), electroshock treatments did not make her politically suspect or dubious, or more prone to totalitarianism, but simply apathetic, deindividuated, and not quite human. Wolfe was a white woman who was hospitalized after a nervous breakdown in 1964, when she was in her early thirties and the mother of two young children. The memory loss was particularly striking for her after electroshock: she could not remember the existence of one of her children, nor could she remember the Kennedy assassination.[90] She perseveres with daily life after she is released from the hospital, but she is unable to feel joy even when she and her husband purchase a first house in the country. While her husband was enchanted by the new place and wanted her to "share his feelings," he had an "automaton for a wife, who had dressed herself attractively for the event, and who had smiled when smiled at, and who had signed her name in a hand that was almost steady, but who had been empty of any feelings."[91] Chief Bromden, the narrator of *One Flew over the Cuckoo's Nest*, an archetypal, countercultural "wise Indian" character whose mind, in this portrait, it is all the more tragic to tamper with, speaks of a "gray zone" after a shock treatment, of wandering around "in a daze" and "living in that foggy, jumbled blur, which is a whole lot like the ragged edge of sleep, that gray zone between light and dark, or between sleeping and waking or living and dying."[92] This image is drained of any of the peacefulness that such zones of indeterminacy, when willingly submitted to, were felt to have by patient narrators during the interwar era. Instead the gray zone here was simply a tragedy, one step away from the "vegetable"[93] McMurphy becomes at the end of the novel after his lobotomy.

Patient advocates and anti-psychiatry activists, in turn, characterized electroshock in purely punitive, almost conspiratorial terms for the ways in which it nullified emotion and inculcated passivity, a perceived affect of psychiatric incarceration.[94] In the 1960s, when Kenneth Donaldson was still a patient at Florida State Hospital in Chattahoochee and was waging his legal battle against involuntary confinement, Chesterfield H. Smith, who was then a lawyer and president of the Florida Bar Association, started to receive letters from other psychiatric patients who claimed to have been incarcerated falsely. In one such letter, from 1965, a man from Miami wrote that after a stay in the Lantana TB Hospital in 1962, he became impotent, something he blamed on the conditions in the hospital and the fact that he believed the food there "was medicated."[95] It was after he made this accusation that he was moved to a ward with a psychiatrist. He described his ensuing shock treatments, administered without his consent. "The effect of shock treatments is to black out all memory," he said. "Sometimes the memory is never regained and sometimes intellectual function is permanently impaired. With no memory the patient is confused, submissive, tractable, and docile. After the first treatment I was a sitting duck, a demented duck."[96] This patient does not suggest that he had become a politically compliant subject as mid-twentieth-century captivity narratives might have asserted, or that a dubious political force was behind these treatments, but by the mid-1960s, as the impetus for deinstitutionalization was gaining momentum, the very fact of enforced docility within the specific institutional context of the hospital in itself was enough to generate outrage. Given how burdened by dystopian imagery ECT had become, it is not surprising that by 1980 the practice had been discontinued in the majority of American mental hospitals.[97]

If biological psychiatry was to be an acceptable form of care, from the standpoint of late twentieth-century patient advocates, it had to be one that enlivened patients, reviving them and restoring them to a life outside of the hospital. As early as 1963, a woman evoked this idea when she wrote to Winfred Overholser to discuss the medical treatment of her mother.[98] The mother was sixty-one years old and had no "very alarming symptoms," but "for a number of years her life narrowed until she did little besides rest, and think about minor physical ailments." About six months prior to writing the letter, her mother had had "shock treatments" and since then "she has been much more active."[99] This is an intriguing description of electroshock therapy, since patients often described the procedure as something that rendered them sedentary. But here a family member viewed it in a positive light because it reanimated the patient.

These reflections on biological psychiatry included a reimagining of the posture of the cure and the purpose of hospitalization. In 1968, Millen Brand wrote *Savage Sleep*, a novel set in the 1940s that offers a retrospective reading of the era of biological psychiatry: the sensibility of the novel is much more circumspect about scientism, and romantic about human capacities for empathy, than perhaps one would have found in the 1940s. The book is set at New State, a fictional state mental hospital. A colleague of protagonist Dr. Marks, Dr. Wellman, argues that a patient needs to be shocked to bring her back "into contact."[100] Dr. Marks questions the very idea of being "out of contact": "'When we dream at night, what's the part of us that remembers the dream?'"[101] He also rejects mental inactivity, evoking a terror of unconsciousness reminiscent of the first patients to receive general anesthesia in the nineteenth century. Though New State is touted as a hospital in which there is a "great cure for insanity—electricity, Metrazol intravenous, and hypodermics of insulin"—Marks struggles with administering ECT: "giving it violated the deepest feelings he had against making people unconscious, but if they said it cured, he would do it."[102]

But Brand's novel goes even deeper than these critiques to question the emotionless register of science itself, something that seems to reprise nineteenth-century debates about the quantitative perspective as an amoral universe and a nostalgia for a preindustrial world in which qualitative perspectives were more predominant than quantitative ones.[103] Dr. Marks even feels disillusioned with doctors' notes, and he questions the utility of the very genre. He reads the file of his patient, Jimmy, and is taken aback to find comments in the vein of: "'Intravenous amytol given . . . Temperature at 4pm 105.7. . . . Patient talking continuously with confused flight of ideas, hypermanic, and fearful. . . . Sedation shows little effect'. . . . Then, without explanation: 'Temperature normal, marked decrease in excitement. Patient in partial contact.'"[104] Coming into "contact" has been reduced to a purely biological process, and this character cannot abide the fragmentary nature of the doctor's note and its bureaucratic, impersonal tone.

Patients, too, were becoming more circumspect about the "militant ideology of the cure," seeing it as tampering with emotional vibrancy and unique selfhood. This was the case for Jane Fry, a male-identified person who wished to be a woman, who faced psychiatric treatment before being transgender was a commonly recognized identity. She wrote a memoir in 1974 about her time as a patient in a psychiatric ward at a V.A. hospital after experiencing a nervous breakdown in 1968 and being discharged from the Navy. While some of the young doctors she met seemed fairly willing to give her female hormone shots as part of her treatment, the older doctors were more reluctant. Their attitude instead was somewhat glib: "if someone wanted to be an umbrella, would you try to make him an umbrella?"[105] In turn, they portrayed gender reassignment simply as an artificial choice, a self-indulgent affectation, and were given to reductive analogies in this vein. The medical establishment had a limited view, from the standpoint of 1968, of what was considered a "need" versus what was considered a matter of aesthetics, debates that still animate today's discussions of gender reassignment and aesthetic surgeries.[106] She insisted that "no transsexual has ever been 'cured' that I know of,"[107] and nor did she want to be cured. And yet, like the patients and family members who hoped for a clarifying moment of diagnosis, she was nonetheless hoping for a more humane and empathetic version of psychiatry to surface.

Even drug advertisers by the late twentieth century were careful to promote their products as agents of self-expression and emotional vibrancy, not institutional lifelessness. Perhaps a more prominent form of biological psychiatry from the standpoint of the 1960s and 1970s was the use of psychopharmaceuticals, beyond the antipsychotic drugs and the major and minor tranquilizers of the earlier postwar era. The drug landscape now featured an array of new medications for ailments such as chronic fatigue, anxiety, mania, and depression.[108] And advertising campaigns for these drugs, as David Herzberg notes, placed psychological illnesses firmly in the realm of choice, medical consumerism, and consumer culture.[109] During the 1960s and 1970s pharmacological companies that manufactured anti-depressant drugs were quite savvy about distancing themselves from and repudiating the benumbed psychiatric patient that might have characterized the psychotropic drugs of the 1950s or even early twentieth-century sleep-inducing medical compounds like paraldehyde.[110] Instead, anti-depressant drugs were "psychic energizers."[111] During a moment when depression was America's most common emotional illness, rather than the "age of anxiety" as some observers characterized the earlier postwar period, medical observers widely commented upon and dissected this ailment. Nathan Kline, a psychoanalytical psychiatrist as well as an early advocate of the use of anti-depressants, evoked a fear of emotionlessness from his vantage point in 1974, perhaps to make the prospect of taking medication more palatable. While he does not use the word "automaton," his writings define a depressed patient as exactly that: "Some withdraw deeply into themselves, becoming dull and lethargic, hiding the pain behind a mask that seems to exhibit no emotion at all."[112] The fear of emotionlessness was striking in itself, perhaps because it evoked institutional life, even if only obliquely. In advertisements for anti-depressants, women's domestic contexts look abysmal, tainted by the inertia of depression, but the implication of the ads is that worse forms of confinement could be had in the mental hospital. The possibility of institutional life as a worse and more dramatic form of imprisonment than being hermetically sealed inside the house lingered. In a 1977 ad for Tofranil, a tricyclic anti-depressant, a woman stares out a rain-soaked window under the caption "copelessness," but it is unclear if the vantage point is confinement in the home or the mental hospital.[113] An advertisement for Haldol, an anti-psychotic drug, was less subtle, showing a dramatic institutional "general hospital" door hovering in the background over a family with the foreboding caption: "Just three weeks ago Mommy entered the hospital for acute schizophrenia" (see Figure 4).[114]

What could the role be, then, of a psychiatric hospital amid these critiques, the deepening expressive individualism of the counterculture, and even medical consumer culture? Psychiatric institutions of this period did not proclaim their ability to cure, but some were still insistent that they could provide activities that would enliven and refresh their patients. One of the ironies of all of these critics' voices that problematized psychiatry is that they

Figure 4. Adver-
tisement, "Mommy
Entered the Hospital,"
*Archives of General
Psychiatry* 35, no. 10
(October 1978): 1186.

started to have purchase at a moment when more experimental methods in
therapeutic culture were being applied at the mental hospital. Another irony
of the structuralist and anti-psychiatry viewpoints is that they took hold at
the same moment that the therapeutic impulse was becoming more diffuse
in American society. Feminist psychiatrists and psychologists, for example,
had tried to make the experience of therapy more positive for women.[115] And
voluntary organizations also took the mission of humanizing medical realms
quite seriously.

To be sure, these therapeutic activities were sometimes ham-handed and
not always successful. In her memoir, Jane Fry noted that the psychiatric

ward of her hospital offered a rather sorry and infantilizing array of activities: "You could watch soap operas on the TV set in the dayroom, or go to the other day room and watch soap operas there. You could also sleep or play pool."[116] A 1972 federal court order had ruled that patients in mental health facilities could no longer work without compensation, and this meant that hospitals that did not have enough money to pay their patients closed down work programs such as hospital farms and laundries. Though these programs were often vulnerable to exploitation, and historically institutions sometimes simply used patients for free labor,[117] they also could be a way for patients to assert their selfhood in the institution; their loss might have meant that more patients simply ended up sitting in front of the television set. However, Fry would have preferred being left alone to being subjected to a style of condescending leisure that she felt was on offer there. The women's auxiliary of the American Legion came to her psychiatric ward to take the patients out for picnics and parties. But she felt that these women "act like you're 14 years old. Instead of trying to get you into a decent conversation like coming up to you and saying, 'What do you think of Nixon?' they come up to you and say, 'Let's play pin the tail on the donkey,' or 'Do you want to sing some songs?'"[118] She was not the only one to notice a garish quality of leisure and fun in a mental hospital where the overall atmosphere was so depressing. Frederick Wiseman's 1967 documentary *Titicut Follies* opens with mental patients at the Massachusetts Correctional Facility for the Criminally Insane in Bridgewater performing in a variety show musical, and the effect is one of surreal gaudiness.[119] Wiseman is a documentarian of institutions, and as such the institution and the setting are the central—and domineering—characters rather than the patients; or, at least, in keeping with Wiseman's structuralist vision, and focus upon the institution rather than the individual, they are filmed quite consciously this way.

Hospital Audiences Incorporated (HAI), by contrast, was an organization that put on musical performances and plays for audiences in institutional settings, including psychiatric hospitals, but also general hospitals, prisons, nursing homes, addiction centers, and other care units, in the belief that the arts provided "uplift, hope and 'refreshment of spirit.'"[120] The executive director of HAI, Michael Jon Spencer, said that he felt people especially needed aesthetic experiences in times of crisis, noting that a Holocaust survivor had remembered that bread was needed "to an extent" but it was his art lessons that "really helped" them to survive in the concentration camps by salvaging their "souls" and their "dignity as human beings." This comment resonates with a common, postwar slippage between the "concentration camp" and modern institutions. "Hospitals, prisons, nursing homes and other rehabilitative settings are miniature or encapsulated societies in perpetual 'crises,'" he wrote. "They are extreme situations in which individuals are separated from families, removed from homes, limited in freedom in varying degrees, and in an environment of general sensory deprivation."[121] This characterization represents a radical departure from the perceived pause from the intensity of modernity that such a removal suggested earlier in the century. A psychiatric patient at St. Luke's Hospital in New York in 1975 wrote to HAI to say that "even under ordinary conditions, it's not often that one gets to see first rate experimental theater; that it was made possible by Hospital Audiences Inc. in an institutional setting was I hope as rewarding to the players as it was to at least this member of their audience." He went on to say that "unfortunately, too often what is [deemed] 'appropriate' [for psychiatric patients] is equated with what is safe ... lifelessly conventional, insipid, and downright dull; in short, what won't get the audience to think terribly much, but rather will leave everyone in a state of narcotized euphoria."[122] What is striking in this patient's letter is a rejection of "narcotized euphoria" in favor of experiencing an array of emotions, from the extreme to the more mundane, and not having life cleansed of its unpleasant aspects, or a more authentic emotional experience, even within the walls of a hospital.

Medical textbooks also suggest that letting a hospitalized patient lie idle was not an acceptable therapeutic practice in this period. In *The Comprehensive Textbook of Psychiatry*, psychiatrist Heinz E. Lehmann discussed a schizophrenic patient, a twenty-year-old woman who had been hospitalized after expressing violence toward her parents. In the hospital, she "had been observed gazing into space with a rapt expression, and had been talking to invisible persons. She had been seen to strike odd postures. Her speech had become incoherent." Staring off into space was now a purely pathological behavior in a hospital rather than something a psychiatrist might describe a patient as being "perfectly content" to do. That said, as this same author noted, "many simple schizophrenics turn into tramps, hoboes, or beatniks. They become increasingly shallow in their emotional responses and are quite content to drift aimlessly through life as long as they are left alone."[123] The 1967 version of being content was a wanderer, a somewhat romantic figure of a social outsider. This description was not a statement of admiration or envy of those with schizophrenia, as the author believed psychiatric support was still needed, but neither was it a disparaging description or a hopeless one. The iconic patient staring into space of the modern period was displaced by the wanderer, the doer, the dissenter, the outsider, but also the authentic, emotionally open communicator of the postmodern period who lived outside of society's structures.

CHAPTER 5

Liberating "Those Whose Ways Are Different"

Kenneth Donaldson had been a patient at Florida State Hospital in Chattahoochee for years when he sued two psychiatrists employed there, claiming that he had in fact received no treatment during his confinement and that they had "intentionally and maliciously deprived him of his constitutional right to liberty."[1] The case eventually appeared before the Supreme Court in 1975 as *O'Connor vs. Donaldson*. Here the Burger Court argued that there was no constitutional basis for the involuntary confinement of the mentally ill unless these individuals posed harm to others or to themselves.

While the majority opinion was reverential about the private sphere and the preferability of the "comforts of one's home to those of an institution," the justices also sought to uphold the diversity of the public sphere. "May the State fence in the harmless mentally ill solely to save its citizens from exposure to those whose ways are different?" the Court asked. "One might as well ask if the State, to avoid public unease, could incarcerate all who are physically unattractive or socially eccentric. Mere public intolerance or animosity cannot constitutionally justify the deprivation of a person's physical liberty."[2]

The Court simultaneously elevated the private sphere as a place of care and the public sphere as a place of cosmopolitanism, animated by an array of ways of being and appearing.[3] While not explicitly likening the mentally ill to an ethnicity, the Supreme Court justices discussed psychiatric patients in terms of their having different ways and customs, they addressed the aesthetic dimensions of the mentally ill as one might address the aesthetic dimensions of racism, and they discussed and circulated an image of a certain type, the "harmless mentally ill," in the idiom of rights that animated social movements based on race. Vulnerable populations seeking rights were increasingly embracing this ethnicity model of oppression, valuing it more highly than biological identities and biological determinism, gay liberationists of the 1970s among them,[4] and it is perhaps this sort of strategic move toward legitimacy and respectability that the Court was engaging in here. In keeping with this broader social logic, the Court did not rule on whether or not Donaldson had the "right to treatment," despite a growing body of federal case law in this period that recognized this right, but was much more concerned with the right to individual liberty from the intrusiveness of the state.[5]

The decision harked back to the well-known legal precedent at the turn of the twentieth century of the right to privacy as the right to be "let alone." Some medical observers were already fretting that a right to privacy would come to take precedence over the right to treatment, or, in broader terms, that a right to self-reliance would take precedence over the state's obligation to protect.[6] This legal precedent, however, had a broader intellectual ambit in the last third of the twentieth century. Hannah Arendt, writing in 1974, claimed that a new and deeper freedom was increasingly demanded: "the right to be free from any mandatory participation in public life, be it something so basic as the duty to vote or to serve as a juror."[7] Though it was a protean idea, anti-statism had a particular urgency in a larger medical context in which the rights of patients to refuse medical treatment, whether a blood transfusion or an artificial respirator, were gaining more attention and were even enshrined in official documents such as the Patient Bill of Rights, which was adopted by the American Hospital Association in 1973.[8] Since participation was a central mode of citizenship in the postwar mental hospital—not to mention American liberalism broadly conceived—the right to be set free from it formed a part of a shifting landscape of both postwar American liberalism and deinstitutionalization.

The Supreme Court furthered a deinstitutionalizing impulse that was present, though more subterranean, in the early postwar era. Deinstitutionalization was accelerating during the second half of the 1960s and was particularly prevalent by the 1970s and throughout the rest of the twentieth century. The deinstitutionalizing project was, in some incarnations, liberationist and associated with a left-leaning counterculture in its depiction of paternalistic institutions as forms of nefarious social control, its renunciation of technocracy and bureaucracy, its profound distrust of state corruptions, and its emphasis on individual autonomy from the carceral state. "The right to treatment" itself was a contested concept for radical civil libertarians, who thought that it implied further medicalization. In this view, even ideas like rehabilitation, a pillar of postwar American liberalism, could be exposed for their paternalistic qualities. Historian Anne E. Parsons shows that policymakers and politicians took up the value of rehabilitation during the early postwar period as a justification to arrest and imprison African American men in particular.[9]

But deinstitutionalization was capacious enough to embody an array of political perspectives that have at their heart individual liberty, even a style of classical liberalism, which broadened the scope from anti-statism to include a renunciation of welfare services and an embrace of self-reliance and voluntarism, something especially urgent during an economic downturn and the ensuing social dislocations of an economy that was beginning to deindustrialize. Both radical and conservative libertarians were invested in self-determination and both hoped for a more perfected domesticity. For radicals domesticity could be a source of subversive politics itself, and for conservatives the domestic realm could compensate for the state's absence, and should be robust anyway as a part of traditional values.[10] Perhaps most relevant to psychiatric hospitals, these ideas suggest a perception of the public sphere as a place of vitality and energy but public institutions as places of atrophy and depression, something befitting an automaton's shelter.

That libertarians of different ideological persuasions could both support deinstitutionalization betokens a deepening fear of the state and medical authority and their perceived overextension in late twentieth-century America. In a departure from second wave feminist depictions of domesticity as repressive, dreary, and soul-crushing, deinstitutionalization elevates the individual family's role as a haven for protection and comfort at the same time as, even if only by default, subordinating the state and political institutions to the market economy. It could be said to instantiate a broader ideological shift from mid-twentieth-century American liberalism that was allied with the welfare state to a late twentieth-century neoliberalism that was dismantling it.[11] Neoliberalism also is relevant to the question of emotional demeanors, as this ideology privileges the productive, active figure and again rejects the automaton, in the same way that countercultural philosophies did, only toward different ends: for entrepreneurialism rather than for social dissent. Psychiatric patients and their families were registering these changes, especially by the late 1960s and the 1970s when the transition to deinstitutionalization was becoming more apparent, and their writings reveal some early impressions of neoliberalism, even without a precise vocabulary for this concept.

While social observers over the course of the twentieth century increasingly felt that institutionalization could create automatons, the transition to deinstitutionalization allows for a meditation upon the more unmoored figures who emerged in its wake, ones who, of necessity, had to be more concerned with material well-being and material survival than the transcendence of material thinking that patients of the interwar era could sometimes appreciate. Their writings, in turn, illuminate a nostalgia for something imprecise that could be described as a yearning for an idealized communitarianism and places of care that ran alongside broader postwar social ideals of self-reliance and active agency.

A sense of placelessness increasingly animated patient and family writings about mental illness. What happens to emotions without a place to express them? Placelessness breeds quite a different and much more unanchored sensibility than the interwar and war era patient writers who were more firmly grounded in institutions and institutional orbits when they contemplated mental illness. Late twentieth-century patient and family writings were becoming more explicitly and directly political not just in their emerging awareness of neoliberalism but in their use of imagery and metaphors: they were now much more likely to view medical tumults within a prism of civil rights broadly construed. Civil rights consciousness had an expanded scope during the late 1960s and throughout the 1970s, and movements proliferated that encompassed not just Black civil rights and those of other racial "minorities" but disability rights as well as more capaciously conceived patient rights.[12] This sort of rights consciousness also could encompass a need for restitution, as well as a sense of redress, reparations that early and midcentury patients did not demand, given a tragic sensibility more commonly harbored by earlier generations when confronting the suffering of mental illness and life hardships more broadly. The more resigned psychiatric subject of the early twentieth century and the ambivalent psychiatric citizen of the mid-twentieth century were becoming displaced by a more active, rights-bearing individual in a more institution-less world. Patients were liberated from the carceral state and potentially from psychiatric labeling, in possession of their rights to be let alone and to emotional expression, though they were also newly uncertain and ambiguous.

The Supreme Court judgment in *O'Connor vs. Donaldson* also could be said to represent a definitive reversal of any lingering nineteenth-century ideals of havens or refuges for the mentally troubled and the institutionalization of care premised on the idea that protection of the mentally ill from the public sphere and broader society was necessary. The ruling suggests an affirmation of the midcentury modernist characterizations of institutions as simply warehouses, as subsocieties that have some kinship with concentration camps, as exposé writers had argued. At the same time, the Court was embracing an earlier postwar ideal of social integration. This model was somewhat out of sync with broader critiques of social integration on the part of "minorities" in this era, as evidenced by the changing character of terms like "community," which by the late 1960s and 1970s tended to have more precise meanings, or more political meanings, such as the "Black community" or the "gay community," or alternative communities such as the commune movements of the 1970s.[13]

Somewhat paradoxically, the Court could be said to have invoked a strategy of privatization in its repudiation of public institutions in order to maintain the diversity of the public sphere. This strategy was in keeping with a broad intellectual and political movement toward privatization in this period, whether this took the form of the primacy of the family and the private sphere as a zone for care or an emphasis on self-authority and experiential authority over other kinds of authority—religious, parental, political, and medical. This elevation of the self propelled some critics to denounce the 1970s in particular as an era of mass self-absorption, characterized by therapeutic cultures that were too confessional, even apolitical. For these often socially conservative commentators, the duties of citizenship were becoming displaced, and alarmingly so, by the rights of the individual.[14] However, broader, more official rights culture of this period also instilled a respect for the self-care of the private sphere over the realm of the institution, such as the United Nations' Declaration on the Rights of Mentally Retarded Persons in 1971.[15] The words of the Declaration on the Rights of Disabled Persons from 1975 are also quite telling in this vein: "Disabled persons are entitled to the measures designed to enable them to become as self-reliant as possible."[16]

What was ideally supposed to replace psychiatric institutions during the 1970s was community psychiatry. Even the World Health Organization, from the standpoint of 1971, praised community care, noting that this approach was the "antithesis of custodial care in large isolated institutes and of an exclusively medical approach which seeks to treat mental illness in the same terms as a physical disease."[17] In the United States, community psychiatry often translated to the development of local mental health centers for those suffering from mental illness who were no longer treated in hospitals. Most of these centers dispensed an array of psychotherapies, and this made it difficult for them to attend to people with severe or chronic mental illnesses, since they did not necessarily provide psychiatrists, not to mention food or housing, and were often semi-institutional or semi-medical settings.[18]

In this community psychiatry model, patients were supposed to be able to live independently while receiving the care they needed. Still, as psychiatrist Milton Greenblatt, commissioner of the Massachusetts Department of Mental Health from 1967 to 1972 and himself an advocate of deinstitutionalization, noted in 1976, the wider community was not always open to receiving individuals with mental illnesses, in stark contrast to the Supreme Court's ideals of diversity within the public sphere. He felt that the "public" actively resisted the release of "'unattractive and misbehaving patients' into the community," fearing that they "burden the welfare rolls, crowd flophouses, sleep in subways."[19] What is striking here is that he highlighted physical appearance as a central factor in why the larger community might stigmatize the mentally ill, an acknowledgment of bodies and comportments that interpreters of discrimination against other "minorities" do not always consider first and foremost, even if intolerance of physical appearance and perceived affect has been a long-standing facet of homophobia and racism.

Moreover, the mentally "well" did not always want to live with the mentally ill and opposed building community homes, cooperative apartments, or halfway houses in their neighborhoods, a kind of "spatialization of prejudice."[20] This was an enduring theme over the course of the postwar period, as the letters of complaint from the neighbors of Saint Elizabeths Hospital about patient noise attest. Greenblatt had reason to fear that deinstitutionalized patients might be going from the "protection of the ward to the oblivion of the gutter."[21] In California, for example, the free clinic model thrived because so many patients who were still quite ill or at least vulnerable had received their releases too early, something that seemed to instantiate Greenblatt's dire predictions.[22]

The number of institutionalized patients did diminish greatly over the course of the postwar period: from 1955 to 1985, there was an 80 percent drop in the population of psychiatric hospitals.[23] It is not that public mental hospitals simply became obsolete: sometimes the remaining institutions could now give more attention to treating acute cases of mental illness and could provide more programming to their patients.[24] But generally, the length of stay in such facilities decreased dramatically, from years to weeks or even days, especially after 1970.[25] And the project of radically improving mental hospitals and giving them more funding that the critics of the hospital landscape during the war and early postwar eras so passionately demanded did not come to fruition.[26] Instead, care for those with mental illnesses became more fragmented. General hospitals became more important, though some of these did not even have dedicated psychiatric wards, just as community health centers could not always meet the needs of people with severe mental illnesses. Instead, the emphasis was on outpatient programs, prevention, and mental health.[27] Some social historians have pointed to a process of transinstitutionalization at work in the late twentieth century: those who could not live with their families or friends, or in hotels, could find themselves in psychiatric units within general hospitals or in nursing homes. They were also vulnerable to incarceration for things like loitering, trespassing, and disorderly conduct. Homeless people with mental illnesses, in turn, became a feature of urban landscapes in the United States from the 1960s onward.[28]

Community psychiatry was also supposed to obviate the need for an isolated, rural hospital on the fringes of society. The move toward integration rejected the salutary potential of a bucolic context in favor of an urban, assimilative model. Greenblatt, for his part, was enthusiastic about the flexibility of community psychiatry for the way it prepared patients for the outside world. It used day hospitals as a bridge into the community, night hospitals for those who could work during the day, and apartments for groups of patients who could help each other. Writing in the 1970s, he renounced the recent past of psychiatric care in his characterization of the mental hospital of the 1930s as a "custodial authoritarian model," wherein hospitals were plagued by "overcrowding, understaffing, hierarchical social organization, autocratic management . . . [in a] remote, barren, and punitive institution." He believed that "people found it depressing to visit such hospitals, and once a patient was referred for admission, his ties to the community were broken."[29] His rereading of the past as hopelessly benighted is in keeping with a more general therapeutic attitude that compared new, progressive treatments to the dark days of the past, bound up with images of patient disengagement, hospital bureaucratization, and automation. "The wards in those days were drab and the patients unkempt and apathetic, sitting in rows or lying on the floor. Activities were minimal, with most of the important daily functions carried out on a mass impersonal basis," he wrote. Some details offer an imaginative historical narrative on his part: "at mealtime the patients queued up at a food line or cafeteria, received their rations, and ate without sociality or even awareness of each other. . . . [The patient] was certainly not a true citizen or living member of any social group."[30] The question of citizenship is intriguing within the ambiguous public sphere of the medical institution, given the uncertain relationship between the figure of the patient and the citizen of a larger polity. But Greenblatt also discounts any possibility of community, solidarity, or other forms of association in the mental hospital.

His observations of institutional life in the twentieth century do resonate with the ideas of some parents of patients who came of age earlier in the twentieth century, who felt that little could be expected from the institution and that they were unfortunate necessities about which nothing could be done. Kenneth Donaldson's parents had signed his commitment papers to Florida State Hospital in 1956 when he was visiting them in Florida from New Jersey during tourist season. He believed that "there was love between my parents and myself; there was no quarrel; there was only a misunderstanding."[31] But he noted that his incarceration was prompted by his parents' "senile imaginings" at which point "'mob rule' took over and the ubiquitous busybodies ballooned innocent imaginings into outrageous imprecations."[32] His "estrangement" from his parents derived from their "fixation that I am nuts."[33] By 1957, Florida State Hospital had declared him a paranoid schizophrenic.[34] In 1963, he received a letter from his then eighty-one-year-old mother, who noted that his confinement was "hard for all of us. You want out and we want you out."[35] But "the doctors said you would have to have strict supervision. You can see we are powerless."[36] Donaldson's mother closed by talking about the weather, as if to find some human commonality, and to comment upon another area of life out of one's control: "A change in the weather on the cool side and high winds—a few sprinkles of rain—Hope you are comfortable Ken. We think of you all the time—we love you—always have and always will. Lovingly, Mom and Dad."[37]

Other letters that his parents wrote to him during his hospitalization about daily life are reminiscent of the style of family writing in asylum letters of the early twentieth century. "I am reading a book . . . about . . . diving in the Dead Sea to try and find some remains of Sodom and Gomorrah—the Wicked Cities," his mother wrote. "It is interesting and I will send it to you if you would like to read it. . . . Dad and I both need new glasses and will go as soon as these colds have gone."[38] When Donaldson's mother died in 1967, his father wrote to him to deliver the news: "Mother passed away Jan. 14th at 6am. She thought of you always and hoped to see you sometime."[39] But he too believed he was powerless in the face of Donaldson's hospitalization: "I am not aloud [sic] to sign any papers so don't write to me to do so. I am glad to hear from you but I am helples [sic] to do as you ask me to do. If the Doctor says you should be aloud to leave the hospital why don't they let you. You of age. . . . This hurts me as well as you so don't write me about it again. I love you but can't do anything for you. Love, Dad."[40]

Kenneth Donaldson was unusual, of course, in that he ended up suing his hospital, but his example still illuminates the situation of patients who thought in more rights-oriented and possibility-seeking ways than did some of his interwar forebears and certainly than his parents, of the same generation, did. His parents' assertions of tough love and their insistence that they were simply following medical advice or fulfilling parental duty do not seem especially affectionate from a late twentieth-century perspective, if they ever would have seemed so. Instead, they exhibit a sensibility of acceptance of the universe's will, only here it was not a peaceful acceptance but more of an assertive, almost aggressive compliance with the way things are.

The banalities of small talk in families and the starkness of the day to day on view in these letters were in fact becoming explicit targets of mental health promoters and psychoanalytical thinkers in this period. In 1965, the National Institute of Mental Health produced a film called *Trouble in the Family*, bemoaning the fact that "people in families were always strangers to one another." If this comment was a truism for many American families in this period, this might have been heightened when one of those family members was contending with mental illness. In this film, family therapist Nathan Ackerman decried family interactions: "what they do is talk about trivial matters . . . the mechanics of everyday living." In family therapy he suggested that families should "do away with the empty mouthings of the day to day and reach out towards the important."[41]

Ackerman's comments betoken something of a utopian expectation for emotional fulfillment in family life, a sentiment that has some kinship with the Supreme Court's thinking about the humanitarian and empathetic capacities of the private or domestic sphere as the preferable space of care. But as deinstitutionalization came to fruition, families also could feel quite ambivalent about these sanguine interpretations of domesticity, sometimes interpreting the demise of social and residential services for the mentally ill as a kind of abandonment. In 1976, Connecticut governor Ella Grasso, a Democrat known for austerity and budget cuts to welfare programs in her state, received a heart-rending letter from a mother about her forty-two-year-old daughter who had suffered from mental illnesses most of her adult life. She had been a patient at Fairfield Hills Hospital several times during the previous twenty years. However, she had been discharged in 1975, and this mother, at the age of sixty-six, did not feel she could look after her daughter in her home. Her daughter was then placed in a nursing home wherein many patients were old and dying, the young people were "so retarded that they border on the line of degeneracy," and there were no facilities in the way of psychiatric rehabilitation.[42] Placement in nursing homes or boardinghouses was again another repercussion of deinstitutionalization.[43] In the face of this, this mother in effect reprised an earlier twentieth-century rhetorical strategy of placing the guileless mentally ill in a different category from the "degenerate," embodying an observation of historian Jonathan Metzl that affirming one's own health often follows a logic of suggesting the spoiled health of another.[44]

If homelessness as an accelerating late twentieth-century problem could be said to engender a sense of hopelessness in its beholders, or a sense that the poor in society were inevitable figures, then it was also important for family members to distinguish their loved ones from these homeless "masses." A similar plaintive letter to Governor Grasso came in 1979 from another mother of a son who had been in and out of state hospitals in Connecticut for eight years. She noted that he was not "able to maintain a residence for very long at any of the hotels or rooming houses in the Hartford area due to his appearance associated with his mental illness."[45] Here she refers specifically to his comportment as a cause of general social intolerance. This woman asked the governor earnestly: "Can you let me know where an individual with a history of mental illness can go to obtain food and shelter where there is none available to him." She even felt compelled to say that the illness was not the son's "fault" and grouped him with other blameless victims: "I have followed with great interest how you have helped tornado victims . . . [yet] there is no relief in sight for the mentally ill that must live on the streets and be exposed to many dangers and hazards besides suffering from hunger and cold."[46]

This strategy of not ascribing blame for mental illness was perhaps heightened in the late twentieth century when new public health campaigns were reiterating this idea. The National Alliance for the Mentally Ill was founded in 1979 by two women from Wisconsin, Beverly Young and Harriet Shelter, and the organization was originally conceived as a protest against the commonly held view that schizophrenia was the fault of aloof and uncaring mothers.[47] That mothers still were absolving themselves of accusation and criticism in the late twentieth century indicates the enduring power and grip of stigma about mental illness and ideas about the family's potential role in it. It also may reveal an atmosphere of renewed social conservatism, social campaigns for "family values," and traditional moralism in the United States during the

1970s, all of which magnified the family's hand in creating or mitigating social problems.[48]

These desperate entreaties sometimes called forth a nostalgia for an idealized version of the mental hospital. One of the oft-noted and almost clichéd observations about the deepening importance of therapeutic culture in the twentieth century is that it had displaced religion, and yet perhaps spirituality was reemerging, or was forced to reemerge, in the face of deinstitutionalization, at the same time as it was more magnified, in an era of a more intense sociocultural presence of a renewed evangelical Christianity, and a political religious presence in the form of the Christian Right and the New Right.[49] In 1976, Governor Grasso received a letter from the wife of a clergyman in which she noted that she had seen an upswing of phone calls to her husband, often in the middle of the night, and he would "pray" for them and "read scripture to these stricken souls."[50] She attributed the increase in these numbers of desperate calls to the closing of the Undercliff "halfway house" for mentally ill patients. "From the serenity of beautiful grounds, unlocked doors, and the caring staff at Undercliff," she said, "the only alternative for most is a place which has many criminally insane, locked doors, padded cells, strait jackets, and harsh, repressive measures."[51] She also noted that her husband, though spiritually wise, was "not in any way trained as a psychiatrist," which suggests just how deeply therapeutic culture had permeated society, if even a preacher's wife felt the need for medical expertise and therapeutic training. "We are anxious that these people receive medication and proper help when they need it," she noted.[52]

Families could recognize, implicitly, the limits of domestic privatization strategies and their writings pondered material realities and capitalism writ large rather than the transcendence of capitalism, a possibility that some, facing institutionalization, had contemplated during the interwar era. In 1978, one mother wrote a letter to a programs analyst who was on a committee reviewing legislative programs in Connecticut. She told the story of her twenty-two-year-old son who had spent two years at Children's Village in Hartford with "undiagnosed emotional difficulties" and then spent another year at a group home. As a young adult, he had spent more than a year in the Institute of Living, which at the time was a residential psychiatric facility, where he was diagnosed with "chronic, undifferentiated schizophrenia."[53] As this family's health insurance could not cover the cost of the institute after their son reached adulthood, he was then admitted to Norwich State Hospital. This mother felt that Norwich was "little more than a holding operation which engages primarily in administering psychotropic drugs, a science still in its infancy." The custodial, industrial imagery and the massification of psychiatry here are especially salient. While she and her family had "no quarrel with the use of such drugs," they yearned for, in addition, "individualized treatment and accompanying support services which do not now exist,"[54] in other words the right to treatment beyond a purely medical model.

A facet of undersupported state institutions, as this woman noted, was reduced psychotherapy services. Kenneth Donaldson, too, wished that in Florida State Hospital doctors had not been reduced to dispensers of what many patients considered dubious medicines. Donaldson noted in 1964 that when he was at that hospital "very few [patients] show any understanding of why they are here" and characterized the doctors' attitudes as, "Now, you imbeciles, take your meds." He felt that doctors "who are dedicated to their job are so badly outnumbered that they are ineffectual."[55] He even suggested that the abuse of medications was among the central problems of the state hospital and that these drug-dispensing practices gave "much glee and satisfaction to the scientifically inclined sadist,"[56] again a revival of the "scientist at the bedside" doctor image from the turn of the twentieth century. These conversations were larger than just Kenneth Donaldson, though, as an array of prominent court cases during the 1970s and 1980s were also taking up the issue of the right to refuse treatments and psychiatric medications, including antipsychotic drugs, as well as the right to be free from physical restraint.[57]

But Donaldson did not have an explicit economic analysis of hospitalization: he simply sought humanist treatment and wanted to dispense with the oppressive parts of institutionalization altogether. Ironically, in the early 1970s, Florida State Hospital produced a film that intertwined an economic analysis of the hospital's treatment programs with a libertarian one in the name of creating a patient who could be a productive and "useful member of society" and not "just . . . sit in a chair." Once back in society, former patients could become "gainfully employed" and "become taxpayers and not just continue to be a burden on the people of the state of Florida."[58] Deinstitutionalization could be seamlessly interwoven with the kind of self-reliance and active affect that informed late twentieth-century neoliberalism.

While libertarian patient activists who were proponents of deinstitutionalization did have a particular ideological perspective and their writings tend to be politically charged, other patients and their families were trying to make sense of the phenomenon of deinstitutionalization often without a larger political vocabulary. The parents of the twenty-two-year-old in Connecticut wished that Norwich had the "time and the staff to provide individualized psychotherapy."[59] This mother was under no illusion about why the services she sought did not exist: for her it was not a matter of a particular philosophy of treatment but of overburdened public institutions with scanty resources. The phenomenon of deinstitutionalization was not something that generated much public commentary in the United States during the 1970s, and this must have made it hard to contemplate in a larger socioeconomic framework, or to have a language with which to analyze it. She knew that this was a time of a taxpayers' revolt and yet for her "cutting rather than improving services to the handicapped and the mentally ill in our society is a crime worse than murder."[60] As another mother yelled out in frustration to the director of the Creedmoor Psychiatric Center in Queens, New York, in 1978, who felt that the hospital was hamstrung by a dearth of funds and staff: "All I hear is budgets! Budget is not important: my son, these people, are important!"[61]

Activist patients had an animating tension in the form of the hospital. But how can one be critical of or wish to destroy an institution that does not really exist anymore? Despairing families sometimes grasped or hoped for an institutional environment that they knew was not forthcoming, and neither could they conceive of what this would look like. Another 1978 letter writer in this vein, to First Lady Rosalynn Carter, who had made mental health one of her signature issues, and to Governor Grasso, asked forthrightly: "Where do thirty-one-year-old emotionally ill American citizens go for long term and adequate care?" Her brother had been diagnosed with schizophrenia, and his family had come to the heartbreaking conclusion that "there is no cure and no humane place wherein he can live out the remainder of his life with dignity . . . that the outlook is so hopeless devastates us." She described his family as "unable to shoulder the burden of 150$ per day" of a private hospital, so their brother lived at Connecticut State Hospital where he "wasn't receiving any care at all" and "suffered grievous abuse." Finally, she said that the "deplorable conditions" there "defy description and consequently, we and others remain angry, frustrated, and desperate."[62]

Late twentieth-century families faced a unique political moment in terms of the erosion of the social services that had once characterized the welfare state. And those who still did have access to institutional settings did not necessarily see them as salutary, as the example of Connecticut State Hospital suggests. As early as 1965, in a letter to Minnesota governor Karl Rolvaag of the Minnesota Democratic-Farmer-Labor Party, who made addressing the plight of the mentally disabled one of his central issues, a woman said of her nephew at Rochester State Hospital that he is "not well but he is not crazy and there should be other places for such people other than mental institutions."[63]

But there were not always "other places," and the trend toward deinstitutionalization demanded a greater sense of voluntarism in the family. In testimony to a California mental health advocacy group in 1979, the mother of a twenty-year-old with a profound mental illness pointedly asked: "Has the state decided that mental illness no longer exists?" From her point of view, care was geared to the "more well, cooperative patient. The street becomes the home of the really ill person. Street and jail." Her son was living at home and it was "most unsatisfactory for all concerned," but what were the "alternatives. Any?"[64]

For their part, patients, even those who were not explicitly activist, were more assertively declaring their rights during this period, inflected with a sense of consumer choice, willingness to litigate, and broader civil rights consciousness. It was out of step with the political moment to feel that mistreatment at the hands of the medical establishment was simply inevitable. Medical malpractice suits proliferated during the 1970s, and not just in the realm of mental health.[65] In turn, organizations for patients' rights and to combat psychiatric abuse proliferated, among them, the Insane Liberation Front from Portland, Oregon, formed in 1970, the Network Against Psychiatric Assault in San Francisco in 1972, and the Mental Patients Rights Association in Florida in 1977, comprised of former patients who sometimes self-identified as survivors. Most of these organizations emphasized "negative" rights, especially the right not to be locked up, though not always. In a handbook published by the Mental Patients' Liberation Front in Boston in 1970, patients declared the right to "patient-run facilities."[66] The right to health care did have synergies with broader civil rights. Patients tended to trade in the language of civil rights rather than the perhaps more capacious category of human rights, seeing some allegiance with other "minorities" in the 1960s and 1970s, particularly African Americans but also women, gays, and Indigenous Americans, which perhaps instilled more of a critical consciousness.[67] While in the early and mid-twentieth century patient captivity narratives were imbued with a deep sense of woe, as well as graphic descriptions of wrongs and violence, and, after World War II, Holocaust metaphorization and totalitarian imagery, these earlier captivity narratives did not contain the same degree of protest or the same critical consciousness about their circumstances—they did not suggest a need for restitution for them as these later twentieth-century ones would.

When patients spoke in the idiom of civil rights, it was as if to proclaim that having them would engender tangible change. Even as early as 1960, a man from Minnesota wrote to Democratic governor Orville Freeman, identifying himself as one of the "unfortunates" who had been "railroaded into an institution." He said that he was picked up by a policeman at his home in 1956 and "denied my civil rights," among them the privilege to have visitors.[68] Another letter writer to Governor Rolvaag in 1966 spoke of his "incarceration," proclaiming that "the political machinery in this State has prospered to[o] long at the expense of the honesty and dignity of the mislead [sic] citizen," and for the "past year I have been surrounded by such needless suffering and despair that it actually sickens me."[69] These letters also demonstrate a shifting sense of justice in this period, one that encompassed outrage against a more abstract medical or political system. The concept of the "system" was evolving from an eclectic concept and metaphor during the early 1960s into a more menacing idea by the late 1960s, particularly as American leftists used the term, and this more nefarious use of the term is on display here.[70]

Perhaps the civil rights consciousness that had seeped into these letters was indicative of a heightened political awareness beyond the hospital walls and a deeper sense of identification between psychiatric patients, particularly white patients, and other "minorities," resonant with a larger posture of white middle-class American activism during the 1960s in particular. In her retrospective and best-selling memoir, *Girl, Interrupted*, recalling her time at McLean Hospital in 1968, Susanna Kaysen wrote that "the world didn't stop because we weren't in it anymore; far from it. Night after night tiny bodies fell to the ground on our TV screen: black people, young people, Vietnamese people, poor people." What she witnessed of "the sixties" was decontextualized, fragmentary imagery and a mediated version. Still she remembers something enlivening about observing the upheavals of the period from a remove: "People were doing the kinds of things we had fantasies of doing: taking over universities and abolishing classes . . . sticking their tongues out at policemen. We'd cheer them on, those little people on our TV screen. . . . We thought eventually they'd get around to 'liberating' us too. 'Right on!' we'd yell at them."[71]

During the late 1960s and 1970s, libertarian critics accused the government of invading the lives of individual Americans, of overreaching; those of a conservative bent, sometimes called "neoconservatives" by their critics, felt that the government had overextended its tentacles into too many areas of American life, for example, in the perceived excesses of the Great Society welfare state programs and in affirmative action programs.[72] Patient libertarianism had a different flavor and was more imbued with social justice, as more left-leaning libertarianism was. And patients in the vein of Kenneth Donaldson straddled these ideas when they extolled, at least implicitly, a self-reliant ideal.

Still, a notion of restitution, one ironically sought from the state, remained a powerful consolation, as demonstrated in the very act of writing entreaties to government officials. Another patient wrote to Governor Rolvaag in 1965 from Anoka State Hospital, detailing the travails he felt upon being released from his most recent stay at Hastings State Hospital. Anoka tended to house patients who were considered chronic; it received the "hopeless" patients from other state hospitals in Minnesota and their discharge rates were accordingly low.[73] When he sought a job after being in the state hospital he felt "discriminated" against. "This is the Civil Rights era," he proclaimed. "Yet I am still being discriminated against, because of race, religion, creed, etc." He does not say what his race and religion are, but it does appear that he placed his illness within this larger framework of human difference. At Anoka, he claimed, he was "not allowed to do anything . . . except sit . . . and be confined."[74] "Civil rights" implies an attachment to a particular polity, and much as many state hospitals tried to encourage hospital citizenship, it does seem that this patient was speaking more of an atmosphere of civil rights and had an awareness of a transformative historical moment. But this is still more concrete and more explicitly political than war era patients who spoke of a "right" in an abstract realm or as a synonym for a moral right. One woman who had been a patient at Bryce Hospital, or Alabama Insane Hospital as it was sometimes still called, in Tuscaloosa in 1938 pleaded with the governor of Alabama, Frank M. Dixon, to counter the persistent wishes of her husband's family to continue to have her institutionalized. She did feel she needed medical help, though not psychiatric help. "All knowed I not crazy," she wrote, "so pleas see I get my right."[75]

Entreaties to political authorities could even include pleas for empathy and redress for misery; during the earlier postwar period, letters to political officials were characterized more by sorrowful acceptance of one's lot. There is here a sense that the state can be looked to for help as well as an awareness that this help was inadequate and diminishing. A twenty-six-year-old letter writer to Governor Rolvaag in Minnesota asked him for help and release from a state hospital. She wrote that "if you or no one cares the least you could do is try to understand the position I am in. I just can't carry anymore myself. I can't eat because I cry myself to sleep."[76] She said that she was a "young girl and I know there must be a place for me with just the wind in my hair and Freedom and contribution without any more Physical or mental tests . . . I have written a Book since I've been here and now I ask for your help for my Freedom."[77] The woman made it clear that she had been a flight attendant[78] and might want to work again, that she wrote things, and that she was active and alert, as if to show that she had earned rights and freedom. A yearning for restitution and the at times capacious nature of rights culture were on display in her letter, too. She implored the governor: "I ask that I can have back my Health," as if this were his to give her.[79] However, and somewhat paradoxically, she conveys her loneliness as a larger and more abstract than lacking human bonds in a community. She had "no one to pick me up. No lights on the Christmas tree that used to sparkle. No one that would say . . . we care about you."[80]

Even if a subterranean desire for community was still present, a more dominant cultural view persisted that the psychiatric hospital existed merely to churn out indifferent drones and was profoundly detrimental to self-reliance, not to mention indifferent to rights. What had not changed from the early postwar period was the prospect, and reality, of exploitation at the hands of the psychiatric system, as well as the specter of the state hospital in particular. Even with the call for more material resources for the public hospital, the disquiet, even terror, about these institutions still ran deep in the late twentieth century. Exposé knowledge of exploitation inside the hospital was just as chilling and troubling during this period as it had been at midcentury. An arresting example is a 1969 investigation of New Jersey's largest mental hospital, then known as New Jersey State Hospital at Trenton, which exposed the sexual abuse of patients, including the rape of female patients by staff members and the forced prostitution of patients for the male employees.[81]

Phyllis Chesler's portrait of mental hospitals in *Women and Madness* is also unremittingly bleak, rejecting the possibility of solidarity or communion therein. "The state hospital," she declared, "like the poor or workhouse of old, functions as a warning specter. . . . Mental asylums rarely offer asylum. Both their calculated and their haphazard brutality mirrors the brutality of 'outside' society." At their best, she felt that hospitals might provide a special "hotel" or "collegelike" atmosphere for white and wealthy women. But at their worst she called them "families bureaucratized: the degradation and disenfranchisement of self, experienced by the biologically owned child (patient, woman), takes place in the anonymous and therefore guiltless embrace of strange fathers and mothers. In general, in psychiatric wards and state hospitals, 'therapy', privacy, and self-determination are all either minimal or forbidden."[82] Second wave feminists, particularly white women, condemned the family as another institution that could be a zone of oppression. These ideas are in keeping with some of the period's most prominent critics of psychiatry, most centrally British critics who also became important figures in the American anti-psychiatry movement.[83]

It was not just feminist critics who deplored mental hospitals as institutions: exposé works in the vein of Albert Deutsch's *The Shame of the States* had similar, late twentieth-century parallels, often more salacious ones. By the mid-1960s, such accounts shared Deutsch's belief in the sincerity of the intentions of the doctors and administrators therein but were more likely to see the institution as inevitably dehumanizing for everyone involved, rather than harbor hope for them through a more robust welfare state, again expressing a stance of implicit self-reliance. An arresting example is Frank Leonard's novel *City Psychiatric* (1965), based on his experiences as an attendant at Bellevue Mental Hospital in New York City.[84] The suggestive book cover unapologetically trafficked in the "pornography of violence," selling it as "BRUTAL" and "ANGRY" and "APPALLING," a novel to expose the "stinging truth . . . the inner workings of such a hospital . . . the beatings, the filth, the poverty, the callous brutality and terrifying violence," as well as the "alcoholics and psychopaths, sexual deviates, juvenile delinquents, would-be suicides, the feeble-minded and the senile—all the cast-offs and victims of a vast city . . . a raw human drama."[85] There is something of an anti-urban aesthetic in his exposé, as though all of the frightened imaginings about the American city during the 1960s—their perceived criminality, riots, and violence—could be distilled into one spot: the mental hospital.[86] This "hell on earth" that he created was City Psychiatric, an unnamed public psychiatric receiving hospital in a large city. The novel suggests that most attempts at displaying humanity toward the sick and the troubled were hampered by the unbearable and miserable atmosphere of the institution that all but encouraged a casual callousness, an all-encompassing structuralist vision that seems to reprise Michel Foucault's ideas of the inherent repressions of the institution.[87]

Other exposé accounts in the late twentieth century abandoned the notion of good public intentions gone awry so characteristic of mid-twentieth-century liberalism and instead advanced an idea of the institution as an agent of a mass, stultifying bureaucratization more characteristic of late twentieth-century libertarianism. In *Prisoners of Psychiatry* (1972), Bruce J. Ennis, the lawyer who represented Kenneth Donaldson and legal director of the American Civil Liberties Union (ACLU), wrote that the inmates of the nation's psychiatric hospitals—he estimated their number to be 750,000, 400,000 of whom were in state hospitals and the rest spread out in V.A. hospitals, private hospitals, and general hospitals with psychiatric wards—"will be physically abused, a few will be raped or killed, but most of them will simply be ignored, left to fend for themselves in the cheerless corridors and barren back wards of the massive steel and concrete warehouses we—but not they—call hospitals."[88] This blatant imagery of confinement held an extra urgency during the 1960s and 1970s when prison riots and prisoners' rights were gaining attention in sociocultural conversations, at the same time as many observers noted the waning ideal of rehabilitation and a turn toward more punitive measures in the nation's prison systems.[89] Ennis felt that it was hard to "imagine a more depressing environment than the sullen corridors and empty hours of a state mental hospital. . . . The patient will wear the same clothes as the other patients, eat the same food, receive the same medication, watch the same TV shows, and fall asleep in a long room filled with 50 or 60 metal beds exactly alike."[90] This description recalls the denunciations of suburbia and social conformity in the early postwar period, except here he offers a more assertive, nightmarish vision of conformity in a bureaucratic setting, perhaps best symbolized by the common state-issued clothing: hospital-manufactured dresses.[91]

Ennis goes on to refer to the long "empty hours" in the hospital, identifying a space of shapeless or dimensionless time as a central oppression, not the liberating solace it sometimes could be considered in the interwar years. This work also attributes a sense of nefarious intentionality to the institution, one that was seldom ascribed in earlier works when more common reference points were ill fate and luck. "Coercive psychiatry has a comfortable niche in society," Ennis wrote. "How would we tame our rebellious young, or rid ourselves of doddering parents, or clear the streets of the offensive poor, without it?"[92] This kind of commentary again suggests a minority consciousness that animated the late twentieth century, with the mentally ill taking their place alongside other vulnerable groups in society, here with perhaps a clearer sense of an existing conspiracy against them.

As with the war and early postwar era generations, late twentieth-century critics of the hospital as an institution took up Holocaust imagery, but it was more graphically expressed in the 1960s and 1970s both for the moral shock that it could elicit and for the affirmation of the rights of the individual in the face of the ultimate industrial system out of sight. Frederick Wiseman's 1967 documentary *Titicut Follies* explicitly compared the Bridgewater State

Hospital, a correctional institution in Massachusetts, to a concentration camp. His images are stark and unrelenting, especially of naked inmates being searched, wandering aimlessly about, defecating and urinating on the floor. Screams from the isolation room punctuate this narrative and provide the soundscape of this hospital. Orderlies and guards use tear gas to control patients, an image particularly resonant of the concentration camp. The State of Massachusetts censored the film in 1968 for twenty-five years, officially for violating Massachusetts privacy laws, even though the staff and patients at Bridgewater had given their consent to be filmed.[93]

The Holocaust as a metaphor had by now suffused American postwar intellectual and political rhetoric to such an extent that observers in the vein of Hannah Arendt noted that reality in the postwar period always existed in comparison with the Holocaust, engendering in individuals an inability to "confront reality on its own terms because they had always some parallels in mind that 'helped' them to understand those terms." She meant this in relation to the ways that Americans understood their own politics or foreign policy, especially the Vietnam War, and how it was that distinguished American foreign policy figures could come to conclude that in global politics "every gesture of reconciliation was a 'second Munich.'"[94] But this reception and interpretation of reality were striking in more intimate institutional contexts for patients making sense of their experiences. In 1976, a group of patients with schizophrenia hospitalized on a National Institute of Mental Health (NIMH) clinical research unit in the National Institutes of Health (NIH) Clinical Center in Bethesda, Maryland, were asked to depict their experience of the seclusion room in drawings as part of an art therapy program. The patients were asked to draw a self-portrait, pictures of their psychiatric illnesses, and pictures of delusions/hallucinations. Many patients chose to represent the seclusion room experience visually.[95] In one image that was particularly laced with the Holocaust, a patient drew a seclusion room as a "gas chamber with patient waiting for gas to be turned on" (see Figure 5).[96]

Knowing about the Holocaust, fascism, and genocides inevitably shaped how writers and political figures thought, felt, or represented in the postwar period. American radicals during the 1970s, among them members of the New Left and Black Power, for example, accelerated this kind of speech and metaphor, especially as the disappointments of the war in Vietnam and American racism began to appear entrenched and unchanging.[97] And it is not uncommon, of course, for social movement thinkers, in their critiques of the United States, to liken Americans to subtle and sophisticated fascists

Figure 5. Harriet Wadeson and William T. Carpenter, "Impact of the Seclusion Room Experience," *Journal of Nervous and Mental Disease* 163, no. 5 (November 1976): 325. Reproduced with the permission of Wolters Kluwer Health, Inc.

and thereby the more calculating and less honest ones. In fact pointing to an innate fascism could be a way of overcoming an analytical frustration about the slipperiness of systems of power and abstract bureaucracy. Historian Daniel T. Rodgers notes that American intellectuals became increasingly preoccupied during the postwar period, after the publication of Gramsci's *Prison Notebooks*, with the insidiousness of power and the facelessness of hegemony.[98] Critiques of psychiatry can be seen as particularly provocative antidotes to the facelessness of power and hegemony, in that they do suggest the workings of a fascist system and name a clear oppressor, perhaps shaped by the reality that psychiatric patients were in fact explicit Nazi victims in the euthanasia program and could trace a lineage to Nazism in a way that other vulnerable groups did more rhetorically.[99]

Was the possibility that patients could find themselves in an emotionally intense, appalling, and contradictory community about which one could feel bemused, intrigued, and ambivalent gone by the late twentieth century? Did the structuralist viewpoints of activists against psychiatry and patient advocates necessarily offer representations of the mental hospital as an inherently corrupt institution that nothing, not even altruistic organizations like

Hospital Audiences Incorporated, could mitigate? In a structuralist vision, the individual subject is necessarily muted, a fragment of the institution and systems.[100] This structuralist idea resonates with the principle tenets of social psychiatry in the 1970s and 1980s, as well as its attention to social ills and environmental problems such as poverty and racism and their contributions to mental distress.[101] From the vantage point of the late twentieth century, structuralism was a wide-ranging philosophical position, eliciting commentary from both left- and right-leaning thinkers. Leftists tended to see in dominating structures the possibility for a kind of inherent violence. As historian David Courtwright notes, "moral leftists" in the United States, rather than denying the existence of evil, tended to locate it within oppressive systems rather than individuals, while moral conservatives, as philosopher Cornel West notes, tended to locate evil within the actions of the individual.[102]

Patient narratives and memoirs suggest that the psychiatric institution was emblematic of the complete dissolution of the individual, a structuralist thought that ironically could take them toward desiring and inhabiting a more profound individualism. One perhaps unintentional corollary of structuralist thinking and deinstitutionalization was this greater recourse to privatization and domesticity. Did the quest to illuminate the exploitations of the vulnerable inadvertently contribute to an abandonment of state protections for mentally ill people, which simply dovetailed with a neoliberal ideology gaining ground in the final third of the twentieth century?

Social critics of individualism and narcissism and the turn inward, especially of the "Me Decade" 1970s, felt that these trends were happening independently of deinstitutionalization in the wake of the perceived failure of utopian politics of the 1960s and were phenomena that further illuminated tensions between the individual and the community.[103] Historian Thomas Borstelmann has spoken of a "hyperindividualism" that characterized the 1970s, given a new focus on interiority in this moment, but one that did not transmogrify into introspective arts and literature. Instead, he argues that it simply created an excessive emphasis on self-improvement and self-expression at the expense of communitarianism.[104] Other theorists of neoliberalism such as historian Lisa Duggan have noted a "shrinking of the public sphere" and the diminishing links between a private self and public realm, as well as the high and perhaps impossible expectations then placed upon the family.[105] Duggan, however, does not indict introspection as self-absorption or see individualism as propelling the shrinking public but instead the eroded responsibilities of government and the demise of the welfare state.

Therapeutic cultures also were becoming more diffuse in the United States in the wake of deinstitutionalization. During the 1970s, a number of books about self-improvement, personal growth, and achieving personal intimacy became best sellers.[106] Sociologist Micki McGee has argued that the financial crisis of the 1970s facilitated the strengthening of the idea of self-help: if people could not achieve financial well-being, they were more apt to turn to other ideas about fulfillment and self-realization.[107] Self-empowerment became an end in itself. But self-help, as well as other kinds of alternative therapeutic cultures, was not necessarily geared toward those suffering from mental illnesses, especially since in some ways self-help discounted the existence of biological mental illness, or at least medical labeling.[108] From the standpoint of the era of the 1970s itself, cultural critics such as historian Christopher Lasch lamented that this very proliferation of therapies had not diminished the therapeutic impulse or the culture of experts but had instead established a "therapeutic state" that contributed to the "culture of narcissism," again at the expense of the concept of community. For him, the postwar period was punctuated by a shift from mass social conformity to mass social narcissism and self-realization, and the New Left had become distracted from the critiques of capitalism that the Old Left had offered, again calling into question the compatibility between citizenship and therapeutic selfhood.[109] The discussion of narcissism that animated the 1970s—and indeed continues to animate twenty-first-century America amid an alleged "narcissism epidemic"—is actually a long-standing conversation in the United States. As early as 1942 Karen Horney was desperately trying to set psychoanalysis apart from self-admiration or "dead-end ruminations about oneself."[110]

Perhaps what was unique to the 1970s era were the tensions between domesticity and the state. To return to *O'Connor vs. Donaldson* (1975), the judgment said that the "mere presence of mental illness does not disqualify a person from preferring his home to the comforts of an institution."[111] Just as the hope of a better, more fulfilling domesticity existed for thinkers on both ends of the political spectrum, the hope of better cures, and sometimes even a better institution, also existed.

In a psychiatric hospital, unlike in the home, a patient might be thrown into incidental interactions with individuals representing a broad spectrum of ways of being. Sometimes, even during a period of more widespread rebellion against authority and the institution, this hospital stay offered glimmers of community. In 1973, a high school student wrote to *Ms.* magazine to tell her story, a common consciousness-raising strategy among feminists in this period, in response to an article about mental health that had appeared in *Ms*. She confided that she had just spent two months in an unnamed psychiatric ward in an unnamed hospital. Prior to this she had been raped three times and had been feeling that "I had deserved it and was worthless and unclean. Reasoning that since I was worthless I had no right to live, I attempted suicide a number of times." It was her guidance counselor at school, a nun, who persuaded her father to commit her. "I shall be eternally grateful to her," she wrote, "for she saved my sanity if not my life. Those two months were the most rewarding of my entire life. The women, patients, and staff, gave me advice, self-support, friendship, love and a sense of self-worth through small gestures, in group therapy and the long talks we had far into the AM."[112]

Was it rare, as this letter seems to indicate, to have had an ultimately assuaging experience in a psychiatric hospital or, in the case just mentioned, in a psychiatric ward of a larger general hospital? In 1976, in the venue of an activist publication, a young woman who self-identified as a "deaf, 18 year old Native American lesbian feminist" wrote a letter to *Speak Out*, a feminist newsletter from Albany, New York, to talk about her "struggle to survive through 6 months of being locked up in McLean's [McLean] Hospital in Belmont, Massachusetts." She tells the story of being "knocked out with Thorazine" and "locked into rooms, in isolation," for "defying the system." However, she also wrote that during her time in maximum security it was a psychiatric nurse there who "saved her life. A woman who gave me back my strength and courage to keep fighting, by recognizing my feelings and experiences as being very real." This nurse "helped me learn the psychiatric system to use it against itself, so I could get out without being destroyed. She was the only woman within that system who felt I and other women in McLean's were important enough to take a courageous, active part in freeing us from that patriarchal institution!"[113] While clearly seeing this woman as an exception, and while decrying the hospital as a system, this letter writer also located political acts of resistance within private acts of sympathy.

Those who remained in mental hospitals in the era of deinstitutionalization—those who were not seeking out the often meager community resources or making do with family members and friends—were forced to be in the public world of the institution, sometimes with little sense of individualism or community, let alone a balance between the two. In an untitled silent film from the 1960s showing the admission of a male patient to Utica State Hospital, he is interviewed, has a shower, and wraps up his possessions. He is put in a bed and reads *Time* magazine;[114] he is neither robotic nor unwilling, just more resigned than anything else. This is a film made by the hospital for a hospital audience: obviously it was not intended to unsettle the prospective patients with an exposé in Frederick Wiseman style. Still, it is worthwhile remembering that while intellectuals, patient advocacy movements, and patients who were highly politicized and often justifiably disillusioned with their care options rebelled against and launched damning critiques of psychiatric institutionalization during this period, and while there were some intriguing, if inchoate, departures from these dominant viewpoints, other patients may not have been aware of, or simply disengaged from, these debates. For them, resignation might have continued to be a default mode, a demeanor of ambivalence.

Withdrawing from the Fray
at the End of the Century

During the mid-1990s, in the midst of a harrowing suicidal depression, writer Daphne Merkin took herself to a hospital in midtown Manhattan to consult with a psychiatrist who was the head of an inpatient depression unit. When he suggested to her that it would be a good idea to check in to the hospital, she felt a "surge of relief" because she knew that she could "no longer remain on the outside."[1] Once inside, she "felt strangely safe" and remembers "feeling most protected against my despair" when watching TV with her fellow insomniacs late at night. She referred to "those cozy hours when the unit was cast in darkness" and then the feeling, when watching the evening news, that "all the catastrophes and crises seemed to take on an almost anthropological cast, so far removed were they from the constricted life of the universe I now inhabited." She was not lonely in the hospital, even though she had often felt that way at home. When she woke up "feeling bleak," she knew that life in the hospital "did not require me to put on a face to greet the world."[2] She felt comforted by the pause that the hospital offered; time took on a "different, less imperative dimension, [receded] into the background." The day seemed to "never really [start] up."[3] Mostly "you were at leisure to perambulate in your own mind, peeking in at various nooks and crannies." She had, it seemed, "withdrawn from the fray."[4]

Hers is not a romantic or nostalgic portrait of her time in the ward. She once pondered, for instance, the "beige linoleum" floor all around her, how it "shone with an incongruous brilliance" after the cleaners left, and yet no one "paid such loving attention to [patients]." She characterized the atmosphere for patients as one of "benign neglect."[5] After three weeks she developed an "aversion" to being there. She did not want to make the unit, "with its harsh fluorescent lights and endless expanses of waxed linoleum, its tasteless food and unchanging days,"[6] her home.

And yet, her writing seems to come from another era, in its acceptance of a pause from the clamors of life in society in a space of hospital introspection. She does not express fears of apathy or of becoming an institutionalized automaton, or characterize the people surrounding her in this way, nor does she dread being stripped of individualism. She does not identify with larger social and political turmoil in her midst but feels reassuringly absented from it.

How do we make sense of Merkin's account as an early twenty-first-century memoir? Her book was not without precedence in the late twentieth century. In 1990, writer William Styron, reflecting on how his depression had become unbearable in the 1980s and how the "struggle with disorder" in his mind might have had a "fatal outcome," said that the hospital was his "salvation."[7] It was here, in this "austere place with its locked and wired doors and desolate green hallways—ambulances screeching night and day ten floors below—I found the repose, the assuagement of the tempest in my brain, that I was unable to find in my quiet farmhouse."[8] The hospital offered him "sequestration" and "safety," as the knives that he normally wanted to "plunge" into his breast were here "bendable plastic." In a passage that stands in dramatic contrast to *O'Connor vs. Donaldson*, he notes that the hospital also gave him the "mild, oddly gratifying trauma of sudden stabilization—a transfer out of the all too familiar surroundings of the home, where all is anxiety and discord, into an orderly and benign detention where one's only duty is to try and get well." For him, the "real healers were seclusion and time."[9]

He stayed in this hospital, which goes unnamed in the book, for seven weeks. Though he writes that he was privileged to be at one of the "nation's best"[10] hospitals, again, his was not a romantic portrait. He called it "hardly a vacation spot" and felt that all hospitals possessed a "stupefying dreariness" with "subairline food" and lousy TV programs in the vein of *Dynasty*. He could not stand the activities such as group therapy, which made him "seethe" owing to a "condescending and bullying"[11] psychiatrist, or the "organized infantilism" of art therapy wherein the patients were enjoined by an overly perky young teacher to draw pictures with crayons on mural paper.[12] And yet he felt strongly that the hospital should be "shorn of its menacing reputation" and should not be "considered the method of treatment of last resort."[13]

It is of course easier for a famous writer in a top-tier hospital to make this assessment, but his narrative is also fascinating for its seemingly anachronistic qualities. Perhaps a fantasy of a better psychiatric hospital in the wake of deinstitutionalization responds to unresolved yearnings for refuge, for suspended time, and for inactivity rather than activity. And perhaps this longing reflects a perceived dearth of institutions that responded to these needs for comfort, camaraderie, and belonging at the turn of the twenty-first century, the now fading and greatly diminished psychiatric institutions among them.

Styron's meditations provide a striking contrast to the observers who analyzed the Willard State suitcases, who noted that the suitcase owners would "certainly have done better if they had been treated with kindness and persistent care, and been given a chance to live in the outside world."[14] The quest for kindness toward people with mental illnesses has been an enduring one, but this comment also reflects a quintessentially end of the twentieth-century idea, reinforced by decisions in the vein of *O'Connor vs. Donaldson*, that people in mental distress are necessarily better-off outside the hospital than they are inside it.

And yet the yearning for refuges from suffering, on display in these patient narratives, was becoming especially urgent in a neoliberal context. Merkin's work in particular is a retrospective telling, written amid some disillusionment with the deinstitutionalization era and at a moment when critics decried that individualism and an American "narcissism epidemic"[15] had overtaken any sense of community or civic and social bonds. These late twentieth-century social disappointments might have informed these works, in particular an acknowledgment of the dearth of possible communitarianism in contemporary social life, something that millennium era and early twenty-first-century social observers felt that Americans were deeply craving, and still insist that they are missing, from Amatai Etzioni's *The Spirit of Community* (1993), to Robert Putnam's *Bowling Alone* (2000), to Patrick Deneen's Trump era cri de coeur, *Why Liberalism Failed* (2018).[16] These communitarians fear excessive individualism, consumerism, and an oppressive state and call for a sense of obligation toward others, one that they hope will spring forth organically among members of the body politic rather than having it demanded of them by the state or enforced by social engineering or even violence. This longing for organic forms of community life in the United States has fostered an array of political dispositions, and as with different styles of libertarianism, these are not easy to place in a liberal-left-conservative prototype.

As the psychiatric hospital as an institution has become less commonplace, gone perhaps are the horrors captured in *The Shame of the States* and *Titicut Follies*, and gone are the social and spatial boundaries that separated the mentally ill and the mentally "well." However, gone too are places of potential sanctuary for the emotionally vulnerable, and gone is the ability to take a "pause" from the postindustrial, information age, "late" capitalism, which solicits energy and activity as a resource for productivity.[17] The state's protective impulses that characterized the mid-twentieth-century liberal welfare state, tainted by charges of benevolent or more violent kinds of paternalism, also diminished in the era of deinstitutionalization. Perhaps it is always impossible to distill and disentangle protection from paternalism, since it can become so easily bound up with bureaucracy and exploitation and suffused with unequal power relationships. But acknowledging this does not preclude yearnings for sympathetic witnesses or civic bonds and collective obligations. In her 1998 memoir of depression, *Willow Weep for Me: A Black Woman's Journey Through Depression*, Meri Nana-Ama Danquah tells her first therapist that "'I'm tired . . . I'm so tired of everything. I feel like I just want the world to stop spinning for a while, so I can take a break.'"[18] Hers was hardly a statement of yearning for hospitalization—indeed, the prospect terrified her—but it bears some resemblance to interwar era sentiments and patient evaluations of their feelings. And it was a need that the asylum was, at least in theory, designed to accommodate.

Harboring mental tumults without a place to express them or to take shelter from them was the potential lot of the "postmodern" patient. As journalist Meghan O'Rourke writes, "Today's version of the sanatorium is the Internet, where you find a vaporous world of fellow-sufferers, companions in isolation and fear and frustration."[19] There is, of course, a palpable presence of the "mad" in Internet cultures, in websites, for example, that encourage people to discuss their experiences with mental illness, and these venues have themselves provided solace to those who are suffering, perhaps owing to their anonymity or their capacity to share testimonials.[20] In O'Rourke's depiction, though, the Internet is more of an audience than a community, and certainly not a place. As literal as it is, perhaps the physicality of a place does matter after all.

By the century's end, the plummeting numbers of deinstitutionalized patients were quite stark.[21] Some states did indeed try to respect the mission of community care and rehabilitation by integrating federal entitlement programs for medical care with community mental health services.[22] But the Reagan administration had renounced plans under Jimmy Carter's Mental Health Systems Act of 1980 to set up 1,500 small clinics across America rather than large public hospitals, something that would have provided federal funding for these clinics.[23] Between 1980 and 1988, domestic spending more broadly in the United States dropped by more than a third, and some of this spending was directly relevant for people suffering with mental illness.[24] Transinstitutionalization continued, to general hospitals and nursing homes most centrally, and to prisons at worst, while homelessness accelerated.[25] As early as 1984, an American Psychiatric Association report, *The Homeless Mentally Ill*, denounced the effects of deinstitutionalization on people with mental illnesses, particularly the rise of homelessness.[26] In his 1994 study *The Homeless*, sociologist Christopher Jencks blamed the rise in homelessness in contemporary America on theorists of social control such as Michel Foucault and Erving Goffman, who had been so unrelenting in their portraits of the mental hospital as an embodiment of social oppression, a position that has been supported by some medical historians.[27] For these observers, the "shame of the states" inside the "total institution" was at least better than homelessness.

In fact, a sense of powerlessness or that there was nowhere to turn ironically bred in some patients and their observers a desire to return to the era of the institution. In a 2002 interview about mental illness in their family, the Mosers discussed their forty-eight-year-old son David, who suffered from schizophrenia. They told a harrowing story of the night he broke into his parents' house and beat them badly, almost killing one of them. The son disappeared; he later went to jail. The Moser family felt "angry on behalf of our son and the thousands like him who have suffered needlessly for years when court-mandated treatment could have relieved the terrible symptoms of their mental illnesses."[28]

Sociologist David Karp has noted that "it frequently shocks family caregivers that they cannot get a person hospitalized when the severity of their illness seems so transparently clear. In the middle of a family crisis, debates about the 'rights' of the mentally ill seem irrelevant."[29] How did it come to be that a concept of "human rights" could be so bloodless, and such an abstraction, that in the name of respecting its principles people were left to suffer? It is a logical question, given these testimonials. However, it is somewhat of an ahistorical question that ignores the legacy of the exploitations of the carceral state over the course of the twentieth century. The question also neglects a recognition of the many elements of both horror and solace that mental institutions have encompassed.

Human rights for the mentally ill have tended to enshrine privacy rights and the right to be let alone above the rights to care and protection, again reinforcing broader privatization strategies, in the broadest sense of the term, of the late twentieth century. A document given to Saint Elizabeths Hospital patients in the 1980s, for instance, states that the first patient right is to "privacy and dignity," including visiting "in private with family and friends," conducting "private telephone conversations," and having access to medical records in accordance with the Privacy Act of 1974, as well as mailing and receiving unopened correspondence. These privacy rights came before item number 15 on the list, which was "safe, sanitary, and humane living conditions," as though these were incidental compared to the integrity of patient privacy.[30] Moreover, there was no mention of a "right" to the solace of a community, perhaps because even with patient recreation activities as forms of gentle social engineering there was never a guarantee of something so elusive. Still, this enumeration of rights provides a stark contrast to the document the Brattleboro Retreat patient received, some forty years earlier, "How to Keep Sane in a Hospital for Mental Patients," that promoted an ideal of resignation and reminded the patient simply to make the best of the situation.

Though a promoter of psychopharmaceuticals and a critic of psychiatric institutionalization, psychiatrist Nathan Kline also feared a loss of communal selfhood in the face of deinstitutionalization. In 1974, he wrote that among the aged who are experiencing mental deterioration, "loneliness is the most acute problem. People need a sense of community, a sense of belonging to a group that provides strength and comfort while giving a larger focus to their lives."[31] He was distressed by the prospect of "those who find themselves aged and alone in that furnished room in the midst of an uncaring city. . . . Their mates are dead, their children scattered to far places, their life connections all broken off or fast disappearing. Sometimes one sees such people feeding the pigeons in the park, and one can sense by their very attitude that it is almost their only outlet."[32] Could the community of the asylum be an alternative to lonely urbanism, or even function, as in this portrait, as a type of anti-urbanism in late twentieth-century American life?[33] Though not expressly calling for reinstitutionalization to recapture these lost communities, by the 1980s, some mental health professionals also were starting to doubt the efficacy of community mental health care, even as they recognized its attempts to forswear dependency on hospitals.[34]

Patients themselves, in non-retrospective accounts at the century's end, expressed some ambivalence about the existence of the institution, reflecting on the strangely compelling parts of existing in public space with other sufferers, something that I have suggested was more likely to animate patients from the vantage point of the interwar era. While Susan Sontag famously gave expression to a sense of universal loss in leaving the "kingdom of the well" for the "kingdom of the sick,"[35] there also could be a feeling of wistfulness in the other direction as well. In 1991, Governor Lowell Weicker of Connecticut, a politician known for his advocacy of the rights of people with disabilities, and who wanted to render disability a central civil rights issue, received a remarkable unpublished essay about what it is like to be diagnosed with schizophrenia and being in and out of hospitals for thirty-five years. During one of this patient's first breakdowns, he was taken to Fairfield Hills State Mental Hospital in Connecticut, where, he noted, some graffiti on a brick wall said, "'If you are here, we hope you are still alive.'" In his telling, the psychiatric hospital, as in interwar era perceptions of them, was a place where "you have plenty of time to think about your personal emergency in the nuthouse. Captive in a psychological zoo, you roll with the punches through strange days adjusting to the wacky environment created by squeezing so many psychotics into one place at one time."[36]

Life beyond the hospital for him was both wonderful and discombobulating. After this "intense company and companionship of the ward, I found myself 'alone' again, aging quietly in the suburbs of New York City. The contrast between the great outdoors and the stifling ward was absolute and startling. To live beyond the locked doors of the hospital was a great relief and an even greater freedom to savor."[37] This is hardly a ringing endorsement for the existence of psychiatric hospitals: they are so confining that they make one grateful for daily life, or for the things previously taken for granted. And yet it was the subsociety of the hospital that forced this reconsideration. He was still reflecting on his fellow patients in the hospital, who "take me in stride. They have their own 'visions' which they have shared with me. Our somewhat similar sufferings have made us friends behind the walls of mental institutions."[38] According to him, "you make friends out of absolute necessity not to be alone in crazyness."[39] And he now often thought about the "tortured faces I have seen in the nuthouse. We were alone together facing the unfaceable. We helped each other discover our own humanity that enabled us to reach out through the madness and be friends concerned about each other's well being." He even felt that he had "healed from breakdowns and psychotic episodes not through the institutional efforts of shrinks as much as from other human beings classified as schizophrenics. They were my profound company in times of utmost distress," perhaps because he "saw myself in other schizophrenics I was herded together with. Something inexplicably good occurred between us on the wards together where the night is long and the day promises no relief other than in the power of a friend's eyes."[40] This letter recalls meditations on the emotional intensity of the "thrown-ness" inside the asylum from the interwar era. Was the hospital one of the only late twentieth-century institutions that allowed for this kind of embrace of strangers?

This is not to suggest that critiques of psychiatric institutions and the establishment that animated 1960s and 1970s counterculture had simply dissipated into nostalgia by the century's end. The story I have told throughout this book has been one of resignation and apparent passivity giving way to a more hopeful and active sensibility. Ironically, it might have been the hospital itself, in encouraging ideals of participation and activity, that eroded the ideal of a passive, resigned, and potentially deferential institutional subject.

An engagement with science that the hospital embodies also, at least on the surface, contributed to a more hopeful and active sensibility. But there were ample fissures in ideas about psychiatric cures and scientific values writ large, ones that became especially pronounced in the early post–World War II era when patients and their advocates cast more doubt on the nature of these cures, seeing them as being implicated in enforced patient passivity and apathy, even in the name of overcoming these states. Especially during the last third of the twentieth century, social critics challenged and questioned the psychiatric establishment, sometimes by juxtaposing it against the insights engendered by mental illnesses.

Radical movements like "anti-psychiatry" went even further, condemning the "militant ideology of the cure" itself as being anything but utopian and something that simply integrated a patient into the "medical-industrial" system, reimagining and radicalizing the critiques of those at midcentury who found psychosurgery anti-humanist. The anti-psychiatry critique did not abate during the waning decades of the twentieth century. In his 1986 book, Lenny Lapon, for example, condemned psychiatrists as "mass murderers in white coats," referring to a "psychiatric genocide" in Nazi Germany and in the United States.[41] While the patient voices that I have uncovered here do complicate the anti-psychiatry vision, and even pose a challenge to it, the movement was still condemning medicalization and the category of madness by the century's end, illuminating the social construction and reification of mental illness. In so doing, the anti-psychiatry movement on the one hand and the supporters of biological models of psychiatry on the other exemplified larger debates regarding the nature of reality that so ignited broader American social thought in the late twentieth century. Social constructionists believed that meanings in general were socially created rather than inhering in phenomena in the world.[42] They were unlikely to agree with psychiatrist

Harvey L. Ruben, who pronounced in 1986 that "there is such a thing as mental illness. We did not invent it."[43]

Imagery of the automaton and the validation of an array of emotional expression were still quite striking in anti-psychiatry rhetoric by the end of the twentieth century. Activist Leonard Roy Frank, the cofounder of the Network Against Psychiatric Assault, found himself with a large platform to talk about anti-psychiatry ideas in the *Hospital and Community Psychiatry* in 1986, published by the American Psychiatric Association. Frank, an editor of *Madness Network News*, a paper of the Mental Patient Liberation Movement, had been an involuntary psychiatric patient in the early 1960s at Twin Pines Hospital outside of San Francisco and came to think that electroshock treatment in particular should always be voluntary. Here, Frank took aim at biological psychiatry, faulting it for a "loss of creativity, apathy." And he spoke against the major tranquilizers, such as Thorazine, as well as anti-depressants in the vein of lithium, among others, suggesting that these drugs were responsible for "zombielike states" in psychiatric facilities and even among deinstitutionalized people.[44] Where once during the interwar era a general sense of emotionlessness could connote peacefulness, and then by the midcentury connoted amoral and reckless scientists, as well as a dubious political comportment, it had become, by the late twentieth century, a simpler, more aesthetic form of terror of an inability to express an array of emotions and by the century's end a person whom psychiatry had rendered less than fully human.

Anti-psychiatry ideas were increasingly open to challenge by the end of the twentieth century, though, and not just on the part of medical practitioners. Skepticism about the reality of mental illness also could seem a callous disregard of people's suffering.[45] After legal scholar and author Elyn Saks, who suffered from schizophrenia, left the Institute of Pennsylvania Hospital where she had stayed for three months during the early 1980s, she was hoping to live her life beyond the hospital and without anti-psychotic medications. After her release, she was visiting her parents in Miami and felt that she was exerting a "constant effort to keep reality on one side and delusions on the other." Her father, however, delivered a "'buck up—get tough'" speech to her, telling her that she did not have "terminal cancer" and that schizophrenia was a "piece of cake by comparison."[46] The fact that he could still make this argument in the 1980s shows not only how enduring the theme of the perceived willful character or self-indulgence of mental illness was but how compelling the need to see illness as "real" and biological could be among those who were trying to ascertain care and sympathy.

Perhaps this is why during the final decades of the twentieth century the National Alliance of the Mentally Ill (NAMI) continued to follow the "same as any other sickness" model of the midcentury, acknowledging the biological beings of those with mental illnesses. A poster that NAMI created in 1999 for elementary students said, "Brains can get sick, too" but with "treatment they can get better!"[47] As an advocacy group of parents and friends of those with mental illness or mental disabilities, NAMI drew from more of a model of liberal rights, even consumer rights, than a radical activist model of anti-psychiatry. NAMI started with about 250 members in 1979 but had about 140,000 members by 1993. It supported the Americans with Disabilities Act in 1990 and sought greater insurance coverage for those with mental illness.[48] In its original incarnation, the organization was primarily for people who felt that psychiatry had harmed their loved ones. But it would come to subscribe to the view that mental illness was a biological condition, rooted in biochemical problems in the brain.[49] Harboring a reverential tone about mental illness, NAMI discouraged irony or dark or casual humor, something that once animated interwar era patient cultural expression and arguably encouraged a more critical posture toward the hospital and therapeutic cultures writ large. In a 1999 board game that NAMI developed for middle schoolers, for example, a student could move forward a point if he/she "resisted the urge to laugh" when "your friends called someone a 'mental'" but needed to "move back 2" if "you used 'nut house' to refer to a psychiatric hospital."[50]

If NAMI embraced medicalization, other late twentieth-century critics continued to feel apprehensive about its encroaching quality. Strikingly, most of this uneasiness was about biological psychiatry outside of the context of a psychiatric hospital. Sometimes this took the form of anxiety about pathologization of ordinary emotions and traits; the classification of "kinds" of people that appear to call into existence and change those who have been classified; or a general sense of "psychiatrization" of all society.[51] For example, philosopher Lou Marinoff was alarmed by the expanding categories of mental illness, noting the proliferation of DSM disorders. Others felt that selling psychoactive drugs was the corollary of selling mental disorders.[52] As literary critic Eric Cazdyn points out, the majority of the world's population would consider the idea of "too much medical care" something of a luxury.[53] These fears of the overextension of health care are not just Western; they are contemporary and specific to the end of the twentieth century and turn of the twenty-first, as interwar era patients did not voice the same disquiet about the intrusiveness of the medical realm. Perhaps they were more willing to think of themselves as part of a scientific community of knowledge and did not have the same anxiety about the role of the patient overcoming the role of the citizen, as the mental hospital as an institution tried to suggest that the two were quite intertwined.

Even amid the psychopharmaceutical revolution of the late twentieth century that at least on the surface made the hospital irrelevant, those experiencing mental distress still felt a substantial ambivalence about biological psychiatry. During the 1990s, feminist sociologist Kate Millett received testimonials primarily from women about their experiences with psychiatric hospitalization and with psychotropic drugs at a moment when third-generation psychopharmacology was just coming into being.[54] Though Millett was known for her academic study of patriarchy and memoirs about sexuality in the 1970s, she also became a central figure within the American anti-psychiatry movement after she wrote her 1990 memoir, *The Loony-Bin Trip*, which discusses her psychiatric hospitalization, her diagnosis of bipolar disorder, and her struggles with lithium, which she felt produced "blanked-out women" who "only mumbled to themselves."[55] This iteration of the automaton spoke to the complicated second wave feminist relationship to the psychiatric establishment, and especially to psychotropic drugs: as historian David Herzberg notes, liberation from "mother's little helper" was a key platform of second wave feminism,[56] and this could be a template transposed upon other drugs.

One testimonial that Millett received came from a woman who acknowledged the exploitations of involuntary institutionalization, while still calling for a nuanced view of psychiatry in the broadest sense. In 1992 she told Millett that she felt a huge catharsis after reading *The Loony-Bin Trip*; she had been haunted by a memory of her own forced psychiatric treatments in 1977 when she was "handcuffed and taken from my . . . home and put in a Patrol Wagon. My children and neighbors watched this once bright affable mother of three . . . stunned." She avowed that the "memory of horror will never leave." While she believed Millett was right in noting "how anxious everyone is to 'get you help,'" nonetheless the "low side"[57] of depression, in her experience, was unstintingly awful. In fact, in this woman's portrait, the terror of that intense depression equaled, though perhaps did not justify, the terror of involuntary hospitalization. She characterized her low side as a state of ination with "no music, no words, no colors or flowers. No love. My only wish was to cease to exist. Somehow I never actually attempted suicide, although I thought of nothing but it." This is not to say this letter writer romanticized psychiatric treatment; in fact, she recalled that while taking anti-psychotic medications she "walked with the mental patient gait. The Stelazine Shuffle. I hated the woman treating me."[58] Nonetheless, she noted, she reached different conclusions about her experiences than Millett did about hers and even appeared to find some solace in categories of mental illness. "I feel somehow comforted to 'give away' that high behavior to 'mania' and the disappearance of myself to 'Depression,'" she wrote. "I believe I was 'mad.'"[59]

This letter marks an implicit departure from anti-psychiatry thinkers who were wary of medical taxonomy as an intellectual tradition. If there was a human rights violation to contemplate in this view, perhaps it was not treating the suffering. This discussion again illuminates fraught ideological disputes about the existence of biological mental illness in late twentieth-century psychiatry, most poignantly on display in the 1984–1985 case of Rafael Osheroff, a forty-two-year-old patient suffering from depression admitted to Chestnut Lodge in 1979, who received psychoanalytically oriented psychotherapy and then sued the hospital for negligence, as he believed his depression worsened under this treatment.[60]

David Herzberg has referred to the 1990s as the "age of antidepressants,"[61] which highlighted in a highly public way the biochemical causes of illness, again reinforcing images of biological beings who existed outside of institutional contexts. A new generation of drugs used primarily as anti-depressants, most famously Prozac (1987), a selective serotonin reuptake inhibitor, betokened a shift in the conception of biological concepts of illness and feelings themselves, which now could be perceived as consequences of neurochemistry, as simply a matter of adjusting one's serotonin levels, a more purely materialist view.[62] As Tipper Gore said in 1999, when discussing her own depression, serotonin levels were low in depressed people, and "your brain needs a certain amount of serotonin and when you run out of that, it's like running out of gas."[63]

By the 1980s and 1990s, the existence of psychopharmaceuticals that purported to adjust these levels provoked both approval and dissent, as well as a debate about the ethics of enhancement, and even allegations of posthumanism (in this instance an individual dependent on scientific intervention that tampers with an authentic self) in their wake. For some, these drugs could restore psychiatry to the more grandiose hopes ascribed to psychosurgeries in the interwar era; others compared psychopharmaceutical success to antibiotics in their profound sociocultural influence.[64] In the 1970s and 1980s, when psychiatric publics were newly digesting deinstitutionalization, there was still some grasping around at another kind of institution; by the end of the century, that hope for the future seemed not to be social but biological. If there were not always other places for loved ones, there was still a hope of better medicine. In this rendering, psychopharmaceuticals were not the nefarious agents of political complicity but abettors of an enlivened or at least renewed agent, something that countercultural critics and anti-psychiatrists insisted could only come from the natural self.

Such positive portraits coexisted with emerging alarm about the nature of anti-depressants, including patient testimonials of their unsettling and disturbing experiences or dearth of emotional expression while taking them, at the 1991 Food and Drug Administration (FDA) Prozac Hearings, in just one prominent example. In fact, much as psychopharmaceuticals hold an iconic place in pop culture, literary culture, and psychiatric lore, many observers who contemplated them—and biological or "neurochemical selfhood" more broadly—did not unequivocally embrace them.[65] "The decade of the brain," as a proclamation issued by President George H. W. Bush in 1991 on behalf of the National Institute of Mental Health named the 1990s,[66] was not without its dissenters, or at least those who hesitated to ascribe so much of the individual will to the brain. It is difficult to know where to place "brainhood" in relation to "selfhood," let alone possessive individualism; brainhood could be said to heighten it. As sociologist Nikolas Rose writes, in a neuro-ontology, human beings are not brains but have brains; for him, a new kind of biologization, or a new kind of biopolitics and biological citizenship, had taken shape in the late twentieth century and especially in the early twenty-first century as psychiatry increasingly became bound up with the realm of neuroscience, as well as brain activities said to correspond to emotional states such as those offered in PET scans and MRIs.[67] Scientific medicine in this incarnation again occupies civic and public life quite dramatically; psychiatry, as Charles Barber ominously put it, was "in our blood streams."[68] Patients also shared in these fears of becoming bodies rather than individuals. "We expect more from our bodies than previous generations did,"[69] pronounced historian Jonathan Sadowsky. And yet, we are also wary of being reduced to biological material, or becoming, as journalist Ethan Watters has put it, a "batter of chemicals we carry around in the mixing bowls of our skulls."[70]

Psychosurgeries took on an extra dimension of urgency amid this mood of ambivalence about biological psychiatry, given the fraught historical legacy that has been so difficult for these treatments to shed. Though biological psychiatry such as electroconvulsive therapy as a treatment largely disappeared from most American psychiatric hospitals by 1980, it was revived later in that decade and during the 1990s, upon the recommendation of the American Psychiatric Association that suggested that ECT could relieve the symptoms of severe depression.[71] For writer and mental health activist Andy Behrman, ECT was a last resort. He was hospitalized at Gracie Square Hospital in New York City during the mid-1990s after struggling with what was then still called manic depression throughout his twenties. He was unsettled by the prospect of memory loss after ECT. Any connotations of brain damage, naturally, "scare[d] the shit out of me. Am I going to become a permanent zombie, forced to return to the suburbs to live with my parents?"[72] There is no political allegory here per se: becoming a "zombie" will not make him a potential Nazi, as it might have been conjured during the war era, just a failure at adult life, a non-productive member of society, and was discomfiting for this alone. After his first treatment, he notes in a somewhat ambivalent register that "my brain has been reset like a windup toy."[73]

Yet for every call to resist devolving into biochemistry or simply biological material, there was another call to biology. Danquah, for example, felt that her friends ascribed too much to the social context of her feelings, to such an extent that they felt her depression should be easily vanquishable when it was anything but. She had conversations with Black women about her depression in the vein of, "'What do you have to be depressed about? If our people could make it through slavery, we can make it through anything.'"[74] Perhaps the medical model could at least offer assurances of a "right" to mental illness. In her account of bipolar disorder, anthropologist Emily Martin says of the medical model: "I often heard from my psychiatrist that my problems were related to my neurotransmitters, and I always found this comforting. I took this to mean that my problems were not entirely within my control."[75] This comment suggests a need to have an unintentional self validated, and perhaps this was even more poignant for African American patients who were still not permitted the "luxury" of mental illness.

Contemporary contradictions surrounding neurochemical selfhood are quite compelling during a moment when some social observers of the early twenty-first century have noted an age of "anti-scientific revolution,"[76] wherein science and its empirical and objective habits of mind are readily questioned, discarded, and politicized, whether this is about vaccinations or global warming. At the same time, literary critic David B. Morris has argued that Americans now "live in a culture saturated with scientific explanations and assumptions," including assumptions about cures.[77] Literary critic Eric Cazdyn disputes claims about the casualness of the cure with his take on chronicity, arguing that there is a "new chronic mode in medicine" that has displaced utopian curing with practical management.[78] He argues that both utopian medical cures and utopian, revolutionary politics have fallen out of favor as strategies or hopes. "Chronicity," from the standpoint of the late twentieth and early twenty-first centuries, in this interpretation, has become a mode of acceptance of late or chronic capitalism, in the sense that planetary, economic, and health crises are largely taken for granted as chronic, and this pervasive sense of acceptance precludes radical possibilities in the vein of political revolutions and medical cures alike.[79] This idea of twenty-first-century chronicity seems curiously akin to a sensibility of inevitable sorrow that animated the interwar era.

But the idea of cures has been more complicated for mental illness, especially since the anxiety about what the cure could produce has been so striking over the course of the postwar period and fears of scientism have run alongside and complicated these utopian aspects of the cure. Psychiatrist and historian Robert J. Lifton notes that the "image of cure lends itself to the restorative myth of state violence,"[80] a compelling observation about twentieth-century totalitarianism and its legacies. While a psychiatric observation of the late twentieth century is that Americans have unequivocally and uncritically embraced the idea of being "better than well,"[81] which some bioethicists see as a uniquely American ideal and late twentieth-century identity, there has always been substantial disquiet and uncertainty about this ideal, a ready willingness to acknowledge the post-humanist nightmare lurking in the fantasy of enhancement.

I also have suggested that an uneasiness with cures, psychiatric treatments, and psychiatric hospitalizations has been bound up, since the late modern postwar period, with a dread of the automaton. One area where contemporaries are not so contradictory is in their confidence in the idea that engagement and activity are always preferable to disinvestment and inertia, a confidence that I hope this book has troubled simply by demonstrating that interwar era patients and their observers could perceive inertia as a kind of peacefulness. This cultural and medical anxiety has grown even more profound over time, from a politically dubious and socially conformist automaton at midcentury to a robot who is aesthetically and creatively offensive in the late twentieth century.

The automaton was still a disquieting figure at the turn of the millennium—even if one less likely to be institutionalized. The "flattened" emotions that some claimed they experienced with psychopharmaceuticals are striking here. For example, Danquah said that when she was taking Zoloft, "there was no good or bad, I just stopped feeling. It was like being glued on top of the fence that separated pain from pleasure; nothing could transport me to the other side, either side."[82] Emily Martin notes that to some degree "madness" itself has become conflated with the idea of the automaton: a contemporary anthropological "study describes the fear of madness as the terror of looking into the eyes of a mentally ill person and seeing no answering comprehension."[83] Moreover, as Edith Sheffer notes in her work on autism, while overemotional women were once pathologized in the nineteenth century, a more prominent social apprehension in the early twenty-first century has become underemotional boys, and they are the ones who now get pathologized.[84] But perhaps this anxiety about underemotionality that she so powerfully evokes transcends little boys and is a more all-encompassing one about contemporary automatons who cannot produce and cannot feel. Perhaps the twenty-first-century incarnation of the automaton is the much deplored image of a zombie staring at a screen instead of talking face-to-face, an embodiment of the "digital affect,"[85] rather than the blithely oblivious staring out an institutional window.

Does the contemporary automaton carry with it the same sensibility of resignation as the interwar era automaton did? The acceptance of the way things are was predicated on the idea that life was inherently tragic. But this tragic sensibility altered to a more optimistic one, or at least a more expectant one, entrenched in a more firmly scientifically utopian hope, during an era of midcentury biological psychiatry, until those utopian dreams too were exposed for their shortcomings. But this did not mean that midcentury Americans returned to simple acceptance of the suffering and misfortunes of life as inevitabilities. In fact, the political realities of the time, most prominently the possibilities of global totalitarianism, demanded that one be alert and awake and self-aware enough not to succumb to dangerous inertia and massification, just as the social and political tumults of the late twentieth century, and the overthrowing of traditions and received wisdom, demanded a sense of activism and resistance rather than passivity and acquiescence.

Moreover, the "public" that public mental health messages were trying to reach changed over time as well. By the late twentieth century, this public was perhaps more cynical about government advice and the culture of experts, about the advertisements of "big pharma," and perhaps even more so about the specter of the mental hospital, and often owing to well-documented, historical precedence. Why should anyone trust the government, or the market, or even human institutions with good intentions for establishing communities, given their multiple and chronicled failings and exploitations over the course of the twentieth century? And what human institutions were even on anyone's radar in the late twentieth century? The exposé stories about the midcentury psychiatric hospital are not especially well known today. When critic Lisa Duggan argued that a neoliberal vision was animated by "attacks on public institutions and spaces for democratic public life" during the 1980s and 1990s, she probably did not have the psychiatric hospital in mind.[86] And yet the founders and observers of some of these public institutions did indeed have democracy on their minds, especially the relationship between the individual and the community. Perhaps Freud's well-known lament that finding an accommodation between the claim of the individual and the "cultural claims of the group"[87] presents an irreconcilable conflict is most uniquely on view from within a psychiatric hospital.

On the surface, the more widespread use and prescription of psychopharmaceuticals powerfully suggest the existence of a readily available cure, as well as the overthrow of both psychotherapy and the hospital by the medical model, as though the hospital was simply a distant force or an anachronism that nobody gave thought to any longer by the century's end, other than as an extreme threat that loomed in the background as it had in the psychopharmaceutical ads of the 1970s.[88] But just as the trajectory of biology overthrowing psychoanalysis was never definitive or unambiguous, even in earlier eras of biological psychiatry, the rejection of the hospital ideal was never definitive either, at least in the diffuse sense that patients and families yearned for communal settings of solace. One of Millett's 1992 letter writers told her that she had been diagnosed as manic depressive in 1986 and that she had "lost a job over it, been incarcerated forcibly, been stereotyped as 'crazy', and all the while my family insists it never happened and we won't talk about it." This woman had recently taken in a roommate because "I wanted someone to talk to, someone to share the deepest, most intimate and awkward thoughts—feelings—of my life. But all I find myself is alone, still depressed, angry to the point of erupting and still walking on the edge."[89] Institutions like the asylum were supposed to make a patient suffering like this feel as though she had a haven from misunderstanding and taciturn family members, from life on the streets, or from the judgments of others and a compassionate witness to all the troubles that others could not understand.

Perhaps it makes sense, then, that there is a mass fascination with the abandoned asylum, since these institutions can represent that diffuse, never realized hope for the care of the mentally ill or for ideals in caring relationships. They also represent the withering away of the concept of a curative environment, and perhaps even the death knell of the philosophy of nineteenth-century environmentalism and moral treatment that undergirded the asylum. The erosion of the asylum suggests a diminishment of faith in institutional care that so thickly populated this nineteenth-century American landscape, whether in the form of almshouses or orphanages.[90] Perhaps the reason twenty-first-century observers are so moved by the ruins of asylums is not solely a prurient or voyeuristic fascination with paranormal activity and ghost sightings or an enchantment with "creepiness," the strange, the sad, and the compelling in people and in buildings alike. Instead, maybe these are not just "abandoned asylums" but abandoned solidarities, sensibilities, and modes of being. Some of these old asylums are being razed to make room for condominiums or other business spaces in the face of much controversy. Asylums are, after all, spiritual sites, if only as sites of death.[91] But outside the contemplation of patient deaths and unclaimed bodies, they are also important sites simply for the contemplation of mental life and its vulnerability and the communities that might assuage them.

When in the 2010s photographer Jon Crispin photographed and displayed the contents of the suitcases of patients left behind at Willard State Hospital in upstate New York between the 1910s and 1960, one twenty-first-century observer described these photos as "chilling"; another described them as "haunting."[92] There is no denying that lives inside the asylum might have been terribly sad and that they might have felt torn asunder from their loved ones and their life before the institution. But why is it "chilling" to see the personal effects of former asylum patients, such as toothbrushes, pieces of clothing, hairbrushes, and family photographs and letters? Is it simply the stark fact of seeing material objects that once belonged to someone now dead, a blurring of life and death? Is this an instance of intertextuality, as the suitcases so powerfully recall concentration camp imagery?[93] Or does this suggest a sense of twenty-first-century protest versus the asylum rather than an earlier twentieth-century pragmatic necessity of accepting it, or simply living it? (See Figure 6.)

Part of the reason these institutions seem so chilling to contemporary observers is that they allegedly enforced the creation of apathetic automatons, a perfect demeanor for contemporary ghosts. How can this lingering fear of

Figure 6. Thelma R's suitcase, Willard State Suitcases. Photo Credit: Jon Crispin
©2020. From the Willard Suitcases Project, willardsuitcases.com.

the automaton be reconciled to contemporary observers who nonetheless
yearn for a more perfected hospital and are drawn to the very sites of them?
It is telling that abandoned asylums themselves have been portrayed whim-
sically and with a sad, disappointed nostalgia, as much as haunting. Some of
these hospitals had life spans that roughly corresponded with the twentieth
century and can be considered mementos of the previous century as well. In
a photograph of Manteno State Hospital in Illinois, for example, which closed
in the 1980s, the sunlight in the abandoned room makes it look as though
there are lights on an empty dance floor (see Figure 7).[94] Could a resurrected
asylum be a form of contemporary humanism?

These perfected hospitals, as many hopeful patients and their caregivers
find out painfully, often do not exist or are as elusive as attempts to revive
and update nineteenth-century forms of moral treatment. This recognition
itself could all but enforce a position of resignation, only now divorced from
the institution. What did resignation look like at the turn of the twenty-first
century? Do older voices about inevitability still exist, or have these been
definitively rejected for rendering one an automaton? Daphne Merkin, upon
deciding not to return to the hospital to get ECT, wrote that even though she

Figure 7. Manteno State Hospital. Photo Credit: Phil Tkacz.

still often thought of committing suicide, "I still live on, take my meds, fight with my daughter, watch dopey TV shows, struggle with writing this book, go to therapy."[95] As this passage suggests, a twenty-first-century incarnation of resignation is perhaps a species of chronicity, of management, of getting through the day to day. But what seems only a passive or a chronic state can, in this respect, be imbued with a hopefulness of endurance, or being philosophical. Wisdom can yet be—often has to be—distilled from resignation.

NOTES

Introduction

1. Letter, October 2, 1928, Superintendent's Correspondence, 1921–1942, Racine County, Racine County Institutions, Box 1, Folder 5, Racine Series 58, State Historical Society of Wisconsin, University of Wisconsin–Parkside Libraries, Archives Department, Kenosha, WI, p. 1. She is quoting the matron, using indirect speech, when she says "extremely nervous and hard to handle."

2. Letter, n.d., but presumably January 1929, given the dates of the surrounding letters. Superintendent's Correspondence, Racine County Institutions, p. 1.

3. Letter, March 13, 1929, Superintendent's Correspondence, Racine County Institutions, p. 1.

4. Eugen Bleuler's work was not published in English until 1950. He argued that dementia praecox, or "the schizophrenias," was a physical disease for which there was no cure. See Bleuler, *Dementia Praecox, or, Group of Schizophrenias* (New York: International Universities Press, [1911] 1950), 40.

5. Lillian A. Cole, "Institutionalitis," *Mental Hospitals* 6, no. 2 (February 1955): 16–17. I use "asylum" when talking about early twentieth-century sources and "mental hospital" for midcentury ones to capture the language of the times. I also think the literal meanings of those labels merit our attention.

6. Christopher Payne and Oliver Sacks, *Asylum: Inside the Closed World of State Mental Hospitals* (Cambridge, MA: MIT Press, 2009), 5.

7. See Marc Augé, *Non-Places: Introduction to an Anthropology of Supermodernity* (London: Verso, [1992] 1995). Augé considers roads, railways, highways, and airports as "non-places" characterized by ephemerality (34, 78). For a discussion on the distinction between places and spaces, see Wilfred M. McClay, "Introduction: Why Place Matters," in *Why Place Matters: Geography, Identity, and Civic Life in Modern America*, ed. McClay and Ted V. McAllister (New York: Encounter Books, 2015), 1–6 at 3. Here he notes that places tend to be imbued with "human meaning" while spaces connote something more "inert, a mere space."

8. Susan Neiman, *Why Grow Up? Subversive Thoughts for an Infantile Age* (New York: Farrar, Straus, and Giroux, 2014), 3.

9. On the automaton as being a slightly "off" human, see Minsoo Kang, *Sublime Dreams of Living Machines: The Automaton in the European Imagination* (Cambridge, MA: Harvard University Press, 2011), 4.

10. See, for example, Richard Noll, *American Madness: The Rise and Fall of Dementia Praecox* (Cambridge, MA: Harvard University Press, 2011), 19; James Moran, "Architectures of Madness: Informal and Formal Spaces of Treatment and Care in 19th Century New Jersey,"

in *Madness, Architecture and the Built Environment: Psychiatric Spaces in Historical Context*, ed. Leslie Topp, James E. Moran, and Jonathan Andrews, (New York: Routledge, 2007), 151–171; and Gerald N. Grob, *The Mad Among Us: A History of the Care of America's Mentally Ill* (New York: Free Press, 1994), 23–53. On psychoanalysis's minimal impact in these institutions, see Nathan Hale, *The Rise and Crisis of Psychoanalysis in the United States: Freud and the Americans, 1917–1985* (New York: Oxford University Press, 1995), 58.

11. Curing in psychiatry has always been fraught and uncertain, reminiscent of oncology, wherein being mentally "healthy" is akin to being in a state of remission. See Alex Beam, *Gracefully Insane: The Rise and Fall of America's Premier Mental Hospital* (New York: Public Affairs, 2001), 169. On psychosurgeries, see Chapter 2; Mical Raz, *The Lobotomy Letters: The Making of American Psychosurgery* (Rochester, NY: University of Rochester Press, 2013); and Jonathan Sadowsky, *Electroconvulsive Therapy in America: The Anatomy of a Medical Controversy* (New York: Routledge, 2016).

12. See Chapter 3, as well as exposé literature such as Albert Deutsch, *The Shame of the States* (New York: Arno Press, [1948] 1973).

13. For a conservative view on rights as a kind of entitlement, see James T. Patterson, *Grand Expectations: The United States, 1945–1974* (New York: Oxford University Press, 1996), 562–592. On the interaction of civil and human rights, and a deepening awareness of the suffering of others, particularly by the late twentieth century, see Mark Philip Bradley, *The World Reimagined: Americans and Human Rights in the Twentieth Century* (Cambridge: Cambridge University Press, 2016), 223ff. On the emergence of the Black body as a bearer of rights and the synergies between this idea and the right to health care, see Dennis A. Doyle, *Psychiatry and Racial Liberalism in Harlem, 1936–1968* (Rochester, NY: University of Rochester Press, 2016), 13. On rights consciousness more broadly, see Michael Schudson, *The Rise of the Right to Know: Politics and the Culture of Transparency, 1945–1975* (Cambridge, MA: Harvard University Press, 2015), 26, 175.

14. On midcentury liberalism, see Jefferson Cowie, *The Great Exception: The New Deal and the Limits of American Politics* (Princeton, NJ: Princeton University Press, 2016), 9 and Anne E. Parsons, *From Asylum to Prison: Deinstitutionalization and the Rise of Mass Incarceration After 1945* (Chapel Hill: University of North Carolina Press, 2018), 56. On neoliberalism, see Chapter 5, and Wendy Brown, *Undoing the Demos: Neoliberalism's Stealth Revolution* (Brooklyn, NY: Zone Books, 2015), 17, 31, 37, 100.

15. On contemporary ambivalence about biochemistry and critiques of it, see Charles Rosenberg, "Contested Boundaries: Psychiatry, Disease and Diagnosis," *Perspectives in Biology and Medicine* 49, no. 3 (2006): 407–424 at 417 and the introduction to Charles E. Rosenberg and Janet Golden, eds., *Framing Disease: Studies in Cultural History* (New Brunswick, NJ: Rutgers University Press, 1992), xvi.

16. On cultural histories that have tried to establish the critical capacities of the consumer, see, for example, Susan Smulyan, *Popular Ideologies and Mass Culture at Mid-Century* (Philadelphia: University of Pennsylvania Press, 2010); Elena Razlogova, *The Listener's Voice: Early Radio and the American Public* (Philadelphia: University of Pennsylvania Press, 2011); and Nan Enstad, "Popular Culture," in *A Companion to American Cultural History*, ed. Karen Halttunen (New York: Blackwell, 2008), 356–370. Writing about the Tuskegee experiments, Susan M. Reverby urges historians to think beyond the lens or framework of voice and agency, of suffering and resistance, or of victimization and resistance, specifically pertaining to African American medical history. See Reverby, "Suffering and Resistance, Voice and Agency: Thoughts on History and the Tuskegee Syphilis Study," in *Precarious Prescriptions: Contested Histories of Race and*

Health in North America, ed. Laurie B. Green et al. (Minneapolis: University of Minnesota Press, 2014), 261–275 at 262. See also Walter Johnson, "On Agency," *Journal of Social History* 37, no. 1 (Fall 2003): 113–124.

17. See Paul V. Murphy, *The New Era: American Thought and Culture in the 1920s* (Lanham, MD: Rowman and Littlefield, 2012), 22.

18. See Sandra Charron, "Forget Mental Health, We Need to Talk About Mental Illness," *Huffington Post*, June 3, 2015, http://www.huffingtonpost.ca/sandra-charron/mental-illness -mental-health-stigma_b_7500116.html.

19. See Roy Porter's classic essay, "The Patient's View: Doing Medical History from Below," *Theory and Society* 14, no. 2 (March 1985): 175–198. On oral history and the patients' perspective, see Michelle Winslow and Graham Smith, "Ethical Challenges in the Oral History of Medicine," in *The Oxford Handbook of Oral History*, ed. Donald A. Ritchie (Oxford: Oxford University Press, 2011), 372–392 at 377. On historiography that uses oral interviews with patients, here in a British context, see Kerry Davies, "'Silent and Censured Travellers?' Patients' Narratives and Patients' Voices: Perspectives on the History of Mental Illness Since 1948," *Social History of Medicine* 14, no. 2 (2001): 267–292 at 272. For a broader call to chronicle more of the patient's perspective, see Gail Hornstein, *To Redeem One Person Is to Redeem the World: The Life of Frieda Fromm-Reichmann* (New York: Free Press, 2000), 152. A critical mass of historians of psychiatry have indeed heeded this call to do history from the patient's perspective, in and beyond American contexts. See, for example, Matthew Gambino, "Erving Goffman's Asylums and Institutional Culture in the Mid-Twentieth Century United States," *Harvard Review of Psychiatry* 21, no. 1 (January/ February 2013): 52–57 at 53. On patients using the state as a resource, and assertions of citizenship, see Martin Summers, *Madness in the City of Magnificent Intentions: A History of Race and Mental Illness in the Nation's Capital* (New York: Oxford University Press, 2019), 11, 86–87. See also Lykke de la Cour, "'She Thinks This Is the Queen's Castle': Women Patients' Perceptions of an Ontario Psychiatric Hospital," *Health and Place* 3, no. 2 (1997): 131–141; André Cellard and Marie-Claude Thifault, *Une toupie sur la tête: Visages de la folie a Saint-Jean-de-Dieu au tournant du siècle dernier* (Montreal: Boreal, 2007); Geoffrey Reaume, *Remembrance of Patients Past: Patient Life at the Toronto Hospital for the Insane, 1870–1940* (Don Mills, ON: Oxford University Press, 2000), 5, 74. On material culture and memory, see Dolly MacKinnon and Catharine Coleborne, "Seeing and Not Seeing Psychiatry," in *Exhibiting Madness in Museums: Remembering Psychiatry Through Collection and Display*, ed. Coleborne and MacKinnon (New York: Routledge, 2011), 3–13 at 12.

20. Peter Bartlett and David Wright, eds., *Outside the Walls of the Asylum: The History of Care in the Community, 1750–2000* (London: Athlone Press, 1999), vii.

21. See the introduction to L. S. Jacyna and Stephen T. Casper, eds., *The Neurological Patient in History* (Rochester, NY: University of Rochester Press, 2014), 6.

22. Akihito Suzuki, *Madness at Home: The Psychiatrist, the Patient, and the Family in England, 1820–1860* (Berkeley: University of California Press, 2006), 2.

23. See Gerald N. Grob, *Mental Illness and American Society, 1875–1940* (Princeton, NJ: Princeton University Press, 1983), 179, 180, 187. Here he notes that during the early decades of the twentieth century, psychiatrists lost sight of institutionalized patients while instead thinking about mental disease as an abstraction, thus ensuring that patients became "invisible entities." See also Grob, *The Mad Among Us*, 124.

24. Michael Pettit, "Becoming Glandular: Endocrinology, Mass Culture, and Experimental Lives in the Interwar Age," *American Historical Review* 118, no. 3 (October 2013): 1052–1076 at 1057.

25. Lisa M. Hermsen defines an "autopathography" as an "autobiography focused on or inspired by the influence of a disability, disease, or disorder on the author's life." See Hermsen, *Manic Minds: Mania's Mad History and Its Neuro-Future* (New Brunswick, NJ: Rutgers University Press, 2011), 82. As Gail Hornstein notes, despite the success of many memoirs of mental illness, most first-person accounts have not attracted much attention. See Hornstein, *Agnes's Jacket: A Psychologist's Search for the Meanings of Madness* (Ross-on-Wye, Herefordshire: PCCS Books, 2012), xiii, 159.

26. See Suzuki, *Madness at Home*, 2 and Joseph Melling et al., "Families, Communities, and the Legal Regulation of Lunacy in Victorian England: Assessments of Crime, Violence, and Welfare in Admissions to the Devon Asylum, 1845–1914," in *Outside the Walls of the Asylum*, ed. Bartlett and Wright, 153–18 at 153.

27. For a reflection on the category of "lived experience," see Deborah Doroshow, Matthew Gambino, and Mical Raz, "New Directions in the Historiography of Psychiatry," *Journal of the History of Medicine and Allied Sciences* 74, no. 1 (January 2019): 15–33.

28. For commentary on institutional histories and the tradition of social histories in the historiography of American psychiatry, see Mark S. Micale and Roy Porter, "Introduction: Reflections on Psychiatry and Its Histories," in *Discovering the History of Psychiatry*, ed. Micale and Porter (New York: Oxford University Press, 1994), 3–36 at 11. They argue that a 1960s ethos of "anti-statism and anti-institutionalism" has shaped the historiography, emphasizing bleak institutions and confinement, and that the political orientations of these social histories were consciously activist, though they do not suggest that their own history shares in any kind of political consciousness. On this theme, see also Jacyna and Casper, *The Neurological Patient in History*, 6. For historiography that emphasizes social control and the carceral state, see, for example, Ian Dowbiggin, *The Quest for Mental Health: A Tale of Science, Medicine, Scandal, Sorrow, and Mass Society* (New York: Cambridge University Press, 2011); Andrew Scull, *The Insanity of Place/The Place of Insanity: Essays on the History of Psychiatry* (New York: Routledge, 2006); Lisa Appignanesi, *Mad, Bad, and Sad: A History of Women and the Mind Doctors from 1800 to the Present* (London: Virago, 2009); and Parsons, *From Asylum to Prison*, esp. 18 for her definition of the "carceral state." On patient agency and resistance, even in everyday actions, see Elizabeth Lunbeck, *The Psychiatric Persuasion: Knowledge, Gender, and Power in Modern America* (Princeton, NJ: Princeton University Press, 1994) and Joel Braslow, *Mental Ills and Bodily Cures: Psychiatric Treatment in the First Half of the Twentieth Century* (Berkeley: University of California Press, 1997). On patient engagement with the state and patient citizenship, see Summers, *Madness in the City of Magnificent Intentions*.

29. I note here a growing body of cultural and intellectual history in the historiography of American psychiatry in the past ten years. See, for example, Michael E. Staub, *Madness Is Civilization: When the Diagnosis Was Social, 1948–1980* (Chicago: University of Chicago Press, 2011); Sadowsky, *Electroconvulsive Therapy in America*; Deborah Weinstein, *The Pathological Family: Postwar America and the Rise of Family Therapy* (Ithaca, NY: Cornell University Press, 2013); David Herzberg, *Happy Pills in America: From Miltown to Prozac* (Baltimore: Johns Hopkins University Press, 2010); Martin Halliwell, *Therapeutic Revolutions: Medicine, Psychiatry, and American Culture, 1945–1970* (New Brunswick, NJ: Rutgers University Press, 2013); and Troy Rondinone, *Nightmare Factories: The Asylum and the American Imagination* (Baltimore: Johns Hopkins University Press, 2019). On intellectual histories of psychiatry in the European tradition, see, for example, Jan Goldstein, *Console and Classify: The French Psychiatric Profession in the Nineteenth Century* (Cambridge: Cambridge University Press, 1987); Dagmar Herzog, *Cold War Freud: Psychoanalysis in an Age of Catastrophes* (Cambridge: Cambridge University

Press, 2017); and Jane Kromm, *The Art of Frenzy: Public Madness in the Visual Culture of Europe, 1500–1850* (London: Continuum, 2002).

30. On gothic culture and horror culture that have sprung up around the history of psychiatry, see Jenell Johnson, *American Lobotomy: A Rhetorical History* (Ann Arbor: University of Michigan Press, 2014), 7 and Rondinone, *Nightmare Factories*, 25, 187. For the Milledgeville video, see "Greatest Asylum Ghost Pics! Haunted Central State Hospital Milledgeville Georgia!" https://www.youtube.com/watch?v=VsbA4KJQho0. Milledgeville was one of the largest mental hospitals in the United States; it had a capacity of about 15,000 patients at its height during the early postwar era. See Scull, *The Insanity of Place/The Place of Insanity*, 117.

31. See "Pet Show Is a Howling Success," *Mental Hospitals* 9, no. 3 (March 1958): 22; "Volunteer Teaches Puppet Making," *Mental Hospitals* 9, no. 3 (March 1958): 22; and B. F. Peterson and Sidney H. Acuff, "An Experiment in Living," *Mental Hospitals* 6, no. 11 (November 1955): 8–9. This periodical was called *Mental Hospitals* between 1951 and 1965, and would later be called *Psychiatric Services*.

32. On the relationship between history and violence, see Henry Rousso, *The Latest Catastrophe: History, the Present, the Contemporary* (Chicago: University of Chicago Press, 2016), 63.

33. On the possibilities and impossibilities of community formation in concentration camps, see, for example, Tara Zahra, *The Lost Children: Reconstructing Europe's Families After World War Two* (Cambridge, MA: Harvard University Press, 2011), 85. On gulag communities, see Steven A. Barnes, *Death and Redemption: The Gulag and the Shaping of Soviet Society* (Princeton, NJ: Princeton University Press, 2011), 7. On the concept of a wartime "solidarity of the shaken," see Jan Patocka, *Heretical Essays in the Philosophy of History* (Peru, IL: Open Court, [1990] 1996), 131–136. On the idea of the mental hospital as a "subsociety," see Eugene Talbot and Stuart C. Miller, "The Mental Hospital as a Sane Society: Treating Patients as People," *Transaction* (September/October 1965): 2.

34. On these themes, and the idea that disability is the form of diversity that we all eventually share, see Rayna Rapp and Faye Ginsburg, "Enabling Disability: Rewriting Kinship, Reimagining Citizenship," in *Going Public: Feminism and the Shifting Boundaries of the Private Sphere*, ed. Joan Scott (Urbana: University of Illinois Press, 2004), 178–200 at 179.

35. Here she is talking about a refinery worker during the 1970s. Lillian Rubin, *Worlds of Pain: Life in the Working-Class Family* (New York: Basic Books, 1976), 39.

36. Jessie Redmon Fauset, *There Is Confusion* (Boston: Northeastern University Press, [1924] 1989), 179.

37. On ideals of emotional expression and "emotional communities," see Lucien Febvre, "Sensibility and History: How to Reconstitute the Emotional Life of the Past," in *A New Kind of History: From the Writings of Lucien Febvre*, ed. Peter Burke (New York: Routledge, 1973), 12–26. See also Barbara Rosenwein, *Emotional Communities in the Early Middle Ages* (Ithaca, NY: Cornell University Press, 2006), 1–25 and Peter N. Stearns, "Evaluating the Victorian Emotional Style: Causes and Consequences," in *American Cool: Constructing a Twentieth-Century Emotional Style* (New York: New York University Press, 1994), 58–94. See also Alon Confino, *Foundational Pasts: The Holocaust as Historical Understanding* (Cambridge: Cambridge University Press, 2012), 129. Finally, see Daniel Wickberg, "What Is the History of Sensibilities? On Cultural Histories, Old and New," *American Historical Review* 112, no. 3 (June 2007): 661–684 at 669. For him "sensibilities" is something of a protean concept, a "loose affiliation of . . . categories of perception, emotional states, a collective or cultural orientation, moral presupposition, and matters of taste and style."

38. On the censoring of patient mail, among other erosions of patient citizenship rights, see Jack D. Pressman, *Last Resort: Psychosurgery and the Limits of Medicine* (Cambridge: Cambridge University Press, 1998), 163.

39. As historian Joel Braslow has noted, patients' voices within medical notes are "thin, barely audible," and "even when heard, they are almost always refracted through the doctors." Braslow, *Mental Ills and Bodily Cures*, 10. See also Sander L. Gilman, *Difference and Pathology: Stereotypes of Sexuality, Race, and Madness* (Ithaca, NY: Cornell University Press, 1985), 217 and Jacyna and Casper, *The Neurological Patient in History*, 5–6.

40. I am referring specifically here to the institution of the Health Insurance Portability and Accountability Act (HIPAA) in 1996, laws that took effect in 2003. Here, in one example, is a document that describes regulations about access to Illinois's state hospitals. Mental health patient records are closed in Illinois and to access them one needs the patient to sign a release of information: http://www.newberry.org/records-state-mental-hospitals-illinois-state-archives -part-1. On HIPAA itself, see http://www.hhs.gov/ocr/privacy/. For a discussion of the significance of HIPAA, see Anita L. Allen, *Why Privacy Isn't Everything: Feminist Reflections on Personal Accountability* (Lanham, MD: Rowman and Littlefield, 2003), 115; Anita Allen, *Unpopular Privacy: What Must We Hide?* (New York: Oxford University Press, 2011), 114; and Nancy Tomes, *Remaking the American Patient: How Madison Avenue and Modern Medicine Turned Patients into Consumers* (Chapel Hill: University of North Carolina Press, 2016), 268, 394. Finally, see Susan C. Lawrence, *Privacy and the Past: Research, Law, Archives, Ethics* (New Brunswick, NJ: Rutgers University Press, 2016), 14, 15, 50, 66, 111, 118.

41. As Susan C. Lawrence notes, privacy, in general, is a particularly modern and postmodern preoccupation, associated with the rise of bureaucratic states and individual rights. See *Privacy and the Past*, 66. Michael Schudson, in turn, discusses how forcing the NAACP to be open about its membership rolls during the 1950s would have exposed its members to grave danger. See Schudson, *The Rise of the Right to Know*, 275. On the modern tensions in American privacy cultures, between the desire to be left alone and the desire to be known, see Sarah Igo, *The Known Citizen: A History of Privacy in Modern America* (Cambridge, MA: Harvard University Press, 2018), 9.

42. Lawrence, *Privacy and the Past*, 14, 111.

43. "Dear Governor," January 13, 1941, Box 1, Folder 13, Container SG12205, State Institution Files, Dept.: Alabama Governor (1939–1943: Dixon), Alabama Dept. of Archives and History, Montgomery, AL, pp. 1–4 at 4.

44. Darby Penney and Peter Stastny, *The Lives They Left Behind: Suitcases from a State Hospital Attic* (New York: Bellevue Literary Press, 2008), 16.

45. Ibid, 13.

46. Ibid., 31. See also Nathan Flis and David Wright, "'A Grave Injustice': The Mental Hospital and Shifting Sites of Memory," in *Exhibiting Madness in Museums*, ed. Coleborne and MacKinnon, 101–115, especially 102 for their discussion of Danvers State Hospital in Massachusetts. On anonymous graves in abandoned asylums, see Matt Van der Velde, *Abandoned Asylums* (London: Jonglez Publishing, 2016), 222. He notes here that there are 55,000 patients at 17 sites interred anonymously in New York State. He calls these the graves of "thousands of tortured souls" and speaks of them as having been "stripped of dignity" (224).

47. See, for example, on the Remembering with Dignity project in Minnesota, Jennifer Brooks "In Graveyards of State Hospitals, Names Replace Numbers," *Star Tribune*, October 21, 2013, http://www.startribune.com/politics/statelocal/228496201.html.

48. See Elizabeth Lunbeck, "Empathy as a Psychoanalytic Mode of Observation: Between Sentiment and Science," in *Histories of Scientific Observation*, ed. Lorraine Daston and Elizabeth Lunbeck (Chicago: University of Chicago Press, 2011), 255–275 at 256. This is not to claim empathy as an unqualified source of goodness but to allow for a more dialogical relationship between the observer and the observed than voyeurism, the "pornography" of human pain, or the Orientalizing or fetishizing of patients.

49. Here I am indebted to Gail Hornstein's "Bibliography of First-Person Narratives of Madness in English": http://www.gailhornstein.com/files/Bibliography_of_First_Person_Narratives _of_Madness_5th_edition.pdf.

50. See Fernando Vidal, "Brainhood, Anthropological Figure of Modernity," *History of the Human Sciences* 22, no. 1 (2009): 5–36. Gail Hornstein conceives of memoirs of mental illness as a kind of protest literature against psychiatrists and particular treatments, something that has not been the case with memoirs of physical illnesses such as cancer. See Hornstein, *Agnes's Jacket*, 163. The addition of other patient voices that I will explore, such as their personal correspondence, adds more layers of motivations to writing beyond protest, though I do not discount the sometimes express and more implicit political motivations for writing.

51. For a discussion on psychiatrists and morality, see Michael Dudley and Fran Gale, "Through a Glass, Darkly: Nazi Era Illuminations of Psychiatry, Human Rights, and Rights Violations," in *Mental Health and Human Rights: Vision, Praxis, and Courage*, ed. Michael Dudley et al. (Oxford: Oxford University Press, 2012), 211–236 at 223. See also Tod Chambers, *The Fiction of Bioethics* (New York: Routledge, 1999). Chambers shows that it is now common in bioethics to engage with narrative and students are given literature as a springboard to debate concepts of informed consent, euthanasia, etc. (see pp. 1–2).

Chapter 1

1. Jane Hillyer, *Reluctantly Told* (London: Wishart and Company, [1926] 1927), 17.

2. Noll, *American Madness*, 92–93. He likens it to terminal cancer on page 4, while noting that "manic-depression insanity" offered "qualified hope" (99). By the 1930s, as American psychiatry became more interested in Freudian concepts and retreated somewhat from Kraepelinian ideas, the term "schizophrenia" became adopted as the diagnostic term of preference; schizophrenia contained the hope of a cure, while dementia praecox did not (5).

3. Andrew Scull shows that the suicidal and those no longer in possession of self-control were not patients at sanatoriums. He discusses the Battle Creek Sanitarium in Michigan as a prototype of such an institution in the United States. See Scull, *Madness in Civilization: A Cultural History of Insanity from the Bible to Freud, from the Madhouse to Modern Medicine* (Princeton University Press, 2015), 272.

4. Hillyer, *Reluctantly Told*, 74. As Susan J. Hubert notes, Hillyer's memoir bears traces of the similarly titled *A Mind That Found Itself* by Clifford Beers, published in 1908, a best-selling account of his hospitalization for depression with an eye to reform. He would go on to found the National Committee for Mental Hygiene in 1909. See Hubert, *Questions of Power: The Politics of Women's Madness Narratives* (Newark: University of Delaware Press, 2002), 68 and Mary Elene Wood, *The Writing on the Wall: Women's Autobiography and the Asylum* (Urbana, IL: University of Illinois Press, 1994), 136.

5. On "moral treatment" specifically, see Grob, *The Mad Among Us*, 27, 65, 69. For an interpretation of "moral treatment" as an aspect of social control and management, see Scull, *The Insanity of Place/The Place of Insanity*, 76, 108. See also Benjamin Reiss, *Theaters of Madness:*

Insane Asylums and Nineteenth-Century American Culture (Chicago: University of Chicago Press, 2008), 7. Finally, see Nancy Tomes, *A Generous Confidence: Thomas Story Kirkbride and the Art of Asylum Keeping, 1840–1883* (Cambridge: Cambridge University Press, 1984), 87 on "moral treatment" as straddling scientific and religious values.

6. On late nineteenth-century ideas of custodial care displacing mid-nineteenth-century hopes of moral cures, see Noll, *American Madness*, 19. See also Grob, *Mental Illness and American Society*, 291–292. And on exposés of the harsh realities of asylum life in the late nineteenth century, see Anne Harrington, *Mind Fixers: Psychiatry's Troubled Search for the Biology of Mental Illness* (New York: W. W. Norton, 2019), 6. Jack D. Pressman notes that even as late as the 1930s and 1940s, state mental hospitals were primarily custodial institutions rather than treatment institutions. See *Last Resort*, 162. For a primary document, see Abraham Myerson, *The Inheritance of Mental Diseases* (Baltimore: Williams and Wilkins, 1925), 11. Andrew Scull writes, in turn, that the "specter of chronicity" and the "horde of the hopeless" were quite prominent in the public imagination of the asylum, especially in the late nineteenth and early twentieth centuries. See Scull, *The Insanity of Place/The Place of Insanity*, 108. On curability in the early nineteenth century, see Grob, *The Mad Among Us*, 29, 103; and on chronicity as an emerging, depressing reality of mental hospitals during the late nineteenth and early twentieth centuries, see p. 127.

7. On construction, see Susan Burch and Hannah Joyner, *Unspeakable: The Story of Junius Wilson* (Chapel Hill: University of North Carolina Press, 2007), 43. On patient populations, see Parsons, *From Asylum to Prison*, 47.

8. Murphy, *The New Era*, 22. See also Hale, *The Rise and Crisis of Psychoanalysis in the United States*, 58; Dorothy Ross, "Freud and the Vicissitudes of Modernism in the United States, 1940–1980," in *After Freud Left: A Century of Psychoanalysis in America*, ed. John Burnham (Chicago: University of Chicago Press, 2012), 163–188 at 167; Joel Pfister, "Glamorizing the Psychological: The Politics of the Performances of Modern Psychological Identities," in *Inventing the Psychological: Toward a Cultural History of Emotional Life in America*, ed. Joel Pfister and Nancy Schnog (New Haven, CT: Yale University Press, 1997), 167–200 at 167–168, 172.

9. Gerald Grob also notes that psychiatry was one of the lowest-paid specialties in American medical care between 1927 and 1932. See Grob, *Mental Illness and American Society*, 266. See also Andrew Scull, *Psychiatry and Its Discontents* (Berkeley: University of California Press, 2019), 165–166.

10. Scull, *The Insanity of Place/The Place of Insanity*, 89. Even though the United States joined World War I late in the conflict, about 130,000 Americans died during the war. See Nathan Miller, *New World Coming: The 1920s and the Making of Modern America* (New York: Scribner, 2003), 16. On mental hygiene, see Harrington, *Mind Fixers*, 76 and Grob, *Mental Illness and American Society*, 144–178.

11. On the "expansion of the domestic sphere" into medical spheres, see Margaret Humphreys, *Marrow of Tragedy: The Health Crisis of the American Civil War* (Baltimore: Johns Hopkins University Press, 2013), 14. On the reorganization of health from the home to the hospital between 1900 and the 1930s, see Robert Orsi, *Thank You, St. Jude: Women's Devotion to the Patron Saint of Hopeless Causes* (New Haven, CT: Yale University Press, 1996), 162.

12. See Gerald Grob, "The History of the Asylum Revisited: Personal Reflections," in *Discovering the History of Psychiatry*, ed. Micale and Porter, 260–281 at 276. See also Dowbiggin, *The Quest for Mental Health*, 72 and Parsons, *From Asylum to Prison*, 33.

13. Letter August 21, 1924, Box 14, Folder 4 1919–1924, Bellevue Place Records, Batavia, Illinois State Historical Library, Springfield, pp. 1–2 at 2. Bellevue Place opened in 1867 as a private rest home and sanatorium for women and operated until 1965.

14. The Racine County Insane Asylum opened in 1889 and was alternately known as the Gatliff Asylum. In 1933, the census reported on the educational levels of the patient population admitted to state hospitals in the United States. Out of a total of 65,077 people recorded, 2,771 were college graduates, 9,440 were high school graduates, and 37,800 were "common school" graduates. See William Lane Austin, director, Bureau of the Census, prepared under Dr. Leon E. Truesdell, *Mental Patients in State Hospitals* (Washington, DC: U.S. Government Printing Office, 1934), table 26: First Admissions to State Hospital, by Education and Sex, 1933. Census figures also suggest an overwhelmingly white population among the patients in Wisconsin. In 1923, for example, there were 9,091 patients in state hospitals in Wisconsin: 9,017 white, 50 "Negro," 19 "Indian," and 1 "Chinese." See W. M. Steuart, director, Bureau of the Census, *Patients in Hospitals for Mental Disease* (Washington, DC: U.S. Government Printing Office, 1924), table 68: Color/Race of Patients in Hospitals for Mental Disease, January 1, 1923, by Divisions and States, 116.

15. As Gerald Grob points out, between 1890 and 1940, the number of long-term, chronically ill patients in American mental hospitals had increased dramatically, and many were elderly. Moreover, he notes that between 1903 and 1940, the number of mentally ill patients in state hospitals increased from 150,000 to 445,000. See Grob, *Mental Illness and American Society*, 180, 181. See also Gerald Grob, *From Asylum to Community: Mental Health Policy in Modern America* (Princeton, NJ: Princeton University Press, 1991), 6. Finally, see Grob, *The Mad Among Us*, 120. Grob notes that the aged were more likely during this period to be committed to a mental hospital rather than a poorhouse and that commitment to a hospital might have carried less stigma than pauperism (181). Gail A. Hornstein notes a 25% increase in the number of psychiatric patients in the early twentieth century, including those suffering from schizophrenia or epilepsy and the "senile" elderly, owing to the expansion of the categories of mental illness, new diagnostic methods, and the waning importance of extended family as agents of care. See Hornstein, *To Redeem One Person Is to Redeem the World*, 88.

16. "Dear Mother," June 24, 1922, Box 2, Folder 1, Superintendent's Correspondence, Racine County Institutions, p. 1.

17. See Thomas R. Cole, *The Journey of Life: A Cultural History of Aging in America* (Cambridge: Cambridge University Press, 1992), xxvi. On a style of resignation as fatalism and acceptance of God's will, prevalent in the nineteenth century, see Emily K. Abel, *The Inevitable Hour: A History of Caring for Dying Patients in America* (Baltimore: Johns Hopkins University Press, 2013), 136.

18. John Williams, *Stoner* (New York: New York Review of Books, 1965), 4.

19. Henry Collins Brown, *A Mind Mislaid* (New York: E. P. Dutton, 1937), 10. The Bloomingdale Asylum catered primarily to wealthy patients. For details, see Grob, *The Mad Among Us*, 37.

20. Brown, *A Mind Mislaid*, 28.

21. "Dear Friend," January 12, 1924, Box 1, Folder 4, Superintendent's Correspondence, Racine County Institutions, pp. 1–8 at 8.

22. "Dear Mrs. Overson," November 9, 1924, Box 1, Folder 2, Superintendent's Correspondence, Racine County Institutions, p. 1.

23. Letter, October 14, 1924, Box 1, Folder 2, Superintendent's Correspondence, Racine County Institutions, p. 1.

24. Letter, November 12, 1924, Box 1, Folder 2, Superintendent's Correspondence, Racine County Institutions, p. 1.

25. Letter, April 19, 1931, Box 1, Folder 1, Superintendent's Correspondence, Racine County Institutions, pp. 1–5 at 3.

26. On the idea of campuses, see Hornstein, *To Redeem One Person Is to Redeem the World*, 96, 173. By contrast, the newly formed psychopathic hospitals of the turn of the century seemed to have more distinctive medical identities. See Noll, *American Madness*, 27. See also Elizabeth Lunbeck's study on the Boston psychopathic hospital, *The Psychiatric Persuasion*. On the hotel model, see Pressman's discussion of the McLean Hospital and the recreational facilities and luxury foods offered there in *Last Resort*, 246. On hotels as historical places of fellowship, see A. K. Sandoval-Strausz, *Hotel: An American History* (New Haven, CT: Yale University Press, 2007), 232.

27. Letter, August 21, 1924, Box 14, Folder 4, 1919–1924, Bellevue Place Records, pp. 1–2 at 1.

28. "My dear Doctor!" October 4, 1926, Box 14, Folder 7, 1925–1928, Bellevue Place Records, p. 1.

29. "Dear Friend," January 12, 1924, Box 1, Folder 4, Superintendent's Correspondence, Racine County Institutions, pp. 1–8 at 8.

30. Roland Marchand, *Creating the Corporate Soul: The Rise of Public Relations and Corporate Imagery in American Big Business* (Berkeley: University of California Press, 1998), 59, 73; Lynn Dumenil, *The Modern Temper: American Culture and Society in the 1920s* (New York: Hill and Wang, 1995), 4.

31. "Dearest Mother," May 27, 1923, Box 2, Folder 1, Superintendent's Correspondence, Racine County Institutions, pp. 1–2.

32. See Gail Caldwell, *Let's Take the Long Way Home: A Memoir of Friendship* (New York: Random House, 2010), 123.

33. See George Paulson, *Closing the Asylums: Causes and Consequences of the Deinstitutionalization Movement* (Jefferson, NC: McFarland and Company, 2012), 105. Edward Shorter describes depression as being about an "inability to feel" rather than "sad feelings." See Shorter, *How Everyone Became Depressed: The Rise and Fall of the Nervous Breakdown* (New York: Oxford University Press, 2013), 2.

34. Letter, October 9, 1924, Box 2, Folder 2, Superintendent's Correspondence, Racine County Institutions, p. 1.

35. According to Hannah Decker, it is Kraepelin's legacy that propelled American psychiatrists to adhere very closely to a medical model of mental illness. Decker, *The Making of DSM-III: A Diagnostic Manual's Conquest of American Psychiatry* (New York: Oxford University Press, 2013), 3. On the *Statistical Manual for the Use of Institutions for the Insane*, published in 1918, which then had twenty-two diagnostic categories, see Andrew Skodol, "Diagnosis and Classification of Mental Disorders," in *American Psychiatry After World War Two (1944–1994)*, ed. Roy W. Menninger and John C. Nemiah (Washington, DC: American Psychiatric Publishing, 2000), 430–458 at 430.

36. According to Horatio M. Pollock, 400,000 patients with mental illnesses were being cared for in institutions after 1936, and 340,000 of these were in state hospitals. Pollock, *Family Care of Mental Patients: A Review of Systems of Family Care in America and Europe* (Utica, NY: State Hospitals Press, 1936), 13.

37. W. M. Garvin, "The Attitude of State Hospitals Toward Relatives and Friends of Patients," *State Hospital Quarterly* 7, no. 1 (November 1921): 5.

38. Ibid., 6.

39. W. M. Garvin, "The Attitude of State Hospitals Toward Relatives and Friends of Patients," *State Hospital Quarterly* 7, no. 1 (November 1921): 5, 6, 8.

40. For a historical overview of the idea of "benevolent deception" in the doctor-patient relationship, see Daniel K. Sokol, "How the Doctor's Nose Has Shortened over Time: A Historical Overview of the Truth-Telling Debate in the Doctor-Patient Relationship," *Journal of the Royal Society of Medicine* 99, no. 12 (December 2006): 632–636.

41. Letter from the Superintendent of the Sheppard and Enoch Pratt Hospital, Towson, Maryland, Ross McC. Chapman, M.D., October 24, 1932, Adolf Meyer Collection Patient Records Series XV, Patient Correspondence, Patient 1, Alan Mason Chesney Medical Archives, Johns Hopkins University, Baltimore. Note regarding medical records: each medical file at the Adolf Meyer Collection is cited using a numeric code, generated by the author-researcher, that bears no relation to the original number. Scholars wishing to access these records should contact the Alan Mason Chesney Medical Archives. For a historical view of Sheppard Pratt, see F. Barton Evans III, *Harry Stack Sullivan: Interpersonal Theory and Psychotherapy* (London: Routledge, 1996), 34. Chapman was hired by Harry Stack Sullivan, a psychoanalytical psychiatrist, who was at Sheppard Pratt from 1922 to 1930. See also Bliss Forbush, *The Sheppard & Enoch Pratt Hospital, 1853–1970* (Philadelphia: J. B. Lippincott, 1971), 103.

42. Letter from the Superintendent of the Sheppard and Enoch Pratt Hospital, Towson, Maryland, Ross McC. Chapman, M.D. November 1, 1932, Adolf Meyer Collection Patient Records Series XV, Patient Correspondence, Patient 1, p. 1.

43. Kathleen Brian, "'Occasionally Heard to Be Answering Voices': Aural Culture and the Ritual of Psychiatric Audition, 1877–1911," *History of Psychiatry* 23, no. 3 (2012): 305–317 at 312. On mania, dementia, and melancholia, see Noll, *American Madness*, 25. Noll also discusses other possible diagnoses at the turn of the century such as paresis, linked to syphilis, paranoia, general neuroses, psychopathic states, insanity due to exhaustion, "infectious insanity" (rabies, typhoid fever, small pox), and "imbecility, idiocy" (*American Madness*, 91).

44. On medical case histories being written in the third person and rendering patients "mute objects," see Jennifer Terry, *An American Obsession: Science, Medicine, and Homosexuality in Modern Society* (Chicago: University of Chicago Press, 1999), 18. Some theorists emphasize the surfeit of objectivity that characterizes medical notes. See Arthur Kleinman, *The Illness Narratives: Suffering, Healing, and the Human Condition* (New York: Basic, 1988), 130. On published letters of hospital superintendents, see Anne Kirk, *Chronicles of Interdict No. 7807* (Boston: Meador, 1937), a story of a woman's stay in the Louisiana Retreat Asylum as well as the State Insane Asylum in Jackson in the 1910s.

45. On the late nineteenth-/early twentieth-century "rest cure," see Hornstein, *To Redeem One Person Is to Redeem the World*, 89. On the rural asylum ideal, see Lisa Guenther, *Solitary Confinement: Social Death and Its Afterlives* (Minneapolis: University of Minnesota Press, 2013), 8.

46. See Thorstein Veblen, *The Theory of Business Enterprise* (1904), 108, available online at https://archive.org/details/theorybusinesse00veblgoog/page/n10. Frederick Taylor, *Principles of Scientific Management*, 1911. See chapter 1, "Fundamentals of Scientific Management," available online at https://www.marxists.org/reference/subject/economics/taylor/principles/ch01 .htm. On Fordism in the 1910s and 1920s, see Miller, *New World Coming*, 180–181 and Dumenil, *The Modern Temper*, 6. See also Mark Seltzer, *Bodies and Machines* (New York: Routledge, 1992), 157. On the increase of mechanization, and the growing American economy during the 1920s, see Murphy, *The New Era*, 16, 88. On ambivalence about and the fear of futurism in this

period, see Lawrence R. Samuel, *Future: A Recent History* (Austin: University of Texas Press, 2009), 41.

47. Murphy, *The New Era*, 1. See also Warren Susman, *Culture as History: The Transformation of American Society in the Twentieth Century* (Washington, DC: Smithsonian Institution Press, [1973] 2003), 106, 111. Finally, on modernist orientations toward the new, see Berber Bevernage, *History, Memory, and State-Sponsored Violence* (New York: Routledge, 2012), 14. For a primary source, see Willa Cather, *Not Under Forty* (Lincoln: University of Nebraska Press, [1922] 1988).

48. Brand is most well known for the screenplay he wrote for the movie version of Mary Jane Ward's novel *The Snake Pit* (New York: Random House, 1946) in 1948. But before this he wrote novels about the mental hospital experience, drawing on research he conducted as a psychiatric aide. His central character is placed in a mental hospital upon the death of a beloved brother. Primarily, it is a story of her escape from the asylum and her attempts to survive in Depression era New York City, though there are some vivid evocations of asylum life early in the novel. Millen Brand, *The Outward Room* (New York: Simon and Schuster, 1937), 3.

49. Brand, *The Outward Room*, 15. Jane Hillyer, too, repudiated mania for a sense of peace. See Hillyer, *Reluctantly Told*, 33.

50. The Bloomingdale Asylum moved to White Plains in 1895. The name was changed to New York Hospital Westchester Division in 1936. The Westchester Division operated under the general hospital license of New York Hospital and not as a private psychiatric hospital. See Steven S. Sharfstein et al., *Textbook of Hospital Psychiatry* (Arlington, VA: American Psychiatric Publishing, 2009), 364.

51. William Seabrook, *Asylum* (New York: Harcourt, Brace and Company, 1935), 3, 42, 43–44.

52. Brown, *A Mind Mislaid*, 53.

53. Mark S. Micale, ed., *The Mind of Modernism: Medicine, Psychology, and the Cultural Arts in Europe and America, 1880–1940* (Stanford, CA: Stanford University Press, 2004), 2.

54. Literary critic Lauren Berlant has argued that "cognitive overload in the urban everyday" has been one of the dominant tropes of American modernity. Berlant, *Cruel Optimism* (Durham, NC: Duke University Press, 2011), 9.

55. Otniel E. Dror, "Creating the Emotional Body: Confusion, Possibilities, and Knowledge," in *An Emotional History of the United States*, ed. Peter N. Stearns and Jan Lewis (New York: New York University Press, 1998), 173–194 at 178.

56. Here I am thinking of Clifford Beers's classic work, *A Mind That Found Itself* (1908). Memoirist Lawrence M. Jayson believed that the pressures of advanced industrial capitalism had contributed to his hospitalization during the 1930s. See Jayson, *Mania* (New York: Funk and Wagnalls, 1937), 214. Henry Collins Brown believed that many of the patients at Bloomingdale were there owing to "business troubles." See *A Mind Mislaid*, 46–47.

57. Diseases of the nerves in particular held some prestige during the late nineteenth century, as they signified overwork and a strong work ethic among the middle-class labor force. Laura Salisbury and Andrew Shail, introduction to *Neurology and Modernity: A Cultural History of Nervous Systems, 1800–1950*, ed. Salisbury and Shail (London: Palgrave Macmillan, 2010), 1–40 at 35. On asylums as self-sustaining communities with farms, gardens, and patient work, see Payne and Sacks, *Asylum*, 4.

58. Howard Brick, *Transcending Capitalism: Visions of a New Society in Modern American Thought* (Ithaca, NY: Cornell University Press, 2006), 16. See also Michael Denning's reflection

on the "aesthetics of social significance" in *The Cultural Front: The Laboring of American Culture in the Twentieth Century* (New York: Verso, 1997), 83. On the model of prisons as social debt, see Caleb Smith, *The Prison and the American Imagination* (New Haven, CT: Yale University Press, 2009), 41. If prison follows the model of social debt, what sort of capitalist logic did the asylum follow, if any?

59. Seabrook, *Asylum*, 146. Here he conveys the atmosphere of the asylum as an alluring, but potentially dubious, womb.

60. See Helen Horowitz, *Wild Unrest: Charlotte Perkins Gilman and the Making of "The Yellow Wall-Paper"* (New York: Oxford University Press, 2010), 3. For further details on the rest cure, see pp. 127 and 141. On Charlotte Perkins Gilman and depression, see p. 206. Andrew Scull notes that neurologists at the turn of the century were attempting to establish themselves as a psychiatric alternative, owing to a focus on nervous and mental disorders. See Scull, *Madness in Civilization*, 276.

61. This diagnosis was never made explicit at least from the standpoint of 1934, though her husband had speculated about it, as did some of her doctors. On this, see Appignanesi, *Mad, Bad, and Sad*, 229. Appignanesi also notes Craig House's "sumptuous[ness]," a place where patients could use swimming pools, tennis courts, and the golf course.

62. Letter, March 19, 1934, Box 1, Folder 2, Craig House Medical Records on Zelda Fitzgerald, Department of Rare Books and Special Collections, Princeton University Library, Princeton, NJ, p. 1.

63. Margaret Wilson [an ex-patient from Blackmoor], *Borderland Minds* (Boston: Meador, 1940), 24, 37.

64. On Haskell, see Scull, *Madness in Civilization*, 232–233. He felt he had been forced into the Pennsylvania Hospital for the Insane while sane, while Packard felt that her husband had railroaded her into Illinois State Hospital. On Packard, see Wood, *The Writing on the Wall*, 28, 34.

65. Wilson, *Borderland Minds*, 37.

66. Susman, *Culture as History*, 118.

67. Brown, *A Mind Mislaid*, 18.

68. "Dear Mrs. Overson and all," August 22, 1922, Box 2, Folder 3, Superintendent's Correspondence, Racine County Institutions, pp. 1–4 at 2.

69. "Dear Mother," July 30, 1922, Box 2, Folder 1, Superintendent's Correspondence, Racine County Institutions, pp. 1–3 at 1.

70. On speed and adrenaline and car culture, see Enda Duffy, *The Speed Handbook: Velocity, Pleasure, Modernism* (Durham, NC: Duke University Press, 2009), 111ff. See also T. J. Jackson Lears, *Fables of Abundance: A Cultural History of Advertising in America* (New York: Basic Books, 1995), 180.

71. Brown, *A Mind Mislaid*, 107.

72. See Samuel, *Future*, 34. See also the first line of William Faulkner's short story "Death Drag," from 1928: "The airplane appeared over town with almost the abruptness of an apparition." Faulkner, "Death Drag," in *The Portable William Faulkner* (New York: Viking, 1946), 585.

73. "Dear Mother," July 30, 1922, Box 2, Folder 1, Superintendent's Correspondence, Racine County Institutions, pp. 1–3 at 3.

74. "Dear Mother," June 3, 1932, Box 1, Folder 1, Superintendent's Correspondence, Racine County Institutions, pp. 1–4 at 2.

75. Ibid., 3.

76. Hillyer, *Reluctantly Told*, 139.

77. J. H. van den Berg, *The Psychology of the Sickbed* (New York: Humanities Press, 1972), 71–72.

78. On the drinking comment, see Wilma Wilson, *They Call Them Camisoles* (Los Angeles: Lymanhouse, 1940), 44, 130; on the towels, see p. 50. Camarillo operated from 1936 to 1997 and was known for its treatment of alcoholics and therapy for schizophrenia. Evelyn S. Taylor and Mary E. Holt, *Camarillo State Hospital* (Charleston, SC: Arcadia, 2019), 39–40. On the perceived connections between alcoholism and "insanity," see Lisa McGirr, *The War on Alcohol: Prohibition and the Rise of the American State* (New York: W. W. Norton, 2016), 20.

79. Wilson, *They Call Them Camisoles*, 82.

80. Charles E. Goshen, "A Review of Psychiatric Architecture and the Principles of Design," in *Psychiatric Architecture: A Review of Contemporary Developments in the Architecture of Mental Hospitals, Schools for the Mentally Retarded and Related Facilities*, ed. Goshen (Washington, DC: American Psychiatric Association, [1959] 1961), 1–6 at 3.

81. Wilson, *They Call Them Camisoles*, 69. On the sense of smell in history and the idea of the "deodorization project" of Western culture, see Mark S. R. Jenner, "Follow Your Nose? Smell, Smelling and Their Histories," *American Historical Review* 116, no. 2 (April 2011): 335–351 at 338.

82. Noll, *American Madness*, 25.

83. Susan Lamb, *Pathologist of the Mind: Adolf Meyer and the Origins of American Psychiatry* (Baltimore: Johns Hopkins University Press, 2014), 101. As with many other American psychiatric thinkers in the 1920s, White distinguished between the "mentally ill," whose treatment was temporary, and the "insane," whose treatment required custody. On White's eclectic psychiatry, combining biological psychiatry with psychoanalytic methods, while rejecting some of the gloomier aspects of Freudianism, see Hale, *The Rise and Crisis of Psychoanalysis in the United States*, 23. See also Arcangelo R. T. D'Amore, "WA White—Pioneer Psychoanalyst," in *William Alanson White: The Washington Years, 1903-1937: The Contributions to Psychiatry, Psychoanalysis, and Mental Health by Dr. White, While Superintendent of Saint Elizabeths Hospital*, ed. D'Amore (Washington, DC: U.S. Dept. of Health, Education, and Welfare, 1976), 69–91 at 71. Finally, see Hornstein, *To Redeem One Person Is to Redeem the World*, 97 and Summers, *Madness in the City of Magnificent Intentions*, 126. See p. 191 on the shift from diagnosing and curing insanity to preserving mental health.

84. Letter "My Dear ——," October 9, 1920, Folder S, 1920, Records of Superintendent William Alanson White, Personal Correspondence, 1906-1937, Entry 32, Records of St. Elizabeths Hospital, RG 418, National Archives, Washington, DC, pp. 1–2 at 1. In the body of this book I have chosen to call the hospital Saint Elizabeths, since after 1916 the name of the hospital generally appears as St Elizabeths without the period. However, the archival collections at the National Archives regarding the hospital refer to it as "St. Elizabeths" so I have chosen to keep this title when referring to the archival documents. On the history of the name and spelling of the hospital, see Matthew Gambino, "'These Strangers Within Our Gates': Race, Psychiatry, and Mental Illness Among Black Americans at St Elizabeths Hospital in Washington, D.C.," *History of Psychiatry* 19, no. 4 (January 2009): 387–408, at 403.

85. Erving Goffman, *Stigma: Notes on the Management of Spoiled Identity* (New York: Penguin, 1963), 83. See Lunbeck, "Empathy as a Psychoanalytic Mode of Observation," 261. I note here that the pessimistic Freudian view of transforming "hysterical misery into common unhappiness" is not necessarily the view that took hold in the United States. See Joseph Breuer and Sigmund Freud, *Studies in Hysteria* (Boston: Beacon Press, [1895] 1964), 232. During the interwar

years, ego psychology was quite popular in America and, according to Edward Shorter, encompassed American analysts' sense of progressive spirit and belief in improving their patients' lives. Shorter, *A History of Psychiatry: From the Era of the Asylum to the Age of Prozac* (New York: Wiley, 1998), 169.

86. This hospital was sometimes known as the Gallinger Municipal Hospital Psychopathic Ward. James Duffy, *The Capital's Siberia* (Middleton, ID: Boise Valley Herald, 1939), 3.

87. Ibid., 7.

88. Ibid., 16.

89. Wilson, *They Call Them Camisoles*, 24.

90. Marian King, *The Recovery of Myself: A Patient's Experience in a Hospital for Mental Illness* (New Haven, CT: Yale University Press, 1931), 17. The foreword to King's memoir was written by Adolf Meyer, a psychiatrist at Phipps. He was a professor of psychiatry at Johns Hopkins from 1910 to 1941 and wished to unite the various fields of the asylum physician, the neurologist, and the general practitioner to establish a different kind of mental health discipline. On Meyer's rejection of what Susan Lamb calls the mind-body dualism and adaptation of the "bio-psycho-social" model, see *Pathologist of the Mind*, 5, 249. As Mary Elene Wood notes, it was common for asylum autobiographies to appear with introductions by psychiatrists who often attested to their professional abilities in curing patients with mental illnesses. See Wood, *The Writing on the Wall*, 125.

91. King, *The Recovery of Myself*, 18.

92. Ibid., 58.

93. Ibid., 71–72. King's memoir is a kind of conversion narrative from a hostile view of therapy to an embrace of it. See, for example, p. 119. This conversion narrative was a common trajectory in mental illness memoirs of the turn of the twentieth century. See Anne C. Rose, *Psychology and Selfhood in the Segregated South* (Chapel Hill: University of North Carolina Press, 2009), 8.

94. Jayson, *Mania*, 5.

95. Ibid., 1.

96. Ibid., 89.

97. Ibid., 32–33.

98. C. G. Jung, *Jung Contra Freud: The 1912 New York Lectures on the Theory of Psychoanalysis*, ed. Sonu Shamdasani (Princeton, NJ: Princeton University Press, 2012), 110, 112.

99. On the ritual of the confession, see William Ian Miller, *Humiliation: And Other Essays on Honor, Social Discomfort, and Violence* (Ithaca, NY: Cornell University Press, 1993), 170. Foucault famously emphasized the coercive aspects of confession and the succumbing to expanding realms of social authority. See Michel Foucault, *The History of Sexuality, Volume 1: An Introduction* (New York: Random House, 1978), 60–62.

100. See Thomas Bender's entry on "community" in *A Companion to American Thought*, ed. Richard Wightman Fox and James T. Kloppenberg (New York: Blackwell, 1998), 137. See also Susman, *Culture as History*, 109, 173. On the participatory ethic, see Razlogova, *The Listener's Voice*, 5. On the collectivism expressed in American cultural sources in the 1930s, see Cowie, *The Great Exception*, 147.

101. Arthur P. Noyes and Lawrence C. Kolb, *Modern Clinical Psychiatry* (Philadelphia: W. B. Saunders, [1934] 1963), 335.

102. Susman, *Culture as History*, 172.

103. Jayson, *Mania*, 111.

104. *Out of the Shadows*, 8mm color, 1930, New York State Archives Series B1581-97, Utica Psychiatric Center (NY) training and publicity motion pictures and videotapes, 1930–1989, Albany, NY, https://www.youtube.com/watch?v=7RENS5bif0M.

105. "My Dear Sir," August 6, 1930, Folder Wh-Wy, "Personal," Records of Superintendent William Alanson White, Personal Correspondence, Entry 32, RG 418, pp. 1–2 at 1. This hospital had around 4,000 patients as of 1924. See "Dr. W. A. White Mender of Brains," *Sunday Telegram*, 1921, Folder U-V, "Personal," 1921, William Alanson White, Personal Correspondence, Entry 32, RG 418, p. 1. Again, census figures give some sense of the white patient majority hospitalized in the District during this period, though with a sizable African American "minority." Of the 3,931 hospitalized patients in 1923, 3,028 were white, 897 were "Negro," 1 "Indian," 3 Chinese, and 1 Japanese. See Steuart, *Patients in Hospitals for Mental Disease*, table 68.

106. Colonel Bell Burr, *Practical Psychology and Psychiatry: For Use in Training Schools for Attendants and Nurses in Medical Classes* (Philadelphia: Davis, 1921), 218.

107. Gambino, "These Strangers Within Our Gates," 388.

108. Hillyer, *Reluctantly Told*, 72.

109. Mary de Young, *Madness: An American History of Mental Illness and Its Treatment* (Jefferson, NC: McFarland, 2010), 155. As Martin Summers notes, some states, notably Virginia and North Carolina, did have public asylums just for African Americans. Beyond these institutions, he notes that there were limited psychiatric services in general hospitals that served African American communities. See Summers, "Diagnosing the Ailments of Black Citizenship: African American Physicians and the Politics of Mental Illness, 1895–1940," in *Precarious Prescriptions*, ed. Green et al., 91–114 at 99. In terms of a nationwide statistic, in 1923, according to the Federal Census Bureau, Black resident patients numbered 20,084, and made up of 7.6% of the total patient population, while white patients numbered 244,968, or 92% of the total population. See Horatio M. Pollock, "Mental Disease Among Negroes in the United States," *State Hospital Quarterly* 11, no. 1 (November 1925): 47–66 at 49. On the anxiety caused by desegregation in intimate spaces more broadly, see Jeff Wiltse, *Contested Waters: A Social History of Swimming Pools in America* (Chapel Hill: University of North Carolina Press, 2007), 4, 154–181.

110. Hillyer, *Reluctantly Told*, 103.

111. Ibid., 104.

112. Brown, *A Mind Mislaid*, 19.

113. See Chad Heap, *Slumming: Sexual and Racial Encounters in American Nightlife, 1885–1940* (Chicago: University of Chicago Press, 2009), 17, 86, 189.

114. Susan M. Schweik, *The Ugly Laws: Disability in Public* (New York: New York University Press, 2009), 86. On medicine as spectacle, see Elizabeth Stephens, *Anatomy as Spectacle: Public Exhibitions of the Body from 1700 to the Present* (Liverpool: Liverpool University Press, 2011), 92. Stephens argues that medicalization destroyed the freak show as "unusual bodies" were moved into medicalized settings. Recent historiography on insane asylum visiting has tried to nuance the motivations of the visitors beyond simple voyeurism, illuminating the practice of the visit as a cultural and educational phenomenon of institutional tourism within a climate that saw spectatorship as a valuable form of education and scientific enlightenment. See Janet Miron, "'In View of the Knowledge to Be Acquired': Public Visits to New York's Asylums in the Nineteenth Century," in *Permeable Walls: Historical Perspectives on Hospital and Asylum Visiting*, ed. Graham Mooney and Jonathan Reinarz (Amsterdam: Rodopi, 2009), 243–267.

115. Brown, *A Mind Mislaid*, 33, 34.

116. Wilson, *They Call Them Camisoles*, 59, 60.

117. Ibid., 217.

118. On the conventions of the captivity narrative, see Gordon M. Sayre, ed., *American Captivity Narratives* (Boston: Houghton Mifflin, 2000), 12. On sentimental and domestic fiction, see Wood, *The Writing on the Wall*, 15.

119. Wilson, *Borderland Minds*, 85.

120. In fact, Grob notes that in 1930, the mortality rate for those in asylums was five times that of the general population. See Grob, *The Mad Among Us*, 126. According to him, the leading causes of death within the asylum then were heart disease, pneumonia, paresis, tuberculosis, arterial diseases, and nephritis. On epidemic disease, see Noll, *American Madness*, 32.

121. On the concept of the "good death," see Abel, *The Inevitable Hour*, 3. Abel argues, contra historian Philippe Ariès, that many relatives resisted the professionalization of death in medical institutions even during the twentieth century and wanted their fatally ill family members to die in the home. This dynamic might have been true for families with members in an asylum as well. Though Abel does not deal with them in her study, she notes that asylums are also important sites of death and dying and merit a separate study (see p. 7).

122. "Dear Madam," July 27, 1931, Box 1, Folder 1, Superintendent's Correspondence, Racine County Institutions, pp. 1-2.

123. Letter, July 29, 1931, Box 1, Folder 1, Superintendent's Correspondence, Racine County Institutions, p. 1.

124. Letter, October 11, 1932, Box 2, Folder 3, Superintendent's Correspondence, Racine County Institutions, pp. 1–2.

125. Letter, October 13, 1932, Box 2, Folder 3, Superintendent's Correspondence, Racine County Institutions, pp. 1–2.

Chapter 2

1. Paul Starr, *The Social Transformation of American Medicine* (New York: Basic Books, 1982), 5. Aaron Lecklider suggests that American audiences also encountered science in venues of working-class spectatorship, such as Coney Island. See *Inventing the Egghead: The Battle over Brainpower in American Culture* (Philadelphia: University of Pennsylvania Press, 2013), 15ff.

2. Anne Hunsaker Hawkins, "Myth of a Cure and the Process of Accommodation: *Awakenings* Revisited," *Medical Humanities Review* 8, no. 1 (1994): 9–21 at 11.

3. On possessive individualism, see the discussion of the popular American perception of Nietzsche's concept of the self-sovereign "ubermensch" in early twentieth-century America in Jennifer Ratner-Rosenhagen, *American Nietzsche: A History of an Icon and His Ideas* (Chicago: University of Chicago Press, 2012), 111. For a broader discussion of political theory, see C. B. MacPherson, *The Political Theory of Possessive Individualism Hobbes to Locke* (London: Oxford University Press, 1962), 270.

4. Wendy Kline, *Building a Better Race: Gender, Sexuality, and Eugenics from the Turn of the Century to the Baby Boom* (Berkeley: University of California Press, 2001), 59; Grob, *Mental Illness and American Society*, 172–173. Here he notes that from 1907 to 1940, 18,552 people living in state hospitals had been surgically sterilized. See also Summers, *Madness in the City of Magnificent Intentions*, 80. On scientific engagement and utopianism, see the introduction to Burnham, ed., *After Freud Left*, 26 and Andrew Jewett, *Science, Democracy, and the American University: From the Civil War to the Cold War* (Cambridge: Cambridge University Press, 2012), 10. On the shift from insanity to maladjustment, see Lamb, *Pathologist of the Mind*, 101.

5. Shorter, *How Everyone Became Depressed*, 17; Josephine Jackson, *Outwitting Our Nerves: A Primer on Psychotherapy* (New York: Century, 1921), 7. She defines "nerves" quite amorphously as an array of both physical and emotional, or neurotic, troubles.

6. Letter, April 19, 1931, Box 1, Folder 1, Superintendent's Correspondence, Racine County Institutions, pp. 1–5 at 3.

7. Letter, February 2, 1931, Box 1, Folder 4, Superintendent's Correspondence, Racine County Institutions, p. 1.

8. On mind cure movements, including Christian Science, New Thought, and the Emmanuel Movement that animated the second half of the nineteenth century, see Dowbiggin, *The Quest for Mental Health*, 83. See also Rosenberg, "Contested Boundaries," 416. On holism, see Halliwell, *Therapeutic Revolutions*, xii. On the origins of psychiatry in lay healing, hypnotism, theology, philosophy, literature, etc., see Micale and Porter, "Introduction: Reflections on Psychiatry and Its Histories," 5.

9. "Dear Sir," April 9, 1921, Folder Personal U-V, Records of Superintendent William Alanson White, Personal Correspondence, 1906–1937, Entry 32, RG 418, pp. 1–6 at 6.

10. Ibid., 2.

11. See Paul Hahn and Z. M. Lebensohn, "New Trends in Hospital Design," *American Journal of Hospital Psychiatry* 104, no. 8 (February 1948): 561. On food and daily details about Worcester, see Enoch Callaway, *Asylum: A Mid-Century Madhouse and Its Lessons About Our Mentally Ill Today* (Westport, CT: Praeger, 2007), 5.

12. "Dear Sir," April 9, 1921, 2.

13. Ibid., 3.

14. Ibid., 4.

15. Ibid., 4.

16. Lunbeck, *The Psychiatric Persuasion*, 11, 152. See also Grob, *Mental Illness and American Society*, 135, 141.

17. "Dear Sir," April 9, 1921, 4.

18. Ibid., 5, 6.

19. "Dr. W. A. White Mender of Brains," 1.

20. Braslow, *Mental Ills and Bodily Cures*, 92.

21. Scull, *The Insanity of Place/The Place of Insanity*, 138–141. Scull argues that this theory was an attempt to secure psychiatry's scientific status. For a study of Cotton himself, see Andrew Scull, *Madhouse: A Tragic Tale of Megalomania and Modern Medicine* (New Haven, CT: Yale University Press, 2005), 81–96, 115.

22. See William James, "The Varieties of Religious Experience," 1901–1902, 15, https://www.gutenberg.org/files/621/621-pdf.pdf.

23. "My Dear Mr. Overholser," March 9, 1939, Folder 4, Entry 54, St. Elizabeths Hospital, Records of the Superintendent, Supt. Overholser, RG 418, National Archives, Washington, DC, pp. 1–9 at 3. Overholser was superintendent until 1962. During his time at the hospital, he was also a professor of psychiatry at George Washington University and the president of the American Psychiatric Association from 1947 to 1949. On this, see Grob, *From Asylum to Community*, 10. On his philosophy as a superintendent, see Winfred Overholser, *St. Elizabeths Hospital* (Washington, DC: U.S. Government Printing Office, 1958), 14. On Saint Elizabeths' therapeutic techniques, see Gambino, "Erving Goffman's Asylums and Institutional Culture in the Mid-Twentieth Century United States."

24. Hornstein, *To Redeem One Person Is to Redeem the World*, xii.

25. "My Dear Mr. Overholser," March 9, 1939, 3.

26. Ibid., 4.

27. Ibid., 5.

28. Insulin therapy was premised on the idea that insulin could balance the adrenaline in the brain since adrenaline was perceived to be implicated in many brain disorders of the period. See Grob, *Mental Illness and American Society*, 296.

29. "My Dear Mr. Overholser," March 9, 1939, 7.

30. Ibid., 8.

31. Ibid., 8.

32. Ibid., 9.

33. See Grob, *The Mad Among Us*, 165. He notes that by 1940 the inpatient population was 500,000, the majority of whom were considered "chronic." See Grob, *Mental Illness and American Society*, 288.

34. Harry A. Laubert, "Experiences with Family Care of Psychiatric Cases," in Pollock, *Family Care of Mental Patients*, 74–90 at 88. On orphans in 1930s American culture, see John Kasson, "Behind Shirley Temple's Smile: Children, Emotional Labour, and the Great Depression," in *The Cultural Turn in U.S. History: Past, Present, and Future*, ed. James W. Cook et al. (Chicago: University of Chicago Press, 2008), 185–216.

35. On early twentieth-century immigrant and working-class people and their emotional investments in extended families, mutual aid societies, and ethnoreligious communities, see Cowie, *The Great Exception*, 38. On African American families, see Heather Andrea Williams, *Help Me to Find My People: The African American Search for Family Lost in Slavery* (Chapel Hill: University of North Carolina Press, 2012), 10–12.

36. For example, 1937 census figures reveal that of the 411,814 state hospital patients on the books at the beginning of the year, the vast majority were hospitalized, while only 603 were in "family care." William Lane Austin, director, Bureau of the Census, *Patients in Hospitals for Mental Disease* (Washington, DC: U.S. Government Printing Office, 1939), table 3, Movement of Patient Population in State Hospitals by Class of Patients and Sex: 1937 and 1936, p. 5.

37. Summers, *Madness in the City of Magnificent Intentions*, 228. Jack D. Pressman notes a dearth of treatments especially for patients in the grip of psychotic episodes, who had only "traditional resources" as treatment options. See *Last Resort*, 214, 219.

38. On medication, see Hornstein, *To Redeem One Person Is to Redeem the World*, 239. See also Deutsch, *The Shame of the States*, 107. Zigmond M. Lebensohn notes an exception: mute catatonics under the influence of sodium amytal were able to speak. See Lebensohn, "The History of Electroconvulsive Therapy in the United States and Its Place in American Psychiatry: A Personal Memoir," *Comprehensive Psychiatry* 40, no. 3 (May/June 1999): 173–181 at 173.

39. On medication, see Edward Shorter and David Healy, *Shock Therapy: A History of Electroconvulsive Treatment in Mental Illness* (New Brunswick, NJ: Rutgers University Press, 2007), 5. On Henry Cotton, see Hornstein, *To Redeem One Person Is to Redeem the World*, 240–241.

40. Ellen C. Philtine, *They Walk in Darkness* (New York: Liveright Publishing, 1945), 48, 40, 46. Philtine was the pseudonym of a woman whose husband had worked at Pilgrim State Hospital in Brentwood, New York, which, just after World War II, had become the world's largest mental hospital. The novel was set in the 1930s. On Pilgrim State, which housed more than 11,000 patients by 1950, see Pressman, *Last Resort*, 173.

41. Albert Q. Maisel, "Bedlam, 1946," *Life*, May 6, 1946, 102. The photos in Maisel's article had their origins with World War II conscientious objectors who were sent to work in mental

hospitals during the war and, under the auspices of the Mental Hygiene Program, provided information for exposé literature. See Steven Taylor, *Acts of Conscience: World War Two, Mental Institutions, and Religious Objectors* (Syracuse, NY: Syracuse University Press, 2009). For other examples of exposé literature, and another conscientious objector, see Frank L. Wright, *Out of Sight, Out of Mind* (National Mental Health Foundation, 1947), https://www.disabilitymuseum .org/dhm/lib/detail.html?id=1754. On the Philadelphia State Hospital at Byberry during these years, see Parsons, *From Asylum to Prison*, 1, 27–29.

42. Deutsch, *The Shame of the States*, 90. For more details on Deutsch, and how he was subsidized by Clifford Beers and the National Council on Mental Hygiene (NCMH), see Grob, *From Asylum to Community*, 73 and "The History of the Asylum Revisited," 261.

43. Deutsch, *The Shame of the States*, 40.

44. Ibid., 70.

45. Ibid., 42.

46. Ibid., 96.

47. On this, see Kirsten Fermaglich, *American Dreams and Nazi Nightmares: Early Holocaust Consciousness in Liberal America, 1957–1965* (Waltham, MA: Brandeis University Press, 2006), particularly her discussion of Stanley Milgram (88).

48. Deutsch, *The Shame of the States*, 96. Observations about abuse were also made outside the exposé genre. In 1950, a man from Chisholm, Minnesota, wrote a shocking exposé about the treatment of patients at Rochester State Hospital in Minnesota to the State Civil Service Department, explaining why he left his job there as a psychiatric aide. See "Dear Sirs," May 16, 1950, Box #114.B.15.5 (B), Rochester State Hospital, Superintendent's Office Correspondence, Government Records, Minnesota State Archives, Minnesota Historical Society, St. Paul, pp. 1–4 at 1.

49. Robert Meister, *After Evil: A Politics of Human Rights* (New York: Columbia University Press, 2011), 212.

50. Deutsch, *The Shame of the States*, 110.

51. Cole, "'Institutionalitis.'"

52. Deutsch, *The Shame of the States*, 42, 184.

53. See Halliwell, *Therapeutic Revolutions*, 136.

54. Braslow, *Mental Ills and Bodily Cures*, 126, 152. The operation did not fall into more general disuse until the mid-1950s, particularly in the wake of the introduction of chlorpromazine in 1954. On lobotomy's decline, see Elliot S. Valenstein, *Great and Desperate Cures: The Rise and Decline of Psychosurgery and Other Radical Treatments for Mental Illness* (New York: Basic Books, 1986), 272, 284. As Hannah Decker points out, judicial decisions had even found lobotomies in violation of the First Amendment because they interfered with mentation. Decker, *The Making of DSM-III*, 25.

55. Pressman, *Last Resort*, 2. According to Gerald Grob, by 1951, 18,608 people had undergone psychosurgery since its introduction in 1936. See Grob, *From Asylum to Community*, 130.

56. Pressman, *Last Resort*, 147.

57. On Fulton, see Braslow, *Mental Ills and Bodily Cures*, 126. Pressman traces modern neurophysiology to World War I, as doctors tried to make sense of the function of the damaged frontal lobes of soldiers. See *Last Resort*, 51. On Fulton and Jacobsen's experiments on chimpanzees, see 64–66. Finally, see Walter Freeman and James W. Watts, *Psychosurgery: In the Treatment of Mental Disorders and Intractable Pain* (Springfield, IL: Charles C. Thomas, [1942] 1950), 19.

58. Valenstein, *Great and Desperate Cures*, 233, 291. See also Halliwell, *Therapeutic Revolutions*, 201–202. Lobotomy became more of a "mass" or "assembly line" operation when its

technique was changed in 1946 from the standard "prefrontal" lobotomy of the 1930s and early 1940s, which required a surgical suite, a neurosurgeon, and a nursing staff, to the "transorbital" lobotomy of 1946 onward, which accessed the frontal lobes through the eye socket, something that could be done by Freeman by himself, in his office. See Pressman, *Last Resort*, 337, on transorbital lobotomies. Finally, see Raz, *The Lobotomy Letters*, 7, 83ff.

59. Freeman and Watts, *Psychosurgery*, 504.

60. Walter Freeman and James W. Watts, "Prefrontal Lobotomy in the Treatment of Mental Disorders," *Southern Medical Journal* 30, no. 1 (January 1937): 23–31 at 30.

61. Walter Freeman and James W. Watts, "Psychosurgery During 1936–1946," in *From Madness to Mental Health: Psychiatric Disorder and Its Treatment in Western Civilization*, ed. Greg Eghigian (New Brunswick, NJ: Rutgers University Press, 2010), 285. I will not discuss Freeman and Watts except to provide context because they have already been written about extensively by the historians I cite here, and also because neurology is quite a distinctive enterprise from psychiatry. While there was some overlap between neurologists and alienists in the early twentieth century, after 1934 there was a split between the licensed specialties of psychiatry and neurology. See Noll, *American Madness*, 17.

62. Freeman and Watts, "Psychosurgery During 1936–1946," 285.

63. Freeman and Watts, *Psychosurgery*, 504.

64. Raz, *The Lobotomy Letters*, 38.

65. Pressman, *Last Resort*, 213. Though, as Mical Raz notes, lobotomy enabled some patients to resume life at home, in their own communities. See *The Lobotomy Letters*, 2.

66. Lester Drubin, "Further Observations on Sixty-Two Lobotomized Psychotic Male Veterans at the Veterans Hospital, Northport, New York," *Journal of Nervous and Mental Disease* 113, no. 3 (March 1951): 254.

67. On the article in the *New England Journal of Medicine*, "The Surgical Treatment of Certain Psychoses," see Valenstein, *Great and Desperate Cures*, 147. On Dannecker, see p. 156. As Gail Hornstein notes, lobotomy was written up enthusiastically in the *New York Times*, *Reader's Digest*, *Time*, *Life*, and *Newsweek*. See *To Redeem One Person Is to Redeem the World*, 242.

68. This article was written by Waldemar Kaempffert, the science editor for the *New York Times*, in 1941, who argued that the lobotomized were no different from the rest of humanity. See Scull, *Madness in Civilization*, 317.

69. See John Drury Ratcliff, *Science Yearbook of 1942* (New York: Doubleday, Doran, 1942), 99. See also Gretchen J. Diefenbach et al., "Portrayal of Lobotomy in the Popular Press: 1935–1960," *Journal of the History of the Neurosciences* 8, no. 1 (1999): 60–69 at 65.

70. Thomas B. Henry, "Brain Operation by D.C. Doctors Aids Mental Ills," *Washington Evening Star*, November 20, 1936, A-2.

71. Pressman, *Last Resort*, 198. A lobotomy did not cure patients of a specific disease: it just transformed their physiological and psychological characteristics, something that he argues was perceived as a medical advance (see p. 10).

72. Ibid., 10–11, 384. Pressman also shows how lobotomy inadvertently helped engender the notion of "peer review" in scientific or psychiatric circles (see p. 14).

73. Hornstein, *To Redeem One Person Is to Redeem the World*, 239. On World War II, see Dowbiggin, *The Quest for Mental Health*, 135.

74. Harry Stack Sullivan was among the first American psychiatrists to use psychoanalytic treatment on those suffering from psychoses. Sullivan worked at Maryland's Sheppard and Enoch Pratt Hospital and was a founder of the William Alanson White Institute, an independent

psychoanalytic institute, in 1943. On his reaction to lobotomy, see Paul E. Stepansky, *Freud, Surgery, and the Surgeons* (New York: Routledge, 1999), 198–199. Jonathan Sadowsky notes that Sullivan was among the most vocal critics of biological psychiatry. See *Electroconvulsive Therapy in America*, 91.

75. Quoted in Pressman, *Last Resort*, 367. In 1947 David Rioch was an analyst at Chestnut Lodge, a private sanatorium in Maryland, and had publicly denounced the practice as being a form of "partial euthanasia."

76. Hornstein, *To Redeem One Person Is to Redeem the World*, 242.

77. Pressman, *Last Resort*, 2.

78. Ibid., 200.

79. Raz, *The Lobotomy Letters*, 4, 44ff.

80. "Post Lobotomy," *Pomo News* 5, no. 9 (September 19, 1952): 3 from F 3886:49, Mendocino State Hospital, Mental Hygiene-Hospitals, California State Archives, Office of the Secretary of State, Sacramento. This hospital existed from the 1890s to 1972. It followed the cottage plan, designed to give the hospital a more domestic feeling, and encompassed drug and alcohol rehabilitation, as well as an array of therapeutic regimes, such as industrial therapy.

81. Shorter, *A History of Psychiatry*, 227. Braslow notes in his study that 12% of patients died from lobotomy surgery at Stockton State Hospital (which stopped performing the surgery in 1954), while others faced seizures, incontinence, and confusion afterward. And by 1960, only 23% of lobotomized patients were able to leave the hospital. See Braslow, *Mental Ills and Bodily Cures*, 168–169.

82. See, for example, Edward Shorter's portrait of Joseph Kennedy in *The Kennedy Family and the Story of Mental Retardation* (Philadelphia: Temple University Press, 2000), 1–2, 10. On p. 33 he writes that Joe Kennedy determined that his daughter Rosemary, who had a cognitive disability, would get a lobotomy as "one last desperate measure before sending her away." Halliwell, by contrast, argues that Kennedy was aware of the risks involved in the operation. See *Therapeutic Revolutions*, 201.

83. Braslow, *Mental Ills and Bodily Cures*, 133–134; see also p. 12. Andrew Scull argues that the desire to see doctors as "desperate" or to see their mistakes as "good intentions ... gone wrong" is characteristic of a Whiggish approach to the history of psychiatry in general. See *The Insanity of Place/The Place of Insanity*, 10.

84. Letter, April 9, 1948, Records of the Superintendent, Administrative Files, 1921–1964, Folder 16: Lobotomy, Entry 7, RG 418, St. Elizabeths Hospital, National Archives, Washington, DC, pp. 1–3 at 3.

85. Ibid., p. 2. A lobotomy is sometimes called a "leucotomy," which follows the same principles of cutting away the connections to and from the prefrontal cortex.

86. Letter from Samuel L. Silk, April 28, 1948, Records of the Superintendent, Administrative Files, 1921–1964, Folder 16: Lobotomy, Entry 7, RG 418, St. Elizabeths Hospital, p. 1.

87. Pressman, *Last Resort*, 10.

88. Noll, *American Madness*, 198.

89. Letter, April 28, 1956, Records of Supt. Overholser, Folder 8, Entry 7, RG 418, St. Elizabeths Hospital, pp. 1–6 at 2, 3.

90. Ibid., 4.

91. Raz, *The Lobotomy Letters*, 47, 57–58. See Winfred Overholser, "What Is Past Is Prologue," St Elizabeths Hospital Documents, Records of the Superintendent, 1855–1967, Folder 14, Entry 7, RG 418, pp. 1–4 at 2.

92. Letter, April 28, 1956, 5, 6.

93. Scull, *The Place of Insanity/The Insanity of Place*, 131.

94. Letter, September 6, 1946, Records of the Superintendent, Administrative Files, 1921–1964, Folder 16: Lobotomy, Entry 7, RG 418, St. Elizabeths Hospital, pp. 1–2 at 2.

95. Ibid., 1.

96. Hugh T. Carmichael was the coauthor of *Prospects and Proposals: Lifetime Learning for Psychiatrists*, published by the American Psychiatric Association in 1972, and *Continuing Education and Psychiatrists*, published in 1975 by the National Institute of Mental Health. In 1938, he conducted a well-received study about the reliability of diagnosis. See Decker, *The Making of DSM-III*, 134. The Illinois Neuropsychiatric Institute, a part of the University of Illinois–Chicago, offered one unit for psychiatry and one for neurology and neurosurgeries. See this online pamphlet from 1942, courtesy of the University of Illinois Library and Archives: http://archives.library.illinois.edu/erec/University%20Archives/5238815/5238815_01_NeuropsychiatricInstitute.pdf.

97. "Lobotomy Notes," Hugh T. Carmichael Articles and Papers, 1941–1975, American Psychiatric Association Foundation, Melvin Shabin, MD, Library and Archives, American Psychiatric Association, Washington, DC, pp. 1–17 at 1.

98. Ibid., 2.

99. Freeman and Watts, *Psychosurgery*, 249.

100. Ibid., 251–252, 256.

101. On the phrase "calculus of suffering," see Martin S. Pernick, *A Calculus of Suffering: Pain, Professionalism and Anesthesia in Nineteenth-Century America* (New York: Columbia University Press, 1985).

102. On doctor's notes as humanitarian narratives and their resonation with realist novels, see Thomas Laqueur, "Bodies, Details, and the Humanitarian Narrative," in *The New Cultural History*, ed. Lynn Hunt (Berkeley: University of California Press, 1989), 176–204 at 182. Mark S. Micale notes that by the late nineteenth and early twentieth centuries, Western psychiatry's case studies became much more literary in orientation and were often quite accessible for a more a general audience. See Micale, *The Mind of Modernism*, 7. On the "golden age" of American sociology, see Jeffrey Escoffier, "Homosexuality and the Sociological Imagination: The 1950s and 1960s," in *A Queer World: The Center for Gay and Lesbian Studies Reader*, ed. Martin Duberman (New York: New York University Press, 1997), 248–261.

103. Edward Hunter, *Brain-Washing in Red China: The Calculated Destruction of Men's Minds* (New York: Vanguard, 1951), 10. On the trope of the "emotionless" Chinese, see Norman Kutcher, "The Skein of Chinese Emotions History," in *Doing Emotions History*, ed. Susan J. Matt and Peter N. Stearns (Urbana: University of Illinois Press, 2013), 57–73 at 57.

104. On menticide, see Joost Meerloo, *The Rape of the Mind: The Psychology of Thought Control, Menticide, and Brainwashing* (New York: World Publishing, 1956), 13. On totalitaria, see pp. 106, 116–117, 124.

105. Hannah Arendt, *The Origins of Totalitarianism* (San Diego: Harcourt Brace Jovanovich, 1951), 443.

106. See Matthew Dunne, *A Cold War State of Mind: Brainwashing and Postwar American Society* (Amherst: University of Massachusetts Press, 2013), 5, 232. On brainwashing casting doubt upon the American national character, see Staub, *Madness Is Civilization*, 72. On the brainwashing of American soldiers during the Korean War, see Catherine Lutz, "Epistemology of the Bunker: The Brainwashed and Other New Subjects of Permanent War," in *Inventing*

the Psychological, ed. Pfister and Schnog, 245–267 at 255–256 and Timothy Melley, *The Covert Sphere: Secrecy, Fiction, and the National Security State* (Ithaca, NY: Cornell University Press, 2012), 71. These cases were not written about and made known to the American public until after the conflict, though, in the form of Hunter's book and Virginia Pasley's *21 Stayed: The Story of the American GIs Who Chose Communist China—Who They Were and Why They Stayed* (New York: American Book-Stratford Press, 1955).

107. On Freeman's medical utilitarianism and his defense of lobotomies in the name of helping both the individual and society, see Raz, *Lobotomy Letters,* 42.

108. Frank G. Slaughter, *Daybreak* (London: Universal Book Club, 1958), 31. In his 1946 novel, *All the King's Men* (New York: Harcourt, Brace, and Company, 1946), Robert Penn Warren includes a lobotomy scene that also advances the comparison between lobotomy and soul murder (336).

109. Slaughter, *Daybreak,* 31.

110. Ibid., 32.

111. Michaela Hoenicke Moore, *Know Your Enemy: The American Debate on Nazism, 1933–1945* (Cambridge: Cambridge University Press, 2009), 12, 183.

112. On the fear of the "masses" in the interwar period, see José Ortega y Gasset's famous work, *The Revolt of the Masses* (New York: W. W. Norton, [1932] 1994). See also Stefan Jonsson, *Crowds and Democracy: The Idea and Image of the Masses from Revolution to Fascism* (New York: Columbia University Press, 2013), 8, 16, 63. During the war, see Max Horkheimer and Theodor Adorno, "The Culture Industry: Enlightenment as Mass Deception," in Horkheimer and Adorno, *Dialectic of Enlightenment* (New York: Continuum, [1944] 1987), 127. For Benjamin Alpers, the image of the automaton expressed broader American social anxieties about mass society and the "regimented crowd." See Alpers, *Dictators, Democracy, and American Public Culture: Envisioning the Totalitarian Enemy, 1920s–1950s* (Chapel Hill: University of North Carolina Press, 2003), 103, 105.

113. Harry Stack Sullivan, *The Collected Works,* vol. 1, *The Interpersonal Theory of Psychiatry* (New York: W. W. Norton, 1964), 149. Neo-Freudians were particularly interested in the emotional weight of the experiences of the first years of life. See Harrington, *Mind Fixers,* 91.

114. Quoted in Scull, *The Insanity of Place/The Place of Insanity,* 135. On Lewis as a figure who blended psychoanalytical and biological psychiatry, see Michael J. Aminoff and Larry R. Faulkner, eds., *The American Board of Psychiatry and Neurology: Looking Back and Moving Ahead* (Arlington, VA: American Psychiatric Association Publishing, 2012), 53–54.

115. Irving Wallace, "The Operation of Last Resort," *Saturday Evening Post,* October 20, 1951, 24–25, 80–95 at 95.

116. Ibid., 24.

117. On questions of the "nature of man" and the fundamental human anthropology that animated the American midcentury, see Mark Greif, *The Age of the Crisis of Man: Thought and Fiction in America, 1933–1973* (Princeton, NJ: Princeton University Press, 2015), 4–5, 61.

118. For an analysis of science fiction film classics like *Invasion of the Body Snatchers* (1956) and *Brain Eaters* (1958), see Sharon Packer, *Neuroscience in Science Fiction Films* (Jefferson, NC: McFarland, 2014), 114. See also Priscilla Wald, *Contagious: Cultures, Carriers, and the Outbreak Narrative* (Durham, NC: Duke University Press, 2008), 189.

119. John Lahr, *Tennessee Williams: Mad Pilgrimage of the Flesh* (New York: W. W. Norton, 2014), 357.

120. Tennessee Williams, *Suddenly Last Summer* (New York: Dramatists Play Service, [1958] 1986), 14.

121. Ibid., 15.

122. Sylvia Plath, *The Bell Jar* (London: Faber and Faber, [1963] 1966), 185. For details on McLean, see Beam, *Gracefully Insane*, 2, 13.

123. Freeman and Watts, "Prefrontal Lobotomy in the Treatment of Mental Disorders," 25.

124. Insulin therapy began to be used in the United States in 1936 and by the early 1940s most institutions were employing it. It produced a state of hypoglycemic shock but no seizures while Metrazol and electric shock both produced convulsions. As Joel Braslow notes, a complete course of insulin could entail fifty to sixty days in a coma, a coma that was considered rehabilitative. See *Mental Ills and Bodily Cures*, 96–99. Metrazol treatment followed a similar course as that of insulin therapy but substituted a synthetic form of camphor for insulin. Hornstein notes that by 1942 more than 75,000 patients were treated with one of the shock treatment methods. See *To Redeem One Person Is to Redeem the World*, 241.

125. Shorter, *A History of Psychiatry*, 213. Jonathan Sadowsky notes that by 1941, 42% of American mental hospitals were using ECT machines. See *Electroconvulsive Therapy in America*, 47.

126. Lebensohn, "The History of Electroconvulsive Therapy in the United States and Its Place in American Psychiatry," 176. Muscle relaxants became more common before ECT treatments, and the procedure became more refined, during the 1960s (see p. 178).

127. Hornstein, *To Redeem One Person Is to Redeem the World*, 241. See also Scull, *Madness in Civilization*, 317. These historians tend to emphasize the negative effects of electroshock therapy, such as memory loss, while Edward Shorter offers a more positive take on the practice in *Shock Therapy*, 104.

128. Letter to Dr. Petersen, 1953, Superintendent's Office Correspondence, Box #114.B.15.5 (B), Rochester State Hospital, Government Records, p. 1.

129. Whitehorn would go on to write, for the American Psychiatric Association, *Psychiatry and Medical Education* (1951) and *The Psychiatrist, His Training, and Development* (1953), as well as *Effective Psychotherapy with the Schizophrenic Patient* (New York: Jason Aronson, 1975), 107ff. On Whitehorn, see Scull, *Psychiatry and Its Discontents*, 153.

130. "Third Year Course in Psychiatry," October 25, 1955, Fourth Meeting, Box #505554/2008-038, Folder 6: Third Year Lectures, Lex Smith Papers, Alan Mason Chesney Medical Archives, Johns Hopkins University, Baltimore, pp. 1–21 at 8.

131. Ibid., 9.

132. Ibid., 18.

133. Ibid., 20.

134. Ibid., 18. This medical lecture is emblematic of the idea that psychoanalytical and biological psychiatry were not always or solely oppositional. On this idea, see Sadowsky, *Electroconvulsive Therapy in America*, 94.

135. Letter, August 30, 1956, Records of Supt. Overholser, St. Elizabeths Hospital Records, Folder 8, Entry 7, RG 418, pp. 1–3 at 3.

136. Letter, July 13, 1956, File 14, Box 2, General Correspondence, Fan Mail, 1956–66, Fredric Wertham Papers, Manuscript Division, Library of Congress, Manuscript Collections, Washington, DC, pp. 1–7 at 1.

137. Ibid., 1, 2.

138. Ibid., 2.

139. Ibid., 3.

140. Ibid., 4.

141. Ibid., 5.

142. Harold Maine, *If a Man Be Mad* (New York: Doubleday, 1947), 411. "Harold Maine" was a pseudonym for Walker Winslow.

143. Letter, "Gentlemen," January, 1956, Box 2, Folder 7, Kenneth Donaldson Papers, MS 1677, Manuscript and Archives, Yale University Library, New Haven, CT, pp. 1–4 at 1.

144. When conscientious objectors during World War II were assigned to be attendants in mental hospitals, they were ideally supposed to rectify this cruelty. On this, see Grob, *From Asylum to Community*, 120. One letter writer to Governor Earl Warren attested to electric shock treatments given by what she considered "hardened and unscrupulous doctors" and attendants who made up the shock lists and used ECT as a form of punishment. See "Dear Governor Warren," July 25, 1952, Box F3640: 2749, Earl Warren Papers, Administrative Files, Dept. of Mental Hygiene, Camarillo State Hospital, California State Archives, Office of the Secretary of State, Sacramento, pp. 1–19 at 5 and 6.

145. Peter G. Cranford, *But for the Grace of God: The Inside Story of the World's Largest Insane Asylum* (Milledgeville, GA: Old Capital Press, 2008), 191. At this time, Milledgeville had a capacity of about 15,000 patients. See Scull, *The Insanity of Place/The Place of Insanity*, 117. It was also the subject of exposé journalism by Jack Nelson in 1959 in the *Atlanta Constitution*.

146. Cranford, *But for the Grace of God*, 192.

147. Ibid., 158.

148. Ibid., 189.

149. "Dear Governor," February 2, 1957, Box 4, Folder: Mental Files, 1955–1960, Hastings and Moose Lake Hospitals, Orville L. Freeman Papers, Minnesota State Archives, Minnesota Historical Society, St. Paul, p. 1. Hastings State opened in 1901 and was closed in 1978 and specialized in treating drug addictions and was modeled on the "cottage" system. Dr. Walter Freeman visited the hospital in 1949 to perform lobotomies. See Michael Resman, *Asylums, Treatment Centers and Genetic Jails: A History of Minnesota's State Hospitals* (Saint Cloud, MN: North Star Press of St. Cloud, 2013), 151, 154. Orville Freeman was the Democratic governor of Minnesota between 1955 and 1961; I discuss him in more depth in the next two chapters.

150. See, for example, Lecklider, *Inventing the Egghead*, 162–163. The figure of the "scientist at the bedside" was particularly prevalent in the late nineteenth century and at the turn of the century as it pertained to the anti-vivisection movement. On this, see Joanna Bourke, *The Story of Pain: From Prayer to Painkillers* (New York: Oxford University Press, 2014), 235–240.

151. "Former Mental Patient," "A Subjective Account of Electroshock Treatment," *The Attendant* 2, no. 11 (November 1945): 81.

152. Ibid., 84.

153. Judith Kruger, *My Fight for Sanity* (London: Hammond and Hammond, 1959), 61. The baby appears to have been born in the late 1940s or early 1950s (see p. 7). The hospital in the book is unnamed but presumably somewhere in or outside of Philadelphia, where she and her husband were living.

154. Nancy Tomes, "Feminist Histories of Psychiatry," in *Discovering the History of Psychiatry*, ed. Micale and Porter, 348–383 at 375. Here she is citing Elaine Showalter, who argues that in England and the United States women outnumbered men as ECT patients. Showalter also notes that lobotomy has been more often recommended for and administered to women.

Elaine Showalter, *The Female Malady: Women, Madness, and English Culture, 1830–1980* (New York: Pantheon Books, 1985), 207, 209. In his study of Stockton State Hospital in California, Joel Braslow noted that 85% of the 241 lobotomies performed there were on women. See *Mental Ills and Bodily Cures*, 154. Ian Dowbiggin states that between 1949 and 1951 in the United States, 60% of all patients who underwent lobotomies were women. See *The Quest for Mental Health*, 119.

155. Ralph Ellison, *Invisible Man* (New York: Vintage, [1952] 1995), 235–236.

156. Ibid., 237.

157. Ibid., 249.

158. Shorter and Healy, *Shock Therapy*, 9, 148–149, 153, 242. On electricity's connotation of lethalness in American history, see Sadowsky, *Electroconvulsive Therapy in America*, 24 and Seltzer, *Bodies and Machines*, 11. On patient reaction to electroshock in America, see Dale Peterson, ed., *A Mad People's History of Madness* (Pittsburgh: University of Pittsburgh Press, 1982), 241.

159. Mary Jane Ward, *The Snake Pit* (New York: Random House, 1946), 43. On the novel's impact, see Sadowsky, *Electroconvulsive Therapy in America*, 51. In the novel the hospital is called Juniper Hall. Rockland State opened in 1927, and at its peak during the 1950s it housed 9,000 patients and was one of the world's largest mental hospitals. See Deutsch, *The Shame of the States*, 84.

160. Ellison, *Invisible Man*, 233.

161. Vincent J. Daly, *Understanding Mental Illness: A Patient's Manual for Group Therapy* (Whitfield, MS: Mississippi State Hospital, 1950), 25.

162. Katrina Firlik, *Another Day in the Frontal Lobe: A Brain Surgeon Exposes Life on the Inside* (New York: Random House, 2006), 183.

163. Sadowsky, *Electroconvulsive Therapy in America*, 71.

164. Plath, *The Bell Jar*, 1.

165. Grob, *From Asylum to Community*, 90.

166. Alex Wellerstein, "States of Eugenics: Institutions and Practices of Compulsory Sterilization in California," in *Reframing Rights: Bioconstitutionalism in the Genetic Age*, ed. Sheila Jasanoff (Cambridge, MA: MIT Press, 2011), 29–59 at 50. On Warren's establishment of a Department of Mental Hygiene, and its programs, see Kevin Starr, *Embattled Dreams: California in War and Peace, 1940–1950* (New York: Oxford University Press, 2002), 270.

167. "Dear Gov," April 20, 1949, Box F3640:2777, Earl Warren Papers, Administrative Files, Dept. of Mental Hygiene, Camarillo State Hospital, pp. 1–5 at 1.

168. Ibid., 2.

169. Ibid., 4.

170. Robert J. Lifton, *The Nazi Doctors: Medical Killing and the Psychology of Genocide* (New York: Basic Books, 1986), 14.

171. Grob, *From Asylum to Community*, 149; Edward Shorter, *Bedside Manners: The Troubled History of Doctors and Patients* (New York: Simon and Schuster, 1985), 247; Herzberg, *Happy Pills in America*, 18.

172. *Proceedings of the Second Annual Public Hearing on Mental Health*, held by the New York State Senate Committee on Public Health in the Senate Chamber, The Capitol, Albany, New York, January 28, 1958, Senator George R. Metcalf, Chairman, Box 10, Folder 27, pp. 1–12 at 11, Mike Gorman Papers, 1946–1989, MS C 462, Modern Manuscripts Collection, History of Medicine Division, National Library of Medicine, Bethesda, MD.

173. On the impact of Thorazine, see Herzberg, *Happy Pills in America*, 8, 17–18. See also Tomes, *Remaking the American Patient*, 236.

174. Annual Report of the Northampton State Hospital, March 25, 1957, Department of Mental Health, Annual Reports of the Northampton State Hospital Collection, Massachusetts Archives, Boston, 9.

175. Slaughter, *Daybreak*, 241.

176. Andrew Scull challenges the role of drugs in the process of deinstitutionalization, placing his explanatory emphasis instead on new social policies that I will explore as context in Chapters 3 and 4. See *Madness in Civilization*, 369.

177. Henri Laborit, a French naval surgeon, used this phrase in 1951. See Judith Swazey, *Chlorpromazine in Psychiatry* (Cambridge, MA: MIT Press, 1974), 105.

178. David Walton Allen as told to his son Terence Beckington Allen, *Shrink! A Freudian Psychoanalyst Speaks About His Career in Psychiatry* (San Francisco: Redactors' Press, 2004), 52. He seems to be using "catatonia" in the sense of being in a stuporous state, though catatonia's meanings are more capacious than this and can also encompass agitation. See Edward Shorter, *What Psychiatry Left Out of the DSM-5: Mental Disorders Today* (New York: Routledge, 2015), 27.

179. "Dear Governor," January 6, 1956, Box 4, Folder: Mental Files 1955–1960, Assistance and Friendly Correspondence, Hastings and Moose Lake Hospitals, Orville L. Freeman Papers, Minnesota State Archives, Minnesota Historical Society, St. Paul, p. 1. It should be said that while Thorazine does reduce psychosis, it also has some serious effects, such as muscular twitches and what some patients and doctors called a "Thorazine shuffle," a noticeable, shuffling gate. On said effects, see Tanya Luhrmann, *Of Two Minds: An Anthropologist Looks at American Psychiatry* (New York: Vintage, 2001), 226.

180. Scull, *The Insanity of Place/The Place of Insanity*, 137. On the ethos of science and mistrust in science, see Hannah Arendt, "The Archimedean Point," in *Thinking Without a Banister: Essays in Understanding, 1953–1975* (New York: Schocken, 2018), 417 and "Values in Contemporary Society," 440.

181. Benno Muller-Hill, *Murderous Science: Elimination by Scientific Selection of Jews, Gypsies, and Others in Germany, 1933–1945* (New York: Oxford University Press, 1988), 89. See also Jacob Darwin Hamblin, *Arming Mother Nature: The Birth of Catastrophic Environmentalism* (New York: Oxford University Press, 2013), 17. Joel Isaac notes that objectivity and scientism in the United States have long been seen, especially in the immediate post–Civil War era, as ideologically charged, reinforcing cultures of experts. See Isaac, *Working Knowledge: Making the Human Sciences from Parsons to Kuhn* (Cambridge, MA: Harvard University Press, 2012), 15.

182. Martin Halliwell, *Therapeutic Revolutions*, 103. On scientism, see Jewett, *Science, Democracy, and the American University*, 4, 327, 272. He also notes that critics of scientism were making their voices heard in the New Deal era.

183. David Serlin, *Replaceable You: Engineering the Body in Postwar America* (Chicago: University of Chicago Press, 2004), 102. See his discussion of the positive publicity surrounding the reconstructive surgery of the Hiroshima Maidens in the United States. See also Grob, *From Asylum to Community*, 22.

184. Peter Bacon Hales, *Outside the Gates of Eden: The Dream of America from Hiroshima to Now* (Chicago: University of Chicago Press, 2014), 5.

Chapter 3

1. On this theme, see Babette Faehmel, *College Women in the Nuclear Age* (New Brunswick, NJ: Rutgers University Press, 2012), 7. On the concept of "therapeutic community," see Grob, *The Mad Among Us*, 227.

2. For a primary source on these themes, see, for example, Robert A. Nisbet, *Community and Power* (New York: Galaxy Books, [1953] 1962). For historiography, see Sandra Opdycke, "The Spaces People Share: The Changing Social Geography of American Life," in *The Columbia History of Post–World War Two America*, ed. Mark C. Carnes (New York: Columbia University Press, 2007), 11–36 at 18; Lizabeth Cohen, "From Town Center to Shopping Center: The Reconfiguration of Community Marketplaces in Postwar America," in *The Gender and Consumer Culture Reader*, ed. Jennifer Scanlon (New York: New York University Press, 2000), 245–261; and Elaine Tyler May, "Gimme Shelter: Do-It-Yourself Defense and the Politics of Fear," in *The Cultural Turn in U.S. History*, ed. Cook et al., 217–241 at 223. For a more general discussion, see Alan McKee, *The Public Sphere: An Introduction* (Cambridge: Cambridge University Press, 2005), 2. Finally, on African American communities and participation during the civil rights era, see Peniel E. Joseph, *Dark Days, Bright Nights: From Black Power to Barack Obama* (New York: Basic Books, 2010), 6.

3. I note that consensus culture did have another, more positive valence in this period, as a means of avoiding ideological extremes. See Jewett, *Science, Democracy, and the American University*, 283. On the need to resist "un-American" collectivist ideas, see May, "Gimme Shelter," 222. See also Nisbet, *Community and Power*, 191, 201. On mass consumer society, see Erich Fromm, *The Art of Loving* (New York: Continuum, [1956] 2008), 77.

4. On the tensions between excessive individualism and conformity in American culture, see Wilfred M. McClay, *The Masterless: Self and Society in Modern America* (Chapel Hill: University of North Carolina Press, 1994), 3. See also Jewett, *Science, Democracy, and the American University*, 298.

5. Eli Zaretsky, "Domesticity and Psychoanalysis," in *Intimacy*, ed. Lauren Berlant (Chicago: University of Chicago Press, 2000), 378–404 at 385. See also Eli Zaretsky, "Psychoanalysis, Authoritarianism, and the 1960s," in *Psychoanalysis and Politics: Histories of Psychoanalysis Under Conditions of Restricted Political Freedom*, ed. Joy Damousi and Mariano Ben Plotkin (New York: Oxford University Press, 2012), 233–259 at 238 and Ellen Herman, *The Romance of American Psychology: Political Culture in the Age of Experts* (Berkeley: University of California Press, 1995), 19.

6. On the resurgence of psychoanalysis, see Grob, *From Asylum to Community*, 17, 95. While after the war many European psychiatrists continued to follow Kraepelin, American psychiatrists turned away from him and advocated psychotherapy. Decker, *The Making of the DSM-III*, 3; and Karl Menninger, *The Vital Balance: The Life Process in Mental Health and Illness* (New York: Penguin, 1963), 294. On American psychoanalysts' questioning of Freudian orthodoxy, see Noll, *American Madness*, 265.

7. Herzberg, *Happy Pills in America*, 15; Hale, *The Rise and Crisis of Psychoanalysis in the United States*, 253. On the DSM-I, see Decker, *The Making of the DSM-III*, xvii, 3 and Grob, *From Asylum to Community*, 97.

8. Decker, *The Making of the DSM-III*, 3.

9. Herzberg, *Happy Pills in America*, 32–33. The 1957 statistic is from Alan Horwitz, *Anxiety: A Short History* (Baltimore: Johns Hopkins University, 2013), 119. See also Scull, *Madness in Civilization*, 384.

10. On film, see, for example, *Spellbound*, directed by Alfred Hitchcock (1945). On popular psychoanalysis, see Robert Lindner, *The Fifty-Minute Hour: A Collection of True Psychoanalytic Tales* (New York: Bantam, 1955). This quotation is from the inset of the book. On psychoanalytic thought in the mass media, see Eva Illouz, *Cold Intimacies: The Making of Emotional Capitalism*

(New York: Polity, 2007), 53. On the presence of psychoanalysis in pop culture, see Rachel Devlin, *Relative Intimacy: Fathers, Adolescent Daughters, and Postwar American Culture* (Chapel Hill: University of North Carolina Press, 2005), 21 and Jonathan Metzl, *Prozac on the Couch: Prescribing Gender in the Era of Wonder Drugs* (Durham, NC: Duke University Press, 2003), 14.

11. See Alfred Kazin, *Contemporaries* (Boston: Little, Brown, 1958), 370. See Trilling's well-known 1955 essay "Freud and the Crisis of Our Culture" (Boston: Beacon Press, 1955). On intellectuals' admiration for Freudian ideas in the 1950s, see Ross, "Freud and the Vicissitudes of Modernism in the United States," 172ff.

12. On the mental health of nations, see Eva Illouz, *Saving the Modern Soul: Therapy, Emotions, and the Culture of Self Help* (Berkeley: University of California Press, 2008), 157 and Herman, *The Romance of American Psychology*, 173ff. On anthropology, see John S. Gilkeson, *Anthropologists and the Rediscovery of America, 1886–1965* (Cambridge: Cambridge University Press, 2010), 5 and Scull, *Madness in Civilization*, 351. On anthropologists' analysis of "national character," see Jewett, *Science, Democracy, and the American University*, 293, 342. On psychiatry in the face of psychology and social work, see Grob, *From Asylum to Community*, 92 and *The Mad Among Us*, 276.

13. Noll, *American Madness*, 266. Edith M. Stern and Samuel W. Hamilton, *Mental Illness: A Guide for the Family* (New York: National Association for Mental Health, 1954), 58. Some private establishments, such as the Menninger Clinic, Chestnut Lodge, Austen Riggs, and the McLean Hospital, maintained that psychoanalysis was necessary, including for patients with schizophrenia. On this, see Scull, *Madness in Civilization*, 341. Jonathan Metzl notes that in 1955 the number of patients in state hospitals reached its highest point: 559,000 were institutionalized out of a general population of 165 million. See Metzl, *The Protest Psychosis: How Schizophrenia Became a Black Disease* (Boston: Beacon, 2009), 13.

14. Mike Gorman, *Every Other Bed* (New York: World Publishing Company, 1956), 13.

15. David Maraniss, "Afterword: Uncle Phil's Brain," in *Nothing to Hide: Mental Illness in the Family*, ed. Jean J. Beard and Peggy Gillespie (New York: New Press, 2002), 272.

16. Ibid., 273.

17. Ibid., 274.

18. Ibid., 275. A topectomy is a variation on a lobotomy—a removal of more specific areas of the frontal lobes as a means of treatment.

19. Ibid., 277.

20. Jerome K. Myers and and Bertram H. Roberts, *Family and Class Dynamics in Mental Illness* (New York: John Wiley and Sons, 1959), 205. They also discuss a 1952 study which found that the wealthy accepted the idea of neurosis to a certain extent and felt entitled to be served by institutions, while the poor were more cynical about neurosis and only consulted medical help for ailments beyond neurosis(see p. 52).

21. Siegfried Wenzel, *The Sin of Sloth: "Acedia" in Medieval Thought and Literature* (Chapel Hill: University of North Carolina Press, 1967), 31.

22. Karen Horney, *Self Analysis* (New York: W. W. Norton, 1942), 29.

23. Myers and Roberts, *Family and Class Dynamics in Mental Illness*, 208. They argue that "pulling yourself together" is a particularly working-class mentality with regard to therapy.

24. Kristin Gay Esterberg, "From Illness to Action: Conceptions of Homosexuality in *The Ladder*, 1956–1965," *Journal of Sex Research* 27, no. 1 (February 1990): 65–80. Esterberg argues that the challenge to viewing homosexuality as a mental illness did not emerge among activists until after 1964

25. Stern and Hamilton, *Mental Illness*, 1. First published in 1942, and revised several times between then and 1962, I am quoting here from the 1954 version. Her exposé piece is titled "Our Ailing Mental Hospitals" and was published in both *Survey Graphic* and *Reader's Digest* in August 1941. Available online at https://archive.org/stream/surveygraphic30survrich /surveygraphic30survrich_djvu.txt.

The insistence that mental illness was just like physical illness was quite common in advice literature for families. See Karl R. Beutner and Nathan G. Hale, *Emotional Illness: How Families Can Help* (New York: G. P. Putnam's Sons, 1957), 15.

26. Vincent G. King, "Space: A Fundamental Concept in Design," in *Psychiatric Architecture*, ed. Goshen, 21–22 at 22.

27. See Silvano Arieti, "Manic-Depressive Psychosis," in *American Handbook of Psychiatry*, vol. 1, ed. Arieti (New York: Basic Books, 1959), 419–454 at 427.

28. Ian Stevenson and William M. Sheppe, "The Psychiatric Examination," in *American Handbook of Psychiatry*, vol. 1, ed. Arieti, 215–234 at 220.

29. On this, see, for example, the introduction to Frank Biess and Daniel M. Gross, eds., *Science and Emotions After 1945: A Transatlantic Perspective* (Chicago: University of Chicago Press, 2014), 2, 5.

30. However, it did not enjoy the same success as Thorazine; it was not as fast-acting, even if it did have fewer side effects. See Grob, *From Asylum to Community*, 149.

31. See *St. Elizabeths Hospital: Mental Patients from Northern Virginia: Hearing Before a Subcommittee of the Committee on Education and Labor House of Representatives Eighty-Fifth Congress First Session on H.R. 6638 A Bill to Provide for the Admission and Treatment of Mental Patients from Northern Virginia at St. Elizabeths Hospital Hearing Held in Washington, DC, August 1, 1957* (Washington, DC: U.S. Government Printing Office, 1958), 14. On the expansion of the VA system, and Saint Elizabeths as more a civilian institution in the postwar period, see Summers, *Madness in the City of Magnificent Intentions*, 232.

32. Dr. Waldrop, Serpasil Study, January 15, 1955, Folder 1, St. Elizabeths Records of the Medical Records Branch: Clinical Notes Relating to the Serpasil Geriatric Project, 1954–1955, Entry 70, RG 418, National Archives, Washington, DC.

33. Henry Davidson, "A Psychiatric Word Clinic: Session IV: Words Describing Withdrawal or Indifference," *Psychiatric Services* 9, no. 3 (March 1958): 12.

34. Dr. Waldrop, Serpasil Study, October 5, 1954.

35. Dr. Waldrop, Serpasil Study, November 5, 1954.

36. Dr. Waldrop, Serpasil Study, December 4, 1954.

37. On conceptualizations of a distinctive Black emotionality and psyche from the late nineteenth century to the mid-twentieth century, see Summers, *Madness in the City of Magnificent Intentions*, 84–85, 179, 250, 266, 271–274. In a similar vein, in *The Wretched of the Earth* (New York: Grove/Atlantic, [1961] 2007), Frantz Fanon famously noted that to the Algerian School of Psychiatry, which attempted to justify European colonialism in Algeria, the North African was a "lobotomized European" (36).

38. Halliwell, *Therapeutic Revolutions*, 211, 208. *Ebony* reported in 1949 that in New York, Illinois, and California, "colored admissions" to asylums exceeded white ones by two to one. See "Insanity," *Ebony* (April 1949): 19, Box 3, Folder 4, 1946–1949, Lafargue Clinic Records, Sc MG 141, Schomburg Center for Research in Black Culture, Manuscripts, Archives, and Rare Books Division, New York Public Library, Harlem. Kenneth Clark, too, noted in *Dark Ghetto:*

Dilemmas of Social Power (New York: Harper and Row, 1965), 83, that Harlem ranked first in admissions to state hospitals.

39. On deference, see Gambino, "'These Strangers Within Our Gates,'" 394. Martin Summers shows that physical restraints and seclusion were more likely to be used on African American patients than on white patients at Saint Elizabeths during the early twentieth century. See *Madness in the City of Magnificent Intentions*, 164. On conditions in segregated wards, see Metzl, *The Protest Psychosis*, 40.

40. On the slow pace of desegregation, see Gambino, "'These Strangers Within Our Gates,'" 394. Southern hospitals in particular took a full decade after *Brown* to desegregate. On this, see Halliwell, *Therapeutic Revolutions*, 227. As Martin Summers points out, though, Saint Elizabeths' ward integration was complete by 1956. See *Madness in the City of Magnificent Intentions*, 250. Superintendent Overholser, however, was an incrementalist when it came to racial change. He argued in 1948, for example, that the racial integration of Virginia hospitals could be harmful to patient care. See Rose, *Psychology and Selfhood in the Segregated South*, 157. It should be noted, too, that private psychiatric hospitals in the early postwar period tended not to admit African American patients. Metzl, *The Protest Psychosis*, 40.

41. Quoted in Robert Bendiner, "Psychiatry for the Needy," April 1948, 22–26 at 24, Box 3, Folder: Reprints re Lafargue Clinic, Lafargue Clinic Records. See also document dated November 5, 1949, p. 1, Box 92, Folder 2, Fredric Wertham Papers.

42. See "Insanity," 21. Martin Summers also writes about the early and mid-twentieth-century underuse of outpatient mental health services by African Americans and their over-representation in in-patient services, particularly in public hospitals. See "Diagnosing the Ailments of Black Citizenship: African American Physicians and the Politics of Mental Illness, 1895–1940," in *Precarious Prescriptions*, ed. Green et al., 91–114 at 91–92.

43. See Zora Neale Hurston, "What White Publishers Won't Print," *Negro Digest*, April 1950, 1.

44. On midcentury racial liberalism, see Lily Geismer, *Don't Blame Us: Suburban Liberals and the Transformation of the Democratic Party* (Princeton, NJ: Princeton University Press, 2015), 9. Literary critic Claudia Tate has argued that both historians and literary scholars tend to view their African American subjects as purely political beings, thereby marginalizing emotional realms. See *Psychoanalysis and Black Novels: Desire and the Protocols of Race* (New York: Oxford University Press, 1998), 4, 5. More recently, Badia Ahad has written about a long-standing presumption in American thought and culture that African American women in particular lack a complex emotional and psychological life. On this, see "Confessions," in *Rethinking Therapeutic Culture*, ed. Timothy Aubry and Trysh Travis (Chicago: University of Chicago Press, 2015), 85–95 at 86. Ahad also notes that psychoanalysis was a preoccupation of modernist African American intellectuals and writers, just as it was for their white counterparts. See Badia Sahar Ahad, *Freud Upside Down: African American Literature and Psychoanalytic Culture* (Urbana: University of Illinois Press, 2010), 2.

45. Mari Jo Buhle, *Feminism and Its Discontents: A Century of Struggle with Psychoanalysis* (Cambridge, MA: Harvard University Press, 1998), 171. The National Mental Health Act created the National Institute of Mental Health in 1949. See Scull, *The Insanity of Place/The Place of Insanity*, 94. Professional psychiatric organizations enlarged and proliferated during this period as well, such as the American Psychiatric Association in 1946 and the Group for the Advancement of Psychiatry. See Groh, *From Asylum to Community*, 78, 24 and Scull, *Psychiatry and Its Discontents*, 162.

46. Elizabeth J. Donaldson, "*The Snake Pit*: Mary Jane Ward's Asylum Fiction and Mental Health Advocacy," in *Literatures of Madness: Disability Studies and Mental Health*, ed. Donaldson (London: Palgrave Macmillan, 2018), 109–126 at 109. For details on Rockland, see p. 111.

47. Though organizations in the vein of the National Committee on Mental Hygiene also attempted to educate the public through awareness campaigns, prevention, and community programs during the interwar years. See Grob, *From Asylum to Community*, 82.

48. "Dear Sir," March 22, 1946, Box F3640: 2745, Administrative Files, Dept. of Mental Hygiene, Camarillo State Hospital, 1945–1946, Earl Warren Papers, pp. 1–4 at 1, 2–3.

49. Ibid., 4.

50. Ibid., 3–4.

51. Ibid., 4.

52. "Mrs. Buchanan to Work with Group Affairs," *Pomo News* 1, no. 46 (March 22, 1949): 1–7 at 7, F 3886:45 Mendocino State Hospital, Mental Hygiene-Hospitals, California State Archives.

53. Pressman, *Last Resort*, 151.

54. Letter to Dr. Overholser from a patient in CT-2B, [1955–60], Folder 1, St. Elizabeths Hospital, Records of the Superintendent: Administrative Files, Ca 1921–1964, Entry 7, RG 418, p. 1.

55. Erving Goffman, *Asylums: Essays on the Social Situation of Mental Patients and Other Inmates* (New York: Anchor Books, 1961), 13. On Goffman, see Halliwell, *Therapeutic Revolutions*, 212. For an alternate view, see Gambino, "Erving Goffman's Asylums and Institutional Culture in the Mid-Twentieth Century United States," 53–54. For other examples of patient family gratefulness toward superintendents, see Letter, June 3, 1951, Superintendent's Office Correspondence, Rochester State Hospital Documents, Box 114.B.15.5 (B), Folder: Rochester State Hospital, p. 1; and Letter, April 9, 1952, Box F3640: 2768, Administrative Files, Department of Mental Hygiene, Patton State Hospital, 1951–1952, Earl Warren Papers, pp. 1–2.

56. Herman C. B. Denber, *Research Conference on Therapeutic Community Held at Manhattan State Hospital Ward's Island, New York* (Springfield, IL: Charles C. Thomas, 1960), 21. Denber was the director of Psychiatric Research at Manhattan State Hospital, Ward's Island, New York. Vermont State Hospital, which is in Waterbury (now affiliated with the University of Vermont), opened in 1890, at first for the criminally insane and later for those suffering from an array of mental disorders, including alcoholism, epilepsy, and depression.

57. Kathleen Doyle, *Public Affairs Pamphlet No. 172: When Mental Illness Strikes Your Family* (New York: Public Affairs Committee, 1951), 26.

58. Quoted in John Cumming and Elaine Cumming, "Social Equilibrium and Social Change in a Large Mental Hospital," in *The Patient and the Mental Hospital*, ed. Milton Greenblatt et al. (Glencoe, IL: Free Press, 1957), 49–71 at 55. On asylum architecture mirroring domestic spaces, see Leslie Topp et al., eds., *Madness, Architecture, and the Built Environment: Psychiatric Spaces in Historical* (New York: Routledge, 2007), 6.

59. J. Sanbourne Bockoven, "Some Relationships Between Cultural Attitudes Toward Individuality and Care of the Mentally Ill: An Historical Study," in *The Patient and the Mental Hospital*, ed. Greenblatt et al., 517–534 at 525.

60. Deutsch, *The Shame of the States*, 27.

61. Mike Gorman, "Misery Rules in State Shadowland," *Daily Oklahoman* series reprint (July–October 1946): 7, http://profiles.nlm.nih.gov/ps/access/TGBBGW.pdf.

62. Frieda Fromm-Reichmann, "Loneliness," *Psychiatry: Journal for the Study of Interpersonal Processes* 22 (February 1959): 3.

63. Ibid., 2.

64. Denber, "A Therapeutic Community," 65, in Denber, ed., *Research Conference on Therapeutic Community*.

65. Deutsch, *The Shame of the States*, 79.

66. Gorman, "Misery Rules in State Shadowland," 3.

67. Goffman, *Asylums*, 359.

68. Stern and Hamilton, *Mental Illness*, 53.

69. *Mental Hospital*, directed by Layton Mabrey, 1953. Produced by the University of Oklahoma, for the Oklahoma State Department of Health and Mental Health. Distributed by the International Film Bureau,
https://archive.org/details/mental_hospital. The film was made in Central State Hospital in Norman, Oklahoma, or the Norman State Hospital, which was known in the 1950s for its overcrowding. Mike Gorman notes that the hospital had only one doctor for every seven hundred patients. See "Misery Rules in State Shadowland," 9.

70. See "Vocation Camp for Psychiatric Patients: VA Hospital, Fort Meade, South Dakota," in Department of Medicine and Surgery Information Bulletin: Psychiatry and Neurology Division, Office of the Chief Medical Director Veterans Administration, Washington, DC, John Milne Murray Papers, Box 16, Folder 2, U.S. Veterans Administration, Library of Congress, Manuscript Division, Washington, DC, pp. 20–22. Other examples that I cite here are taken from the Commonwealth of Massachusetts, *Annual Report of the Northampton State Hospital* for March 25, 1957, Department of Mental Health, Annual Reports of the Northampton State Hospital Collection, Massachusetts Archives, Boston,13.

71. See pamphlet titled "This Is Radio Therapy," Missouri State Hospital, No. 4, Farmington, Missouri, Photos of "Miss X," a patient in dance therapy, in "Film Programs as Therapy for Mental Shut-ins: A Scientifically Developed Formula Now Winning Wide Favor as Patient-Care Factor"; "Some Uses of Psychodrama at St. Elizabeth's Hospital"; "Creative Work by the Wednesday Group at St. Elizabeth's Hospital," all in Folder 2, Entry 7, Annual Reports, 1942–1946, St. Elizabeths Hospital Papers, Administrative Files, Entry 7, RG 418.

72. Mortimer Gross, "Therapy in a State Hospital Regressed Ward," *Journal of Nervous and Mental Disease* 120, no. 5 (November/December 1954): 325.

73. See Barry Edginton, "A Space for Moral Management," in *Madness, Architecture, and the Built Environment*, ed. Topp et al., 85–104 at 87. Portions of the Retreat, such as Lawton Hall, were designated for "mild psychoneurotic or borderline cases," predominantly from the "business and professional classes," and sought to offer an "environment conducive to rest and relaxation." See Esther M. Swift, *Brattleboro Retreat: 1834–1984, 150 Years of Caring* (Brattleboro, VT: The Retreat, 1984), 98.

74. Letter, April 21, 1949, Box 10, File 1, George Amsden (1870–1966) Papers, 1898–1953, Medical Center Archives of New York-Presbyterian/Weill Cornell Medicine, New York, pp. 1–4 at 1, 2.

75. Goffman, *Asylums*, 13.

76. Letter, April 21, 1949, 1.

77. Anne Sexton, "Ringing the Bells," in *To Bedlam and Part Way Back* (Boston: Houghton Mifflin, 1960), 40.

78. H. Warren Dunham and S. Kirson Weinberg, *The Culture of the State Mental Hospital* (Detroit: Wayne State University Press, 1960), 120.

79. Ibid., 204.

80. Russell K. Hampton, *The Far Side of Despair: A Personal Account of Depression* (Chicago: Nelson-Hall, 1975), 43.

81. Paul Hackett, *The Cardboard Giants* (London: Victor Gollancz, 1953), 18.

82. Ibid., 303.

83. On the "comfortable concentration camp," see Betty Friedan, *The Feminine Mystique* (New York: Dell, 1962), 305. On tranquilizers, see p. 20. On Friedan's influence on the feminist critique of psychiatry, see Tomes, "Feminist Histories of Psychiatry."

84. Friedan, *The Feminine Mystique*, 301.

85. Richard E. Gordon, Katherine K. Gordon, and Max Gunther, *The Split Level Trap* (New York: Bernard Geis, 1960), 18.

86. Letter, August 21, 1956, Folder 8: Inquiries, Records of the Superintendent, Entry 7, RG 418, St. Elizabeths Hospital, pp. 1–2 at 1.

87. Ibid., 2.

88. Peter D. Kramer, *Listening to Prozac: A Psychiatrist Explores Antidepressant Drugs and the Remaking of the Self* (New York: Penguin, 1993), 39, 270.

89. Andrea Tone, *The Age of Anxiety: A History of America's Turbulent Affair with Tranquilizers* (New York: Basic Books, 2008), xvi, 106. See also Herzberg, *Happy Pills in America*, 7, 47–48. Herzberg shows that Miltown's critics thought the drug might diminish white-collar men's initiative.

90. Louis Menand, "Freud, Anxiety, and the Cold War," in *After Freud Left*, ed. Burnham, 189–207 at 200.

91. Letter, August 21, 1956, 2. The drug she is referring to here is Meratran, a central nervous system stimulant. During the 1940s, it was mostly used to treat senile dementia, though it was trialed for depression and schizophrenia. See William A. G. Begg and A. Arnaud Reid, "Meratran: A New Stimulant Drug," *British Medical Journal* 1, no. 4973 (April 28, 1956): 946–949.

92. Richard Yates, *Revolutionary Road* (New York: Vintage, [1961] 2008), 53. On midcentury domesticity, see, for example, Rebecca Jo Plant, *Mom: The Transformation of Motherhood in Modern America* (Chicago: University of Chicago Press, 2010), 88.

93. Cohen, "From Town Center to Shopping Center," 247.

94. "How to Keep Sane in a Hospital for Mental Patients," [late 1940s], Box 10, Folder 6, George Amsden Papers.

95. On deepening religion, see George M. Marsden, *The Twilight of the American Enlightenment: The 1950s and the Crisis of Liberal Belief* (New York: Basic Books, 2014), 97ff. See Gretta Palmer and Howard Whitman, "Is Psychoanalysis at War with God?" *Cosmopolitan* (June 1947): 26, 113–118, Box 3, Folder 4, 1946–1947, Publicity News Clippings, Lafargue Clinic Records.

96. Erving Goffman, *The Presentation of Self in Everyday Life* (New York: Anchor, 1959), 18.

97. Letter, December 26, 1943, Box 10, Folder 2, George Amsden Papers, pp. 1–4 at 4.

98. Abigail Cheever, *Real Phonies: Cultures of Authenticity in Post–World War Two America* (Athens: University of Georgia Press, 2010), 18–19.

99. Moran, "Architects of Madness," 164.

100. Dr. Kiracofe to Dr. E. D. Griffin, August 26, 1954, Folder 1: Mandatory Letters and Complaints, Entry 7, Records of the Superintendent of St. Elizabeth's Hospital, Administrative Files, 1921–1964, RG 418.

101. Letter, August 18, 1954, Folder 1: Mandatory Letters and Complaints, Entry 7, Records of the Superintendent of St. Elizabeth's Hospital, Administrative Files, 1921–1964, RG 418.

102. Duval was the acting superintendent at this time. Letter, August 27, 1954, Folder 1: Mandatory Letters and Complaints, Entry 7, Records of the Superintendent of St. Elizabeth's Hospital, Administrative Files, 1921–1964, RG 418.

103. *Voluntary Admission and Treatment of Patients at St. Elizabeths Hospital Hearing Before Subcommittee No. 2 of the Committee on Education and Labor House of Representatives 80th Congress Second Session on H.R. 4553 and H.R. 6289 Bills to Provide for the Voluntary Admission and Treatment of Mental Patients at Saint Elizabeths Hospital with Report on H.R. 6289 December 2, 1947* (Washington, DC: U.S. Government Printing Office, 1948), 19. William C. Woodward was the chairman of the Sub-Committee on Mental Disorders, District of Columbia Bar Association.

104. George Cotkin, *Existential America* (Baltimore: Johns Hopkins University Press, 2003), 60ff.

105. On communists, see Herbert Philbrick's confessional *I Led Three Lives: Citizen, "Communist," Counterspy* (New York: McGraw-Hill, 1952) and J. Edgar Hoover, *Masters of Deceit* (New York: Pocket Books, 1959). On class mobility, see Lionel Trilling, *Sincerity and Authenticity* (Cambridge, MA: Harvard University Press, 1971), 16. On race, see Allyson Hobbs, *A Chosen Exile: A History of Racial Passing in American Life* (Cambridge, MA: Harvard University Press, 2014), 4. On Jewish "passing" and fluid identities, see Daniel Itzkovitz, "Passing Like Me: Jewish Chameleonism and the Politics of Race," in *Passing: Identity and Interpretation in Sexuality, Race, and Religion*, ed. Maria Carla Sanchez and Linda Schlossberg (New York: New York University Press, 2001), 38–64.

106. See Goffman, *The Presentation of Self in Everyday Life*, 17–19.

107. Bruno Bettelheim, *The Informed Heart: Autonomy in a Mass Age* (New York: Free Press, 1960), 137.

108. Hortense Powdermaker, "The Channeling of Negro Aggression by the Cultural Process," in *Personality in Nature, Society, and Culture*, ed. Clyde Kluckhohn and Henry A. Murray (New York: Knopf, 1950), 473–484 at 481. On rituals of segregation, see Rose, *Psychology and Selfhood in the Segregated South*, 155. See also Walter A. Adams, "Segregation-Integration: Patterns of Culture and Social Adjustment," *American Journal of Orthopsychiatry* 28, no. 1 (January 1958): 15. On the "façade of acquiescence" in the face of racism, see Jay Garcia, *Psychology Comes to Harlem: Rethinking the Race Question in 20th Century America* (Baltimore: Johns Hopkins University Press, 2012), 85. On emotional facades before white people more broadly, see Jonathan Scott Holloway, *Jim Crow Wisdom: Memory and Identity in Black America Since 1940* (Chapel Hill: University of North Carolina Press, 2015), 16.

109. On the alleged passivity of the "masses," see Andrew Ross, *No Respect: Intellectuals and Popular Culture* (New York: Routledge, 1989), 106, 116. On perceptions of the masses as being uniquely susceptible to persuasion, see Sarah Igo, *The Averaged American: Surveys, Citizens, and the Making of a Mass Public* (Cambridge, MA: Harvard University Press, 2007), 109.

110. See Daniel Horowitz, *Consuming Pleasures: Intellectuals and Popular Culture in the Postwar World* (Philadelphia: University of Pennsylvania Press, 2012), 30–36 and Alpers, *Dictators, Democracy, and American Public Culture*, 108. For primary sources, see T. W. Adorno, *The Authoritarian Personality* (New York: Harper and Bros., 1950), 748, 759, 760. See also Max Horkheimer and Theodor Adorno, *Dialectic of Enlightenment: Philosophical Fragments* (Palo Alto, CA: Stanford University Press, 2002), 94–137.

111. Carol R. Murphy, "Religion and Mental Illness" [pamphlet] (Wallingford, PA: Pendle Hill, 1955), 5, 6.

112. See, for example, Marshall McLuhan, *Understanding the Media: The Extensions of Man* (New York: McGraw-Hill, 1964), 47, 346. The motif of extreme passivity and catatonia was likewise prevalent in 1950s alien invasion films. See, for example, Susan L. Carruthers, *Cold War Captives: Imprisonment, Escape, and Brainwashing* (Berkeley: University of California Press, 2009), 15.

113. Greif, *The Age of the Crisis of Man*, 49. See also Eric Josephson and Mary Josephson, eds., *Man Alone: Alienation in Modern Society* (New York: Laurel, 1962), 9–53 at 27.

114. On mechanized warfare, see Halliwell, *Therapeutic Revolutions*, 79. On Hiroshima, see Martin Woessner, *Heidegger in America* (Cambridge: Cambridge University Press, 2011), 76.

115. Nathan W. Ackerman, *The Psychodynamics of Family Life: Diagnosis and Treatment of Family Relationships* (New York: Basic Books, 1958), 4.

116. Erich Fromm, *Escape from Freedom* (New York: Farrar and Rinehart, 1941), 186, 253. On the perception that Nazis were automatons, see Alpers, *Dictators, Democracy, and American Public Culture*, 99.

117. Letter to Fromm, March 4, 1942, Erich Fromm Papers, Reel 1, ZL-340, Manuscripts and Archives Division, New York Public Library, Astor, Lenox, and Tilden Foundations, New York, pp. 1–3 at 1.

118. Ibid., 2.

119. Ibid., 3.

120. Fromm, *The Art of Loving*, 78–79.

121. Hornstein, *To Redeem One Person Is to Redeem the World*, 242.

122. George Cotkin, *Feast of Excess: A Cultural History of the New Sensibility* (New York: Oxford University Press, 2015), 107.

123. On popularity culture, see C. Wayne Gordon, *The Social System of the High School: A Study in the Sociology of Adolescence* (Glencoe, IL: Free Press, 1957), 107. See also a 1952 Encyclopedia Britannica film, *Keeping Mentally Fit*, available online at https://www.youtube.com/watch?v=fwJGbhQpaJU. For details on Stanton and Schwartz's study, see the review by Lucy D. Ozarin, *Psychiatric Services* 5, no. 10 (December 1954): 10. During the time that they investigated Chestnut Lodge, the institution helped those who had been diagnosed with schizophrenia, manic depression, and alcoholism. Alfred H. Stanton and Morris S. Schwartz, *The Mental Hospital: A Study of Institutional Participation in Psychiatric Illness and Treatment* (New York: Basic Books, 1954), 82. For details on the recreational programs that Chestnut Lodge provided in the postwar period, see Chloethiel Woodard Smith, "Developing the Building Program," in *Psychiatric Architecture*, ed. Goshen, 85–96 at 85. On the hotel vision as an aspirational one for a range of institutions, see John Latenser Jr., "The Nebraska Psychiatric Institute: Some Architectural Considerations," in *Psychiatric Architecture*, ed. Goshen, 28–34 at 28.

124. Hornstein, *To Redeem One Person Is to Redeem the World*, 203.

125. Stanton and Schwartz, *The Mental Hospital*, 199.

126. Grob, *From Asylum to Community*, 145.

127. Jean-Christophe Agnew, "The Walking Man and the Talking Cure," in *After Freud Left*, ed. Burnham, 233–245 at 235.

128. Jamie Cohen-Cole, *The Open Mind: Cold War Politics and the Sciences of Human Nature* (Chicago: University of Chicago Press, 2014), 17; Gilkeson, *Anthropologists and the Rediscovery of America*, 250.

129. Chloethiel Woodard Smith, "Architectural Research and the Construction of Mental Hospitals," in *Psychiatric Architecture*, ed. Goshen, 10–15 at 14.

130. Lesley Johnson and Justine Lloyd, *Sentenced to Everyday Life: Feminism and the House-wife* (New York: Berg, 2004), 128.

131. Stanton and Schwartz, *The Mental Hospital*, 122.

132. Carla Yanni, *The Architecture of Madness* (Minneapolis: University of Minnesota Press, 2007), 102. For an unsettling cultural portrait, see the long corridor in the 1962 classic film *Shock Corridor*, directed by Samuel Fuller. Chloethiel Woodard Smith wrote of the "necessary evil of the corridor" and of minimizing its length. See Smith, "Architectural Research and the Construction of Mental Hospitals," 11, 13.

133. Stanton and Schwartz, *The Mental Hospital*, 186.

134. Ibid., 187.

135. Dunham and Weinberg, *The Culture of the State Mental Hospital*, 67.

136. Martin Meeker, *Contacts Desired: Gay and Lesbian Communications and Community, 1940s–1970s* (Chicago: University of Chicago Press, 2006), 83. On integration and race, see David L. Chappell, *A Stone of Hope: Prophetic Religion and the Death of Jim Crow* (Chapel Hill: University of North Carolina Press, 2004), 4. On reintegration into society at large for patients, see Gorman, "Misery Rules in State Shadowland," 9.

137. On the romance of individualism, see Faehmel, *College Women in the Nuclear Age*, 91–92, 138 and Alpers, *Dictators, Democracy, and American Public Culture*, 103.

138. "Insanity," 22.

139. Patients at Mendocino State Hospital in California, for example, could participate in staging operas, ward parties, and a minstrel show, advertised with actors in blackface. Perform-ing in blackface was a way that white patients maintained racial privilege; it also might have been a way for white patients to take on the subject position of an actor in blackface who reveals truths in the format of the figure of the Black "fool" character. These activities were advertised in the following issues of the patient newsletters: *Pomo News* 7, no. 24 (December 17, 1954): 1, 2; *Pomo News* 1, no. 8 (June 29, 1948): 1; *Pomo News* 1, no. 28 (November 16, 1948): 1, 2; *Pomo News* 1, no. 38 (January 25, 1949): 9; *Pomo News* 1, no. 42 (February 22, 1949): 2, all in F 3886:45, Mendocino State Hospital, Mental Hygiene-Hospitals, California State Archives. On the phe-nomenon of minstrel shows in the 1950s, see Smulyan, *Popular Ideologies*, 16ff. Benjamin Reiss shows that the blackface minstrel troupe of patients is a long-standing tradition, stretching back to the nineteenth century, and that white patients who appeared in blackface in these troupes were trying to show that they were capable of rationality in a way that the Black characters they derided were not. See Reiss, *Theaters of Madness*, 52.

140. "How to Keep Sane in a Hospital for Mental Patients," 1.

141. See, for example, Anton T. Boisen, *The Exploration of the Inner World: A Study of Men-tal Disorder and Religious Experience* (Oxford: Willett, Clark, 1936). See also his article, "The Form and Content of Schizophrenic Thinking," *Psychiatry: Interpersonal and Biological Processes* 5, no. 1 (1942): 23–33. The pamphlet by Boisen is undated (but estimated to have been written during the 1950s–early 1960s given the dates of the other documents in the file) and available online at Kansas Memory in the Anton T. Boisen Papers-40, "To Our New Guests," 1964 http://www.kansasmemory.org/item/223252/page/40.

142. Boisen pamphlet, 42.

143. Ibid., 43. This also appeared in Mendocino State Hospital's patient newsletter, *Pomo News* 1, no. 38 (January 25, 1949): 6.

144. "How to Keep Sane in a Hospital for Mental Patients," 2.

145. Letter, September 14, 1944, Box 10, Folder 2, George Amsden Papers, pp. 1–4 at 1 and 2.

146. Maine was first hospitalized in an unnamed island in the Pacific. Maine, *If a Man Be Mad*, 93.

147. Benjamin Looker, *A Nation of Neighborhoods: Imagining Cities, Communities and Democracy in Postwar America* (Chicago: University of Chicago Press, 2015), 54.

148. Hobbs, *A Chosen Exile*, 14.

149. Silvano Arieti, "Schizophrenia," in *American Handbook of Psychiatry*, vol. 1, ed. Arieti, 455–507 at 474.

150. Bruno Bettelheim, "Joey: A Mechanical Boy," in *Man Alone*, ed. Josephson and Josephson, 437–446 at 437. The original essay is from 1959.

151. Rose Spiegel, "Specific Problems of Communication in Psychiatric Conditions," in *American Handbook of Psychiatry*, vol. 1, ed. Arieti, 909–949 at 932.

152. Arieti, "Schizophrenia," 474. Arieti is significant for following a "trauma model" of schizophrenia rather than a strictly medical one, which might have contributed to his willingness to explore other intellectuals and writings in his approach. On Arieti's contributions, see Martin L. Gross, *The Psychological Society: A Critical Analysis of Psychiatry, Psychotherapy, Psychoanalysis and the Psychological Revolution* (New York: Random House, 1978), 95.

153. On "inner" and "other" directedness, see David Riesman, *The Lonely Crowd: A Study of the Changing American Character* (New Haven, CT: Yale University Press, 1950), especially 109ff., 126ff. On other-directedness, see Trilling, *Sincerity and Authenticity*, 66.

154. "Mental Health Is...1 2 3" (National Association for Mental Health, 1951), 2.

155. On the fear of the individual being vulnerable to totalitarianism, see Staub, *Madness Is Civilization*, 26. For a primary source on the fear of adult participation in groups, see Erik Erikson, "Hitler's Imagery and German Youth," in *Personality in Nature, Society, and Culture*, ed. Kluckhohn and Murray, 485–510, especially 485. On the fear of narcissism, see Eugene T. Grendlin, "A Philosophical Critique of Narcissism: The Significance of the Awareness Movement," in *Pathologies of the Modern Self: Postmodern Studies on Narcissism, Schizophrenia, and Depression*, ed. David Michael Levin (New York: New York University Press, 1987), 251–304 at 253. See also Elizabeth Lunbeck, *The Americanization of Narcissism* (Cambridge, MA: Harvard University Press, 2014), 8. Finally, see the discussion on the evolution of and usefulness of community in Daly, *Understanding Mental Illness*, 8, 9, 10.

156. Seyla Benhabib, *Dignity in Adversity: Human Rights in Troubled Times* (Cambridge: Polity, 2011), 74. Here she discusses natural rights as the pre-political claims of individuals.

157. "Dear Governor," January 13, 1941, Box 1, Folder 13, Container SG12205, State Institution Files, Dept.: Alabama Governor (1939–1943: Dixon), 1. Searcy Hospital opened in 1901 and was designed solely for Black patients, remaining segregated in this way until 1969. John S. Hughes notes that the physical accommodations for Black patients were entirely different from those of white patients and that Black patients were treated by more inexperienced doctors. Hughes, "Labeling and Treating Black Mental Illness in Alabama, 1861–1910," *Journal of Southern History* 58, no. 3 (August 1992): 435–460 at 450. On Dixon, see J. Mills Thornton, "Segregation and the City: White Supremacy in Alabama in the Mid-Twentieth Century," in *Fog of War: The Second World War and the Civil Rights Movement*, ed. Kevin M. Kruse and Stephen Tuck (New York: Oxford University Press, 2012), 57.

158. "Dear Governor," January 13, 1941, 2.

159. "Dear Governor," February 1, 1941, Box 1, Folder 13, Container SG12205, State Institution Files, Dept.: Alabama Governor (1939–1943: Dixon), pp. 1–12 at 6 and 10 on patient labor.

160. Ibid., 5.

161. "Dear Governor," January 13, 1941, 4.

162. "Dear Governor," February 1, 1941, 12.

163. "Dear Governor," January 13, 1941, 3.

164. "Dear Governor," February 1, 1941, 12.

165. Braslow has called this a "post-Holocaust sensibility." See *Mental Ills and Bodily Cures*, 53 and Bradley, *The World Reimagined*, 70ff.

166. "Honorable Sir," May 11, 1953, Box F3640: 2769, Administrative Files, Dept. of Mental Hygiene, Agnews State Hospital, Earl Warren Papers, pp. 1–26 at 17. Patton State was opened as the California State Asylum for the Insane and Inebriates in the 1890s and was renamed in 1927. At its peak, it housed 5,600 patients in the mid-1950s and was plagued by overcrowding problems, though it featured an array of recreational and occupational therapies.

167. Ibid., 24.

168. Edward X. Lane, *I Was a Mental Statistic* (New York: Carlton Press, 1963), 19. Martin Summers discusses a common postemancipation narrative of Black people allegedly being unable to adjust to a new status as a citizen. See *Madness in the City of Magnificent Intentions*, 6–7, 72, 94. This mentality lingered into midcentury as a way of calling African American citizenship into question.

169. "Dear Sir," December 29, 1952, F3640: 2744, Administrative Files, Dept. of Mental Hygiene, Agnews State Hospital, Earl Warren Papers, pp. 1–4 at 1. In Ellen Philtine's 1945 novel, *They Walk in Darkness*, she imagines a character who notes that his hospital, the fictional Farland State Hospital, was "nothing but a concentration camp to keep the mentally ill from annoying society" (52). On popular ideas about the Soviet Union, see David A. Smith, "American Nightmare: Images of Brainwashing, Thought Control and Terror in Soviet Russia," *Journal of American Culture* 33, no. 3 (September 2010): 217–229.

170. "Dear Mr. Freeman," December 6, 1960, Box 4, Folder: Mental Files 1955–1960, Cambridge, Fairbault, and Fergus Falls Hospital, Orville L. Freeman Papers, 110.F.6.2F, pp. 1–2 at 1. On Freeman, see Jennifer A. Delton, *Making Minnesota Liberal: Civil Rights and the Transformation of the Democratic Party* (Minneapolis: University of Minnesota Press, 2002). Freeman was known for his Food Stamps program and for being an advocate of accessible education. See Betty McCollum on Freeman in the House of Representatives, March 27, 2003, *United States of America Congressional Record*, p. 7790. Fergus Falls State Hospital was a Kirkbride hospital opened in the 1890s, reaching its peak population of over 2,000 in the late 1930s. See Susan Bartlett Foote, *A Crusade for Forgotten Souls: Reforming Minnesota's Mental Institutions, 1946–1954* (Minneapolis: University of Minnesota Press, 2018), 4. See Resman, *Asylums, Treatment Centers and Genetic Jails*, 111, 123, on the services and activities offered in the hospital, such as the beauty parlor, library, patient plays, and a patient farm.

171. "Dear Mr. Freeman," 2.

172. "Dear Mother," November 23, 1960, Box 4, Folder: Mental Files 1955–1960, Cambridge, Fairbault, and Fergus Falls Hospital, Orville L. Freeman Papers 110.F.6.2F, p. 1.

173. "Ward News," *Pomo News* 3, no. 3 (April 13, 1951): 3, F 3886: 47, Mendocino State Hospital, Mental Hygiene-Hospitals, California State Archives,

Chapter 4

1. "To Governor Freeman," [1956], Box 4, Folder: Mental Health 1955–60, St. Peter Hospital, Orville L. Freeman Papers, 110.F.6.2F, pp. 1–4 at 1. St. Peter State Hospital was a Kirkbride Hospital established in the late nineteenth century, following the moral treatment model, and exists now as the St. Peter Regional Treatment Center. The hospital had patient work crews during this period for the farm who drove horse-drawn plows and patient teams who made clothing. See Resman, *Asylums, Treatment Centers, and Genetic Jails*, 124, 127.

2. "To Governor Freeman," 4.

3. On this theme, see Grob, *Mental Illness and American Society*, 104.

4. Scull, *The Place of Insanity/The Insanity of Place*, 144.

5. Cowie, *The Great Exception*, 9. Here he defines American liberalism, as generated by the Depression and World War II, as being about collective economic rights.

6. Scull, *The Place of Insanity/The Insanity of Place*, 103–105.

7. Grob, *The Mad Among Us*, 258; Metzl, *The Protest Psychosis*, 13. See also Richard G. Frank and Sherry A. Glied, *Better But Not Well: Mental Health Policy in the United States Since 1950* (Baltimore: Johns Hopkins University Press, 2006), 59, 91. The impetus for community-based care was not wholly new in the late twentieth century: psychiatrists such as Adolf Meyer supported community-based aftercare in the early twentieth century. See Ann Braden Johnson, *Out of Bedlam: The Truth About Deinstitutionalization* (New York: Basic Books, 1990), 13.

8. Scull, *Madness in Civilization*, 371. On Medicare and Medicaid, see Grob, *The Mad Among Us*, 265, 290 and Frank and Glied, *Better But Not Well*, 4, 55–56.

9. See, for example, American Psychoanalytic Association, Committee on Community Psychiatry, 1977–78, from the document by Robert S. Wallerstein, M.D., "Psychoanalytic Perspectives on the Problem of Reality," RG 11: Committees, S14 Psychoanalytic Practice and SS01 Community Psychiatry 1969–1988, Folder 1, pp. 1–26, Courtesy of the Oskar Diethelm Library, Institute for the History of Psychiatry, Weill Medical College of Cornell University, New York.

10. On Nixon's "war on cancer" in 1971, see Edward D. Berkowitz, *Something Happened: A Political and Cultural Overview of the Seventies* (New York: Columbia University Press, 2006), 9.

11. On the probing of gay personal experience and its parallels to psychoanalysis, see Terry, *An American Obsession*, 376. On feminist consciousness raising, see Elisabeth Lasch-Quinn, "Liberation Therapeutics: From Moral Renewal to Consciousness Raising," in *Therapeutic Culture: Triumph and Defeat*, ed. Jonathan B. Imber (New Brunswick, NJ: Transaction Publishers, 2004), 3–18. From the vantage point of the 1970s, psychoanalysts in the vein of Heinz Kohut were particularly concerned with a capacity for empathy and introspection, also prominent foci of gay liberationists and women's liberationists during this period. See Kohut, *The Restoration of the Self* (New York: International Universities Press, 1977) and *The Search for the Self* (New York: International Universities Press, 1978). See also Eli Zaretsky, *Secrets of the Soul: A Social and Cultural History of Psychoanalysis* (New York: Vintage, 2005), 314ff., for a discussion of Kohut's reevaluation of narcissism and the development of the psychology of the self.

12. Marshall Berman, *The Politics of Authenticity: Radical Individualism and the Emergence of Modern Society* (New York: Atheneum, 1970), ix. For a more historical overview of the importance of personal authenticity within the counterculture, see Doug Rossinow, "The Revolution Is About Our Lives: The New Left's Counterculture," in *Imagine Nation: The American Counterculture of the 1960s and '70s*, ed. Peter Braunstein and Michael William Doyle (New York:

Routledge, 2002), 99–124 at 110, as well as Doug Rossinow, *The Politics of Authenticity: Liberalism, Christianity and the New Left in America* (New York: Columbia University Press, 1998). For a general overview of the "counterculture," see Theodore Roszak's classic work, *The Making of a Counter Culture: Reflections on the Technocratic Society and Its Youthful Opposition* (New York: Doubleday, 1968).

13. See Gilman, *Difference and Pathology*, 217–238 and Albert Rothenberg, *Creativity and Madness: New Findings and Old Stereotypes* (Baltimore: Johns Hopkins University Press, 1990). For works from the era that consider the affinity between madness, creativity, and sensitivity, see Ronald R. Fieve, *Moodswing: The Third Revolution in Psychiatry* (New York: William Morrow, 1975), 56–60 and Susan Sontag, *Illness as Metaphor* (New York: Farrar, Straus and Giroux, 1977), 31. While American modernist artists celebrated the creative passions of madness, this was more characteristic of bohemian communities in major cities such as Chicago and New York, where psychoanalysis was popular. On this, see Micale, *The Mind of Modernism*, 2. See also Hale, *The Rise and Crisis of Psychoanalysis in the United States*, 58.

14. Howard Brick, *Age of Contradiction: American Thought and Culture in the 1960s* (New York: Twayne, 1998), 66–67; and Matthew D. Tribbe, *No Requiem for the Space Age: The Apollo Moon Landings and American Culture* (New York: Oxford University Press, 2014), 170.

15. Seymour Krim, *Views of a Nearsighted Cannoneer* (New York: E. P. Dutton, 1968), 129. This essay was first written in 1959.

16. Norman A. Cameron, "Psychotic Disorders," in *The Comprehensive Textbook of Psychiatry*, ed. Alfred M. Freedman and Harold Kaplan (Baltimore: Williams and Wilkins, 1967), 665–675 at 668. On the significance of this common reference book, see Shorter, *How Everyone Became Depressed*, 164.

17. Hans Prinzhorn, *Artistry of the Mentally Ill* (New York: Springer-Verlag, 1972), 6.

18. Maraniss, "Afterword: Uncle Phil's Brain," 277.

19. Trilling, *Sincerity and Authenticity*, 171.

20. Phyllis Chesler, *Women and Madness* (New York: Palgrave MacMillan, [1972] 2005), 217.

21. Erich Fromm, *The Revolution of Hope: Toward a Humanized Technology* (Riverdale, NY: American Mental Health Foundation, [1968] 2010), 13.

22. Simon H. Nagler, "Erich Fromm," in *The Comprehensive Textbook of Psychiatry*, ed. Freedman and Kaplan, 351–354 at 354.

23. Buryl Payne, *Getting There Without Drugs: Techniques and Theories for the Expansion of Consciousness* (London: Wildwood House, [1973] 1974), ix.

24. Anthony Brandt, *Reality Police: The Experience of Insanity in America* (New York: William Morrow, 1975), 124.

25. Ibid., 169.

26. Frances Farmer, *Will There Really Be a Morning?* (London: Allison and Busby, [1972] 1974), 34. Western Washington State Hospital is alternately called the Tacoma State Hospital.

27. Ibid., 84.

28. On this, see William Boddy, *New Media and the Popular Imagination: Launching Radio, Television, and Digital Media in the United States* (New York: Oxford University Press, 2004), 52, in which he discusses the gendering of American mass culture and feminine domestic cultural forms such as radio and TV, which were deemed vapid and passive.

29. Susanna Kaysen, *Girl, Interrupted* (New York: Virago, 1995), 21.

30. Brandt, *Reality Police*, 172.

31. Ibid., 188.

32. Ibid., 183.

33. Kenneth Donaldson, *Insanity Inside Out* (New York: Crown, 1976), 134. Florida State Hospital was known, by the 1950s, for overcrowding and a dearth of available psychiatrists to treat thousands of patients (a population of 6,223 in 1952). Sally J. Ling, *Out of Mind, Out of Sight: A Revealing History of the Florida State Hospital at Chattahoochee and Mental Health Care in Florida* (Self-published, 2013), 125.

34. Barbara Field Benziger, *The Prison of My Mind* (New York: Walker and Company, 1969), 82.

35. Ibid., 145.

36. Letter, [1973], Box W5 of 42, Folder: Writings: Women and Madness-Correspondence-Help File-Former Mental Patients, Phyllis Chesler Papers, David M. Rubenstein Rare Book and Manuscript Library, Duke University Archives, Durham, NC, pp. 1–6 at 3.

37. Ibid., 5.

38. Hampton, *The Far Side of Despair*, 56.

39. Ibid., 57.

40. On activity as a fundamental part of social liberalism and communitarianism of the 1960s and 1970s, see Brick, *Transcending Capitalism*, 216. See also Schudson, *The Rise of the Right to Know*, 261.

41. Document dated February 20, 1970, Box 3, Folder 45, Kenneth Donaldson Papers, pp. 1–2 at 2.

42. On left-leaning therapeutic "rap centers," see Michael E. Staub, "Radical," in *Rethinking Therapeutic Culture*, ed. Aubry and Travis, 96–107 at 96. On self-help and individual experience, see Bradley, *The World Reimagined*, 163. On Twelve Step programs and the political character of self-help, see Micki McGee, *Self-Help, Inc.: Makeover Culture in American Life* (New York: Oxford University Press, 2005), 188–190. See also Trysh Travis, *The Language of the Heart: A Cultural History of the Recovery Movement from Alcoholics Anonymous to Oprah Winfrey* (Chapel Hill: University of North Carolina Press, 2009), 143–187. On confessional writing and artists in the 1960s, see Cotkin, *Feast of Excess*, 3, 8, 130, 216–217. On consciousness raising and feminism, see Schudson, *The Rise of the Right to Know*, 265 and Dowbiggin, *The Quest for Mental Health*, 163.

43. Arthur Janov, *The Primal Scream: Primal Therapy: The Cure for Neurosis* (London: Abacus, [1970] 1973), 334.

44. Ibid., 337.

45. Ibid., 338.

46. Ibid., 340.

47. On women's liberation and anger, see, for example, "Rediscovering Anger," in Boston Women's Health Collective, *Our Bodies, Ourselves: A Book by and for Women* (New York: Simon and Schuster, 1971), 17–23 at 21–22.

48. William H. Grier and Price M. Cobbs, *Black Rage* (London: Jonathan Cape, [1968] 1969), 68.

49. Helen Dudar, "Apathy, Despair, Hostility, Seen as Roots of Rioting," *Psychiatric News*, September 1967, Box 91, Folder 5, Fredric Wertham Papers, pp. 9–11 at 11.

50. Metzl, *The Protest Psychosis*, xiii, xvi, 57. This was particularly the case at the Ionia State Hospital for the Criminally Insane in Ionia, Michigan.

51. For a historical overview of the American anti-psychiatry movement, see Norman Dain, "Psychiatry and Anti-Psychiatry in the United States," in *Discovering the History of Psychiatry*, ed. Micale and Porter, 415–444. Not all anti-psychiatry was radical or left leaning. As Dain

notes, Christian Right evangelicals in the 1970s who offered faith healing could themselves be seen as practicing anti-psychiatry. Dain, "Antipsychiatry," in *American Psychiatry After World War Two*, ed. Menninger and Nemiah, 277–298 at 291.

52. Michel Foucault, *Madness and Civilization: A History of Insanity in the Age of Reason* (New York: Vintage, 1973), 59. On Foucault's impact on American anti-psychiatry, see Grob, *The Mad Among Us*, 273–274. See also Gerald Grob, "The Attack of Psychiatric Legitimacy in the 1960s: Rhetoric and Reality," *Journal of the History of the Behavioral Sciences* 47, no. 4 (Fall 2011): 398–416 at 406.

53. On critiques of biological psychiatry, see David J. Rissmiller and Josh H. Rissmiller, "The Evolution of the Anti-Psychiatry Movement in Mental Health Consumerism," *Psychiatric Services* 57, no. 6 (June 2006): 863–866 at 863. See also Shorter, *A History of Psychiatry*, 313. On psychoanalysis, see Grob, *The Mad Among Us*, 277. There were still about 30,000 analysands in the United States by 1978, whose patients were typically upper-middle class and highly educated. See Gross, *The Psychological Society*, 146. Jonathan Metzl has argued against the idea of the 1970s as the era in which psychiatry as a profession split into those who advocated for biological treatments and those who advocated for talking cures, seeing the two positions as more interwoven. See Metzl, *Prozac on the Couch*, 59. Finally, see Shorter and Healy, *Shock Therapy*, 186, for a discussion of the Network Against Psychiatric Assault (NAPA), an organization of former psychiatric "inmates."

54. "Medical-industrial complex" is a play on Eisenhower's famous military-industrial complex speech, which also held enduring power in the midst of criticisms of science for its allegiance with the Vietnam War and the militarization of outer space. On this, see Kelly Moore, *Disrupting Science: Social Movements, American Scientists, and the Politics of the Military, 1945–1975* (Princeton, NJ: Princeton University Press, 2008), 130ff. On the perceived hubris of science, see Tribbe, *No Requiem for the Space Age*, 4, 22; Jewett, *Science, Democracy, and the American University*, 365; and Tomes, *Remaking the American Patient*, 328. A number of health writers and observers have used the term "medical-industrial complex." See Arnold S. Relman, "The New Medical-Industrial Complex," *New England Journal of Medicine* 303, no. 17 (1980): 963–970 and Eli Clare, *Brilliant Imperfection: Grappling with Cure* (Durham, NC: Duke University Press, 2017), 69. On Tuskegee's public disclosure in 1972, see W. Michael Byrd and Linda A. Clayton, *An American Health Dilemma*, vol. 2, *Race, Medicine and Health Care in the United States, 1900–2000* (New York: Routledge, 2002), 417–418.

55. This article was published in the *New England Journal of Medicine*. On the influence of this article, and on Tuskegee, see Tomes, *Remaking the American Patient*, 277.

56. On MKUltra experimentation and the presidential commission to investigate the CIA in 1975, see David H. Price, *Cold War Anthropology: The CIA, the Pentagon, and the Growth of Dual Use Anthropology* (Durham, NC: Duke University Press, 2016), 195ff. See also Bridget Brown, *They Know Us Better than We Know Ourselves: The History and Politics of Alien Abduction* (New York: New York University Press, 2007), 108–110. On Cameron's "depatterning" experiments during the 1950s, more specifically, see John D. Marks, *The Search for the "Manchurian Candidate": The CIA and Mind Control* (New York: Times Books, 1979), 115–136; Shorter, *A History of Psychiatry*, 206; and Sadowsky, *Electroconvulsive Therapy in America*, 53ff.

57. Staub, *Madness Is Civilization*, 70.

58. On the impact of Watergate, see Bruce J. Schulman, *The Seventies: The Great Shift in American Culture, Society, and Politics* (Cambridge, MA: DaCapo Press, 2001), 45; Berkowitz, *Something Happened*, 25ff.; and Schudson, *The Rise of the Right to Know*, 264.

59. On rehumanization, see Paul Ramsey, *The Patient as Person: Explorations in Medical Ethics* (New Haven, CT: Yale University Press, 1970), 5 and Howard M. Spiro et al., *Empathy and the Practice of Medicine: Beyond Pills and the Scalpel* (New Haven, CT: Yale University Press, 1993), 3. On humanist psychologists such as Carl Rogers, Abraham Maslow, and Rollo May, see Jewett, *Science, Democracy, and the American University*, 338. See also Carl Rogers, *On Becoming a Person: A Therapist's View of Psychotherapy* (London: Constable, [1961] 1967), 48 and *On Personal Power: Inner Strength and Its Revolutionary Impact* (London: Constable, [1977] 1978), 17–18. On more positive images of doctors in the earlier postwar era, see Edward Shorter, *Doctors and Their Patients: A Social History* (New Brunswick, NJ: Transaction, 1991), 135; see *Bedside Manners*, 107, on the "unraveling" of the relationship between the modern doctor and patient in the 1960s. For a primary source that offers a positive war era image of doctors, see Lorraine Maynard and Laurence Miscall, *Bellevue* (New York: Julian Messner, 1940), 77. Martin Halliwell notes that in the early to mid-1960s, the more "impersonal specialist or researcher" had displaced the "friendly family doctor." See *Therapeutic Revolutions*, 235. And Nancy Tomes shows that the tradition of questioning medical authority in the United States has been long-standing and animated the early twentieth century long before the 1960s "patients' revolt," often buttressed by a sense of medical consumerism. See *Remaking the American Patient*, 3, 186, 329.

60. On North American women's health movements, see James C. Whorton, *Nature Cures: The History of Alternative Medicine in America* (New York: Oxford University Press, 2002), 219–297; Tomes, *Remaking the American Patient*, 291; and Schudson, *The Rise of the Right to Know*, 273. On second wave feminist demands for more equality and reciprocity in the medical encounter, see Wendy Kline, *Bodies of Knowledge: Sexuality, Reproduction, and Women's Health in the Second Wave* (Chicago: University of Chicago Press, 2010), 58–62; on the primacy of women's experiential knowledge, see Kathy Davis, *The Making of Our Bodies, Ourselves: How Feminism Travels Across Borders* (Durham, NC: Duke University Press, 2007), 1–2, 134. On back-to-nature movements and countercultural communal experiments, see Steven Conn, *Americans Against the City: Anti-Urbanism in the Twentieth Century* (New York: Oxford University Press, 2014), 260–269.

61. The counterculture and science were not always antagonistic but sometimes had more of symbiotic relationship, as when science and technology were quirky, "hip," or experimental. On this theme, see David Kaiser and Patrick McCray, eds., *Groovy Science: Knowledge, Innovation, and American Counterculture* (Chicago: University of Chicago Press, 2016), 5–7. On irrationality as a kind of insight, see Jedediah Purdy, *After Nature: A Politics for the Anthropocene* (Cambridge, MA: Harvard University Press, 2015), 287. On what he calls the "neo-romantic turn" in American culture in the early 1970s, see Tribbe, *No Requiem for the Space Age*, 21, 173.

62. See Tomes, "Feminist Histories of Psychiatry," 359.

63. Chesler, *Women and Madness*, 61.

64. See Scull, *Madness in Civilization*, 373.

65. Letter, [1973], Phyllis Chesler Papers, 1. On the use of "coming out," see Elizabeth Brewer, "Coming Out Mad, Coming Out Disabled," in *Literatures of Madness*, ed. Donaldson, 11–30.

66. Letter, [1973], Phyllis Chesler Papers, 3. Dayton State was sometimes called the Dayton Mental Health Center, or Twin Valley Behavioral Healthcare, in the 1970s, and is in Dayton, Ohio. Longview was another large state hospital in Cincinnati.

67. Ibid., 2.

68. Ibid., 3.

69. Deepening medicalization was also interrupted and contested in the late twentieth century: certain "ailments" such as homosexuality were, as of 1974, demedicalized, even in the wake of the DSM-II in 1968 that expanded the number of possible diagnoses from 106 to 182. See Hannah Decker's account on homosexuality and its removal from the DSM in *The Making of DSM-III*, 210–211. And on the DSM-II more broadly, see p. 21. See also Skodol, "Diagnosis and Classification of Mental Disorders," 432–433.

70. On seeking folk remedies for illnesses, see Berkowitz, *Something Happened*, 10. On populism in American politics during the 1970s, see Thomas Borstelmann, *The 1970s: A New Global History from Civil Rights to Economic Inequality* (Princeton, NJ: Princeton University Press, 2012), 116–119.

71. Letter, October 25, 1973, Box W4, Folder: Help File: Careers, Education, Information, Phyllis Chesler Papers, pp. 1–2 at 2.

72. Ibid., 1.

73. On the theme of health populism, see, for example, Leo W. Simmons, "A Sociologist's Views on Patient Care," *American Journal of Psychiatry* 117 (November 1960): 388.

74. Letter, [1973], Phyllis Chesler Papers, 3.

75. Ibid., 5–6.

76. On labeling theory, see Grob, "The History of the Asylum Revisited," 265.

77. Letter to Phyllis Chesler, December 24, 1972, Box W4, Folder 7: Writings/Women and Madness/Correspondence/Housewives Complaints—Psychiatric History, Phyllis Chesler Papers, p. 1.

78. Thomas Szasz, *Ideology and Insanity: Essays on the Psychiatric Dehumanization of Man* (London: Calder and Boyars, 1973), 213.

79. Letter to Phyllis Chesler, December 24, 1972, 1.

80. David Rosenhan, "On Being Sane in Insane Places," *Science* 179 (January 19, 1973): 250–258. On reactions to this famous article, see Scull, *Madness in Civilization*, 386. According to Scull, reaction was particularly strong among legal scholars who could use this study to call into question psychiatric expert testimony. See Scull, *Psychiatry and Its Discontents*, 203.

81. Interview with Dr. Watts by Harvey Ammerman, 1988, Walter Freeman and James Watts Collection, MS 0803, Box 42, Part 1, Gelman Library, George Washington University, Washington, DC. Lobotomies and other psychosurgeries had not completely died out by the 1970s. By 1971, the psychosurgeries performed tended not to be standard prefrontal lobotomies or transorbital lobotomies; they were more circumscribed, "targeted" psychosurgeries wherein only relatively small areas of the brain were destroyed. See Valenstein, *Great and Desperate Cures*, 284–285. Neuropsychiatrist Frank R. Ervin and neurosurgeon Vernon H. Mark argued that neurosurgery could eliminate violence in society: see *Violence and the Brain* (New York: Harper and Row, 1970), 3.

82. Students for a Democratic Society, "A UCLA Center for Psychosurgery? Unless We Stop It," pamphlet, [1973], pp. 1–19 at 8, Science Service Records, 1920s–1970s, Acc. #90-068, Box 14, Folder RD, Brain Surgery—Lobotomy, Smithsonian Institution Archives, Record Unit 7091.

83. Ibid., 14.

84. Summers, *Madness in the City of Magnificent Intentions*, 123.

85. *One Flew over the Cuckoo's Nest*, directed by Milos Forman (1975).

86. De Young, *Madness*, 214. The movie also appeared shortly after news reports that the Soviet Union had used tranquilizers and involuntary hospitalizations as a form of torture for political dissidents. See Sadowsky, *Electroconvulsive Therapy in America*, 73.

87. Ken Kesey, *One Flew over the Cuckoo's Nest* (New York: Signet, [1962] 1963), 237.

88. *Shock Treatment*, directed by Denis Sanders (1964).

89. On Eagleton, see Herzberg, *Happy Pills in America*, 156 and Sadowsky, *Electroconvulsive Therapy in America*, 118.

90. Ellen Wolfe, *Aftershock: The Story of a Psychotic Episode* (New York: G. P. Putnam's Sons, 1969), 106.

91. Ibid., 115.

92. Kesey, *One Flew over the Cuckoo's Nest*, 242. On the countercultural sense of intrigue with wise "Indians," see Philip Deloria, *Playing Indian* (New Haven, CT: Yale University Press, 1998), 154–181.

93. Kesey, *One Flew over the Cuckoo's Nest*, 269.

94. Shorter and Healy, *Shock Therapy*, 154–55, 158.

95. Letter to Mr. Chesterfield H. Smith, February 3, 1965, Florida Bar Association, Box 2, Folder 19, Kenneth Donaldson Papers, pp. 1–2 at 1. The Lantana TB Hospital as he calls it refers to an institution sometimes called the A. G. Holley State Tuberculosis Hospital in Lantana, Florida, originally opened in 1950, then called the Southeast Florida Tuberculosis Hospital. By the early 1970s, the resident population of TB patients had dropped, and so part of the hospital began to be used for prison work-release programs and for drug addicts and others in the correctional system who needed hospitalization. See Shirley A. Ness, *NIOSH Case Studies in Bioaerosols* (Rockville, MD: Government Institutes, 1996), 5.

96. Letter to Mr. Chesterfield H. Smith, February 3, 1965, 1.

97. Shorter and Healy, *Shock Therapy*, 153.

98. "Dear Dr. Overholser," July 5, 1963, General Correspondence, 1963–1965, Box 3, General Correspondence: 1921–1965, Folder General Correspondence, 1963, July, Winfred Overholser Papers, Library of Congress, Manuscript Division, Washington, DC, pp. 1–2 at 2.

99. Ibid., 1.

100. Millen Brand, *Savage Sleep* (London: W. H. Allen, [1968] 1969), 5. Though a work of fiction, the novel tells the story of John Rosen and his development of "Direct Analysis." Rosen was a psychoanalyst who claimed to have had success in curing schizophrenia through the talking cure; his critics felt he was refusing to acknowledge the biological existence of this disease. See John Rosen, *Direct Analysis* (New York: Grune and Stratton, 1953), 8–9.

101. Brand, *Savage Sleep*, 6.

102. Ibid., 9.

103. Theodore M. Porter, *Trust in Numbers: The Pursuit of Objectivity in Science and Public Life* (Princeton, NJ: Princeton University Press, 1996), 25, 73.

104. Brand, *Savage Sleep*, 218.

105. Robert Bogdan, ed., *Being Different: The Autobiography of Jane Fry* (New York: John Wiley, 1974), 105.

106. Sander L. Gilman, "Judging by Appearances," in *Making the Body Beautiful: A Cultural History of Aesthetic Surgery* (Princeton, NJ: Princeton University Press, 1999), 4–42. During the 1960s, doctors started to implement formal "gender identity" programs for parents and children, and firm gender roles ossified from the more fluid ones they were perceived to be in the 1950s. The doctors that Bogdan encountered might have still been steeped in this kind of thinking. See Joanne Meyerowitz, *How Sex Changed: A History of Transsexuality in the United States* (Cambridge, MA: Harvard University Press, 2004), 125.

107. Bogdan, *Being Different*, 123.

108. Halliwell, *Therapeutic Revolutions*, 293.

109. Herzberg, *Happy Pills in America*, 6, 38.

110. On the impact of Thorazine, see ibid., 17–18. Herzberg places anti-depressants and tranquilizing drugs within the sphere of the medical as well as postwar consumer culture. In the wake of second wave feminism, drug manufacturers were also aware of the critique of tranquilizing drugs as a means of social control. See p. 139.

111. Ibid., 9.

112. Nathan S. Kline, *From Sad to Glad* (New York: Ballantine, 1974), 7. Kline at this point was the head of the research center at Rockland State Mental Hospital in Orangeburg, New York. He had some ambivalence about deinstitutionalization and was not simply an advocate of giving patients drugs so that they could be discharged. For him, patient discharge was not an ideal in itself and he argued that some people needed institutional support. See Thomas Fleming, "The Computer and the Psychiatrist," *New York Times Magazine*, April 6, 1969, 50. Herzberg argues that the early postwar era "age of anxiety" gave way to an "age of depression" by the 1970s. See *Happy Pills in America*, 151. Still, it was not until 1980 that depression was listed as an illness in the third edition of the DSM. See Halliwell, *Therapeutic Revolutions*, 254.

113. Advertisement in *Archives of General Psychiatry* 34, no. 1 (January 1977): 31. Tofranil is the brand name for imipramine, another tricyclic anti-depressant. The drug manufacturer was Geigy pharmaceuticals. The *American Journal of Psychiatry* and the *Archives of General Psychiatry* were two of the most influential American psychiatric journals in the postwar period. On them, see Metzl, *Prozac on the Couch*, 129.

114. Advertisement for Haldol (Haloperiodol), *Archives of General Psychiatry* 35, no. 10 (October 1978): 1186.

115. It should be noted that psychiatry was nonetheless growing in this period. While there were fewer than 5,000 American psychiatrists in 1948, by 1976 there were more than 27,000, the majority of whom practiced psychoanalysis. See Andrew Scull, *Madness: A Very Short Introduction* (Oxford: Oxford University Press, 2011), 89. On women, see, for example, Lisa Appignanesi's discussion of Judith Herman, a psychiatrist and civil rights and women's movement activist, who argued that the psychiatric profession had misdiagnosed abused women. See Appignanesi, *Mad, Bad, and Sad*, 424–426. Jonathan Metzl discusses more cynical observers who did not feel that feminist critiques of psychoanalysis helped shift ideas about gender in psychiatry. See Metzl, *Prozac on the Couch*, 130.

116. Bogdan, *Being Different*, 112.

117. Harrington, *Mind Fixers*, 115–116.

118. Bogdan, *Being Different*, 118.

119. *Titicut Follies*, directed by Frederick Wiseman (Cambridge, MA: Zipporah Films, 1967). Wiseman was an attorney and he filmed this documentary with anthropologist John Kennedy Marshall.

120. Michael Jon Spencer, "A Case for the Arts," MS C 493, Box 64, File 4, 1975, Bertram Brown Papers, National Library of Medicine, Bethesda, MD, pp. 1–7 at 6.

121. Ibid., 6.

122. Letter from a Psychiatric Patient in St. Luke's Hospital, February 23, 1975, Bertram Brown Papers, p. 1.

123. Heinz E. Lehmann, "Schizophrenia. IV. Clinical Features," in *The Comprehensive Textbook of Psychiatry*, ed. Freedman and Kaplan, 621–648 at 632.

Chapter 5

1. Supreme Court of the United States, *O'Connor vs. Donaldson*, 1975, MS C 493, Box 17, File 1, 1975, Bertram Brown Papers, pp. 1–14 at 1. See the transcript for *O'Connor vs. Donaldson*, http://caselaw.lp.findlaw.com/scripts/getcase.pl?court=US&vol=422&invol=563. Justice Burger quoted from postwar narratives of social control and captivity in making this decision, among them Deutsch's *The Shame of the States* and David Rothman's *The Discovery of the Asylum: Social Order and Disorder in the New Republic* (Piscataway, NJ: Transaction, 1971). Donaldson was released in 1971, at the age of sixty-two. It was then that he filed a lawsuit against Doctors O'Connor and Gumanis and received funds for compensatory and punitive damages in *Donaldson vs. O'Connor* in 1974. But O'Connor and Gumanis appealed to the U.S. Supreme Court, which agreed to hear the case in 1975. The ACLU took up Donaldson's case and argued his positions. See Robert G. Meyer and Christopher M. Veaver, *Law and Mental Health: A Case-Based Approach* (New York: Guilford Press, 2006), 134. Witnesses said that Donaldson had spent most of his time at the hospital in a large room that housed sixty patients, most of whom were under criminal commitment. As a Christian Scientist, he sometimes refused to take his medication. For more details, see Bernard Schwartz, *The Unpublished Opinions of the Burger Court* (New York: Oxford University Press, 1988), 311.

2. *O'Connor vs. Donaldson*, 12.

3. See the meditation on cosmopolitanism as "conditional hospitality" in Giovanna Borradori, *Philosophy in a Time of Terror: Dialogues with Jürgen Habermas and Jacques Derrida* (Chicago: University of Chicago Press, 2003), 163.

4. On the aesthetic dimensions of discrimination against those with disabilities, see Schweik, *The Ugly Laws*, 23–62. On an ethnic model of conceiving of gay oppression, see Christopher Nealon, *Foundlings: Lesbian and Gay Emotion Before Stonewall* (Durham, NC: Duke University Press, 2001), 5.

5. Jeffrey D. Fields, "O'Connor vs. Donaldson," *Hofstra Law Review* 4, no. 2 (1976): 527, 530. On other important cases in the lead-up to this Supreme Court case, see Paulson, *Closing the Asylums*, 170. One of Donaldson's lawyers was Morton Birnbaum, who, in 1960, wrote an article for the *ABA Journal* on the "constitutional right to treatment." See Grob, *From Asylum to Community*, 290. See also Grob, "The Attack of Psychiatric Legitimacy in the 1960s," 408–409. Thomas Szasz noted that Donaldson refused earlier attempts to release him from the hospital and that he had rejected both electroshock and psychotropic drugs, so it was problematic to frame the case as being about the "right to treatment." Instead, Szasz argues that Donaldson wanted to make a dramatic point about psychiatric incarceration during a moment when the ethos of the period was drifting in his favor, given that federal appellate courts were already making decisions in this vein. Thomas Szasz, *Psychiatric Slavery* (Syracuse, NY: Syracuse University Press, [1977] 1998), 27–28, 51. Another of Donaldson's counsels, American civil rights lawyer Bruce J. Ennis, wrote *Prisoners of Psychiatry: Mental Patients, Psychiatrists, and the Law* (New York: Harcourt Brace Jovanovich, 1972), 89. Ennis was less concerned with the right to treatment and more concerned with forcible incarceration. See John Parry, *Criminal Mental Health and Disability Law, Evidence and Testimony: A Comprehensive Reference Manual for Lawyers, Judges, and Criminal Justice Professionals* (Chicago: American Bar Association, 2009), 18. On the Supreme Court avoiding the "right to treatment," see Jonas Robitscher, "Moving Patients out of Hospitals—In Whose Interest?" in *State Mental Hospitals: What Happens When They Close*, ed. Paul I. Ahmed and Stanley C. Plog (New York: Plenum Medical Book Company, 1976), 141–175 at 147–148.

6. Samuel D. Warren and Louis D. Brandeis, "The Right to Privacy," *Harvard Law Review* 4, no. 5 (December 15, 1890): 193–220. The Supreme Court was perhaps more interested in the "negative right" to be let alone rather than a "positive right" to have something in particular such as treatment. On this distinction, see Michael Dudley et al., "Mental Health, Human Rights and Their Relationship: An Introduction," in *Mental Health and Human Rights*, ed. Dudley et al., 1–49 at 10 and 19. On medical commentators, see Hornstein, *To Redeem One Person Is to Redeem the World*, 171.

7. Hannah Arendt, "Public Rights and Private Interests," in *Thinking Without a Banister*, 510. On the theme of anti-statism, see Margaret R. Somers, "The Privatization of Citizenship: How to Unthink a Knowledge Culture," in *Beyond the Cultural Turn: New Directions in the Study of Society and Culture*, ed. Victoria E. Bonnell and Lynn Hunt (Berkeley: University of California Press, 1999), 121–161 at 121.

8. On the Patient Bill of Rights, see Tomes, *Remaking the American Patient*, 279, and Igo, *The Known Citizen*, 174. As Igo points out, the bill casts the patient as a rights-holder, with the right to refuse treatment.

9. Parsons, *From Asylum to Prison*, 46.

10. Noninstitutional contexts for psychiatry were increasingly important to psychoanalysis such as a psychiatrist's private office or an outpatient clinic. On this, see Summers, "Diagnosing the Ailments of Black Citizenship," 99. On radical civil libertarians, see Robitscher, "Moving Patients out of Hospitals," 169. For a primary source, see Rothman, *The Discovery of the Asylum*, 265ff., 295. On conservative libertarianism in 1970s American politics, see Borstelmann, *The 1970s*, 6, 316. See also Roy Porter and David Wright, *The Confinement of the Insane: International Perspectives, 1800–1965* (Cambridge: Cambridge University Press, 2003), 1. Here they suggest that deinstitutionalization as an idea had leftist origins and was overtaken by the right during the late twentieth century. On domesticity as a source of subversive politics, see Richard Candida Smith, *Utopia and Dissent: Art, Poetry, and Politics in California* (Berkeley: University of California Press, 1995), xxiv. On the economic downturn of the 1970s, its slowdowns, layoffs, and inflation, see Berkowitz, *Something Happened*, 53, 69ff.

11. David Harvey offers a succinct definition of neoliberalism as the political and economic practices that serve to advance entrepreneurial freedoms within a broader state framework that emphasizes "strong private property rights, free markets, and free trade." The state here, however, is not nonexistent: its role is to facilitate these things. See Harvey, *A Brief History of Neoliberalism* (New York: Oxford University Press, 2005), 2. On producerism and entrepreneurialism at the heart of neoliberalism, see Michel Foucault, *The Birth of Biopolitics: Lectures at the College de France* (New York: Picador, 2004), 131, 147. See also Quinn Slobodian, *The Globalists: The End of Empire and the Birth of Neoliberalism* (Cambridge, MA: Harvard University Press, 2018), 2 and Brown, *Undoing the Demos*, 17. Here she offers a more capacious definition, emphasizing that neoliberal reason reduces the political character of democracy to an economic one, rendering human beings "market actors" (31). She also illuminates an essential paradox: that neoliberal thinkers valued the family as a "social harbor" even as the dictates of a neoliberal economy erode social institutions to support that family life (37, 100). On the rejection of social welfare programs as a part of neoliberalism, see Clarence Lang, *Black America in the Shadow of the Sixties: Notes on the Civil Rights Movement, Neoliberalism, and Politics* (Ann Arbor: University of Michigan Press, 2015), xi. Finally, for a discussion on the distinction between neoliberalism and libertarianism, see Jennifer Burns, *Goddess of the Market: Ayn Rand and the American Right* (New York: Oxford University Press, 2009), 104.

12. On the proliferation of disability rights in the 1970s, see Duane F. Stroman, *The Disability Rights Movement: From Deinstitutionalization to Self-Determination* (Lanham, MD: University Press of America, 2003), 70ff. On Black, Brown, and Red Power movements during the 1970s, see Schulman, *The Seventies*, 62–66. On Black Power, see Peniel E. Joseph, ed., *The Black Power Movement: Rethinking the Civil Rights–Black Power Era* (New York: Routledge, 2006). On 1960s and 1970s civil rights movements for Mexican and Puerto Rican Americans, see C. Cirstina Mora, *Making Hispanics: How Activists, Bureaucrats and Media Constructed a New American* (Chicago: University of Chicago Press, 2014), 20ff. On Red Power, see Daniel M. Cobb and Loretta Fowler, eds., *Beyond Red Power: American Indian Politics and Activism Since 1900* (Santa Fe, NM: School for Advanced Research, 2007), x–xii. In this collection, see especially Sherry L. Smith, "Indians, the Counterculture and the New Left," 142–160. Finally, on rights consciousness, see Zaretsky, "Psychoanalysis, Authoritarianism, and the 1960s," 254.

13. On ethnic communities in this period, see Brick, *Age of Contradiction*, 120. On communes, see Conn, *Americans Against the City*, 257.

14. On privatization and personal responsibility as they relate to neoliberalism, see Lisa Duggan, *The Twilight of Equality? Neoliberalism, Cultural Politics, and the Attack on Democracy* (Boston: Beacon Press, 2003), 12. For a conservative critique of rights culture, see Mary-Ann Glendon, *Rights Talk: The Impoverishment of Political Discourse* (New York: Free Press, 1991), 104. On anti-expertise movements of the 1960s and their relationship to feminism, see Schudson, *The Rise of the Right to Know*, 13; on deepening doubts about the political establishment after the 1960s, see p. 148. On the New Left's efforts to erode relationships of authority, see Zaretsky, "Psychoanalysis, Authoritarianism, and the 1960s," 240. On counterculturalism and libertarianism, see Cowie, *The Great Exception*, 194. Finally, on self-authority over other kinds of authority, see Smith, *Utopia and Dissent*, xxiv.

15. See *Declaration on the Rights of Mentally Retarded Persons*, Proclaimed by General Assembly Resolution 2856 (XXVI) December 20, 1971, https://www.ohchr.org/EN/ProfessionalInterest/Pages/RightsOfMentallyRetardedPersons.aspx.

Kenneth Donaldson quotes from this declaration in his memoir; see *Insanity Inside Out*, 120. On broader rights culture of the 1970s, including the slogans of political debates such as the "right to choose," the "right to life," the "right to bear arms," and "gay rights," as well as the Equal Rights Amendment, see Cowie, *The Great Exception*, 187.

16. See Declaration on the Rights of Disabled Persons, Proclaimed by the General Assembly Resolution 3447 (XXX), December 9, 1975: https://www.ohchr.org/Documents/ProfessionalInterest/res3447.pdf.

17. Quoted in Dowbiggin, *The Quest for Mental Health*, 180.

18. Over time, these centers were more likely to have social workers rather than psychiatrists, and by 1968 this direction was formalized by Congress, whose legislation was focused more on substance abuse, children, and the aged rather than mental illness per se. See Grob, *From Asylum to Community*, 245, 263–264, 280–281. H. Richard Lamb notes that people with schizophrenia were a low priority in these centers. See *Treating the Long-Term Mentally Ill: Beyond Deinstitutionalization* (San Francisco: Jossey-Bass, 1982), 93. See also Hester Pile and Chris Philo, "Mapping 'Mad' Identities," in *Mapping the Subject: Geographies of Cultural Transformation*, ed. Steve Pile and Nigel Thrift (London: Routledge, 1995), 182–207 at 195.

19. Milton Greenblatt, "Historical Factors Affecting the Closing of State Hospitals," in *State Mental Hospitals*, ed. Ahmed and Plog, 9–20 at 18. Greenblatt was a psychiatrist who spent most of his career with indigent patients in Los Angeles.

20. On this phrase, see Michael Bennett, "Cities in the New Millennium: Environmental Justice, the Spatialization of Race, and Combating Anti-Urbanism," in *Free at Last? Black America in the Twenty-First Century*, ed. Juan Jose Battle et al. (Piscataway, NJ: Transaction, 2006), 247–263 at 253. On the fear of deinstitutionalized patients living in the community, see Rondinone, *Nightmare Factories*, 210.

21. Greenblatt, "Historical Factors Affecting the Closing of State Hospitals," 18.

22. Halliwell, *Therapeutic Revolutions*, 279.

23. As Michael Staub notes, in 1955 there were more than 550,000 patients in state mental hospitals and by 1985 that figure was less than 110,000 persons. Staub, *Madness Is Civilization*, 183. Hannah Decker indicates that there were 80,000 patients in state mental hospitals by 1994. Decker, *The Making of DSM-III*, 26. Andrew Scull argues that in the United States the first large wave of deinstitutionalization occurred in 1965 and mostly affected patients over the age of sixty-five; the next wave occurred after 1973, among younger patients, following the Nixon administration's changes to the Social Security Program, the Supplemental Security Income program, which provided federal benefits to the disabled, including those with a mental disability. Scull, *The Place of Insanity/The Insanity of Place*, 103–105.

24. Grob, *The Mad Among Us*, 266. It is also worth noting here that, as Gail Hornstein points out, hospitalization for mental illness was not covered by insurance in a widespread way until the 1970s. Hornstein, *To Redeem One Person Is to Redeem the World*, 174.

25. See Grob, *The Mad Among Us*, 287. Martin Halliwell also notes that this rate of decline was slower among Black patients, who were more likely than white patients to be hospitalized for life. Halliwell, *Therapeutic Revolutions*, 208, 211.

26. Halliwell, *Therapeutic Revolutions*, 205.

27. See Grob, *The Mad Among Us*, 288. On inadequate community resources, see Grob, *From Asylum to Community*, 3, 271, and Paulson, *Closing the Asylums*, 6.

28. Scull, *Madness in Civilization*, 376–377; Harrington, *Mind Fixers*, 118. On homelessness specifically, see Grob, *The Mad Among Us*, 298, 304 and Decker, *The Making of DSM-III*, 312. See also E. Fuller Torrey, *Nowhere to Go: The Tragic Odyssey of the Homeless Mentally Ill* (New York: Harper and Row, 1988), 4–5, 7 and Neal L. Cohen, *Psychiatry Takes to the Streets: Outreach and Crisis Intervention for the Mentally Ill* (New York: Guilford Press, 1990), 7. On transinstitutionalization, see Dowbiggin, *The Quest for Mental Health*, 181. He notes here that during the 1960s the population in American nursing homes jumped from 470,000 to more than 900,000, and that by 1985 more than 600,000 nursing home residents were diagnosed as mentally ill. Finally, see Parsons, *From Asylum to Prison*, 4–5, 107, 122. Parsons shows that prisons absorbed the functions of mental hospitals. The disproportionate incarceration of psychiatric populations has been the result of the expansion of the criminal legal system. General hospitals and nursing homes, she notes, also served people with mental illnesses increasingly owing to shifts in Medicaid and state funding. State psychiatric populations were predominantly white and middle-aged, while incarcerated psychiatric populations tended to be disproportionately African American and younger.

29. Milton Greenblatt, "The Evolution of State Mental Hospital Models of Treatment," in *Further Explorations in Social Psychiatry*, ed. Berton H. Kaplan et al. (New York: Basic Books, 1976), 29–45 at 30.

30. Ibid., 31.

31. His father had signed the original request to have him committed. See Letter, May 6, 1965, Box 2, Folder 21, Kenneth Donaldson Papers, pp. 1–4 at 3 and 4.

32. Ibid., 4.

33. Letter, June 16, 1965, Box 2, Folder 22, Kenneth Donaldson Papers, pp. 1–5 at 5.

34. Donaldson, *Insanity Inside Out*, 70.

35. Letter, "Dear Kenneth," October 2, 1963, Box 1, Folder 14, Kenneth Donaldson Papers, pp. 1–2 at 2.

36. Ibid., 1.

37. Ibid., 2.

38. Letter, "Dear Kenneth," Oct. 21, 1963, Box 1, Folder 14, Kenneth Donaldson Papers, pp. 1-3 at 3.

39. Letter, "Dear Ken," January 28, 1967, Box 3, Folder 35, Kenneth Donaldson Papers, 1.

40. Letter, "Dear Ken," July 7, 1968, Box 3, Folder 39, Kenneth Donaldson Papers, 1.

41. *Mental Health: Trouble in the Family*, Record Group 381: Records of the Community Services Administration, 1963–1981, Arc ID: 72809/Local: 683, Moving Images Relating to Anti-poverty Programs, Motion Picture, Sound and Video Records Section, Special Media Archives Services Division, National Archives, College Park, MD. For details on Nathan Ackerman and family therapy, see Weinstein, *The Pathological Family*, 27ff., 93, 152.

42. See "Dear Governor Ella Grasso," June 14, 1976, Box 223, Folder A, RG 5, 005:036, Office of the Governor, Pt 1: Subject Files, 1975–1977, Mental Health A-J, Ella Grasso Papers, Connecticut State Archives, Hartford, pp. 1–2 at 1. Grasso was the governor of Connecticut from 1975 to 1980. On her policies and budgets specifically, see Molly A. Mayhead and Brenda Devore Marshall, *Women's Political Discourse: A Twenty-First Century Perspective* (Lanham, MD: Rowman and Littlefield, 2005), 68. Fairfield Hills Hospital, in Newtown, Connecticut, closed its doors in 1995, a product of deinstitutionalization and the perceived need to close down underused state hospitals. Earlier in the twentieth century it was called Fairfield State Hospital. For details on the hospital during its lifetime and closure, see Cheri Revai and Heather Adel Wiggins, *Haunted Connecticut: Ghosts and Strange Phenomena of the Constitution State* (Mechanicsburg, PA: Stackpole Books, 2006), 24–25.

43. Scull, *The Insanity of Place/The Place of Insanity*, 95; Grob, *The Mad Among Us*, 266, 289.

44. Jonathan Metzl, "Why Against Health?" in *Against Health: How Health Became the New Morality*, ed. Jonathan Metzl and Anna Kirkland (New York: New York University Press, 2010), 1–11 at 5.

45. "Dear Governor Grasso," October 27, 1979, Box 558, Folder Mental Health Letters A–G, Ella Grasso Papers, pp. 1–4 at 1.

46. Ibid., 2.

47. On parental blame in cases of mental illness, see H. Richard Lamb, "Continuing Problems Between Mental Health Professionals and Families of the Mentally Ill," in *Families as Allies in Treatment of the Mentally Ill: New Directions for Mental Health Professionals*, ed. Harriet P. Lefley and Dale L. Johnson (Washington, DC: American Psychiatric Press, 1990), 23–30 at 27.

48. On social conservatism, see Matthew D. Lassiter, "Inventing Family Values," in *Rightward Bound: Making America Conservative in the 1970s*, ed. Bruce J. Schulman and Julian E. Zelizer (Cambridge, MA: Harvard University Press, 2008), 13–28. See also Seth Dowland, *Family Values and the Rise of the Christian Right* (Philadelphia: University of Pennsylvania Press, 2015), 149, and Didier Fassin, *Humanitarian Reason: A Moral History of the Present* (Berkeley: University of California Press, 2012), 226.

49. See Philip Rieff, *The Triumph of the Therapeutic: Uses of Faith After Freud* (New York: Penguin, 1966), 33. See also Paul Boyer, "The Evangelical Resurgence in 1970s American Protestantism," in *Rightward Bound*, ed. Schulman and Zelizer, 29–51.

50. "Dear Governor Grasso," July 7, 1976, Box 224, Folder U–V, Ella Grasso Papers, pp. 1–4 at 1.

51. Ibid., 3. The Undercliff Halfway House was a part of the Undercliff Hospital in Meriden, Connecticut. See Connecticut, Department of Finance and Control, *Digest of Connecticut Administrative Reports to the Governor* (vols. 10–12, 1956), 210. See also Richard J. Wiseman, *Riverview Hospital for Children and Youth: A Culture of Promise* (Middletown, CT: Wesleyan University Press, 2015), 100.

52. "Dear Governor Grasso," July 7, 1976, 4.

53. "Dear Dr. Shapiro," July 5, 1978, Box 473, Folder: Mental Health, Ella Grasso Papers, pp. 1–4 at 1. In 1994 the Institute of Living merged with Hartford Hospital as a department of psychiatry within a general hospital. See Sharfstein et al., *Textbook of Hospital Psychiatry*, 359. See also Scull, *Psychiatry and Its Discontents*, 138. The Children's Village is now known as the Village for Families and Children in Hartford, an organization that was once the Hartford Orphan Asylum and is now a community mental health center and an amalgamation of the Connecticut Children's Aid Society. See Carlos Salguero, "Community Mental Health Centers," in *Community Child and Adolescent Psychiatry: A Manual of Clinical Practice and Consultation*, ed. Theodore A. Petti and Carlos Salguero (Washington, DC: American Psychiatric Publishing, 2006), 115–133 at 115.

54. "Dear Dr. Shapiro," July 5, 1978, 3.

55. Letter, October 8, 1964, Box 2, Folder 18, Kenneth Donaldson Papers, pp. 1–18 at 7.

56. Ibid., 10.

57. See, for example, *Rennie vs. Klein*, heard at the United States District Court for the District of New Jersey in 1978. This case established that an involuntarily committed psychiatric patient has a constitutional right to refuse psychiatric medication. On this, see John Monahan and Henry J. Steadman, eds., *Mentally Disordered Offenders: Perspectives from Law and Social Science* (New York: Springer, 1983), 17–18. See also "Dean Brooks, Superintendent and Actor, Talks About Cuckoo's Nest," *Hospital and Community Psychiatry* 28, no. 1 (January 1977): 47.

58. "Florida State Hospital," WSFU-TV, 1973, https://www.floridamemory.com/items/show/253099.

59. "Dear Dr. Shapiro," July 5, 1978, 3.

60. On deinstitutionalization not being widely discussed, see Paulson, *Closing the Asylums*, 1. "Dear Dr. Shapiro," July 5, 1978, 4. On the "tax revolt" of the 1960s and 1970s, see Lisa McGirr, *Suburban Warriors: The Origins of the New American Right* (Princeton, NJ: Princeton University Press, 2001), 205.

61. *Anyplace But Here*, directed by Maurice Murad (CBS News, 1978).

62. "Dear Ms. Carter," May 25, 1978, Box 473, Folder: Mental Health, Ella Grasso Papers, pp. 1–2 at 1. This writer is most likely referring to Connecticut Valley Hospital in Middletown, which was known as Connecticut State Hospital until 1961. This is a public hospital still operational at the time of this writing. See Christina Raffuse, *Mental Health in Connecticut: The Case of Connecticut Valley Hospital* (New Haven: Southern Connecticut State University, 2012). On Rosalynn and Jimmy Carter's interest in mental health during the 1970s, see Lucas Richert, *Break on Through: Radical Psychiatry and the American Counterculture* (Cambridge, MA: MIT Press, 2019), 106–107.

63. "Dear Sir," August 24, 1965, Box 2 111.K.8.8F, Folder Assistance Mental 64-66 (A-D), Assistance and Friendly Files, Karl F. Rolvaag Papers, Minnesota State Archives, Minnesota Historical Society, St. Paul, p. 1. Rolvaag was governor from 1963 to 1967. On his commitment to

liberal social programs, see Millard L. Gleske, *Perspectives on Minnesota Government and Politics* (Minneapolis: Burgess Publishing Company, 1984), 140. Rochester State opened in the late nineteenth century and included an alcoholism treatment program. During the 1950s and 1960s it had an array of patient work and therapeutic activities, such as shoe repair, sewing, farming, and canning. See Resman, *Asylums, Treatment Centers and Genetic Jails*, 124–126.

64. "What the New Mental Health System Has Done to/for the Parents of the Severely Mentally Ill Young Adult," Case Histories 9/79, Folder 7, "Mental Health Patient Advocacy: Case Histories—Schizophrenia, 1973–1988," Box 43, Mental Health Advocacy, Collection of Materials on Mental Health Advocacy in California, (Collection 510), Louise M. Darling Biomedical Library History and Special Collections for the Sciences, University of California, Los Angeles, pp. 1–4 at 4.

65. Berkowitz, *Something Happened*, 9.

66. Philip R. Beard, "The Consumer Movement," in *American Psychiatry After World War Two*, ed. Menninger and Nemiah, 299–320 at 301–302. On the array of patient liberation movements, see Harrington, *Mind Fixers*, 123 and Parsons, *From Asylum to Prison*, 101.

67. Suzanne Fleming argues that these groups had some affinity with the mentally ill because they all lacked social and political power. Fleming, "Shrinks vs. Shysters: The (Latest) Battle for Control of the Mentally Ill," *Law and Human Behavior* 6, no. 3/4 (1982): 355–377 at 356. On the expansion of higher education in the United States in the 1950s and 1960s and a developing critical consciousness, see Schudson, *The Rise of the Right to Know*, 26, 175. On civil rights and the rights to health, see Doyle, *Psychiatry and Racial Liberalism in Harlem*, 13. On the civil rights/human rights distinction, see Carol Anderson, *Eyes Off the Prize: The United Nations and the African American Struggle for Human Rights, 1944–1955* (Cambridge: Cambridge University Press, 2003), 2–4. On the idiom of civil rights that animated American social movements, see Bradley, *The World Reimagined*, 223.

68. "Dear Sirs," March 19, 1960, Box 4, 110.F.6.2F, Folder: Mental Files 1955–1960, Anoka State Hospital, Orville L. Freeman Papers, pp. 1–3 at 1.

69. "Dear Sir," February 17, 1966, Box 2, 111.K.8.8F, Folder Assistance: Mental 64-66, Karl F. Rolvaag Papers, pp. 1–3 at 1. This patient refers to incarceration at "St. Peter's," which probably refers to St. Peter State Hospital.

70. On this theme, see Slobodian, *The Globalists*, 226–227. On the "system" as a somewhat amorphous entity in New Leftist thought, see Greif, *The Age of the Crisis of Man*, 281, and Foucault, *The Birth of Biopolitics*, 163.

71. Kaysen, *Girl, Interrupted*, 92. On white identification with "minorities" during the 1960s, see Grace Elizabeth Hale, *A Nation of Outsiders: How the White Middle Class Fell in Love with Rebellion in Postwar America* (New York: Oxford University Press, 2011).

72. Irving Kristol embodies this "neoconservative" spirit well: see Kristol, *Reflections of a Neoconservative: Looking Back, Looking Ahead* (New York: Basic Books, 1983), 43–49, 73–77 and *Neoconservatism: The Autobiography of an Idea* (New York: Free Press, 1995).

73. Resman, *Asylums, Treatment Centers and Genetic Jails*, 67.

74. "Honorable Governor Rolvaag," November 26, 1965, Box 2, 111.K.8.8F, Folder Assistance: Mental 64-66, Karl F. Rolvaag Papers, pp. 1–3 at 1.

75. "Dear Governor," [1940], Box 1, Folder 2, Container SG12205, Dept.: Alabama Governor (1939–1943: Dixon), State Institution Files, 1939–1942, Alabama Dept. of Archives and History, Montgomery, pp. 1–2 at 2. To give a sense of hospital demography, as of 1939, the hospital had 5,537 patients, of whom 1,938 were listed as "colored." See *Annual Report of the*

Superintendent, Bryce Hospital, Tuscaloosa, Alabama, October 26, 1939, Box 1, Folder 10, Container SG12205, Alabama Dept. of Archives and History, p. 11.

76. Letter, "Governor Rolvaag," [November 1964], Box 2, 111.K.8.8F, Folder Assistance Mental 64-66 (A-D), Karl F. Rolvaag Papers, pp. 1–5 at 1. Follow-up notes showed that she had been hospitalized at St. Peter State Hospital in 1963 and Anoka State Hospital in 1964. Office Memorandum, Dept. of Public Welfare, November 19, 1964, Box 2, 111.K.8.8F, Folder Assistance Mental 64-66 (A-D), Karl F. Rolvaag Papers, p. 1.

77. "Governor Rolvaag," [November 1964], 2.

78. Ibid., 1.

79. Ibid., 4.

80. Ibid., 2.

81. See Arnold A. Rogow, *The Psychiatrists* (New York: Delta, 1970), 183.

82. Chesler, *Women and Madness*, 95. On the significance of Chesler, see Nancy Tomes, "Feminist Histories of Psychiatry," in *Discovering the History of Psychiatry*, ed. Micale and Porter, 348–383 at 353.

83. Critiques of the family were often made by white, middle-class feminists and were not always shared by women of color, who might have been more willing to embrace kinship ties (not to mention larger community bonds) in the face of the severity of American racism. On this, see Marta Caminero-Santangelo, *The Madwoman Can't Speak: Or Why Insanity Is Not Subversive* (Ithaca, NY: Cornell University Press, 1998), 159. On British anti-psychiatry, see, for example, David Cooper, *Psychiatry and Anti-Psychiatry* (London: Tavistock, [1967] 1971), 27.

84. On Leonard, see Staub, *Madness Is Civilization*, 87. On Leonard's condemnation of the inhumane treatment of patients at Bellevue, see Sandra Opdycke, *No One Was Turned Away: The Role of Public Hospitals in New York City Since 1900* (New York: Oxford University Press, 1999), 138.

85. These quotations are all from the inset of the 1965 version of Frank Leonard, *City Psychiatric* (New York: Ballantine Books, 1965).

86. On the urban ills and crisis of the 1960s, see Brick, *Transcending Capitalism*, 224. On the perception of "inner cities" as allegedly inherently violent places, see Mical Raz, *What's Wrong with the Poor? Psychiatry, Race, and the War on Poverty* (Chapel Hill: University of North Carolina Press, 2013), 143. On broader cultural images of urban riots during the 1960s, see Looker, *A Nation of Neighborhoods*, 138.

87. See Foucault, *Madness and Civilization*, 59. This was originally published in 1961 in French and 1964 in English.

88. Ennis, *Prisoners of Psychiatry*, vii.

89. On the waning capacity of the prison to provide rehabilitation, see Heather Ann Thompson, *Blood in the Water: The Attica Prison Uprising of 1971 and Its Legacy* (New York: Pantheon Books, 2016), 80. On the deepening doubts about rehabilitation as an ideal on the part of researchers and policymakers in the 1970s, see Anne-Marie Cusac, *Cruel and Unusual: The Culture of Punishment in America* (New Haven, CT: Yale University Press, 2009), 8, 171.

90. Ennis, *Prisoners of Psychiatry*, 229–230.

91. Dean K. Brooks, "A Bushel of Shoes," *Psychiatric Services* 20, no. 12 (December 1969): 373.

92. Ennis, *Prisoners of Psychiatry*, 230.

93. For details see Staub, *Madness Is Civilization*, 87 and Halliwell, *Therapeutic Revolutions*, 217. See also Simon Cross, *Mediating Madness: Mental Distress and Cultural Representation*

(New York: Palgrave Macmillan, 2010), 83. The legal ban on *Titicut Follies* was overturned in 1991. On Wiseman's institutional vision and his arguments about institutions, see Barry Keith Grant and Frederick Wiseman, *5 Films by Frederick Wiseman* (Berkeley: University of California Press, 2006), 3, 5.

94. Hannah Arendt, *Crises of the Republic* (New York: Harcourt Brace Jovanovich, 1972), 40. On the proliferation of testimony about the Holocaust in America during the 1960s, see Bradley, *The World Reimagined*, 139.

95. Harriet Wadeson and William T. Carpenter, "Impact of the Seclusion Room Experience," *Journal of Nervous and Mental Disease* 163, no. 5 (November 1976): 318.

96. Ibid., 325.

97. For example, the Black Panther Party, in their rhetoric, used the phrase "racist Gestapo pigs" to describe the San Francisco police. See Jose Rios et al., "Revolutionary Heroes," *Black Panther Newspaper*, May 11, 1969, 4. In the New Left activist movement, Students for a Democratic Society activists pondered the similarities between the United States and Nazi Germany. On this, see, for example, Mark Rudd, *Underground: My Life with the SDS and the Weathermen* (New York: Harper, 2009), 28.

98. Daniel T. Rodgers, *The Age of Fracture* (Cambridge, MA: Harvard University Press, 2011), 95.

99. On Nazi psychiatry, see Geoffrey Cocks, "German Psychiatry, Psychotherapy, and Psychoanalysis During the Nazi Period: Historiographical Reflections," in *Discovering the History of Psychiatry*, ed. Micale and Porter, 282–296 at 283–285.

100. On American philosophers of structuralism in the 1960s, such as Peter Caws, see Greif, *The Age of the Crisis of Man*, 305. And see Peter Caws, "What Structuralism Is," in *Structuralism: The Art of the Intelligible* (Atlantic Highlands, NJ: Humanities Press International, 1988), 1–7. See also Borradori, *Philosophy in a Time of Terror*, 63.

101. On social psychiatry, see Decker, *The Making of DSM-III*, 311.

102. David Courtwright, *No Right Turn: Conservative Politics in a Liberal America* (Cambridge, MA: Harvard University Press, 2010), 12; and Cornel West, "Nihilism in Black America," in *Black Popular Culture*, ed. Gina Dent (New York: New Press, 1983), 37–47 at 37.

103. On greater privatization, see the introduction to *Rethinking Therapeutic Culture*, ed. Aubry and Travis, 1–23 at 4, 12. On narcissism, see Lunbeck, *The Americanization of Narcissism*, 12, 14.

104. Borstelmann, *The 1970s*, 4, 12, 125. Also, on the alleged hyperindividualism of late twentieth-century America, see Glendon, *Rights Talk*, 75, 178. Finally, see Schulman, *The Seventies*, 78.

105. Duggan, *The Twilight of Equality?*, 22–42.

106. On "Me Decade" cultural sources such as Richard Bach's young adult book about individual achievement, *Jonathan Livingston Seagull* (1970), see Will Kaufman, *American Culture in the 1970s* (Edinburgh: Edinburgh University Press, 2009), 28.

107. McGee, *Self-Help, Inc.*, 14, 54.

108. On these themes, see Thomas J. Scheff, *Being Mentally Ill: A Sociological Theory* (New York: Aldine, 1984), 49.

109. See Christopher Lasch, *The Culture of Narcissism: American Culture in an Age of Diminishing Expectations* (New York: W. W. Norton, 1979), 127ff., 156–157. On tensions between the Old and New Left, see Beryl Satter, "The Left," in *Rethinking Therapeutic Culture*, ed. Aubry and Travis, 119–131 at 121. Many authors in this collection challenge Lasch's thesis

of depoliticization. See, for example, pp. 4, 11, 12. See also Elizabeth Spelman's essay in this collection, "Privacy," 166–174 at 166, in which she discusses the perceived conflict between self-absorption and citizenship duties.

110. Horney, *Self Analysis*, 29. Nikolas Rose has argued that it was the disciplines of psychology and psychiatry, and the rise of interiorizing ideas, that initially promoted the phenomenon of hyperindividualism at the turn of the twentieth century. Rose, *Governing the Soul: The Shaping of the Private Self* (New York: Routledge, 1990), 216.

111. *O'Connor vs. Donaldson*, 11.

112. Letter, 1973, Box 2, Folder 1: High School Kids' Letters, December 1972–May 1974, *Ms.* Magazine Collection, *Ms.* Letters, 1970–1998, MC 568, Schlesinger Library, Harvard University, Cambridge, MA, p. 1.

113. Letter from "Saralinda," *Speak Out*, March 1976, n.p.

114. *Admission of a Patient*, 8mm color, [late 1960s], New York State Archives Series B1581-97, Utica Psychiatric Center (NY) training and publicity motion pictures and videotapes, 1930–1989, Albany, NY.

Epilogue

1. Daphne Merkin, *This Close to Happy: A Reckoning with Depression* (New York: Farrar, Straus and Giroux, 2017), 186.

2. Ibid., 190.

3. Ibid., 191.

4. Ibid., 192.

5. Ibid., 190.

6. Ibid., 193.

7. William Styron, *Darkness Visible: A Memoir of Madness* (New York: Random House, 1990), 3, 68.

8. Ibid., 68–69.

9. Ibid., 69.

10. Ibid., 72.

11. Ibid., 73.

12. Ibid., 74.

13. Ibid., 72.

14. Penney and Stastny, *The Lives They Left Behind*, 20. While Merkin and Styron can easily be written off as the overprivileged in private hospitals, a stunning British example to make a similar case to theirs, this time from the vantage point of a public hospital, is historian Barbara Taylor's memoir, *The Last Asylum: A Memoir of Madness in Our Times* (London: Hamish Hamilton, 2014), 118. Here she discusses her time as a patient at Friern Mental Hospital in North London, where she had spent some time in 1988 and 1989. One of her most arresting scenes is of former patients returning to the site of Friern after it had been shut down, to look around, take photos, and watch the process of the hospital being converted to townhomes; they would be turned away by security guards, and yet "still they kept coming" (244).

15. See Jean M. Twenge and W. Keith Campbell, *The Narcissism Epidemic: Living in the Age of Entitlement* (New York: Simon and Schuster, 2009). See also Lunbeck, *The Americanization of Narcissism*, 253.

16. Amitai Etzioni, *The Spirit of Community: Rights, Responsibilities, and the Communitarian Agenda* (New York: Crown, 1993), 39; Robert Putnam, *Bowling Alone: The Collapse and Revival*

of American Community (New York: Simon and Schuster, 2000); Patrick Deneen, *Why Liberalism Failed* (New Haven, CT: Yale University Press, 2018).

17. On the acceleration of life in the information era, see Judy Wajcman, *Pressed for Time: The Acceleration of Life in Digital Capitalism* (Chicago: University of Chicago Press, 2015), especially her meditation on the appeals of machine speed (49). On corporate workers who are encouraged to be manic, see Emily Martin, *Bipolar Expeditions: Mania and Depression in American Culture* (Princeton, NJ: Princeton University Press, 2007), 15. On the producerist ethos of Prozac, see Metzl, *Prozac on the Couch*, 174.

18. Meri Nana-Ama Danquah, *Willow Weep for Me: A Black Woman's Journey Through Depression: A Memoir* (New York: W. W. Norton, 1998), 193.

19. Meghan O'Rourke, "What's Wrong with Me?" *New Yorker* (August 26, 2013): 32–37 at 34. On patients who seek support using blogs and websites, in addition to local advocacy groups, see Michael Sayeau, "Blogging," in *Rethinking Therapeutic Culture*, ed. Aubry and Travis, 187–199. On blogging communities and online "families," see PhebeAnn M. Wolfrum, "Going Barefoot: Mad Affiliation, Identity Politics and Eros," in *Literatures of Madness*, ed. Donaldson, 31–49 at 31, 34. On the impact of the Internet on health consumerism in the 1990s, see Tomes, *Remaking the American Patient*, 2, 357, 396.

20. On "mad pride," see Staub, *Madness Is Civilization*, 192. On patient advocacy groups and groups with an anti-psychiatry flavor, such as MadLib, see Martin, *Bipolar Expeditions*, xix.

21. Metzl, *The Protest Psychosis*, 13.

22. Grob, *The Mad Among Us*, 305–307. Even if the Clinton administration's health-care plan had come to fruition, it did not include a recognition of support for sufferers of mental illness. Paulson, *Closing the Asylums*, 67.

23. Monica A. Joseph, *Discrimination Against the Mentally Ill* (Santa Barbara: Greenwood, 2016), 79; and Lawrence Kolb et al., "The National Institute of Mental Health: Its Influence on Psychiatry and the Nation's Mental Health," in *American Psychiatry After World War Two*, ed. Menninger and Nemiah, 207–232 at 224.

24. See Van Gosse, *The World the Sixties Made: Politics and Culture in Recent America* (Philadelphia: Temple University Press, 2003), 13; and Gerald N. Grob, "Mental Health Policy in Late Twentieth Century America," in *American Psychiatry After World War Two*, ed. Menninger and Nemiah, 232–258 at 239. Moreover, Reagan's other domestic policies, including reduced incentives for builders to construct low-income housing, and attempts to reduce federal Supplemental Security Income (SSI) payments to people with disabilities had an impact on people with serious mental illnesses who were trying to live in the community. On this, see Torrey, *Nowhere to Go*, 197.

25. On people diagnosed with schizophrenia in the United States being more likely to be in prisons than in psychiatric care institutions, see *The Protest Psychosis*, 187. On the physical repurposing of state hospitals to prisons, see Parsons, *From Asylum to Prison*, 142, and on homelessness in the 1980s, see p. 124.

26. See H. Richard Lamb et al., *Treating the Homeless Mentally Ill: A Task Force Report of the American Psychiatric Association* (Washington, DC: American Psychiatric Association, [1984] 1992). On the fusion of idealistic deinstitutionalizers and fiscal reformers, see pp. 23–24. According to George Paulson, National Institute for Mental Health data for 1986 suggested that there were 104,800 adult schizophrenics living in state mental hospitals, 269,000 in outpatient care, and 73,500 in nursing homes. But there were also 937,300 whose care was listed as "unknown." See *Closing the Asylums*, 78. Finally, see Judith Lynn Failer, *Who Qualifies for*

Rights? Homelessness, Mental Illness, and Civil Commitment (Ithaca, NY: Cornell University Press, 2002), 12.

27. On Foucault and Goffman, see Christopher Jencks, *The Homeless* (Cambridge, MA: Harvard University Press, 1994), 29. Norman Dain makes a similar argument in "Critics and Dissenters: Reflections on 'Anti-Psychiatry' in the United States," *Journal of the History of the Behavioral Sciences* 25, no. 1 (January 1989): 3–25 at 17.

28. Jean J. Beard and Peggy Gillespie, eds., *Nothing to Hide: Mental Illness in the Family* (New York: New Press, 2002), 114.

29. David Karp, *The Burden of Sympathy: How Families Cope with Mental Illness* (New York: Oxford University Press, 2001), 202.

30. "Patients' Rights Sign, 20th Century," U.S. General Services Administration, *Architecture of an Asylum: St. Elizabeths, 1852–2017*, exhibit at the National Building Museum, Washington, DC, March 25, 2017–January 15, 2018, https://www.nbm.org/exhibition/architecture-asylum-st -elizabeths-1852-2017/. The rights listed here were numbers 8, 10, 7, and 9, respectively. On the impact of the Privacy Act and information privacy in the 1970s, see Igo, *The Known Citizen*, 249, 258. Nancy Tomes argues that in the early 1970s legal activists demanded not only the expansion of medical malpractice laws but also patients' rights to privacy and due process. Tomes, *Remaking the American Patient*, 268, 394.

31. Kline, *From Sad to Glad*, 163. On Nathan Kline's interest in lithium, see Hermsen, *Manic Minds*, 111.

32. Kline, *From Sad to Glad*, 177.

33. On anti-urbanism, and on community as an alternative to the city, see Conn, *Americans Against the City*, 6.

34. On high rates of readmission among deinstitutionalized patients, see Stephen C. Schoonover and Ellen L. Bassuk, "Deinstitutionalization and the Private General Hospital Inpatient Unit: Implications for Clinical Care," *Hospital and Community Psychiatry* 34, no. 2 (February 1983): 135.

35. Sontag, *Illness as Metaphor*, 3.

36. "Witnessing Schizophrenia: 'The True Article,'" 1985, Box 24, Folder: Weicker Constituent Correspondence, Agency Files, Correspondence, Dept. of Mental Health, K-L, RG 005, Subgroup 038, 1991–1995, Constituent Correspondence, Agency Files, Mental Health, Lowell Weicker Papers, Connecticut State Library and Archives, Hartford, pp. 1–21 at 10. Weicker, who had a son with Down Syndrome, became interested in disability issues during the early 1980s while he was a U.S. senator. See Larry A. Jones, *Doing Disability Justice, 75 Years of Family Advocacy* (published privately by www.lulu.com, 2010), 235. See also E. J. Dionne, "Lowell Weicker, Jr.," in *Profiles in Courage for Our Time*, ed. Caroline Kennedy (New York: Hyperion, 2002), 53–69 at 65.

37. "Witnessing Schizophrenia," 11.

38. Ibid., 20.

39. Ibid., 10.

40. Ibid., 21.

41. Lenny Lapon, *Mass Murderers in White Coats: Psychiatric Genocide in Nazi Germany and the United States* (Springfield, MA: Psychiatric Genocide Research Institute, 1986), vii.

42. See, for example, Rodgers, *Age of Fracture*, 6. For a primary source, see Diana Fuss, *Essentially Speaking* (New York: Routledge, 1989), 1–23. On science, see Shawn Lawrence Otto, *Fool Me Twice: Fighting the Assault on Science in America* (New York: Rodale, 2011), 125.

43. Harvey L. Ruben, "American Psychiatry's Fundamental Policy Is to Foster the Patient's Good," *Hospital and Community Psychiatry* 37, no. 5 (May 1986): 503. From his vantage point in 1988, psychiatrist and anthropologist Arthur Kleinman wrote that psychiatric illnesses are "'things' in the real world." *Rethinking Psychiatry: From Cultural Category to Personal Experience* (New York: Free Press, 1988), 10.

44. Leonard Roy Frank, "The Policies and Practices of American Psychiatry Are Oppressive," *Hospital and Community Psychiatry* 37, no. 5 (May 1986): 498. For details on Frank, see Sadowsky, *Electroconvulsive Therapy in America*, 114.

45. Michael Staub cites this as a major reason for anti-psychiatry's undoing. See *Madness Is Civilization*, 171.

46. Elyn R. Saks, *The Center Cannot Hold: My Journey Through Madness* (New York: Hyperion, 2007), 183.

47. NAMI New York State, "Breaking the Silence: A Teaching Package for Health Educators with Cross-Curricular Activities, for Upper Elementary School" (Albany, NY: NAMI, 1999).

48. Beard, "The Consumer Movement," 311.

49. On the idea of biochemical problems in the brain, see Nancy Andreasen, *The Broken Brain: The Biological Revolution in Psychiatry* (New York: Harper and Row, 1984), 30 and Rosenberg, "Contested Boundaries," 412. On NAMI campaigns, see Dowbiggin, *The Quest for Mental Health*, 168–169. Dowbiggin argues that NAMI's approach displaced the confrontational tactics of anti-psychiatry and offered a sort of consensus on biological psychiatry. See also Scull, *Psychiatry and Its Discontents*, 70, 208. Finally, see Agnes B. Hatfield, "The Social Context of Helping Families," in *Families as Allies in Treatment of the Mentally Ill*, ed. Lefley and Johnson, 77–90, at 85.

50. NAMI New York State, "Breaking the Silence: A Teaching Package for Health Educators with Cross-Curricular Activities, for Middle School" (Albany, NY: NAMI, 1999).

51. On psychiatrization, see Didier Fassin and Richard Rechtman, *The Empire of Trauma: An Inquiry into the Condition of Victimhood* (Princeton, NJ: Princeton University Press, 2009), 22. On the classification of people into kinds, see Ian Hacking's well-known essay, "The Looping Effects of Human Kinds," in *Causal Cognition: A Multidisciplinary Debate*, ed. Dan Sperber et al. (Oxford: Oxford University Press, 1996), 352–382 at 352.

52. Lou Marinoff, *Plato, Not Prozac! Applying Eternal Wisdom to Everyday Problems* (New York: HarperCollins, 1999), 20. Ian Dowbiggin notes that the DSM-1 had 106 diagnoses, while the DSM-II had 182 and the DSM-III 265. See *The Quest for Mental Health*, 175. Andrew Scull notes 297 diagnoses in the DSM-IV (*Madness*, 111). For a comprehensive look at the development of the DSM-III, and the erosion of psychoanalytical power through descriptive, empirical science, see Decker, *The Making of DSM-III*. On the elimination of neurotic disorders from the DSM-III, another shift away from psychoanalysis, see Peter D. Kramer, *Ordinarily Well: The Case for Antidepressants* (New York: Farrar, Straus and Giroux, 2016), 48 and Metzl, *Prozac on the Couch*, 53. The DSM-III and DSM-IV were also important because health-care providers and patients needed to list codes on bills and insurance claims. See Scull, *Madness in Civilization*, 389. See also Carl Elliott, "Prozac as a Way of Life," in *Prozac as a Way of Life*, ed. Carl Elliott and Tod Chambers (Chapel Hill: University of North Carolina Press, 2004), 1–18 at 5.

53. Eric Cazdyn, *The Already Dead: The New Time of Politics, Culture and Illness* (Durham, NC: Duke University Press, 2012), 183.

54. Herzberg, *Happy Pills in America*, 13.

55. For her thoughts on asylums, see Kate Millett, *The Loony-Bin Trip* (New York: Simon and Schuster, 1990), 193. On lithium, see 30–31.

56. Herzberg, *Happy Pills in America*, 13.

57. Letter, "Dear Kate Millett," September 29, 1992, LBT 6, File 14, pp. 1–3 at 1, Kate Millett Papers, David M. Rubenstein Rare Book and Manuscript Library, Duke University Archives, Durham, NC.

58. Ibid., 2.

59. Ibid., 3.

60. Kramer, *Ordinarily Well*, 44–45. *Osheroff vs. Chestnut Lodge, Inc.* was heard in 1984 before the Court of Special Appeals of Maryland. Available at https://law.justia.com/cases/maryland/court-of-special-appeals/1985/1016-september-term-1984-0.html.

61. Herzberg, *Happy Pills in America*, 165. Herzberg notes that mild forms of depression were discussed in other eras; neurologist Abraham Myerson, for example, talked about the label "anhedonia" (lack of pleasure) in the 1920s. See p. 153.

62. On Prozac's impact, see Herzberg, *Happy Pills in America*, 13, 150, 175, 179, 184. On serotonin, see Shorter, *How Everyone Became Depressed*, 161 and Scull, *Madness in Civilization*, 392.

63. Quoted in David Healy, *Let Them Eat Prozac: The Unhealthy Relationship Between the Pharmaceutical Industry and Depression* (New York: New York University Press, 2006), 374.

64. Edward Shorter, *Before Prozac: The Troubled History of Mood Disorders in Psychiatry* (New York: Oxford University Press, 2009), 176.

65. Nikolas Rose, *The Politics of Life Itself: Biomedicine, Power and Subjectivity in the Twenty-First Century* (Princeton, NJ: Princeton University Press, 2007), 192. David Healy has argued that a "new biological language in psychiatry" has become a part of popular culture. Healy, *The Antidepressant Era* (Cambridge, MA: Harvard University Press, 1999), 5. On the ambivalent embrace of psychotropic drugs, see Metzl, *The Protest Psychosis*, 109. I would even include Peter D. Kramer's popular *Listening to Prozac* as an ambivalent observer. See his meditation on p. 17.

66. See Scull, *Madness in Civilization*, 392 and Kolb et al., "The National Institute of Mental Health," 225.

67. On "having" brains, see Nikolas Rose and Joelle M. Abi-Rached, *Neuro: The New Brain Sciences and the Management of the Mind* (Princeton, NJ: Princeton University Press, 2013), 22. On neuropolitics, see Rose, *The Politics of Life Itself*, 13. On biological citizenship, see pp. 227, 259. On psychiatry and neuroscience, see Scull, *The Insanity of Place/The Place of Insanity*, 142. On brain imaging, see Martin, *Bipolar Expeditions*, 11. Positron emission tomography (PET), a type of brain imagery, became more common in the early 2000s. Though magnetic resource imaging (MRI) was developed in the 1970s and 1980s, these images again became more a part of popular scientific culture in the 2000s. On the impact of brain imaging and the desire to see the origins of madness, see Scull, *Madness in Civilization*, 409.

68. Charles Barber, *Comfortably Numb: How Psychiatry Medicated a Nation* (New York: Vintage, 2009), 61.

69. Sadowsky, *Electroconvulsive Therapy in America*, 145.

70. See Ethan Watters, "The Americanization of Mental Illness," *New York Times*, January 8, 2010, http://www.nytimes.com/2010/01/10/magazine/10psyche-t.html?pagewanted=all&_r=2&. Some argue that biological selfhood is necessarily depoliticizing or that the very idea distracts from a contextual or a structuralist analysis. See Dan G. Blazer, *The Age of Melancholy: "Major Depression" and Its Social Origin* (New York: Routledge, 2005), 17.

71. On the revival of ECT as a therapeutic practice in the 1980s, see Sadowsky, *Electroconvulsive Therapy in America*, 101.

72. Andy Behrman, *Electroboy: A Memoir of Mania* (New York: Random House, 2002), 221.

73. Ibid., 226.

74. Danquah, *Willow Weep for Me*, 21.

75. Martin, *Bipolar Expeditions*, 13.

76. On this theme, see, for example, Otto, *Fool Me Twice*, 107–138. David Herzberg has argued that "simple models of mood and molecules [have] drowned out more complex arguments" because they have such institutional power behind them, including the pharmaceutical industry. Herzberg, *Happy Pills in America*, 167.

77. David B. Morris, *The Culture of Pain* (Berkeley: University of California Press, 1991), 25.

78. Cazdyn, *The Already Dead*, 9.

79. Ibid., 5, 6, 14. On ideas of the chronic mode outside the medical realm, in broader, contemporary political culture, see Purdy, *After Nature*, 226 and Nancy Fraser, *Fortunes of Feminism: From State-Managed Capitalism to Neoliberal Crisis* (New York: Verso, 2013), 219.

80. Lifton, *The Nazi Doctors*, 471.

81. Carl Elliott, *Better than Well: American Medicine Meets the American Dream* (New York: W. W. Norton, 2003), xi. Peter Kramer coined the phrases "better than well" and "cosmetic psychopharmacology." Kramer, *Ordinarily Well*, 86.

82. Danquah, *Willow Weep for Me*, 202. David Healy, too, notes that "emotional flatness or bluntness" is a side effect commonly reported by patients taking Prozac. Healy, *Let Them Eat Prozac*, 250. A fear of psychopharmacology is that they potentially encourage "social quietism." On this, see David DeGrazia, "Prozac, Enhancement, and Self-Creation," in *Prozac as a Way of Life*, ed. Elliott and Chambers, 33–47 at 43.

83. Martin, *Bipolar Expeditions*, 8.

84. Edith Sheffer, *Asperger's Children: The Origins of Autism in Nazi Vienna* (New York: W. W. Norton, 2018), 248.

85. See, for example, Sherry Turkle, *Alone Together: Why We Expect More from Technology and Less from Each Other* (New York: Basic Books, 2011), 265–271 and Gunn Enli, *Mediated Authenticity: How the Media Constructs Reality* (New York: Peter Lang, 2015), 111.

86. Duggan, *The Twilight of Equality?*, xii.

87. Sigmund Freud, *Civilization and Its Discontents*, trans. James Strachey (New York: W. W. Norton, [1930] 1961), 43.

88. I do not want to overstate this case. As Nathan Hale notes, by 1980, there were still 28,000 psychiatrists, 50,000 psychologists, and 300,000 social workers. See Hale, *The Rise and Crisis of Psychoanalysis in the United States*, 340.

89. Letter, July 15, 1992, LBT 6, Folder 14, pp. 1–2 at 1, Kate Millett Papers.

90. See, for example, Judith A. Dulberger, *"Mother Donit fore the Best," Correspondence of a Nineteenth Century Orphan Asylum* (Syracuse, NY: Syracuse University Press, 1996). See her discussion of deinstitutionalization on p. 174. On "almshouse bodies," see Simon P. Newman, *Embodied History: The Lives of the Poor in Early Philadelphia* (Philadelphia: University of Pennsylvania Press, 2003), 16ff.

91. On this, see Dunham and Weinberg, *The Culture of the State Mental Hospital*, 163.

92. Willard State Hospital was formerly known as the Willard Asylum for the Chronic Insane but changed its name and orientation in 1890 to accommodate the "acute" in addition to the "chronic." See Grob, *The Mad Among Us*, 108–109. For the journalist who called the suitcases "chilling," see this article from the *Daily Mail* online, published June 23, 2013: http://www .dailymail.co.uk/news/article-2338714/The-chilling-pictures-suitcases-left-New-York-insane

-asylum-patients-locked-away-rest-lives.html. Robert Whitaker called the photos "haunting" in Penney and Stastny, *The Lives They Left Behind*, 11. On a larger Internet culture of asylum hauntings, see, for example, http://ca.complex.com/pop-culture/2013/01/crazy-mental-asylums /athens-lunatic-asylum.

93. See, for example, the images of shoes and suitcases that Ulrich Baer discusses in *Spectral Evidence: The Photography of Trauma* (Cambridge, MA: MIT Press, 2005), 135. The contents of the suitcases were displayed at the Exploratorium science museum in San Francisco in an exhibit called *The Changing Face of What Is Normal*, http://www.exploratorium.edu/press-office /press-releases/changing-face-what-normal-mental-health. See also the website for the Willard Asylum suitcases: http://www.willardsuitcases.com/.

94. The photo of Manteno State Hospital is available at http://sometimes-interesting.com /2013/03/01/manteno-state-hospital/.

95. Merkin, *This Close to Happy*, 257.

BIBLIOGRAPHY

Archival Collections

Alabama State Institution Files. Alabama Department of Archives and History, Montgomery.

American Psychoanalytic Association, RG 11. Collection Courtesy of the Oskar Diethelm Library, Institute for the History of Psychiatry, Weill Medical College of Cornell University, New York, NY.

Amsden, George (1870–1966). Papers, 1898–1953. Medical Center Archives of New York-Presbyterian/Weill Cornell Medicine, New York, NY.

Annual Reports of the Northampton State Hospital Collection. Massachusetts Archives, Boston, MA.

Bellevue Place Records. Illinois State Historical Library, Springfield, IL.

Brown, Bertram. Papers. MS C 493. National Library of Medicine, Bethesda, MD.

Carmichael, Hugh T. Articles and Papers. American Psychiatric Association Foundation, Melvin Shabin, MD, Library and Archives, American Psychiatric Association, Washington, DC.

Chesler, Phyllis. Papers. David M. Rubenstein Rare Book and Manuscript Library, Duke University Archives, Durham, NC.

Craig House Medical Records on Zelda Fitzgerald. Box 1, Folder 2. Department of Rare Books and Special Collections, Princeton University Library, Princeton, NJ.

Donaldson, Kenneth. Papers. MS 1677. Manuscript and Archives, Yale University Library, New Haven, CT. Freeman, Orville L. Papers. Minnesota State Archives, Minnesota Historical Society, St. Paul, MN.

Freeman, Walter, and James Watts Collection. MS 0803. Gelman Library, George Washington University, Washington, DC.

Fromm, Erich. Papers. Manuscripts and Archives Division, New York Public Library, Astor, Lenox, and Tilden Foundations, New York.

Gorman, Mike. Papers. MS C 462, Modern Manuscripts Collection, History of Medicine Division, National Library of Medicine, Bethesda, MD.

Grasso, Ella. Papers. Connecticut State Archives, Hartford, CT.

Lafargue Clinic Records. Sc MG 141. Schomburg Center for Research in Black Culture, Manuscripts, Archives, and Rare Books Division, New York Public Library, Harlem, NY.

Mendocino State Hospital, Mental-Hygiene-Hospitals. California State Archives, Office of the Secretary of State, Sacramento, CA.

Mental Health Advocacy. Collection of Materials on Mental Health Advocacy in California, Manuscript Collection no. 510, UCLA Biomedical Library, History and Special Collections Division, Los Angeles, CA.

Meyer, Adolf. Collection. Alan Mason Chesney Medical Archives, Johns Hopkins University, Baltimore, MD.

Millet Personal Papers and Manuscripts. Collection Courtesy of the Oskar Diethelm Library, Institute for the History of Psychiatry, Weill Medical College of Cornell University, New York, NY.

Millett, Kate. Papers. David M. Rubenstein Rare Book and Manuscript Library, Duke University Archives, Durham, NC.

Ms. Letters. 1970–1998, MC 568, Box 2, Folder 1: High School Kids' Letters, December 1972–May 1974. *Ms.* Magazine Collection, Schlesinger Library, Harvard University, Cambridge, MA.

O'Neill, William A. Records. Connecticut State Library and Archives, Hartford, CT.

Overholser, Winfred. Papers. Library of Congress, Manuscript Division, Washington, DC.

Rochester State Hospital. Government Records. Minnesota State Archives, Minnesota Historical Society, St. Paul, MN.

Rolvaag, Karl F. Papers. Minnesota State Archives, Minnesota Historical Society, St. Paul, MN.

St. Elizabeths Hospital. Records. RG 418. National Archives, Washington, DC.

Clinical Notes Relating to the Serpasil Geriatric Project.

Records of Other Superintendents.

Records of Superintendent William Alanson White.

Science Service Records. Smithsonian Institution Archives, Record Unit 7091, Washington, DC.

Smith, Lex. Papers. Alan Mason Chesney Medical Archives, Johns Hopkins University, Baltimore, MD.

Superintendent's Correspondence, Racine Series 58. State Historical Society of Wisconsin, University of Wisconsin–Parkside Libraries, Archives Department. Kenosha, WI.

"Vocation Camp for Psychiatric Patients: VA Hospital, Fort Meade, South Dakota." In Department of Medicine and Surgery Information Bulletin: Psychiatry and Neurology Division, Office of the Chief Medical Director Veterans Administration, Washington, DC. John Milne Murray Papers, Box 16, Folder 2, U.S. Veterans Administration, Library of Congress, Manuscript Division, Washington, DC.

Warren, Earl. Papers. Box F3640. California State Archives, Office of the Secretary of State, Sacramento, CA.

Watts, Dr. Interview by Harvey Ammerman. 1988. Walter Freeman and James Watts Collection, MS 0803, Box 42, Part 1. Gelman Library, George Washington University, Washington, DC.

Weicker, Lowell. Papers. Connecticut State Library and Archives, Hartford, CT.

Wertham, Fredric. Papers. Manuscript Division. Library of Congress, Manuscript Collections, Washington, DC.

Medical Textbooks, Works of Psychoanalysis and Psychology

Ackerman, Nathan W. *The Psychodynamics of Family Life: Diagnosis and Treatment of Family Relationships.* New York: Basic Books, 1958.

Ahmed, Paul I., and Stanley C. Plog. *State Mental Hospitals: What Happens When They Close.* New York: Plenum Medical Book Company, 1976.

Andreasen, Nancy. *The Broken Brain: The Biological Revolution in Psychiatry.* New York: Harper and Row, 1984.

Arieti, Silvano, ed. *American Handbook of Psychiatry.* Vol. 1. New York: Basic Books, 1959.

Becker, Ernest. *The Revolution in Psychiatry: The New Understanding of Man.* New York: Free Press, 1964.

Bingham, June. *Do Cows Have Neuroses?* New York. National Association for Mental Health, [1948] 1958.

Bleuler, Eugen. *Dementia Praecox, or, Group of Schizophrenias.* New York: International Universities Press, [1911] 1950.

Brandt, Anthony. *Reality Police: The Experience of Insanity in America.* New York: William Morrow, 1975.

Breuer, Joseph, and Sigmund Freud. *Studies in Hysteria.* Boston: Beacon Press, [1895] 1964.

Burr, Colonel Bell. *Practical Psychology and Psychiatry: For Use in Training Schools for Attendants and Nurses in Medical Classes.* Philadelphia: Davis, 1921.

Chesler, Phyllis. *Women and Madness.* New York: Palgrave MacMillan, [1972] 2005.

Cooper, David. *Psychiatry and Anti-Psychiatry.* London: Tavistock, [1967] 1971.

Daly, Vincent J. *Understanding Mental Illness: A Patient's Manual for Group Therapy.* Whitfield, MS: Mississippi State Hospital, 1950.

Denber, Herman C. B. *Research Conference on Therapeutic Community Held at Manhattan State Hospital Ward's Island, New York.* Springfield, IL: Charles C. Thomas, 1960.

Deutsch, Albert. *The Shame of the States.* New York: Arno Press, [1948] 1973.

Dunham, H. Warren, and S. Kirson Weinberg. *The Culture of the State Mental Hospital.* Detroit: Wayne State University Press, 1960.

Ennis, Bruce J. *Prisoners of Psychiatry: Mental Patients, Psychiatrists, and the Law.* New York: Harcourt Brace Jovanovich, 1972.

Fields, Jeffrey D. "O'Connor vs. Donaldson." *Hofstra Law Review* 4, no. 2 (1976): 511–530.

Freedman, Alfred M., and Harold Kaplan. *The Comprehensive Textbook of Psychiatry.* Baltimore: Williams and Wilkins, 1967.

Freeman, Walter, and James W. Watts. *Psychosurgery: In the Treatment of Mental Disorders and Intractable Pain.* Springfield, IL: Charles C. Thomas, [1942] 1950.

———. "Psychosurgery During 1936–1946." In *From Madness to Mental Health: Psychiatric Disorder and Its Treatment in Western Civilization,* edited by Greg Eghigian, 285–287. New Brunswick, NJ: Rutgers University Press, 2010.

Freud, Sigmund. *Civilization and Its Discontents.* Translated by James Strachey. New York: W. W. Norton, [1930] 1961.

Fromm, Erich. *The Art of Loving.* New York: Continuum, [1956] 2008.

———. *Escape from Freedom.* New York: Farrar and Rinehart, 1941.

———. *The Revolution of Hope: Toward a Humanized Technology.* Riverdale, NY: American Mental Health Foundation, [1968] 2010.

Greenblatt, Milton, et al., eds. *The Patient and the Mental Hospital.* Glencoe, IL: Free Press, 1957.

Gross, Martin L. *The Doctors.* New York: Random House, 1966.

———. *The Psychological Society: A Critical Analysis of Psychiatry, Psychotherapy, Psychoanalysis and the Psychological Revolution.* New York: Random House, 1978.

Horney, Karen. *Self Analysis.* New York: W. W. Norton, 1942.

Jackson, Josephine. *Outwitting Our Nerves: A Primer on Psychotherapy.* New York: Century, 1921.

James, William. "The Varieties of Religious Experience." https://www.gutenberg.org/files/621/621-pdf.pdf.

Kaplan, Berton H., et al., eds. *Further Explorations in Social Psychiatry.* New York: Basic Books, 1976.

Kline, Nathan S. *From Sad to Glad.* New York: Ballantine, 1974.

Kluckhohn, Clyde, and Henry A. Murray, eds. *Personality in Nature, Society, and Culture*. New York: Knopf, 1950.

Kohut, Heinz. *The Restoration of the Self*. New York: International Universities Press, 1977.

———. *The Search for the Self*. New York: International Universities Press, 1978.

Kramer, Peter D. *Listening to Prozac: A Psychiatrist Explores Antidepressant Drugs and the Remaking of the Self*. New York: Penguin, 1993.

Krim, Seymour. *Views of a Nearsighted Cannoneer*. New York: E. P. Dutton, 1968.

Lamb, H. Richard. *Treating the Long-Term Mentally Ill: Beyond Deinstitutionalization*. San Francisco: Jossey-Bass, 1982.

Lapon, Lenny. *Mass Murderers in White Coats: Psychiatric Genocide in Nazi Germany and the United States*. Springfield, MA: Psychiatric Genocide Research Institute, 1986.

Lasch, Christopher. *The Culture of Narcissism: American Culture in an Age of Diminishing Expectations*. New York: W. W. Norton, 1979.

Lefley, Harriet P., and Dale L. Johnson, eds. *Families as Allies in Treatment of the Mentally Ill: New Directions for Mental Health Professionals*. Washington, DC: American Psychiatric Press, 1990.

Lindner, Robert. *The Fifty-Minute Hour: A Collection of True Psychoanalytic Tales*. New York: Bantam, 1955.

Maynard, Lorraine, and Laurence Miscall. *Bellevue*. New York: Julian Messner, 1940.

Menninger, Karl. *Love Against Hate*. New York: Harcourt Brace Jovanovich, 1942.

———. *The Vital Balance: The Life Process in Mental Health and Illness*. New York: Penguin, 1963.

Noyes, Arthur P., and Lawrence C. Kolb. *Modern Clinical Psychiatry*. Philadelphia: W. B. Saunders, [1934] 1963.

Payne, Buryl. *Getting There Without Drugs: Techniques and Theories for the Expansion of Consciousness*. London: Wildwood House, [1973] 1974.

Pollock, Horatio M. *Family Care of Mental Patients: A Review of Systems of Family Care in America and Europe*. Utica, NY: State Hospitals Press, 1936.

Prinzhorn, Hans. *Artistry of the Mentally Ill*. New York: Springer-Verlag, 1972.

Radical Therapist/Rough Times Collective. *The Radical Therapist*. Harmondsworth, Middlesex: Ballantine Books, [1971] 1974.

Rawlings, Edna I., and Dianne K. Carter. "The Intractable Female Patient." In *From Madness to Mental Health: Psychiatric Disorder and Its Treatment in Western Civilization*, edited by Greg Eghigian, 392–400. New Brunswick, NJ: Rutgers University Press, 2010.

Rogers, Carl. *On Becoming a Person: A Therapist's View of Psychotherapy*. London: Constable, [1961] 1967.

———. *On Personal Power: Inner Strength and Its Revolutionary Impact*. London: Constable, [1977] 1978.

Rogow, Arnold A. *The Psychiatrists*. New York: Delta, 1970.

Rothman, David. *The Discovery of the Asylum: Social Order and Disorder in the New Republic*. Piscataway, NJ: Transaction Publishers, 1971.

Sacks, Oliver. *Awakenings*. London: Gerald Duckworth, 1973.

Schwing, Gertrud. *A Way to the Soul of the Mentally Ill*. New York: International Universities Press, 1954.

Stanton, Alfred H., and Morris S. Schwartz. *The Mental Hospital: A Study of Institutional Participation in Psychiatric Illness and Treatment*. New York: Basic Books, 1954.

Sullivan, Harry Stack. *The Collected Works*. Vol. 1, *The Interpersonal Theory of Psychiatry*. New York: W. W. Norton, 1964.

Szasz, Thomas. *Ideology and Insanity: Essays on the Psychiatric Dehumanization of Man*. London: Calder and Boyars, 1973.

———. *Psychiatric Slavery*. Syracuse, NY: Syracuse University Press, [1977] 1998.

———. *The Therapeutic State: Psychiatry in the Mirror of Current Events*. New York: Prometheus, 1984.

Whitehorn, John C. *Effective Psychotherapy with the Schizophrenic Patient*. New York: Jason Aronson, 1975.

Zilboorg, Gregory. *Psychoanalysis and Religion*. London: George Allen and Unwin, [1962] 1967.

Articles in Medical and Social Science Periodicals and Anthologies

Adams, Walter A. "Segregation-Integration: Patterns of Culture and Social Adjustment." *American Journal of Orthopsychiatry* 28, no. 1 (January 1958): 14–20.

Arendt, Hannah. "The Archimedean Point." In *Thinking Without a Banister: Essays in Understanding, 1953–1975*, 403–418. New York: Schocken, 2018.

———. *Crises of the Republic*. New York: Harcourt Brace Jovanovich, 1972.

———. "Ideology and Terror: A Novel Form of Government." *Review of Politics* 15, no. 3 (July 1953): 303–327.

———. *The Origins of Totalitarianism*. San Diego: Harcourt Brace Jovanovich, 1951.

———. "Public Rights and Private Interests." In *Thinking Without a Banister: Essays in Understanding, 1953–1975*, 506–512. New York: Schocken, 2018.

———. "Values in Contemporary Society." In *Thinking Without a Banister: Essays in Understanding, 1953–1975*, 438–442. New York: Schocken, 2018.

Begg, William A. G., and A. Arnaud Reid. "Meratran: A New Stimulant Drug." *British Medical Journal* 1, no. 4973 (April 28, 1956): 946–949.

Bierer, Joshua. "The Marlborough Experiment." In *Handbook of Community Psychiatry and Community Mental Health*, edited by Leopold Bellak, 221–247. New York: Grune and Stratton, 1964.

Brooks, Dean K. "A Bushel of Shoes." *Psychiatric Services* 20, no. 12 (December 1969): 371–375.

Cole, Lillian A. "Institutionalitis." *Psychiatric Services (Mental Hospitals)* 6, no. 2 (February 1955): 16–17.

"Collie Classes Held at Anoka State Hospital." *Psychiatric Services (Mental Hospitals)* 7, no. 7 (September 1956): 18.

Davidson, Henry. "A Psychiatric Word Clinic: Session IV: Words Describing Withdrawal or Indifference." *Psychiatric Services (Mental Hospitals)* 9, no. 3 (March 1958): 12–14.

"Dean Brooks, Superintendent and Actor, Talks About Cuckoo's Nest." *Hospital and Community Psychiatry* 28, no. 1 (January 1977): 46–48.

Drubin, Lester. "Further Observations on Sixty-Two Lobotomized Psychotic Male Veterans at the Veterans Hospital, Northport, New York." *Journal of Nervous and Mental Disease* 113, no. 3 (March 1951): 247–256.

"Former Mental Patient." "A Subjective Account of Electroshock Treatment." *The Attendant* 2, no. 11 (November 1945): 81–86.

Frank, Leonard Roy. "The Policies and Practices of American Psychiatry Are Oppressive." *Hospital and Community Psychiatry* 37, no. 5 (May 1986): 497–504.

Fromm-Reichmann, Frieda. "Loneliness." *Psychiatry: Journal for the Study of Interpersonal Processes* 22 (February 1959): 1–15.

Garvin, W. M. "The Attitude of State Hospitals Toward Relatives and Friends of Patients." *State Hospital Quarterly* 7, no. 1 (November 1921): 5–10.

Gralnick, Alexander. "Build a Better State Hospital: Deinstitutionalization Has Failed." *Hospital and Community Psychiatry* 36, no. 7 (July 1985): 738–741.

Gross, Mortimer. "Therapy in a State Hospital Regressed Ward." *Journal of Nervous and Mental Disease* 120, no. 5 (November/December 1954): 324–329.

Hahn, Paul, and Z. M. Lebensohn. "New Trends in Hospital Design." *American Journal of Hospital Psychiatry* 104, no. 8 (February 1948): 555–564.

Maraniss, David. "Afterword: Uncle Phil's Brain." In *Nothing to Hide: Mental Illness in the Family*, edited by Jean J. Beard and Peggy Gillespie, 271–277. New York: New Press, 2002.

"Pet Show Is a Howling Success." *Psychiatric Services (Mental Hospitals)* 9, no. 3 (March 1958): 22.

Peterson, B. F., and Sidney H. Acuff. "An Experiment in Living." *Psychiatric Services (Mental Hospitals)* 6, no. 11 (November 1955): 8–9.

Pollock, Horatio M. "Mental Disease Among Negroes in the United States." *State Hospital Quarterly* 11, no. 1 (November 1925): 47–66.

Relman, Arnold S. "The New Medical-Industrial Complex." *New England Journal of Medicine* 303, no. 17 (1980): 963–970.

Ruben, Harvey L. "American Psychiatry's Fundamental Policy Is to Foster the Patient's Good." *Hospital and Community Psychiatry* 37, no. 5 (May 1986): 501–506.

"Saralinda." Letter in *Speakout*. March 1976.

Schoonover, Stephen C., and Ellen L. Bassuk. "Deinstitutionalization and the Private General Hospital Inpatient Unit: Implications for Clinical Care." *Hospital and Community Psychiatry* 34, no. 2 (February 1983): 135–139.

Schreiber, Julius. "The Interdependence of Democracy and Mental Health." *Mental Hygiene* 29, no. 4 (October 1945): 606–631.

Simmons, Leo W. "A Sociologist's Views on Patient Care." *American Journal of Psychiatry* 117 (November 1960): 385–391.

Szalita, Alberta B. "Some Thoughts on Empathy." *Psychiatry* 39 (May 1976): 142–151.

Talbot, Eugene, and Stuart C. Miller. "The Mental Hospital as a Sane Society: Treating Patients as People." *Trans-action* (September/October 1965): 1–4.

"Volunteer Teaches Puppet Making." *Mental Hospitals* 9, no. 3 (March 1958): 22.

Wadeson, Harriet, and William T. Carpenter. "Impact of the Seclusion Room Experience." *Journal of Nervous and Mental Disease* 163, no. 5 (November 1976): 318–327.

Wagner, Philip Sigmund. "A Comparative Study of Negro and White Admissions to the Psychiatric Pavilion of the Cincinnati General Hospital." *American Journal of Psychiatry* 95, no. 1 (July 1938): 167–183.

Museum Exhibits and Material Culture

Architecture of an Asylum: St. Elizabeths, 1852–2017. National Building Museum, Washington, DC. March 25, 2017–January 15, 2018. https://www.nbm.org/exhibition/architectureasylum at elizabeths-1852-2017/.

The Changing Face of What Is Normal. April 17, 2013–April 13, 2014. San Francisco https://www
    .exploratorium.edu/press-office/press-releases/changing-face-what-normal-mental-health
    and https://remedianetwork.net/2014/06/18/suitcase-stories/.
NAMI New York State. "Breaking the Silence: A Teaching Package for Health Educators with
    Cross-Curricular Activities, for Middle School." Albany, NY: NAMI, 1999.
———. "Breaking the Silence: A Teaching Package for Health Educators with Cross-Curricular
    Activities, for Upper Elementary School." Albany, NY: NAMI, 1999.
Willard Suitcases. https://www.willardsuitcases.com.

Architecture and Design

Goshen, Charles E., ed. *Psychiatric Architecture: A Review of Contemporary Developments in the
    Architecture of Mental Hospitals, Schools for the Mentally Retarded and Related Facilities.*
    Washington, DC: American Psychiatric Association, [1959] 1961.

Films

Admission of a Patient. 8mm color, [late 1960s], New York State Archives Series B1581-97, Utica
    Psychiatric Center (NY) training and publicity motion pictures and videotapes, 1930–1989,
    Albany, NY.
Anyplace But Here. Directed by Maurice Murad. CBS News, 1978.
The Cabinet of Dr. Caligari. Directed by Robert Wiene. 1919.
Keeping Mentally Fit. 1952. https://www.youtube.com/watch?v=fwJGbhQpaJU.
Mental Health: Trouble in the Family. Record Group 381: Records of the Community Services
    Administration, 1963–1981, Arc ID: 72809/Local: 683, Moving Images Relating to Anti-
    poverty Programs, Motion Picture, Sound and Video Records Section, Special Media Archives
    Services Division, National Archives, College Park, MD.
Mental Hospital. Directed by Layton Mabrey. 1953. Produced by the University of Oklahoma, for
    the Oklahoma State Department of Health and Mental Health. Distributed by the Interna-
    tional Film Bureau. https://archive.org/details/mental_hospital.
One Flew over the Cuckoo's Nest. Directed by Milos Forman. 1975.
Out of the Shadows. Utica Training Center. New York State Archives, Albany, 1930. New York
    State Archives Series B1581-97, Utica Psychiatric Center (NY) training and publicity
    motion pictures and videotapes, 1930–1989, Albany, New York. https://www.youtube.com
    /watch?v=7RENS5bif0M.
Shock Treatment. Directed by Denis Sanders. 1964.
Spellbound. Directed by Alfred Hitchcock. 1945.
Titicut Follies. Directed by Frederick Wiseman. Cambridge, MA: Zipporah Films, 1967.

Government Documents

Bureau of the Census. *Patients in Hospitals for Mental Disease.* Washington, DC: U.S. Govern-
    ment Printing Office, 1939.
Doyle, Kathleen. *Public Affairs Pamphlet No. 172: When Mental Illness Strikes Your Family.* New
    York: Public Affairs Committee, 1951.
"Mental Health Is…1 2 3." National Association for Mental Health. 1951.
Overholser, Winfred. *St. Elizabeths Hospital.* Washington, DC: U.S. Government Printing Office,
    1958.

Proceedings of the Second Annual Public Hearing on Mental Health. Held by the New York State Senate Committee on Public Health in the Senate Chamber, The Capitol, Albany, New York, January 28, 1958, Senator George R. Metcalf, Chairman.

Steuart, W. M. *Patients in Hospitals for Mental Disease*. Washington, DC: U.S. Government Printing Office, 1924.

Truesdell, Leon E. *Mental Patients in State Hospitals*. Washington, DC: U.S. Government Printing Office, 1934.

Voluntary Admission and Treatment of Patients at St. Elizabeths Hospital Hearing Before Subcommittee No. 2 of the Committee on Education and Labor House of Representatives 80th Congress Second Session on H.R. 4553 and H.R. 6289 Bills to Provide for the Voluntary Admission and Treatment of Mental Patients at Saint Elizabeths Hospital with Report on H.R. 6289 December 2, 1947. Washington, DC: U.S. Government Printing Office, 1948.

Media Sources and Pamphlets

Curtis, Constance. "Mental Hygiene Clinic Planned in Harlem Area." *New York Amsterdam News*, May 18, 1946.

"Dr. W. A. White, Mender of Brains." *Sunday Telegram*, 1921.

Dudar, Helen. "Apathy, Despair, Hostility, Seen as Roots of Rioting." *Psychiatric News*, September 1967.

Fleming, Thomas. "The Computer and the Psychiatrist." *New York Times Magazine*, April 6, 1969, 45–50.

"The Hallucination Has Gone." *Book Find News*, December 1947.

Henry, Thomas B. "Brain Operation by D.C. Doctors Aids Mental Ills." *Washington Evening Star*, November 20, 1936, A-1–A-2.

Hurston, Zora Neale. "What White Publishers Won't Print." *Negro Digest*, April 1950, 1.

"The Illinois Neuropsychiatric Institute and the University of Illinois." June 6, 1942. http://archives.library.illinois.edu/erec/University%20Archives/5238815/5238815_01_NeuropsychiatricInstitute.pdf.

"Insanity." *Ebony* (April 1949): 19–24.

Maisel, Albert Q. "Bedlam, 1946." *Life*, May 6, 1946, 102–118.

Palmer, Gretta, and Howard Whitman. "Is Psychoanalysis at War with God?" *Cosmopolitan* (June 1947): 26, 113–118.

"Racial Prejudice Said Form of Mental Illness." *Memphis World* 028, no. 033 (1958).

Ratcliff, John Drury. *Science Yearbook of 1942*. New York: Doubleday, Doran, 1942.

"Snatched from Madhouse, Girl Sues Ex-Suitor for $75 000." *Sunday American*, 1923.

"To Our New Guests." Anton T. Boisen Papers-40. 1964. https://www.kansasmemory.org/item/223252/page/40.

Novels, Short Stories, Plays, Poetry

Brand, Millen. *The Outward Room*. New York: Simon and Schuster, 1937.

———. *Savage Sleep*. London: W. H. Allen, [1968] 1969.

Fauset, Jessie Redmon. *There Is Confusion*. Boston: Northeastern University Press, [1924] 1989.

Faulkner, William. "Death Drag." In *The Portable William Faulkner*, 585–605. New York: Viking, 1946.

Greenberg, Joanne. *I Never Promised You a Rose Garden*. New York: Holt, Rinehart and Winston, 1964.

Kesey, Ken. *One Flew over the Cuckoo's Nest.* New York. Signet, [1962] 1963

Leonard, Frank. *City Psychiatric.* New York: Ballantine Books, 1965.

Maine, Harold. *If a Man Be Mad.* New York: Doubleday, 1947.

O'Neill, Eugene. *The Emperor Jones.* Cincinnati, OH: Stewart Kidd Co., 1921.

Philtine, Ellen. *They Walk in Darkness.* New York: Liveright Publishing, 1945.

Plath, Sylvia. *The Bell Jar.* London: Faber and Faber, [1963] 1966.

Sexton, Anne. "Ringing the Bells." In *To Bedlam and Part Way Back.* Boston: Houghton Mifflin, 1960.

Slaughter, Frank G. *Daybreak.* London: Universal Book Club, 1958.

Ward, Mary Jane. *The Snake Pit.* New York: Random House, 1946.

Warren, Robert Penn. *All the King's Men.* New York: Harcourt, Brace, and Company, 1946.

Williams, John. *Stoner.* New York: New York Review of Books, 1965.

Williams, Tennessee. *Suddenly Last Summer.* New York: Dramatists Play Service, [1958] 1986.

Yates, Richard. *Revolutionary Road.* New York: Vintage, [1961] 2008.

Memoirs

Allen, David Walton. *Shrink! A Freudian Psychoanalyst Speaks About His Career in Psychiatry.* San Francisco: Redactors' Press, 2004.

Beers, Clifford. *A Mind That Found Itself.* 1908. http://www.gutenberg.org/ebooks/11962?msg=welcome_stranger.

Behrman, Andy. *Electroboy: A Memoir of Mania.* New York: Random House, 2002.

Benziger, Barbara Field. *The Prison of My Mind.* New York: Walker and Company, 1969.

Bogdan, Robert, ed. *Being Different: The Autobiography of Jane Fry.* New York: John Wiley, 1974.

Brown, Henry Collins. *A Mind Mislaid.* New York: E. P. Dutton, 1937.

Cranford, Peter G. *But for the Grace of God: The Inside Story of the World's Largest Insane Asylum.* Milledgeville, GA: Old Capital Press, 2008.

Danquah, Meri Nana-Ama. *Willow Weep for Me: A Black Woman's Journey Through Depression: A Memoir.* New York: W. W. Norton, 1998.

Donaldson, Kenneth. *Insanity Inside Out.* New York: Crown, 1976.

Farmer, Frances. *Will There Really Be a Morning?* London: Allison and Busby, [1972] 1974.

Hackett, Paul. *The Cardboard Giants.* London: Victor Gollancz, 1953.

Hampton, Russell K. *The Far Side of Despair: A Personal Account of Depression.* Chicago: Nelson-Hall, 1975.

Hebald, Carol. *The Heart Too Long Suppressed: A Chronicle of Mental Illness.* Boston: Northeastern University Press, 2001.

Hillyer, Jane. *Reluctantly Told.* London: Wishart and Company, [1926] 1927.

Jayson, Lawrence M. *Mania.* New York: Funk and Wagnalls, 1937.

Kaysen, Susanna. *Girl, Interrupted.* New York: Virago, 1995.

King, Marian. *The Recovery of Myself: A Patient's Experience in a Hospital for Mental Illness.* New Haven, CT: Yale University Press, 1931.

Kirk, Anne. *Chronicles of Interdict No. 7807.* Boston: Meador, 1937.

Klitzman, Robert. *In a House of Dreams and Glass: Becoming a Psychiatrist.* New York: Simon and Schuster, 1995.

Kruger, Judith. *My Fight for Sanity.* London: Hammond and Hammond, 1959.

Lane, Edward X. *I Was a Mental Statistic.* New York: Carlton Press, 1963.

Manning, Margaret. *Undercurrents: A Therapist's Reckoning with Her Own Depression*. San Francisco: HarperSanFrancisco, 1994.

Merkin, Daphne. *This Close to Happy: A Reckoning with Depression*. New York: Farrar, Straus and Giroux, 2017.

Millett, Kate. *The Loony-Bin Trip*. New York: Simon and Schuster, 1990.

Neugeboren, Jay. *Imagining Robert: My Brother, Madness, and Survival*. New York: Henry Holt, 1997.

Rudd, Mark. *Underground: My Life with the SDS and the Weathermen*. New York: Harper, 2009.

Saks, Elyn R. *The Center Cannot Hold: My Journey Through Madness*. New York: Hyperion, 2007.

Seabrook, William. *Asylum*. New York: Harcourt, Brace and Company, 1935.

Slater, Lauren. *Prozac Diary*. New York: Penguin, 1998.

Styron, William. *Darkness Visible: A Memoir of Madness*. New York: Random House, 1990.

Taylor, Barbara. *The Last Asylum: A Memoir of Madness in Our Times*. London: Hamish Hamilton, 2014.

Wilson, Louise. *This Stranger, My Son: A Mother's Story*. New York: G. P. Putnam's Sons, 1968.

Wilson, Margaret. *Borderland Minds*. Boston: Meador, 1940.

Wilson, Wilma. *They Call Them Camisoles*. Los Angeles: Lymanhouse, 1940.

Wolfe, Ellen. *Aftershock: The Story of a Psychotic Episode*. New York: G. P. Putnam's Sons, 1969.

Sociology, Philosophy, Political Science

Adorno, Theodor. *The Authoritarian Personality*. New York: Harper and Bros., 1950.

———. "Selections from Minima Moralia." 1965. In *Can One Live After Auschwitz?*, edited by Mieke Bal and Hent de Vries. Palo Alto, CA: Stanford University Press, 2003.

Agee, James. *Let Us Now Praise Famous Men*. New York: Mariner Books, [1941] 2001.

Berman, Marshall. *The Politics of Authenticity: Radical Individualism and the Emergence of Modern Society*. New York: Atheneum, 1970.

Bettelheim, Bruno. *The Informed Heart: Autonomy in a Mass Age*. New York: Free Press, 1960.

Beutner, Karl R., and Nathan G. Hale. *Emotional Illness: How Families Can Help*. New York: G. P. Putnam's Sons, 1957.

Boisen, Anton T. *The Exploration of the Inner World: A Study of Mental Disorder and Religious Experience*. Oxford: Willett, Clark, 1936.

Boston Women's Health Collective. *Our Bodies, Ourselves: A Book by and for Women*. New York: Simon and Schuster, 1971.

Brandeis, Louis, and Samuel D. Warren. "The Right to Privacy." *Harvard Law Review* 4, no. 5 (December 15, 1890): 193–220.

Cather, Willa. *Not Under Forty*. Lincoln: University of Nebraska Press, [1922] 1988.

Césaire, Aimé. *Discourse on Colonialism*. New York: Monthly Review Press, [1955] 1972.

Clark, Kenneth. *Dark Ghetto: Dilemmas of Social Power*. New York: Harper and Row, 1965.

Deneen, Patrick. *Why Liberalism Failed*. New Haven, CT: Yale University Press, 2018.

Etzioni, Amitai. *The Spirit of Community: Rights, Responsibilities, and the Communitarian Agenda*. New York: Crown, 1993.

Fanon, Frantz. *The Wretched of the Earth*. New York: Grove/Atlantic, [1961] 2007.

Farson, Richard. *The Future of the Family*. New York: Family Service Association of America, 1969.

Friedan, Betty. *The Feminine Mystique*. New York: Dell, 1962.

Goffman, Erving. *Asylums. Essays on the Social Situation of Mental Patients and Other Inmates*. New York: Anchor Books, 1961.

———. *The Presentation of Self in Everyday Life*. New York. Anchor, 1959.

———. *Stigma: Notes on the Management of Spoiled Identity*. New York: Penguin, 1963.

Gordon, C. Wayne. *The Social System of the High School: A Study in the Sociology of Adolescence*. Glencoe, IL: Free Press, 1957.

Gordon, Richard E., et al. *The Split-Level Trap*. New York: Bernard Geis, 1960.

Gorman, Mike. "Misery Rules in State Shadowland." *Daily Oklahoman* series reprint (July–October 1946): 1–12. http://profiles.nlm.nih.gov/ps/access/TGBBGW.pdf.

Grier, William H., and Price M. Cobbs. *Black Rage*. London: Jonathan Cape, [1968] 1969.

Hoover, J. Edgar. *Masters of Deceit*. New York: Pocket Books, 1959.

Horkheimer, Max, and Theodor Adorno. "The Culture Industry: Enlightenment as Mass Deception." In *Dialectic of Enlightenment*, 120–167. New York: Continuum, [1944] 1987.

Hunter, Edward. *Brain-Washing in Red China: The Calculated Destruction of Men's Minds*. New York: Vanguard, 1951.

Illich, Ivan. *Limits to Medicine*. Toronto: McClelland and Stewart, 1976.

———. *Medical Nemesis: The Expropriation of Health*. New York: Pantheon Books, 1976.

Josephson, Eric, and Mary Josephson, eds. *Man Alone: Alienation in Modern Society*. New York: Laurel, 1962.

Kazin, Alfred. *Contemporaries*. Boston: Little, Brown, 1958.

Kristol, Irving. *Neoconservatism: The Autobiography of an Idea*. New York: Free Press, 1995.

———. *Reflections of a Neoconservative: Looking Back, Looking Ahead*. New York: Basic Books, 1983.

Lippmann, Walter. *Public Opinion*. New York: Macmillan, [1922] 1957.

Marks, John D. *The Search for the "Manchurian Candidate": The CIA and Mind Control*. New York: Times Books, 1979.

McLuhan, Marshall. *Understanding the Media: The Extensions of Man*. New York: McGraw-Hill, 1964.

Meerloo, Joost. *The Rape of the Mind: The Psychology of Thought Control, Menticide, and Brainwashing*. New York: World Publishing, 1955.

Mills, C. Wright. *White Collar: The American Middle Classes*. New York: Oxford University Press, [1951] 1956.

Myers, Jerome K., and Bertram H. Roberts. *Family and Class Dynamics in Mental Illness*. New York: John Wiley and Sons, 1959.

Niebuhr, Reinhold. *Children of Light and Children of Darkness: A Vindication of Democracy and a Critique of Its Traditional Defense*. Chicago: University of Chicago Press, [1944] 2011.

Nisbet, Robert A. *Community and Power*. New York: Galaxy Books, [1953] 1962.

Oldenburg, Ray. *The Great Good Place*. New York: Paragon, 1991.

Ortega y Gasset, José. *The Revolt of the Masses*. New York: W. W. Norton, [1932] 1994.

Pasley, Virginia. *21 Stayed: The Story of the American GIs Who Chose Communist China—Who They Were and Why They Stayed*. New York: American Book-Stratford Press, 1955.

Philbrick, Herbert. *I Led Three Lives: Citizen, "Communist," Counterspy*. New York: McGraw-Hill, 1952.

Putnam, Robert. *Bowling Alone: The Collapse and Revival of American Community*. New York: Simon and Schuster, 2000.

Ramsey, Paul. *The Patient as Person: Explorations in Medical Ethics*. New Haven, CT: Yale University Press, 1970.

Rieff, Philip. *The Triumph of the Therapeutic: Uses of Faith After Freud*. New York: Penguin, 1966.

Riesman, David. *The Lonely Crowd: A Study of the Changing American Character*. New Haven, CT: Yale University Press, 1950.

Rios, José, et al. "Revolutionary Heroes." *Black Panther Newspaper*, May 11, 1969, 4.

Scheff, Thomas J. *Being Mentally Ill: A Sociological Theory*. New York: Aldine, 1984.

Schlesinger, Arthur. *The Vital Center: The Politics of Freedom*. Boston: Houghton Mifflin, 1949.

Stern, Edith M. *Mental Illness: A Guide for the Family*. New York: National Association for Mental Health, 1954.

———. "Our Ailing Mental Hospitals." 1941. https://archive.org/stream/surveygraphic30survrich /surveygraphic30survrich_djvu.txt.

Taylor, Frederick. *Principles of Scientific Management*. 1911. https://www.marxists.org/reference /subject/economics/taylor/principles/index.htm.

Veblen, Thorstein. *The Theory of Business Enterprise*. 1904. https://archive.org/details/theory businesse00veblgoog/page/n10.

Whyte, William H. *The Organization Man*. Philadelphia: University of Pennsylvania Press, [1956] 2002.

Wright, Frank L. *Out of Sight, Out of Mind*. National Mental Health Foundation, 1947. https:// www.disabilitymuseum.org/dhm/lib/detail.html?id=1754.

INDEX

Figures are indicated by page numbers followed by fig.

ACKNOWLEDGMENTS

I would like to thank all the archivists and librarians I worked with during my research for this book, scholars who greatly facilitated my efforts and made my research trips more interesting. I especially thank Marjorie Kehoe and Phoebe Evans Letocha at the Alan Mason Chesney Archives at Johns Hopkins University; Roland McDonald at the Alabama Department of Archives and History; Cheryl Schnirring at the Illinois State Historical Library; John Rees at the National Library of Medicine in Bethesda, Maryland; Gabriel Swift at the Department of Rare Books and Special Collections, Princeton University Library; Linda Johnson at the California State Archives; Jeannie Sherman and Paul Baran at the Connecticut State Archives; Tal Nadan at the Brooke Russell Astor Reading Room for Rare Books and Manuscripts at the New York Public Library; Jennifer Brathovde at the Library of Congress, Manuscript Division; Lisa Mix and Elizabeth Shepard at the Medical Center Archives of New York-Presbyterian/Weill Cornell Medicine; Deena Gorland at the American Psychiatric Association Foundation, Melvin Shabin, MD, Library and Archives; Chloe Raub at the Gelman Library, George Washington University; Katie Jean Davey, Brigid Shields, and Tracey Baker at the Minnesota State Archives and Minnesota Historical Society; Laura Micham at the David M. Rubenstein Rare Book and Manuscript Library, Duke University Archives; the reference staff at the Manuscript and Archives, Yale University Library; Cheryl Beredo and Steven Fullwood at the Schomburg Center for Research in Black Culture, New York Public Library; Russell Johnson and Teresa Johnson at the UCLA Biomedical Library, History and Special Collections Division; the archivists and librarians at the Schlesinger Library, Harvard University; Melissa Olson at the State Historical Society of Wisconsin, University of Wisconsin–Parkside Libraries, Archives Department; William Creech at the National Archives, Washington, D.C.; and Mary Markey at the Smithsonian Institution Archives. There are many others who helped me, too, whose names I do not know.

A good chunk of this book was rethought and then rewritten during a visiting scholar fellowship at the Erikson Institute for Education and Research at the Austen Riggs Center in Stockbridge, Massachusetts. There I would especially like to thank Jane Tillman, the director of the institute, for her generosity and insight, as well as Lee Watroba, Kathleen Young, and Barbara Keegan, who were so welcoming and helpful. I am grateful for the conversations I had with Greg Farr, Cécilia Faurie, Heather Forouhar Graff, Sarah Hamilton, Charles Olbert, Jeremy Ridenour, Jennifer Stevens, Amy Taylor, Beth Turner, Daltrey Turner, Hannah Wallerstein, and Elizabeth Weinberg, among many others. I am also grateful for my conversations with patients there, who welcomed me and my family within their community and yard. Many thanks also to the teachers at the Austen Riggs Nursery School, especially Sarah Muil, Stephanie Quetti, and Cara Williams, who helped make my daughter happy there.

This book was conceptualized during a visiting fellowship at the United States Studies Centre at the University of Sydney. For their insights, conversations, and generosity, I especially would like to thank Rodney Taveira, Rebecca Sheehan, Sarah Gleeson-White, and Elizabeth Ingleson, as well as all of my fellow fellows, in particular Benjy Kahan. I would also like to thank Chris Poullaos and Alannah Ball for being so generous and welcoming in the city.

I gratefully acknowledge the Social Sciences and Humanities Research Council of Canada (SSHRC) for their support for this project, as well as Seed Funding from the Faculty of Arts, University of Ottawa.

I would like to thank all of my colleagues in the History Department at the University of Ottawa, among them the "French Ladies," and especially Corinne Gaudin, for our walks and talks. The bulk of this book was written under three department chairs, Kouky Fianu, Eda Kranakis, and Sylvie Perrier, and I would like to thank them for taking on what I'm sure can be a thankless job and for their help. I also thank our department's administration officer, Manon Bouladier-Major. And thank you, of course, to my students.

And I am so glad to know Naomi Davidson! She has read more drafts of this book than anyone outside of my editor; I hope she can see her intellectual fingerprints here. Our "salon" continues from Paris.

I have been fortunate to have some conscientious and interesting research assistants for this book. Thank you to Lindon Assaye, who photographed documents for me, and even read them and had conversations about them with me. Thank you to Professor Derryn Moten for introducing us. I would also like to thank Alley Ryan for her photographs and Professor Edward Schmitt and Melissa Olson for introducing me to her. Thank you to Peggy Ann Brown at the Library of Congress, who understands the "sinking feeling" when you realize you forgot the folder number on a document—thank you for tracking it down for me when I couldn't make it to DC. Peter Rumbles photographed two boxes for me at the Oregon State Archives that I didn't ultimately use, but I am still thankful for his work and also for this background reading. At the University of Ottawa, Madeleine Kloske helped me especially with reconnaissance research during this book's early stages. Meagan Wierda helped me with reconnaissance, health law, photographs of primary sources, and all things technological. Even though I did not end up writing the book I thought I would write when she was helping me, I am grateful for all of the background knowledge that her work gave me and for our conversations. In the final stages I benefited especially from the patient technological help of Sarah Benson, Steph Chevalier-Crockett, and Thea Lewis.

I am very grateful to my editor at Penn Press, Bob Lockhart, for his conscientious attention to this book and his perceptive comments. Thank you also to the two anonymous reviewers for their generous, helpful, and rigorous comments on a long manuscript with nineteenth-century style footnotes, and to everyone who worked to put this book together at the press, particularly Lily Palladino and copy editor Jenn Backer.

I am grateful to colleagues at other universities as well, in particular Sarah Igo and David Steigerwald, among many others, and to Lisa Henderson and Daniel Horowitz, both former graduate school advisors. I owe an enormous debt to Kathy Peiss for her generous writing and academic advice and for sharing her intellectual eclecticism over the years. I also would like to thank Peter Agree for his wisdom, book recommendations, and kindness and for introducing me to Penn Press.

Finally, I am beyond grateful to my family.

9 780812 253573